LIBRARY OF LATIN AMERICAN
HISTORY AND CULTURE

GENERAL EDITOR:
DR. A. CURTIS WILGUS

THE MEXICAN NATION,
A HISTORY

RODRIGO DE CIFUENTES. CORTES GIVES THANKS TO SAN HIPOLITO FOR
THE CONQUEST OF MEXICO

(From M. Cuevas. *Historia de la iglesia en México*)

See p. 157

THE MEXICAN NATION,
A HISTORY

By

HERBERT INGRAM PRIESTLEY, Ph.D.

LIBRARIAN OF THE BANCROFT LIBRARY AND ASSOCIATE PROFESSOR OF
MEXICAN HISTORY AT THE UNIVERSITY OF CALIFORNIA

COOPER SQUARE PUBLISHERS, INC.
NEW YORK
1969

Originally Published 1923
Published by Cooper Square Publishers, Inc.
59 Fourth Avenue, New York, N. Y. 10003
Standard Book Number 8154-0292-9
Library of Congress Catalog Card No. 73-79202

. Printed in the United States of America

To

KENNETH AND ELIZABETH

INTRODUCTION

THE characteristic attitude of most Americans toward Mexico is one of ignorant good will combined with skepticism concerning the value of her culture and the solidity of her political institutions. There can be little, they think, in the social traditions of so turbulent a nation to commend her history to serious study. Nothing could be farther from the actuality. Public opinion to the contrary notwithstanding, Mexico has a consumingly interesting story almost unique in its relationships with the primitive epoch and in its significance for present and future world problems. The roots of her social organization run deep into the beginnings of the indigenous culture which was centuries old when the white man made his advent upon this continent. After that epochal arrival run four hundred years of white domination yet too scantily understood but on the whole not discreditable in comparison with other white men's domination of dependent peoples.

That history, and the progress of the conscient element of Mexico in their century-long struggle toward the fixation of a national entity this book seeks to interpret to the interested American public. Its main theme is the development and significance of the Spanish colonial institution in North America and the trend of political, economic, and social activity since independence which has made Mexico so great a problem in national growth and so continuous a study in international relations.

Something more than a well-meaning ignorant good will is necessary if the United States is to maintain an adequately satisfactory relationship with her nearest Hispanic American neighbor. Assumption of superiority and impatience with the unsuccessful gropings of the Mexicans toward nationality and stability do not constitute essential prerequisites for the solution of the problem created by the geographical juxtaposition of Mexico and the United States, both exemplars of Americanized European culture introduced by the two most successful nations of the modern colonizing epoch, Spain and England. More intimate knowledge is needed in order to understand why Mexico has strayed so far from the established norms of social theory and political organization in her effort to achieve amelioration of modern conditions which are the result of centuries of mistakes and the perplexity of her neighbors as well as of her citizens.

In the effort to contribute toward the popularization of such knowledge the author has allotted approximately half the available space of this volume to a portrayal of the colonial epoch. This is done in order to give adequate perspective to the contribution of Spain in her labor of transmitting to America her spirit and culture, and to set forth the elemental defects of the colonial system of the Old Régime, defects which ministered decisively toward the disruption of the colonial scheme of things and set America apart as the new home of democratic and republican theories and forms.

The contribution of Spain was cultural rather than governmental. Her paternalism, her absolutism, her exclusively monopolistic theory, all served as contributory factors diametrically opposed to those which operated within British America. The republicanism which accompanied independence in the English colonies had been a progressive evolution, while that which developed when Spanish America was freed constituted an abrupt and definitive break with the past in the formal aspects, though in spirit and essence the autocracy of the colonial epoch survived and still rules in the political and social organization in Mexico as elsewhere in Hispanic America. To know how that autocratic mechanism was imposed upon the rudimentary civilization of the primitive Mexicans, how it swept the earlier culture into oblivion, what it contributed and what it lacked of the essentials that satisfy the cravings of human existence, and how it has been warped or modified during a century of so-called republican independence, constitute the elementary lessons to be learned before happy solutions can be found for the constantly shifting problems of international comity.

The profound influence exercised on Mexican political and economic life by geographical conditions makes it essential to present as a first chapter of this book some description of the physical Republic as it exists today. The country possesses such diversified climates, such multifarious products, such wide variations in hydrographic and geological conditions, that her history has been uniquely influenced by them and cannot be well understood unless they are borne in mind. Much the same line of thought explains the need of the following chapter on the ancient Mexicans. Though the Spaniards abruptly obliterated the early culture, its surviving influence in thought and tradition still gives to Mexican society the rudiments of national sentiment and cannot be neglected although events of pre-Cortesian history are now of scant significance. Hence the Aztecs and Mayas are presented as historical background rather than as history, to show the effect of their relatively high cultures as determinant of the character of the Spanish conquest and its tradition as a present influence rather than to digress among legendary or cultural details, however worthy of attention and however intriguing to the interest such primitive factors may be. As yet they belong in the field of anthropology rather than in that of history.

The conquest of New Spain was the work of a social element and not of individuals; so said the garrulous participant Bernal Díaz in his *True History*. It was the most successful incident of the great Spanish expansion during an epoch when a magnificent worldwide enterprise was inspired by unity of purpose with a tremendous driving force. The arms and banners of Charles V were carried around the world in a burst of national enthusiasm which created a new realm unequaled in expanse by any other modern people in so short a span of years. And yet, although it was the work of a society and not of individuals, it is no undue emphasis that uses the names of Hernán Cortés and Antonio de Mendoza as points of high interest in the narrative of the conquest and occupation of New Spain; these two great personalities vivified the movement and crystallized it into a unity. Few of us forget that Cortés was the conqueror of Mexico City, but fewer of us remember that for nearly two decades after the fall of the Aztec capital he was the outstanding figure in a series of brilliant movements which added the vast region of Central Mexico to the Spanish Empire. After his day the actual expansion slowed down perceptibly in spite of the efforts of Mendoza, who became the constructive genius where Cortés had been the adventurous conqueror and explorer. Mendoza the great viceroy presided for fifteen years over the acclimatization of European culture in North America with a genius which made him one of the greatest characters in the history of the Continent. His work was carried on by Luis de Velasco and a long line of less distinquished administrators until the great century of the conquest was ended.

Then came the quieter seventeenth century, a century of decline and decay for the once great empire of Charles V and Philip II. In New Spain the wave of expansion slackened, save in the occasional movements of frontiersmen into newer fields of endeavor. It was a time in which the legacy of European culture found solid expression in the refinements of colonial life. Now the missionary, the teacher, the architect, the painter, and the author, began to contribute with greater fecundity the elements of civilized society founded on the accomplishments of the conqueror, the ruler, the merchant, and the farmer who laid the bases of the colonial world.

But with the advent of the House of Bourbon and the colonial wars of the eighteenth century came a new necessity. The policies of isolation and secrecy and exclusiveness which had permitted Spain to preserve her American empire intact while her power in Europe waned and her institutions decayed, no longer availed in the fierce rivalry for empire between Spain, France, and England. Great reforms became

necessary and were imposed, reforms which struck not at
the error of the principles involved in the unwise colonial
theory of those times, but attempted rather to make those
principles more certain and effective in their application.
The effect was to render the colonial system more obnoxious
and to accentuate inveterate evils. In two outstanding
features did Spain change her colonial policy during the late
eighteenth century. She abandoned temporarily and
timorously the policies of commercial exclusion and monopoly, and she tried the effect of developing a colonial army.
The opening of free trade in 1778 had a shortlived beneficial
result on commerce, farming, and industry, but the reform
was soon discarded amid the confusion of the Revolutionary
epoch, and the recruiting of a colonial army was only seizing
one horn of a dilemma. Spain might keep her colonies from
England by training her colonials to arms, but she could not
keep them from finally turning those arms upon herself.

The first great period of modern European expansion saw
its close in the wars of the American and the Spanish American Revolutions. Those wars were caused by the deep-
seated conviction that no part of the civilized community of
mankind is the legitimate prey of any other part, whether
through colonization or by industrial exploitation. The
conviction brought the decline of the mercantilist theory in
colonization, and with the disappearance of the purely
exploitative policy came the post-Revolutionary theory of
home rule in colonized areas as exemplified by the development of the Dominions of the British Empire. The monopolistic right of a homeland to exploit an economically degraded
colonial raw-product community of exiled nationals whose
place was forever fixed in inferiority of fiscal and industrial
status was gradually and reluctantly discarded. America
came into the European world now as a full-fledged equal in
political and economic rights.

New Spain bore in that emancipation from an exploiting
metropolis a part comparable to that played by the United
States. In the Spanish colonies as well as in the English, the
event of actual separation was determined by the accidental

sequences of political events, but there were in each case deeply rooted evils to be thrown off, and in each of them the social and economic discontent of a newly rising native group was the decisive factor. It was quite as much an accident of political policy that Napoleon should have driven Spain and Spanish America to rebellion as it was that George III should have impelled the American radicals to resist his meddlesome policies; the real reasons for separation were the inherent weaknesses of the theory which sets a metropole over against a colonial domain in economic superiority. That New Spain succeeded less perfectly than the United States in achieving real economic freedom was due to the greater intensity with which the colonial theory had been imposed upon her inhabitants, leaving them farther to progress on the ways of development. Her capacities were less by the measure of difference between Spanish and British autonomy and personal initiative. Her later achievements have been conditioned upon that initial difference, upon the racial characteristics which have rendered the Latin less aggressive than the Anglo-Saxon in the struggle for dominion over nature, and upon the psychology developed by the weaker nation struggling unwisely against the superior forces of a dominant and aggressive neighbor.

In that struggle for separation from Spain there emerged the characteristic personalities of Hidalgo, Morelos, and Iturbide, symbols of an age and an aspiration, as faithfully as the names of Washington and Adams are symbols of the yearning of the American people. Hence through the wars of independence the movement though essentially the work of a whole class, is associated with those characteristic names. By an ironical fate a decade of war for liberal principles was ended by the successful secession of Mexico from Spain under the tutelage of that very element from which the revolutionists had sought relief. Even in victory Mexico has usually let slip the prize so dearly attained by gallant warfare. But in the next stage the essential factors in the two Republics are sharply differentiated; we find the people of the United States moving more certainly toward the amalgamation of a national life than the Mexicans, who emerge slowly into spiritual self-consciousness as a people because they are held back by the bane of personalism, the development of the caudillo period under the sway of such egoists as Bustamante or Santa Anna. We have indeed in our own history our Aaron Burrs and General Wilkinsons and Anthony Butlers, but they had no such enduring influence as the Mexican swashbucklers, nor did they rise so high in the political scale. They were incidental, not habitual. Yet we have had enough of them to help us realize what evils political independence might have brought to the United States had it not been for the prior development of vigorous local autonomy and consent in majority rule as the foundation for a strong central constitution, an abiding spirit of national loyalty and respect for the elementary rules of justice.

Throughout the whole period of Mexican independence runs this baneful influence of personalism, finding public expression in pretended aspiration for either centralist or federalist control, as the political accident may dictate. Along with this struggle of personalities goes the strife for advantage by opposing classes of society hopeful for dominance. The social fabric of colonial times which depended upon inviolate privilege for the landed class, the military oligarchy, or the clerical organization, found itself in secular conflict with a numerically superior but intellectually inferior group composed of native American Spaniards and half-breeds, who moved slowly and uncertainly toward group consciousness and final political domination. Through this warfare, which began with the period of military anarchy and came to its climax in the European Intervention of the sixties, the Spanish tradition of autocratic rule survived all the bewildering applications of diametrically opposed constitutional forms, and the course of Mexican history turns on the perpetual struggle for exercise of the chief executive power, little trammeled by constitutional forms or statutory inhibitions. In the midst of this internal struggle the aggressions of the Anglo-Saxon neighbor in the Texas episode and the subsequent Mexican War fall as a disastrous interlude. The westward sweep of land-hungry Americans could not wait for self-government to mature in Mexico. In international politics the race is to the swift and the battle to the strong. Gómez Farías personifies the rise of the new group in politics, a group discontented in oppression, somewhat as an Andrew Jackson typifies the rise of a new democracy and the advent of the common people of the United States in American political life. Ignacio Comonfort is the symbol of their temporary discomfiture because of their superstitious fear of the old autocratic clerical and military power, while Benito Juárez stands like a Lincoln for the preservation of the national integrity against disruption from within; a veritable savior of his country from subversion to the monarchical and clerical influences which sought on one hand repression of the liberal element and perpetuation of a stratified society as necessary for the preservation of privilege, law and order, and on the other an economic dependence upon France which meant the turning back of the course of history into its old eighteenth century colonial channels.

That personalistic and constitutionalistic struggle, with its misfit application of democratic forms to a society yet sharply caste-stratified through long tradition, set the stage for the advent of such a military hero as Porfirio Díaz. This man usurped the sovereignty precisely at the moment when the American conquest of the West had begun to produce superfluous wealth which sought reïnvestment in lucrative adventures; when American initiative moved strongly toward development of natural resources, having outgrown the more simple land-hunger which marked the period of infiltration of farmers into Texas and the wilful misunderstandings which culminated in the war of conquest which took the great West from Mexico. At that same moment the Mexican energies had reached their lowest ebb; the long struggle between political factions for the triumph of the national integrity had left her prostrate; she had no energies to use in competition with the foreign empire builders who swarmed into Mexico from the United States

with the coming of the railroads. Díaz appropriated the
nation to his own purposes and turned aside from the path
of political evolution to smooth the path of material development. The struggle for rational forms of government
adapted to the needs of the people stopped, while a program
was initiated which promised more rapid returns, greater
splendor, and more solid appearance of success. The ambitions of Díaz for his people were excellent, benevolent, and
laudable, whatever may be said of his egotism, his selfishness, his overweening lust for power. Neither he nor his
enthusiastic admirers ever caught an inkling of the crime he
committed. But his success was transitory because he set
personal ambition against the trend of his country's history
ever since independence by denying it the political evolution
which had barely begun at the fall of Maximilian.

He had only half a program, that of material prosperity.
In the development of that program the old system of
economically privileged classes was perpetuated, the situation for Mexico becoming worse because the new privileged
class became largely foreign in composition. Economic
dependence on the church had been exchanged for economic
dependence upon foreign investors. Díaz had fatuously
believed that the investor who made his money in Mexico
would become a loyal Mexican, as the Europeans who came
to the United States became loyal Americans. Instead,
absentee landlordism was the result, with a ruder awakening
in store than had been the sequel of the unfortunate attempt
to colonize Texas against the sweep of the Westward Movement. The foreigner built railroads, opened mines and farms,
but he took his money away, and only a small residue went
to benefit the Mexican nation in taxes and higher wages.
In spite of apparent political independence, great national
wealth and credit, great reputation for stability and prosperity, Mexico had only changed masters. She fixed upon herself the limitations which left her essentially an eighteenth
century colony, economically, of the United States. The
glow of prosperity only aroused the envy of the people of
Mexico, who saw themselves dispossessed of resources which

they would have been able to develop themselves had they been really masters of their own destinies in capacity as well as opportunity.

As the long dictatorship lengthened in political atrophy and finally fell because like all dictatorships it feared to train a successor, the storm of discontent burst upon the devoted head of him who had done his best to make his country happy. Came then the Revolution of Madero, with the other half of the program, which Díaz had not understood. But Madero lacked the half which Díaz had provided. He could furnish ideals, but could not work them. He believed in the economic independence of his country, but under his hand the movement took on the character of destruction instead of construction. Men thought that the elimination of foreign investments would leave Mexico happy and free. They thought the removal of capitalistic influence, native and foreign, essential to a new and right beginning. The inevitable result was strife, confusion, failure.

Whatever there could have been that was rational in the aspirations of Madero was immersed in blood by the egoistical attempt of the reactionaries, abetted by foreign influence, which sought to return to the halcyon days of Díaz by reïmposing the iron hand in the person of Victoriano Huerta. That attempt to set back the clock happily failed, though it failed through an unworthy agency. Venustiano Carranza was, with slight difference in personality, a true disciple of Madero in ideas and of Díaz in methods. He sought to continue the struggle for economic independence, making himself the protagonist of racial antipathies and of state socialism as a weapon wherewith to fight the money power of foreigners who had made his country prosperous but discontented. The Carranza movement crystallized resistance to foreign economic domination in a program of nationalization of resources. This had been the policy of Díaz with the railroads; in that instance it had been acquiesced in dourly by foreign investors because it was effected by shrewd financial manipulation, whereas the new nationalization, applied to subsoil products by Carranza, moved not through the avenue of purchase, but through the avenue of confiscation. This policy pretended to set the higher good of society above the established conventions of contractual relations, and drew down upon the government which espoused it the wrath of all foreigners and all Mexicans whose vested interests were jeopardized. There is no doubt that the Constitutionalists, as they styled themselves, understood the true economic condition of their country, and that the mechanism they devised would have corrected that condition so far as forms go, had they had the power to enforce their system. But that system attacked the essential form of all successful societies. State socialism may have its roseate aspects, but it has nowhere evolved into a more perfect system of society than that of the capitalistic state. Hence against Carranza it was war to the knife by the stable element in Mexico, whether Mexican, British, French, or American in origin. And the issue could be but one. That was the elimination of the personality which represented the attempted system. Let alone the futility of the proposal to restore national economic independence, or rather to create it, by governmental absorption of private rights, the scheme becomes Utopian and fantastic as it flies in the face of all the material development which had for a generation given the only stability which the nation had enjoyed. Moreover, the impracticability of the reform was not its most obnoxious feature. Added to that was the demonstrated fact that the new element which had seized the power was using the turbulence it had created for the cynical purposes of shameless self-enrichment. The orgy of crime, rapine, and destruction which accompanied the operation of the so-called socialistic state was its surest and most unequivocal condemnation.

The conclusion of the matter is obvious. Reforms which leave unobserved the elemental equities bring their own destruction. If in their conception they break too suddenly with experience, they command no respect, win no friends, and inevitably fail. If they are accompanied by flagrant dishonesty, their end is the surer. But on the other hand the system of colonial exploitation has also failed to satisfy the large proportion of the dominant peoples, and the echoes of the discontent it produces among the dependent peoples ring from every colonized area of the earth. There is somewhere a remedy if there is a goal of success for society. It has not yet been found. It does not lie in the adoption of socialism or communism in dependent states, nor in their free license to utter hostile legislation against the development of natural resources existent in poorly governed areas under control of politically incompetent peoples. Nor does it lie in the exclusion of foreign investments from countries where business organization, exploiting skill, and economic initiative are not developed among the indigenes highly enough to provide society with the raw products and artefacts upon which its normal activities have come to depend. The problem awaits solution in the growth of a new spirit among the exploiting peoples, a spirit which already shows signs of becoming dominant at no remote day, which shall provide for the dependent nation possessing great natural wealth its political and economic opportunity to the limit of its growing capacity, at the same time affording the more highly organized nation full opportunity—mutually profitable opportunity, to assist in the progressive labor of reducing the resources of the earth to the service of mankind.

The author takes this occasion to express his obligation to the numerous authors Mexican and American whose works have been utilized, some of them very lavishly, in the preparation of this book; they are appropriately mentioned in the concluding chapter under the lists of authorities and readings. It is a pleasure to acknowledge gratefully the kindness of a number of persons who have assisted with critical comment and suggestion. President David P. Barrows read and offered pertinent criticism on the introduction and the chapters referring to the period since 1910. Professor Thomas M. Marshall read the chapters which concern the Texan episode. Professors H. E. Bolton and C. E. Chapman have given continuously the inspiration of industry

and devotion to Hispanic American History. Professors
Chapman and Franklin C. Palm read the entire manuscript
and made useful suggestions on matter and style. Miss
Jane E. Swanson, Mr. Rolland A. Vandegrift, and Miss
Catherine Arlett gave me much help, and my wife gave
effective assistance in proof-reading. The author has made
generous use of the aid rendered by them all to lessen materially the number of imperfections which the book will
inevitably be found to contain.

Berkeley, California, October, 1922.

TABLE OF CONTENTS

ILLUSTRATIONS

MAPS

THE MEXICAN NATION,
A HISTORY

THE MEXICAN NATION

CHAPTER I

THE LAND OF NEW SPAIN

THE term "New Spain" was used during colonial times to designate the dependency from which the present Republic of Mexico is politically descended. At first applied to the peninsula of Yucatan by the exploring expedition of Grijalva in 1518, and used by Cortés to designate his early conquest, it came in time to embrace generically nearly all the Spanish possessions in North America, though many wide areas were better known by their special names. On the eastern and western sides the boundaries, being shorelines, have remained well fixed; on both the north and the south they have been subject to the changes incident to the events of political history.

The southern boundary of New Spain was at first indefinite. During the conquest by Cortés that captain pushed southward, by the acts of his associates, well into Central America, where the northward stream of conquest from Panamá and the westward one from the Antilles encountered his. As time went on, the Central American area was segregated under the title "Kingdom of Guatemala." This entity, while not entirely independent of New Spain, was practically so for the purposes of ecclesiastical and civil administration. The ruler of New Spain maintained a more or less close connection with Central America in the twin features of colonial defense, namely, collection of the taxes and provision of armed forces.

In 1549 a line of demarcation was drawn between Guatemala and New Spain. It began "at the bar of Tonala,

1

in 16° north latitude, running thence in the direction of the Gulf of Mexico between the towns of Tapana and Maquilapa, leaving the former on the left and the latter on the right, to a point opposite San Miguel Chimalapa; thence turning and running as far as the Mijes Mountain, situated in 17° 21′ of the same latitude; thence to the town of Usumacinta situated on the river of the same name; thence following up this river to a point opposite Huehuetlán in 15° 30′ of the same latitude, and thence to Cape Three Points on the Gulf of Honduras." In 1599 the line was again changed, being then made to follow generally the 18th degree north latitude. In 1678 the ruler of New Spain took from Guatemala many towns on the coast as far as Huehuetlán, also extending the boundaries of Yucatan. When the boundaries were again shifted, in 1787, the line followed the degree of 17° 49′ north latitude, and was so continued by confirmation of various boundary commissions in 1792, 1794, and 1797. The Spanish government map of 1802 adopted the same line. This left most of the present state of Chiapas in Guatemala; Yucatan was then, as it has usually been, practically independent of New Spain save in matters of finance.

The present irregular southern boundary is, like the northern one, partly artificial, and is the result of treaty negotiations of September, 1882, and April, 1895. It runs from the Pacific Coast at 14° 24′ north latitude up the little Río Zuchiate, thence northeast to the Río Usumacinta, which it follows to about 17° north. Since 1895 the line thence advances east, north, and again east to the northwest side of the Belize line; then from the Bacalar Chica inlet between Yucatan and Ambergris Bay to and up the Río Hondo to the junction of Yucatan and Guatemala.

Sweeping northward from the Isthmus of Tehuantepec along the shore of the Gulf on the east, and along that of the Pacific on the west, the northern boundaries of colonial days were extended indefinitely as far as the Spanish influence could push them. Spain from her first knowledge of the continent claimed it all, and did not until 1670 in her treaty with England recognize the existence of any counterclaims to the area. That date marked the beginning of the retrogression of Spanish tenure on the Atlantic side, Jamaica in the Antilles having been lost in 1655. In the year first named, the Savannah River was constituted the actual boundary between the English colony of Georgia and Spanish Florida. In the interior the line was as varying as political vicissitudes could make it. In the Texan area the Spaniards never occupied territory north of a line drawn from Adaes, San Sabá and El Paso, except at the latter point, where the boundary thrust sharply north to Taos in New Mexico. Louisiana, ceded to Spain by France in 1762 and continuing Spanish until 1801 only, may hardly be called a genuine Spanish colony. It was, indeed, never an administrative unit proper of New Spain, being governed as a part of the captaincy-general of Havana, as were both East and West Florida. These areas were, to be sure, under the supervision of the viceroy of New Spain for matters of general policy and defense.

On the Pacific slope occupation lagged far behind discovery. Though the coast became fairly well known from the Cortesian explorations and the voyages of famous discoverers like Cabrillo and Vizcaíno, and from the numerous voyages of the Manila galleons, there was no occupation of the mainland shore northward of the peninsula of Lower California until 1769, when Upper California was added as an area to be defended against threatened Russian encroachments from Alaska. At this time (1770) Lorenzana, archbishop of Mexico, was fain to write in his *Historia de Nueva España:* "It is doubtful if the country of New Spain does not border on Tartary and Greenland;—by the way of California on the former, and by New Mexico on the latter."

There was, then, no boundary to New Spain on the north during the colonial epoch. In 1819 a convention between Spain and the United States abandoned Florida to the latter country and fixed the limits at the Sabine and Red Rivers, thence to follow the one hundredth degree of longitude to the Arkansas, up the latter to 42° north latitude and thence west to the Pacific; but that line was merely a definition, not a mark of occupation, and was not reaffirmed by Mexico and the United States until political events had made it a nullity. The retrogression of the Spaniards on the Pacific slope had already begun with the loss of Nootka in 1790. After the independence of Mexico in 1821 further losses included Texas and adjacent territory separated in 1836, covering 362,487 square miles; and Arizona, New Mexico, California, Colorado, Nevada, Utah, and part of Wyoming, ceded in 1848-1853, covering 568,103 square miles. The total losses have been about 930,590 square miles. Since 1853 there has been comprised in the neighboring republic an area of some 770,000 square miles, nearly 200,000 square miles less than the area of which she has been deprived.

The present boundary between the United States and Mexico follows the Río Grande from its mouth for 1,136 miles to El Paso, Texas, thence to 31° 47' north latitude. It then runs 100 miles west along the same parallel, then south to 31° 20' north latitude and west on that line to 111° west longitude, "where the line is drawn straight to the Río Colorado, twenty miles below its confluence with the Río Gila. Thence it ascends the Colorado to the old line between Upper and Lower California [1773] whence it goes straight to the Pacific just below San Diego Bay, 674 miles from El Paso and 1833 miles from the mouth of the Río Grande."

Within the confines of the indicated boundaries lies the area which concerns the historian of Mexico in so far as environment and racial characteristics are concerned. The outlying areas of the borderland, as Texas and California, had in the later colonial period large political influence over Mexico's destinies, but contributed none of those elements which go toward the amalgamation or the self-expression of a people.

The land of New Spain—Mexico—is, physiographically speaking, divided by the Isthmus of Tehuantepec into two distinct regions. Below that low watershed the Guatemalan area of Chiapas and the low limestone plateau of Yucatan form a world apart physiographically, ethnologically, and, to perhaps as great a degree socially and historically. Northward of the Isthmus lies the true "Mexico," as it came to be called even during the Spanish supremacy. There the land, bordered on one side by the eastern Sierra Madre and on the other by the western Sierra Madre, rises in graduated terraced plateaus northward through Oaxaca and Puebla to the Plateau of Mexico or Anáhuac, which is from seven to eight thousand feet high. Anáhuac is the third highest plateau in the world, being excelled only by those of Tibet and Bolivia. From Mexico City to El Paso it is so evenly sloping that one might drive a carriage over it, or even farther on, to Santa Fe in New Mexico. There is a fall of only 3,600 feet between Mexico City and El Paso, a distance of 1,225 miles. The levelness of this area and its sharp confination by the converging eastern and western Sierras must have been significant in controlling the migrations of the prehistoric Mexicans, as it has been in historical times in directing conquest and settlement.

The country is broken by great transverse ravines or barrancas, which, formed by running waters in gravelly soil, have cut to the yawning depths which make them distinctive characteristics of the physiography. Along their steep slopes they are wonderfully wooded. Between Guadalajara and Tepic lies the romantic Barranca de Mochititle; between Guadalajara and Colima is the Barranca de Beltrán and in the state of Chihuahua are those of Cobre, Batopilas, and San Carlos. These latter run east and west, disappearing in the Sinaloa lowlands.

The mountain ranges, running parallel with the coast lines, differ greatly in height. The occidental Sierra lies close to the coast and runs at a mean altitude of from 10,000 to 12,000 feet from Oaxaca into Arizona. In Lower California the Sierra de la Giganta is 4,000 feet high on an average, sloping more sharply to the Río Grande than to the Pacific. The eastern Sierra runs from ten to one hundred miles inland from the Gulf coast like a low escarpment rather than a range, being scarcely more than 6,000 feet in height, with lower passes at frequent intervals. Its slope is likewise sharper on the interior than on the exterior side. These mountain ranges present some of the magnificent scenic effects for which Mexico is so justly famous. They have in the main those contrasting features which distinguish the western from the eastern mountains of the United States of America, that is, distinctions which differentiate the newer from the older physical formations. In the south the lake regions of Lake Chapala in Jalisco and Lakes Cuitzeo and Pátzcuaro in Michoacán present natural charm almost indescribable.

Mexico is reputed to be a land of numerous volcanoes, nearly all quiescent, in the territory north of Tehuantepec. They all lie on a line nearly east-west between the two oceans, and are of a comparatively late geologic formation, having been formed later than the ranges of sierras, above which they tower thousands of feet. Popocatépetl and Orizaba or Citlaltépetl are over 17,000 feet high, and are excelled on this continent only by Mt. St. Elias and Mt. McKinley. For a great part of the year their snowcapped crests, and that of Ixtaccíhuatl, not considered a volcano, dominate the surrounding territory with a beauty that partially accounts for the attachment of the Mexican to his soil. "Popo" as he is affectionately called, was in eruption at the time of Cortés' conquest, for Bernal Díaz saw the smoke and red hot stones cast out by him. Mt. Colima, fifty miles from the Pacific Coast, has two cones, one volcanic, and eleven other craters exist in the neighboring Santiago Valley.

The physical formation of the country is responsible for its variations in climate even more than is its expanse in latitude. The height of the central plateau renders its temperature equable indeed. Mexico City, at an elevation of over 7,400 feet, is warmer in winter and cooler in summer than Chicago or New York. People who go from the United States to the Mexican capital are surprised to find that they require normal spring clothing practically the year round. Here is the area known as the tierra fría or cool zone, the altitude of which runs from 7,000 to 9,000 feet and the mean range of temperature from 58° to 64° Fahrenheit. We speak of the climatic variations in Mexico as being vertical rather than latitudinous. That is, variation is affected chiefly by altitude. Above the tierra fría are the arctic peaks of the high mountains, which of course count but slightly in a discussion of populated climatic areas. Below the tierra fría lies the tierra templada, temperate or subtropical in climate, where the altitudes lie between 3,000 and 5,000 feet, and where the mean range of temperature is from 62° to 70° Fahrenheit. The tierra templada conforms to the terraces which rise above the coastal slopes, parts of the central plateau itself being included in it. In this area the rains fall during the summer months, as they do indeed in the tierra fría. Subtropical growth is prolific and varied, temperate zone crops flourishing alongside of the tropical plants. It is a transitional floral area.

The tierra caliente or hot zone, running from sea level to 3,000 feet altitude, and having a mean range of temperature from 77° to 82° Fahrenheit, has given the country its unmerited reputation for torridity. This climatic zone runs along the coast of the Gulf and the Pacific, and penetrates here and there to elevations above the 3,000 foot contour. Sometimes the temperature reaches 100°, or even 104° and the area is frequently infested with fevers and other tropical diseases. The drainage being almost uniformly poor, yellow fever and black vomit are endemic. In the tropical areas are produced the bananas, coffee, indigo, vanilla, hardwoods, and other "colonial products" which are the distinctive contributions of Mexico to agriculture and commerce, as distinguished from the European plants which have been acclimated for centuries, and the almost ubiquitous bean, squash, maize, and chile pepper.

It is generally believed that the average annual rainfall has been decreasing during the last thirty-five years or so. This is the common opinion among Mexican agriculturalists. Matías Romero attributed this phenomenon to the continual decrease of the timber bearing area. Forest trees are destroyed, not alone for timber, but to produce charcoal, the nearly universal fuel. No systematic effort at reforestation has yet been undertaken, though many projects to that end have been formed.

The annual precipitation is very uneven and irregular. Over half the country, principally that part north of the twenty-second parallel, receives less than ten inches annual rainfall. To the southward the precipitation is greater. On the Pacific slope southward from the lower end of Sonora, the fall reaches fifty inches at times, as it does in the Yucatan peninsula. In the tropical belt comprising Tabasco, Chiapas, Campeche, and Vera Cruz, the rainfall runs from forty-five to two hundred inches. But nowhere save in the tropical belt is the precipitation regular enough to permit uniform crop production without irrigation. Artificial watering is essential in practically the entire north except along the Gulf. Even in Oaxaca, Guerrero, and the other southern states, irrigation is needed to stabilize production during temporary droughts.

All through the colonial epoch after about 1543, the spread of the population followed the location of irrigable lands. When the fathers of the religious orders went on their explorations or entradas, or the farmer-miners sought fortunes in wilderness or mountains, the toma de agua, or take-out from a permanent stream was the first prerequisite for the prospective mission or hacienda. Famous were the aqueducts of colonial days which were built by the religious, notably the Jesuits, to bring water from mountain sources to cities or plantations. Before the close of the eighteenth century, it was frequently declared that all the available land had been taken up, and today more than ever before, the advance of agriculture must depend on the general spread of facilities for irrigation. Since the rains are so uneven, and the available streams so few comparatively, there is need of artesian wells, great canals and reservoirs, and distributing systems, which can only be financed by combinations of agriculturalists or by government agencies. This problem, combined with ever recurrent shortages in labor, has until now proven too great, though many studies of it have been made. The initiative of American companies, as in the northern part of Lower California, on the Yaqui River in Sonora, in Vera Cruz and elsewhere, has advanced beyond the accomplishment of Mexican farmers in this development, but where these beginnings have been made the unsettled conditions of the past decade have prevented utilization of the waters provided.

Could the question of abundant water supply find a happy solution, there would still remain that of labor. Since the foreign infiltration under Porfirio Díaz the country has lost much of its patriarchal agricultural character. Factories in several districts have drawn off labor; a goodly number of hands have turned to railroad and smelter work; more potent than these has been the recurrent drawing off of laborers to the United States for the benefits of peace and higher wages. Mexican newspapers never weary of recounting the troubles and privations of Mexican laborers in the United States, in an effort to assist the country by preventing the almost continual exodus. But the effort proves vain when conditions are propitious, and the traditional cry of the hacendado, *"falta de brazos"*—"lack of hands," is as serious a problem for agriculture as the need of water, capital, and modern implements.

Though much of the Republic is ruggedly mountainous, and mineral products are conspicuously present in most parts, agriculture is and has from time immemorial been an extremely important activity of the people. When the Spaniards first arrived, they found the Aztec Confederacy established on the Plateau of Anáhuac and southward thence, the basis of their political organization being that of intensive agricultural production. Under the conquest, agricultural methods took on the extensive character, and were coupled with the grazing industry as the subjugation of the northern frontiers proceeded. The grazing and the farming went hand in hand with the mining industry throughout the mineral producing areas.

From the earliest known times the most important crop in Mexico has been maize or Indian corn. It is considered an indigenous plant, developed in prehistoric times from a grass which was native to the lacustrine region of the center, and spread with the development of primitive irrigation. Its development as a food product is one of the distinguished triumphs of primitive American agriculture. Corn has always been the chief food of the natives, and, like the manioc of the West Indian area, it contributed potently to the permanency of the Spanish conquest. The first adventurers, who came before large-scale importation of European foods began, would have starved long before wheat became acclimated had they not been able to subsist on the new-found American grain. Corn grows in every part of the country. It is usually planted thickly in rows, and matures quickly. When crops failed, famine was almost sure to ensue, though during recent years importation of corn and wheat from the United States has usually prevented destitution from crop failures. No definite figures are available for corn production during the colonial epoch. At the beginning of the nineteenth century the annual crop was estimated at seventeen million fanegas or quintals. In the present epoch the normal annual maize production of 110,000,000 bushels is still below the food requirement of the country; it is possible in certain parts to raise two crops of corn each year, and follow these by a crop of wheat.

Another indigenous food, the bean, is raised in numerous varieties. The annual crop is now valued at over seven million dollars, but is all locally consumed. The garbanzo or chickpea, raised chiefly in the northwest, is practically all exported. The crop is worth over five million dollars. Cotton, which has been commercially produced since the first third of the nineteenth century, grows well in Coahuila and Durango, but pests, droughts, and floods render its production precarious. The crop is used entirely in foreign-owned factories. Sugar production, dating from the early plantings of sixteenth century pioneers, is still remarkably low. The Republic has sugar lands capable of producing over seven million tons, but less than 200,000 tons are manufactured. The industry in the state of Morelos was practically ruined during the Carranza régime.

Tobacco, which was a thriving monopoly during the latter eighteenth century and until the middle of the nineteenth century, yielded normally, prior to the recent revolution, a crop of eleven million kilograms. In 1920 some six million kilograms were grown. Coffee is grown in Tabasco, Oaxaca, Chiapas, and Vera Cruz. Much American capital is invested in it. During the recent Revolution the plantations suffered; the normal crop rises above one hundred million pounds, but during 1919 a million pounds of the Brazilian product were obtained from American importers.

The henequen or sisal hemp crop ranks close in importance after maize. It comes almost entirely from Yucatan and Campeche, and goes largely to make American binder twine and to England. Since 1915, when the Carranza government destroyed the planters' monopoly by introducing a socialistic scheme of production and marketing the fibre, the annual crop has seriously diminished. Other crops, such as guayule, chicle, ixtle, and vegetables such as onions, potatoes, and tomatoes, have for some years been increasing in importance. Bananas worth five million dollars are now annually exported. Such tropical fruits as the mamey, the mango, and others, do not reach the export market. Temperate zone fruits are not successfully grown in significant quantities. The original stocks of pears, peaches, figs, have not been much improved since the days of the sixteenth century missionaries.

The maguey or American agave is perhaps the second most valuable vegetable product. It is used for more purposes than any other plant. It furnishes food, shelter, clothing, medicine, and, unfortunately, the most popular intoxicant, pulque. No doubt this beverage, fermented from the sap, is the most pernicious natural influence in Mexico. The liquor is easily and cheaply produced. Maguey grows with little cultivation, and so tends to supplant legitimate food crops which might be grown in its place. This accentuates the destitution incident to recurrent crop failures. The moral and physical effect of the liquor upon the consumer causes as much social damage as does the cultivation of the plant cause economic disaster. The sodden brutality of the addict is responsible for a large part of the crime which prevails among the lower classes. Spanish law attempted to curb its consumption and prevent its adulteration, but to no avail because of the simplicity of its manufacture. The curse of the lower classes, it forms one of the ingrained obstacles to their regeneration. Frowned upon during recent years, and held in contempt by the upper classes, its use may in time disappear as the great national vice, but the signs of such reform are as yet exceedingly faint.

The amazing mineral wealth of the country has been from time immemorial the theme of many pens. It is for the most part of silver, though gold, and, in these latter years, petroleum—"black gold"—have contributed in large share to the output of wealth. The great mother veins of silver run almost uniformly from northeast to southwest, and lie vertically for the most part, so that the penetration of the surface has gone in many cases to a depth of from 1500 to 2000 feet. Fabulous production has come from some of the mines; one alone has produced a hundred million dollars. Chihuahua, Sinaloa, and Sonora have vast stores of gold and silver yet untouched; successful mines like those of Cananea show marvelous production. The historic mines are grouped about the central plateau; the axis of the metalliferous region lies on a line which might be drawn from Guadalupe y Calvo in southern Chihuahua through Mexico south to Oaxaca. The chief deposits of metal lie in the Pacific range. Until the period of the Revolution the output of silver represented one-third of the world's production, coming, as it did in the colonial epoch, mainly from the mineral districts of Guanajuato, Zacatecas, and San Luis Potosí, regions which even during the recent period of unrest continued great production.

Copper has of recent years been a growing item of national wealth. It exists in large quantities in Lower California, Aguascalientes, and San Luis Potosí. El Boleo, a French mine near Santa Rosalía on the Gulf of California, and the

Cananea mines in Sonora, have been the greatest producers of this mineral.

Iron ores are widely situated. The Cerro del Mercado in Durango is a hill 640 feet high containing over three thousand tons of solid ore down to the level of the plain. Below this to an unknown depth the mineral averages about 70 per cent. of metal. The iron of Mexico is sufficient to supply the world for centuries to come. Coal also occurs in Michoacán, Guadalajara, Oaxaca, Sinaloa, and Coahuila. From English mines in the latter state the Republic now draws its sole supply. Unhappily for manufacture, coal is not located near the iron deposits.

Petroleum, discovered near Tampico about 1900 by English and American geologists, has leaped into the front rank as the producer of wealth in Mexico. Several large companies, English, French, and American, operate huge wells in that region. Since 1906 other important areas have been shown to be oil bearing. They lie along the Coatzacoalcos River in Tabasco and on the northern frontier, in the Perote hills of Coahuila, and elsewhere. In 1920 the petroleum exportations amounted to 153,000,000 barrels, whereas in 1901 the total production was only 10,345 barrels.

During the summer of 1922 it was predicted that the spectacular days of Mexican oil production had reached an end. This was due to the finding of emulsion and water in the Toteco-Cerro Azul pool, where production had previously been phenomenal. It was felt by oil producers that this discovery would lead to the stabilization of the oil industry, causing a cessation of competitive development and duplication of means of extraction and marketing. It was recognized that Mexico's potential oil supply is yet unknown, but that there is no longer incentive for mammoth production. In proportion as the Tampico fields continue to show tendency to develop emulsion and sea-water, the area will fall back upon agricultural pursuits. In this area probably one third of the land owners are Americans. The expected slackening of production would mean a reduction of ten million barrels of light crude oil each month, and a fifty per cent. reduction in the oil-tax receipts of the Republic.

There is an element of tragedy in the almost unbelievable natural wealth of Mexico. The mineral deposits, while marvelous, are not inexhaustible. Mineral development continuously brings impoverishment nearer; the time will come when this country will no longer be sought for its mineral riches. In the meantime, the soil of Mexico will have been denuded of its precious metals largely for the benefit of alien owners. The case is a little better for agricultural development, for agriculture builds up, if properly practiced, instead of destroying. But even so, the creation of agricultural wealth is subject to the economic disadvantage of absentee ownership, and much of the wealth produced finds its level outside of the Republic. As regards natural resources, Mexico is not only a raw products nation, hence continuously a debtor nation, but she is in all essential economic respects still a colonial nation, in spite of her fictitious and rickety political independence. A colonial nation with a formal political independence is an anomaly, even among the heterogeneous protectorates, colonies, and dominions which constitute the world of semi-dependent states today. Whether Mexico is ever to emerge as a real nation among nations, with both political and economic independence, is a question which must concern her own citizens vitally and directly. It is of scarcely less moment to the people of the United States, whose interest is in international justice as well as in material development and prosperity.

THE AZTEC CONFEDERACY AND DEPENDENCIES IN 1521

CHAPTER II

THE ANCIENT MEXICANS

THE peculiar charm of baffling mystery attaches to the story of the ancient Mexicans. Problems of their origins, their relationships, the order of their appearance within the territory, their relative stages of culture, have interested hundreds of observers and writers from the time of Hernán Cortés, and the stream of contributions to the solution of the riddle is increasing rather than diminishing. It is not too sanguine to hope that we are on the eve of archaeological discoveries which will reduce to historical certainty large portions of the story of the primitive cultures of Middle America which now lie shrouded in the mists of legend, mythology, and seemingly contradictory annals and picture writings.

The sources of present knowledge concerning the ancient Mexicans may be conveniently divided into four groups: (1) the various writings and paintings produced prior to the Spanish Conquest; (2) those produced after the Conquest, with which may be grouped certain Spanish writings; (3) the public monuments, buildings, and the inscriptions found on them; (4) the cultural remains distinguished from monuments and inscriptions by the evident fact of their creation for purposes of utility or art or both. The added contributions which we may expect will consist of interpretations of the ideography of the ancient inscriptions on public monuments and in the so-called Codices or pre-Cortesian picture writings, and in the harmonizing of these interpretations with the statements of post-Cortesian writers and with the findings of later students. As these contributions continue to be made to our knowledge, we shall probably find that interest will be concerned rather with peoples and groups of peoples, with epochs of culture and successive waves of culture—with social facts, in a word—rather than with the unique or isolated facts or ideas which are usually held to constitute the body of history. Even so, we may also expect to have more definite knowledge of actual historical characters, to be better able to distinguish them from the creatures of ancient theogony and mythology, than at present.

The burden of the present evidence, both in the ancient writings and paintings, and in the known and understood architectural remains of North America, points to the origin of the Mexican peoples in an area to the north of that of the highest cultural development in the Plateau of Anáhuac and south of there, and to a series of migrations into that area of highest cultural development. Though none of the early writings speak of the plateau areas as having been unpopulated when the successive comers from the north arrived, there is at present such scant knowledge of the first or so-called autochthonous inhabitants that we may safely consider that we have to deal with migratory peoples who developed a large part of their culture after reaching the central part of modern Mexico.

Within the area of the modern Republic there existed, at the time of the Spanish conquest, two broad groups of native culture, which may be roughly classified as savage and barbarian respectively. There were all grades of savagery, while the barbarous cultures partook, in many respects, of the traditionally accepted characteristics of genuine civilization.

The geographical line dividing savages from barbarians was about the twenty-first parallel of north latitude. To the south of it was the sedentary culture or civilization. To the north, the savage, nomadic or semi-nomadic culture. The northern portion, including Lower California, was a region of wild peoples, except the Pueblo Indians of the Gila and the upper Río Grande, whose culture approximated that of the peoples of the sedentary area. The chief peoples of the wild area were the Waicurian and Yuman tribes of the Californian peninsula, the Seris of Sonora and the Island of

Tiburón, the Piman tribes of the west coast and northern central part, the Apaches along the Río Grande and southward, and the Tamaulipecan Indians in the northeast and along the Gulf Coast. It is generally recognized, since the studies of Seler in the middle of the past century, that the Piman group affiliates with the Shoshonean group of the western United States on the one hand and with the Nahuatl peoples of Mexico on the other. The Pápagos of the Colorado Desert, the Yaquis of Sonora, and the Tarahumaras of the Bolsón de Mapimí in Coahuila and Chihuahua, show only a degree less relationship with the Aztecan culture than do the Tepecans, Huichols and Coras, whose homes are nearer the old sedentary agricultural area.

It is usual to speak of the area south of the twenty-first parallel as that of the "empire" of the Aztecs. In the southern part, in the areas now named Chiapas, Tabasco, Yucatan, and Guatemala, lies the area of the Maya-Quiche culture, known to be earlier than the Aztec. In the modern oil region along the Pánuco River and the coast, was a segregated group of Mayans, the Huastecs; the Totonacs just south of them may also have been of Mayan stock. In the highlands of the center, west of the Huastecs and the Totonacs were the Otomis, who are thought by some students to be an autochthonous people whose earlier possession of the central plateau region had been successfully combatted by the Nahuatlan predecessors of the Aztecs (the Toltecs). The Otomis were a primitive warlike people, enemies of the Aztecs and earlier Nahuatlans. Their remnants remain in very primitive state. To the west of the Otomis were the Huichols, Coras, and other tribes affiliated with the "civilized" Nahuatlans, who were grouped, at the time of the Spanish conquest, under the Aztec Confederacy. The Tarascos of Michoacán were surrounded completely by Nahuas and Otomis. They are often spoken of as a branch of the early Nahua peoples, left behind in the legendary migrations of the stocks which ultimately settled in the lake region of the Plateau of Anáhuac. They are by others considered to have been earlier comers than the Nahuas, and perhaps to have transmitted their culture to the latter. The early peoples of Oaxaca, the Zapotecs and Mixtecs, have traditions that they are autochthonous. Their culture was highly developed; in certain respects it ranks with the Nahuan and the Mayan, and is thought by some students to have marked a transitional stage between the two. It has shown more vigor and has had greater durability than either.

The earliest historical population of central Mexico was a group of Nahua tribes to whom the generic name Chichimeca is usually applied. Among these Chichimecas the outstanding group or tribe, which developed the highest culture and the greatest political power, was the Toltec. The historical existence of the Toltecs, and the existence of a Toltec "empire" is now generally conceded, though it has long been questioned whether the word Toltec did not indicate merely a tradition of excellence in agriculture and other symptoms of high development. It is not known even yet just what area the Toltecs dominated, nor quite what was the character of their "empire."

The Toltecs came from the northwest. The whole Chichimecan group first appeared on the Gila and Colorado rivers, within the region of which they founded Huehuetlapallan, a city which was the seat of their powerful "empire." The Toltecs separated from the other Chichimecas and went to found Tlachicatzin, from which they were driven by enemies. They then (in the sixth century of the Christian era) began wanderings which lasted a hundred years; during this time they made frequent long stops, leaving behind at each of them parts of the original group. About the end of the seventh century they reached Tulcanzingo (modern Tulancingo) but in a few years (A. D. 713) they moved westward, founding Tollan (modern Tula) in 752. From this point they spread over the Valley of Mexico. At Atzcapotzalco their artefacts are found in strata above a deposit of archaic remains from which they are sharply distinct in development. Some authorities prefer to see in the Toltecs merely a tribe of primitive Nahuas who were the earliest mountaineers to be affected by proximity to the

Mayas. Others think that the Olmecs, with whom the
Toltecs are occasionally identified, were really a Mayan
tribe that lived to the east and southeast of the Valley of
Mexico, and were driven out by invading northerners.

Toltec "history" is rather uncertain. They had records,
in the Chichimecan Annals of Quauhtitlán, of isolated
events dating as far back as A. D. 245. The Toltec rulers
are recorded from a beginning in A. D. 726. In their period
of glory, A. D. 843, came the miraculous birth of their
divinity Quetzalcoatl, the "Fair God" celebrated in Lew
Wallace's romance. This "Green-feathered Serpent," the
wind god, is confused in the early writings with his chief
priest, who bore the same name. Quetzalcoatl is the most
famous and picturesque member of the Mexican theogony.
First of all, he was a king or chief, a wise and good ruler,
white bearded and robed, who taught the arts and founded
a beneficent religion. Driven out by magic of enemies, he
went away over eastern waters to a land of plenty called
Tlapallan, promising that one day he would return to reconquer the land and rule it. The existence of faith in this
tradition was of material aid to Cortés in his conquest, for
he was nothing loath to pose as the descendant of Quetzalcoatl in the eyes of the superstitious Moctezuma. Even
as late as the coming of Maximilian in 1865 the tradition of
the fair bearded stranger from the east swayed Indian sentiment.

The Toltecs were skilled workers in metals, pottery,
jewelry, and textile fabrics. They were notable builders; to
them are attributed the three great pyramids of San Juan
Teotihuacán and that of Cholula. They were clever astrol-
ogers, medicine-men, musicians, priests. They invented
writing, and created a calendar, perhaps the famous "Aztec"
calendar now in the Museo Nacional of Mexico. They were
above all peaceful men, so peaceful that the trait in the end
brought about their ruin. It is known that they spoke the
Mexican language, that is, they used a Nahua tongue, in
which they were expert. The last of their chiefs, Huemac,
permitted the development of witchcraft and human sacri- /

fice, beginning oppressive intertribal wars which caused the overthrow of the Toltecan power. This event is variously set down, as having occurred in 959, 1018, 1070, or 1116, according to the interpretations of the time-cycles in the records. The generally credited movement of the Toltecs southeastward to help the Mayas of Mayapán to defeat the rulers of Chichen Itza in 1196 coincides with the appearance in northern Yucatan about A. D. 1200 of architectural influences of Mexican origin very closely approximating in character the remains of Tula. The Toltecs who remained in the Valley of Mexico after the fall of their "empire," became the landed aristocrats, the "old families," with whom the nobles of the barbarian conquerors sought matrimonial alliances to augment their authority and prestige.

The Chichimecas, that is those other than the Toltecs, were barbarian hunting tribes, chiefly cave-dwellers. They were a stock related, as has already been said, to the Toltecs, whose superior culture they admired and imperfectly absorbed. Their traditional leader and deity was Xolotl, named after their celestial dog. Their first king at Quauhtitlán began to reign in 687. They entered and possessed the Toltec area without great opposition about the twelfth century. Xolotl was their original distributor of landed estates to the principal lords who aided his conquests. Some of these estates were passed on from those early bestowals to descendants still in possession at the time of the Cortesian conquest. The earliest Chichimecas were followed by related tribes; of these the Acolhua, who founded Tezcoco near the shore of the lake of the same name, rose in time to the hegemony of the civilizations of the plateau area, and retained their leadership of the political confederacy until only a short time, some fifty years, before the arrival of the Spaniards. The great epoch of Chichimecan or Acolhuan supremacy and highest culture centers about the personal character of their great king Nezahualcoyotl, who died in 1472. This king, whose name means "The Hungry Coyote," had a career strikingly like that of David, "the sweet singer of Israel." Both were hunted and persecuted when young men by jealous kings, both went into exile and had miraculous escapes from death through benefit of popular sympathy. Both gained thrones and established splendid reigns, Nezahualcoyotl epitomizing Solomon's rather than David's reputation in the latter aspect. Both were psalmists of genuine poetical feeling and expression. Both believed and taught that there was one true God. "Both consented to the execution of an elder son and heir because of palace intrigue," and each of them caused a worthy follower to be slain that he might possess his wife. In each case the child of dishonor inherited the throne just before political decay ensued. Nezahualpilli was the last great Tezcocan king; but here the analogy ends for the son of the "Hungry Coyote" was no Solomon.

The last of the migratory Nahua peoples who possessed Anáhuac, the "Valley of Waters," the Aztecs or Mexica, were late arrivals among the tribal groups called generally Chichimecan. They may have begun their migratory movement from California, in Aztlán, north of the Gulf of that name, or, more remotely, from farther north. Traces of their stays have been noted in Arizona, New Mexico, and in northern Mexico, though these may perhaps be more safely attributed to Toltecan or general Chichimecan cultures. Certainly they built Casas Grandes in Chihuahua, whence southward their migration is safely traceable. Arriving in the Valley of Mexico perhaps about the middle of the eleventh century, they wandered unwelcome for a period among their unneighborly but closely related predecessors, who had absorbed the available lands about the lakes then so essential to the welfare of their primitive agricultural civilization. After their arrival, one of their leaders named Cuauhcoatl and two others went forth to search for a location. They came out, says the legend, at a place called Acatitla, in the center of which was a tenochtli or cactus, with an eagle perched on its crest. At the base of the cactus was the nest of the cuauhtli, made from the feathers of various other birds. Then Cuauhcoatl returned to his people and said: "We have been to reconnoitre the road and the swamp; but there they drowned Axoloa; Axoloa died, as I saw, because he sank in the swampy field of reeds where the cactus is located, upon which stands the eagle with his nest at the base forming a pillow of many and varicolored feathers. There is where the water is found. In this way the swamp was formed where Axoloa sank." Cuauhcoatl also told how on another day Axoloa appeared to him and said to him: "I have been to see Tlaloc, the rain god, who called to me to say that his beloved son Huitzilopochtli (the war god) had arrived here, and this place is to be his seat and domicile. He shall be the protector of our lives in the land." After this account, all the Mexica went to see the tenochtli, and in that place they erected their altar, laid out their gardens, and made their arrows.

Here then, on a swampy island in Lake Tezcoco were laid in 1325 the foundations of Tenochtitlán, a miserable group of grass huts destined to grow into the stone-built City of Mexico with two hundred thousand inhabitants before being conquered by the Spanish nearly two hundred years later. For a time the unwelcome newcomers were subject to their neighbors, refuge from whom was probably quite as much an incentive to their choice of a swampy stronghold as was the advice of their eponymous hero Tenoch. As they grew in numbers and strength they emerged from bondage, and, once free, formed an alliance with two neighboring related groups. These were the Tecpanecs of Tlacopán and the Acolhuas of Tezcoco, original dominators of the earlier Chichimecan immigration under Xolotl. In the confederacy the Aztecs continued in a secondary position, with the Tecpanecs third, until, under the immediate predecessors of Motechuhzoma (Moctezuma) II, they achieved undisputed supremacy in war and government, Tezcoco retaining the cultural ascendancy until the conquest.

During the palmy days of Aztec supremacy the area dominated or effectively influenced by them extended roughly between the eighteenth and twenty-first degrees of north latitude on the Atlantic Ocean, and from the fourteenth to the nineteenth on the Pacific. Within this area numerous tribes were independent, or gave only temporary and grudging allegiance, which was thrown off at the first propitious moment. The Tlascaltecs, Tarascans, and Chiapanecs were independent; the peoples of Guatemala, Soconusco, and Oaxaca yielded only temporarily under duress. Along the eastern waters the recently conquered Huastecs and Totonacs near Vera Cruz were the first to assist Cortés in his projected conquest of Tenochtitlán in retribution for successful Mexican expeditions. Within their original boundaries, the three nations associated in the Aztec Confederacy maintained their control independent each of the other. Outside these bounds, conquests were conducted and shares distributed by fifths, two fifths being the share of both Aztecs and Tezcocans, the Tecpanecs contributing and receiving only one fifth, because of their relative weakness and unimportance. The Aztecs, holding the chief power at the time of the advent of Cortés, and evidently aiming at absolute control, had won by their arrogance the hatred of many neighboring peoples, and their hegemony might have been soon destroyed by these latter even if the Spanish conquest had not then ensued. The arrival of the Europeans was aupiciously timed for success.

Fixed order of succession of events in Aztec life is held to have begun with the founding of Tenochtitlán. It was about 1350 that expansion and development became possible by acquisition of water rights from Chapultepec. This removed the people from dependence on the brackish waters of Lake Tezcoco. From that time on, Tenochtitlán waxed great. The first notable warrier chieftain of the Confederacy, Acamapichtli, ruled from 1376 to 1396. The great Itzcoatl, from 1427 to 1440, Tizoc, from 1482 to 1486, and the two Moctezumas, from 1440 to 1469 and from 1502 to 1520, respectively, were the great expansionists of the nation.

The latter monarch, or better *chief of men*, had been a priest before his election to the magistracy, and he had developed a stern theocratic government in which he was more feared than loved by his subjects and allies; hatred on the part of the conquered but unassimilated peoples was universal, and served as the entering wedge for the disruption of the Aztec Confederacy.

We know more about the social and political organization of the Aztecs, whose central city was Tenochtitlán, than we do about any of the other highly developed Indians of Mexico, for the reason that the early Spanish writers studied them more effectively than the other groups. Moreover, the Aztecs undoubtedly affected materially the social and political life of the lesser civilized peoples. They are then, if not typical, the best representatives of early Mexican culture, and while our knowledge of the other peoples is often indirect or allusive, we are safe in assuming that in few essentials did they differ materially from, and certainly not in complexity or height of development, the dominant element of the Nahua group.

There are two schools of thought regarding the character of the institutions developed by the Aztecs. Lewis H. Morgan and A. F. Bandelier leaned to the opinion that the words "empire," "lord," "king," employed freely by the Spanish writers from Cortés down, and followed by William H. Prescott, are misconceptions of social and political development among the Mexicans. They argue that Cortés, himself steeped in imperial phraseology and conceptions, used familiar descriptive terms in reporting to his emperor a new life of which he had inadequate understanding. His normal tendency would be to over-exalt what he saw, in order to enhance the fame of his own prowess in the hope of material reward. In reality, think these writers, the Aztec "empire" was a "loosely bound confederacy of democratic Indian tribes." This opinion is adhered to by John Fiske the historian, and by many leading American ethnologists. Most other writers incline to the idea that the Aztecs and like tribes had real monarchical institutions. The difference is not of material importance, as it consists largely in mere terminology, and our misconceptions, influenced by this, are increased by the fact that the Spaniards were poor observers of institutions, and various authors used varying terms to describe the same office or social function. It is certain that governmental offices among the Aztecs were not differentiated as we understand them to be, and that as a matter of fact the terms "empire" and "republic" are each inapplicable. As a matter of fact Mexico was governed by a priestly oligarchy, and had a normal tribal organization below it.

Tenochtitlán, having many thousand inhabitants, was a complex or conglomerate of smaller units. The lowest significant social unit was the calpulli, a clan, descended from one early ancestor and inhabiting and owning in common a well-defined plot of land. The calpulli excluded members of other calpulli from its lands, which were inalienable and indivisible. Each calpulli was sovereign within its own limits. It was the basis of the tribal organization, though within these limits individual families had distinct holdings without permanent proprietary rights. In war, which was more conspicuously than was agriculture the main business of the Aztecs, each calpulli or clan marched to conflict under its own distinctive emblem. Each had its own god, and its own place of worship. There were in the city about twenty such clans, which were divided into four general divisions.

The officers by whom government was executed were generically called tecuhtli; they were individuals who had acquired merit and distinction through valor, and held their designation for life regardless of official positions. They might hold any office for which they were properly designated. The title tecuhtli was an honorific.

The clan governed itself by a council of the old men, but met on important occasions as a whole, like the Saxon folk-moot. It had a civil chief, and a war chief; the latter led the clan to battle, and taught the young men arts of war. The great war chief or tlacatecuhtli was elected, either by the tribal council or by a special committee of elders and priests, from within a designated group, but the office was not hereditary by right from father to son. Brothers frequently succeeded brothers. The civil chief, called the "snake-woman," supervised and distributed the clan lands, and had charge of food supplies. He seems to have been a minor importance during the final native period. There was also a "speaker" or clan representative in the tribal or general government.

The twenty-or-so clans made up the tribe, and were directly active in its government. For certain military and ceremonial purposes the tribe was also considered as divided into four major quarters, which we should call phratries. These are considered to have been originally clans which divided by segmentation into four or five, thus accounting for the twenty clans and four large brotherhoods of the early sixteenth century. The tribal council, composed, according to at least three early Spanish writers, of twenty members, exercised important powers. It met regularly at short intervals, and upon call in emergencies, and probably held the highest political power. The phratry commanders were elected by their phratries. They had judicial functions as well as military. From among their number (four) the head war chief was invariably elected. Government was chiefly conducted in a great council house (tecpan). Each phratry had a "school house" where the arts of war were taught, and an armory where war materials were stored. These were adjacent to the temples.

The chief interest in the Aztecs centers about the ancient tecpan or temple enclosure, near the site of the modern National Palace, the Zócalo or Plaza de la Constitución, and a block or so only from the Cathedral. Within the Serpent Wall which inclosed this area were located the principal shrines, accessory buildings, arsenals, and workshops associated with religion. Here were the most notable artistic monuments, for religion was art, and art religion. Below ground in this space have been found the most noteworthy examples of religious art attributed to Aztec origins. Three of these, the Calendar Stone or Stone of the Sun, the Sacrificial Stone or Stone of Tizoc, and the statue of Coatlicue the Earth Goddess, are interestingly described by Spinden.

The Calendar Stone, a porphyritic monolith, weighs over twenty tons, the disk being some twelve feet in diameter. It was carried or drawn by men for many miles to be placed before the Temple of the Sun. Originally it was placed disk side up and used as a sacrificial block. It is at one and the same time a symbol of the sun, marked with the divisions of the year, and a record of the Aztecan cosmogonic myth and the creations and destructions of the world. In the center is the face of Tonatiuh (the Sun God), in the circle called Olin, sign of the present age of the world. Four rectangles, beginning at the upper right hand corner and proceeding toward the left, represent the day signs of the four previous ages. They are 4 Ocelotl (jaguar), 4 Ehecatl (wind), 4 Quauhtli (rain), and 4 Atl (water). They refer to legends of destructions of the world successively by jaguars, hurricane, volcanic fire, and flood. The fifth or present sun or age will end with the day 4 Olin, shown in the central symbol. Next comes a circle bearing the signs of the twenty days of the Aztec months. Outside this band are three others probably representing conventionalized sun-rays, the turquoises and the eagle feathers supposed to decorate the real sun. Outside are two feathered snakes, tails at top, and the heads each showing a human profile meeting at the bottom. The day-sign 13 Acatl (reed) between the tails is variously interpreted as the day the present sun began or the date when the stone was first set up, or as the beginning of the year 1479, in which was completed a cycle of 416 years since the original departure from Aztlán. It may well be, however, that this stone is of Toltec rather than Aztec origin.

The Sacrificial Stone is clearly Aztecan. It is a large black-green drum-shaped stone with a small semi-spherical pit in the center of one face, with a drain running to the edge. On this face there is also a sun calendar. The stone was used for human sacrifices, but not for gladiatorial combats. Around the side of the stone are fifteen groups of figures, each a conqueror and his captive. The victor each time appears as either Huitzilopochtli or Tezcatlipoca, emblematic of the Mexican tribe or successive tribal chiefs. Above the head of each captive is the glyph which represents a defeated town or district. The stone represents the Mexican conquests down to the time of the war-chief Tizoc, who is himself represented as victor in one of the groups, his conquest being the district of Matlazinco in the Valley of Toluca.

The statue of Coatlicue, Earth Goddess, or Mother of the Gods, is a horrendous sample of barbarous imagination in religious sculpture. Spinden's description says: "The feet are furnished with claws. The skirt is a writhing mass of braided rattlesnakes. The arms are doubled up and the hands are snake heads on a level with the shoulders. Around the neck and hanging down over the breast is a necklace of alternating hands and hearts with a death's head pendant. The head of this monstrous woman is the same in front and back and is formed of two serpents' heads that meet face to face. The forked tongue and the four downward pointing fangs belong half and half to each of the two profile faces."

Indeed the Aztec religion was grewsome, grim, unlovely, with scant relief in amenable ideas or hopeful concepts. Religion was a matter of fear and horror. It had not become refined enough to develop decorative art. The gods were a legion, devoted to every conceivable human activity or physical force of nature or the divisions of time and space. The cosmogony was centered about Earth represented as gaping jaws, Sea as a circumambient great serpent, and Underworld represented as a Death's Head. Sun, Moon, and Venus, important in calendrical computations, were chief among the astral deities.

The great Aztec gods were, however, those of war, agriculture, and political destiny. Head of them all was Huitzilopochtli, the war god. With him was Tezcatlipoca, who belonged to all the Nahua tribes, Tlaloc the rain god, who antedated the Nahua period, and Quetzalcoatl the "Feathered Snake," probably the oldest of them all.

Quetzalcoatl and Tlaloc represent the early period, no doubt the Toltec influence, or perhaps the common Chichimecan tradition, whereas the other two, Huitzilopochtli and Tezcatlipoca, represent the more warlike activities of the Mexicans, after their number had increased to the point where subsistence had to be obtained by recourse to conquest or raiding, and their cult was encouraged by a priest-craft which sought to rule through inculcation of fear at home and terror abroad. It was the practice of human sacrifices to these gods, and the ceremonial cannibalism connected therewith, that had won for the Mexicans the bitter hatred of neighboring tribes. These practices, with all their accompanying evils, are adduced as proof that the Aztecs were a decadent people when Cortés reached them. Such a speculation is bootless, as we have scant evidence showing that tribes once committed to cannibalism have ever risen to cultural significance in civilization after outgrowing this custom, which is based originally on sheer necessity for food.

The Mayas, who dwelt to the southeast of the Aztecs, in and near Yucatan, appear on the page of American history about the beginning of the Christian era. They had even then developed a wonderfully accurate system of computing time, an indication of their wide removal from savagery. Indeed, they had developed the capacity to compute time not only by lunar and solar recurrences, but it is fairly certain that they were able to predict eclipses, and they may have recorded planetary conjunctions and other astronomical phenomena. Their calculations based on observations of Venus will, when sufficiently studied, furnish important checks on what has so far been deduced from their periods of art, their inscriptions on monuments, and their traditional history, as recorded in the books of Chilan Balam or digests of the ancient chronicles. Their earliest cities with identifiable dates were Tikal, located in northern Guatemala, and Copán, situated in western Honduras. Both were great and important in the third century. Other great cities of the south, of a little later date, were Palenque, Yaxchilan or Menché, Piedras Negras, Seibal, Naranjo, and Quirigua. The period of highest development in this group was between the years 300 and 600 A. D. After the latter date the cities named were apparently abandoned and the Mayas moved northward to settle in northern Yucatan.

The records of Chilan Balam extend back to the year 160

A. D., or not more than four or five years earlier or later. These records are in the Mayan tongue, but are preserved in Spanish script, in the form of abstracts made shortly after the Spanish conquest. The Mayas had developed their calendar and their system of hieroglyphs prior to 160 A. D. An early date, somewhat doubtful, on a statuette at Tuxtla, corresponds to our chronological year 113 B. C. Another on the Leiden plate is 47 A. D. The inscription at Uaxactan in northern Guatemala, interpreted by Sylvanus G. Morley, is also earlier than 160 A. D.

From 160 to 358 may be called the Mayan Early Period. During this epoch began the great cities of the south already mentioned. In them enormous mounds were built up, and temples constructed thereon. Date monuments (stelae) and altars were set up. Their art, moving forward from its archaic forms, was in a transitional stage, the age of the serpent.

From 358 to 455 may be called the Middle Period. It still shows traces of archaic art, as did the Early Period, but the monuments show purity of style and straightforwardness of presentation without over decoration or flamboyant features. The Great Mound at Copán, and the monuments at Naranjo and Piedras Negras belong to this period.

In the Great Period, 455 to 600, a number of new cities rose; architecture became more refined. The inscriptions left during this period show that intricate astronomical studies were being made, and that isolated periods of history showing traditional correlation with other periods and dates grow less common and finally cease. The inscription of an initial series of dates in this period gives the first opportunity for correlation with European chronology.

Spinden calls the period from 600 to 960 a Transition Period. It was apparently during this epoch that the older Mayan cities of the southern area were deserted, and migration northward in Yucatan began. There was a complete cessation of production of pictorial art, though there is some evidence of changing styles of architecture. The first abandonment of Chichen Itza came just before the initiation of this period, which saw the building of one or two cities south of Uxmal. The Maya chronicles show that the nation was then inhabiting a land called Chakanputun, which may have been in the central part of Yucatan.

The land of Chakanputun was abandoned by the Itza group of Mayas, who reëstablished Chichen Itza during a period lying between 960 and 1195. About the same time two other cities, Mayapán and Uxmal were founded, and a league of the three was organized, under the leadership of Mayapán. Other cities flourished at the same time, Izamal being the only one of them concerning which much is known. The art of this period became highly formalized, as did the architecture. Decoration of buildings took the characteristic form of mask panels, containing a face in a rectangular area, built up out of separately carved blocks. Geometrical figures were also introduced.

The period of Mexican influence, 1195 to 1442, was initiated by a civil war between the cities of the League of Mayapán, and closed with the total destruction of that city about 100 years before the coming of the Spaniards, by the aid of seven Toltec interventionists. Possibly they obtained Chichen Itza as compensation for their intervention, for that city at once began to show marked Toltecan influences in art and architecture. A notable example of such an intrusion is the Great Ball Court flanked by temples, a structural ensemble found often in the Toltecan cities, but, among the Mayas, only at Uxmal and Chichen Itza. The Ball Courts were used for a religious athletic exercise something like basket ball. Possibly this Toltec influence ended by the middle of the fourteenth century. It evidently came from the people who inhabited Tula, Teotihuacán, and Cholula. The incidence of this art intrusion coincides with the traditional period of the migration of the Toltecs from Anáhuac, about 1195.

The Modern Period of the Mayas extends from the probable date of the close of the period of Toltecan influence, 1442, down to the present time. In all, it has been a period of decay, first political, then intellectual. Nobles and priests at first kept up the old culture, but its development was arrested because of lack of a powerful protecting state, for the Mayas were split in fratricidal war after the fall of Mayapán. Some of the Itzas returned to the south and set up a city, Tayasal, on an island in Lake Petén, where Mayan culture survived until 1696. Traces of former grandeur continue among several of the Mayan tribes, but known history among these peoples goes only about two hundred years back of the Spanish conquest. Though the Maya tongue is currently spoken, no natives have been able to read the old picture-writing which holds the key to early Mayan history. Spinden inclines to the opinion that there is no basis for the claim that the coming of the white man snuffed out a culture that was about to develop into real civilization, for with the glories of Mayapán the apex of Mayan culture had been passed, and was not, if we may judge by historical analogies, likely to return. Many other archaeologists lean to a contrary opinion, holding that the culture acquired in isolation by these Americans was guarantee of power of development which would have very likely shortly matured a high type of original civilization. At any event, the Mayas were unable to offer effective resistance to the conquest when it came upon them.

The ruin of the Aztec power had been foretold by the mythical, mystical Quetzalcoatl. Moctezuma, chief of men, was consumed by a superstitious assurance that this cataclysm would occur in his own time. Signs and portents convinced him of it. When he heard of the coming of the maritime expeditions of Córdova and Grijalva to Yucatan in 1517 and 1518, he was so sure of ruin swift impending that he sought at once the aid of witchcraft for escape from fate. There came a great and terrifying comet, and the diviners were called upon to tell its portent. Luckless the wights who foretold evil, for it swiftly overtook them by torture or starvation. Profound despair seized the chief of men, who began to plan making costly presents to induce the unwelcome fair-faced ones to depart from his shores.

For a long time the idea of the impending dissolution of

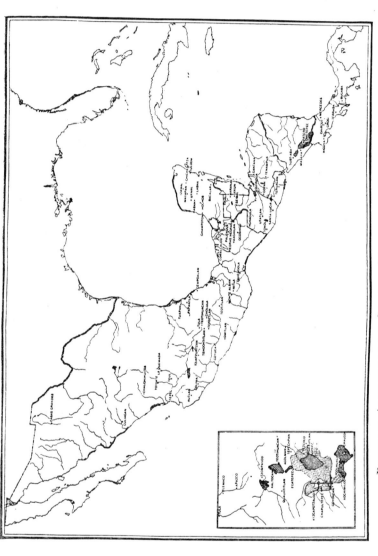

PRINCIPAL ARCHAEOLOGICAL SITES OF MEXICO AND CENTRAL AMERICA

(Reproduced by permission, from H. J. Spinden, *Ancient Civilizations of Mexico and Central America*)

the Aztec power had been gaining ground. Supernatural events were held to signify it. In 1505 widespread famine seemed a portent of worse disasters. In 1507 an eclipse of the sun and an earthquake presaged troubles to come. In 1510 Lake Tezcoco, without cause by flood, earthquake, or tempest, had suddenly risen above former levels, inundating the capital. In 1511 one of the towers of the great teocalli, House of God, in Tenochtitlán, had burst into mysterious flames that consumed it. Comets in daylight, shooting stars, weird night noises, and mysterious lights all presaged doom. The sister of the chief, princess Papantzin, having died and been buried in 1509, was miraculously resurrected three days after death, and came to Moctezuma bringing him warnings from the tomb. It must be confessed that these rather dramatic harbingers of destruction come to us through the medium of the minds of such church writers as Durán and Clavigero, or the Europeanized Tezózomoc, so that it may well be doubted whether Moctezuma was as thoroughly convinced of disaster before the event as we have been led to believe. However that may be, the fates had decreed the end of the greatest of the North American native confederacies, at the hands of the man whose exploits were soon to make him the most renowned captain of the entire Spanish conquest.

CHAPTER III

THE INVASION OF THE MAINLAND

AMERICAN discovery was just a quarter of a century old when the intrusion of the Spaniards into the land of New Spain began. The outward thrust of the conquering race had for a time been slowed down by inadequate opportunities for expansion within the insular area. Columbus had planted an ill-fated colony at La Navidad on the north side of the island of La Española (Haiti) on his first voyage in 1492. This had been absolutely destroyed during his nine months' absence in Spain. Upon his return in 1493 he founded Isabela a few miles to the eastward on the north coast, but the first permanent Spanish settlement in the New World was Santo Domingo, founded in 1496 on the south side of the island. His attempt during the fourth voyage, begun in 1502, to effect a mainland establishment, Santa María de Belén, in Veragua, brought renewed misfortune. It remained for his rivals and successors to set the Spanish foothold firmly on the continent.

It soon became evident that the original plan to give Columbus governmental authority over the immense lands and seas which he had discovered was an administrative absurdity. His admiralty and viceroyalty, conceded by the Spanish monarchs in 1492, would have made him master in time of the whole American continent. It was only natural then that the difficult Bishop Fonseca, who had charge of equipping ships for the new discoveries, should listen willingly to projects framed by the companions of Columbus for independent voyages for trade, exploration, and conquest. In 1495 and for a few succeeding years any Spaniard might at his own expense undertake trade and barter in the Indies. Voyages by Alonzo de Ojeda, and by Pedro Alonzo Niño and

34

Cristóbal Guerra, were made to the South American coast in 1499. Vicente Yáñez Pinzón also in that year began a voyage in which he discovered the same coast as far as eight degrees south, and Diego de Lepe about the same time went over much of the same route. Cristóbal Guerra in 1500 performed a second voyage to the Pearl Coast. In the same year Rodrigo de Bastidas reached the coast of Darien. In 1504 Juan de la Cosa reached the Gulf of Darien, then called Urabá, and sailed 200 miles up the Atrato River.

In 1508 Ponce de León undertook to conquer Puerto Rico. Esquivel began in 1509 to pacify Jamaica for Diego Columbus. In 1508 Ocampo circumnavigated the island of Cuba, and in 1511 Diego Velázquez undertook its occupation. The spread of colonizing energy was now to reach the mainland.

In 1508 Alonzo de Ojeda and Diego de Nicuesa were given contracts to make settlements on the continent in areas to be known as Urabá and Veragua, lying on either side of the modern Gulf of Darien. In 1509 each of these captains sailed and attempted to found two colonies, Ojeda at Cartegena and San Sebastián, and Nicuesa at Belén and Nombre de Dios. Both attempts failed, and the survivors of the two groups united at Santa María de la Antigua del Darien. This was the nucleus from which the mainland occupation for a time advanced.

At Santa María the salient figure by 1511 was Vasco Núñez de Balboa. In 1514 he was superseded in authority by Pedrarias de Ávila, who came as governor of the mainland territory, now to be known as Castilla del Oro. The coming of Pedrarias marked the further removal of the mainland settlements from the tutelage of the authorities of La Española.

In 1513, under the urge of prospective disaster from the coming of Pedrarias, Balboa had effected the discovery of the Pacific, and held hazy tenure as royal adelantado over the South Sea, Panamá, and Coiba, lands sloping toward the Pacific, until he was reduced to nonentity by Pedrarias, and in 1519 executed by him. In that same year the homicide governor himself built Panamá and Nombre de Dios, which marked the end of expansion from Santa María. Henceforth Panamá became the base of operations northward and southward. In 1524 Pedrarias founded Bruselas, Granada, and León, all in Nicaraguan territory, but further expansion in that direction was checked for a time by the southward sweep of the Cortesian conquest of Mexico.

The movement into Mexico had been preceded by northward slave-hunting voyages and searches for a strait to the East Indies. Discovery of the Gulf and mainland coasts had brought into shadowy existence a group of luckless colonial territories north of the Cortesian conquests. In 1512 Juan Ponce de León began an attempt to settle the "Island" of Florida, but had definitely failed by 1521. Slavers and strait hunters in the first fourth of the century ran the whole Atlantic coast. In 1519 Alonzo de Pineda coasted the Gulf, and his master, Garay, was authorized to colonize Amichel reaching from Florida to Vera Cruz. The project had failed by 1523. Lucas Vázquez de Ayllón was in 1523 made adelantado of lands lying north of Florida. His settlement, at San Miguel de Gualdape, was another ghastly failure. Again in 1526 Pánfilo de Narváez sought to explore and settle between the Río de las Palmas and the Cape of Florida; once more disaster ensued, leaving the upper Gulf coast free from Spanish aggression for a decade after 1528.

These last named efforts at colonization, unsuccessful because of inept leaders or inhospitable coasts and treacherous seas, had been synchronous with the successful enterprise of Hernán Cortés. That movement began in two simple slave-hunting voyages from Cuba. The first, in 1517, was led by Francisco Hernández de Córdova, who took three vessels to the point of Yucatan, where, at Catoche, he fought the Indians in a battle, receiving wounds which cost him his life shortly after his return to Cuba. He had brought two natives with him, from whom the adelantado, Velázquez, must have learned as much as he did from Córdova. The second expedition, under the lead of Juan de Grijalva, coasted from Yucatan to San Juan de Ulloa in 1518, that is, it covered all the sea-space which Cortés later followed and even went north to the Pánuco River, but failed of results, save to bring home a little gold, from lack of initiative and audacity.

The near successes of Córdova and Grijalva had warmed the heart of Diego de Velázquez of Cuba to pursue the indicated path of fortune. To carry his plans to fruition he chose for his expeditionary the young Estremaduran, Hernán Cortés, who had led an active life in the island possessions since 1504.

Cortés organized and partly paid for a fleet which was loaded with adventurers and provisions acquired by force, persuasion, and appeals to cupidity in the Cuban ports of Baracoa, Mocaca, Trinidad, and Havana. Velázquez bore the greater part of the expense of the expedition, but at the moment of its departure from Baracoa repented of his choice of leader, and attempted to remove Cortés from command. But the wily Estremaduran had won the hearts of his followers, and departed with them in spite of his superior. The fleet sailed for Cozumel on February 18, 1519. On the Yucatan coast Cortés in middle March performed, according to the orders of Velázquez, an act of humanity which served him in good stead later on. This was to rescue one Gerónimo de Aguilar, a Spanish ecclesiastic, who had been captured some years before while on a voyage from Darien to La Española, and had, with a sole companion named Guerrero, escaped the cannibalism of which eighteen of their companions had been victims. Aguilar had learned the Maya tongue, and was hence a valued acquisition to the party. His utility was enhanced when, on the Tabasco coast, the Spaniards, after victory over the natives, were presented with a number of female slaves. Among these was Doña Marina, a young Aztec woman, who had been enslaved among the Mayas and could speak their language as well as her native Aztec. With these two interpreters, Cortés was able to hold direct verbal converse with Moctezuma's people later, an advantage which Córdova and Grijalva had not enjoyed.

Sailing up the Gulf coast, the Spaniards reached the site of San Juan de Ulloa on April 21. Here the presence of crowds of Indians on the shore induced them to land. Shortly after this was done some ambassadors from Moctezuma, leading four thousand Aztecs bearing messages and gifts, came to the Spanish camp. The Mexican monarch had been kept apprised of the movements of the strangers ever since the first landing of Córdova in 1517, and it was his determination to ward off danger by preventing the Europeans from penetrating farther into his domains.

But Cortés was not to be denied access to the Aztec capital. While he was establishing a new base at a healthier site than that first chosen, he learned that the Aztec "empire" was torn with dissensions, and that Moctezuma's enemies would welcome and even assist in effecting its disintegration. Although the Spanish party was itself divided beween loyalty to Velázquez and loyalty to Cortés, the audacious leader was able to persuade his own partisans to continue occupation of the coast and plan further conquests instead of returning to Cuba as the Velázquez sympathizers in his party urged. The rebellious movement was made as regular as possible by the establishment of the city of Vera Cruz, with a municipal council, and the choice of Cortés as captain-general and chief justice. Outwardly, the expedition now had the semblance of a royally sanctioned enterprise. The recalcitrant Velázquez men were coaxed, promised, wheedled, threatened, and sent inland on expeditions, to prevent their desertion.

It was soon discovered that the Totonac Indians of Cempoalla, northward along the coast, were anxious to free themselves from Moctezuma's control. Marching to their chief city, Cortés adroitly brought them into conflict with Aztec tax collectors, and then espoused their cause. They became Spanish vassals, and assisted in building the new Vera Cruz, while some thirty other Totonac villages followed their example.

Cortés was well aware that his old friend and former master, Velázquez, would not lightly give up control of the expedition should it prove successful, so he sent to Spain his loyal followers Portocarrero and Montejo bearing exquisite presents for the Emperor, Charles V, and a detailed account of his activities. The Velázquez contingent, fearful of the enterprise against an obviously powerful native empire, and deterred from the hazards of an inland conquest by the lack of official sanction, formed a design of seizing one of the ships, returning to Cuba, and helping Velázquez to apprehend the emissaries of Cortés. To prevent the success of this plot, happily discovered, Cortés and his most venturesome partisans sank their ships in the roadstead, after denuding them of cordage, anchors, and other accessories which opportunely served a later purpose of the conquest.

The royal City of the True Cross was left under command of Juan de Escalante when Cortés, with some 450 followers, a few small cannon and fifteen horsemen, set out on August 16, 1519, on his famous inland march. The first objective after the painful ascent from the torrid coast into the Plateau of Anáhuac was the notable so-called republic of Tlascala. Its people were blood relatives of the Aztecs, but had long since separated from them, and had recently been successful in repelling incursions of Moctezuma's hosts, which came annually to capture prisoners for sacrifice to Huitzilopochtli.

After several notable successes in arms against the Tlascalans, whose councils were divided concerning the proper course to pursue with the Spaniards, Cortés succeeded in winning the allegiance of this warlike people. From that time forth the hereditary enemies of Moctezuma became faithful allies of the "messengers of the sun" and served them with a loyalty and efficiency worthy a better reward than they ever received. The Tlascalan alliance reduced the hazard of an arduous inland journey, and made feasible the conquest of a splendid empire so rich that its actual glories seemed well nigh inconceivable.

Pressing inland from Tlascala, the Spanish adventurer, full of conviction that he was an agent of Divine Providence commissioned to proselytize for Christ and enrich his Emperor, now followed by a force alleged to have numbered one hundred thousand Tlascalan warriors, advanced upon the sacred city of the Plateau of Anáhuac, Cholula. This town, allied with the Aztec empire, but full of fear since the successes of the Spaniards against Tlascala, received the bearded strangers with apparent cordiality and respect. Very shortly, however, the Cholulans, obeying Moctezuma's known desire to prevent the arrival of the Spaniards, began to plan their destruction. If it had not been for Marina, the faithful mistress of Cortés, who discovered and exposed the treachery, the conquest of Mexico might have awaited some later band of adventurers. Cortés, meeting deceit with deception, called together the plotters, reproached them for their proposed treachery, and turned upon them his cannon and his terrifying horsemen. Hundreds, if not thousands, of Cholulans paid with their lives for the proposed duplicity of their leaders in a day of carnage that blots the luster of Spanish glory. The deed measures the scant disparity between the grades of culture of victor and victim.

By November 1 the terrible strangers were ready to resume the approach to Tenochtitlán. Reaching Lake Tezcoco, they advanced upon the island citadel over the Iztapalapán causeway, from which they could see the numerous lacustrine suburbs of Moctezuma's capital. The panorama amazed them. Tenochtitlán, with its towers and temples, its causeways and aqueducts, its palaces and gardens, was like the realization of a wonderful dream. On November 8, the "chief of men," shod among his barefoot retainers, received the foreigners near the portals of the city, and, yielding to superstition instead of attempting to repel them, led them into his stronghold and lodged them in "a large and handsome house," the palace of the former King Axayácatl. Here shortly after the first visits of greeting had been exchanged, Cortés realized that he was actually in a most dangerous position, for should the Mexicans choose, they might easily starve his party to death without striking a blow or losing a man. Hence he took as an excuse for strategic duplicity an act of treachery which had been committed at Moctezuma's behest when one of his captains, Quauhpopoca, had killed two Spaniards sent from Vera Cruz to escort him thither to give in his allegiance to Juan de Escalante, commander of the port. Complaining of this act, which had occurred while he was at Cholula, Cortés seized the person of Moctezuma, compelled him to live in the Spaniards' quarters, and undertook to govern the Mexicans through him.

It would now have been possible to proceed with the subjugation of the empire and the accumulation of riches; but, with the coming of spring, arrived disconcerting news from the coast. About April 1, Pánfilo de Narváez had reached San Juan de Ulloa with sixteen vessels and 1500 men, bent on punishing Cortés and assuming control of the conquest for Governor Velázquez. A journey to the coast to meet him became imperative. Cortés left Pedro de Alvarado in Tenochtitlán with some eighty former partisans of Velázquez or others of doubtful allegiance or disability for the march. With his effective forces he set forth early in May for the coast where, near Cempoalla, he succeeded by a masterstroke night-attack and his seductive blandishments in overcoming Narváez and attaching the latter's soldiers to his own cause.

Returning to Tenochtitlán with his forces greatly swelled after the defeat of Narváez, Cortés was perturbed to find that Alvarado, fearing treachery by the Aztecs, had emulated his leader's procedure at Cholula, and had massacred the flower of the Mexican nobility on the occasion of a festival to the god Tezcatlipoca. The little garrison, after heroic self-defense, was about to succumb from fighting and lack of food; even the added forces brought by Cortés could not remove the danger. In vain the perplexed leader tried his astuteness. Thinking to mollify the Aztecs, he released to them the brother of Moctezuma, Cuitláhuac, who believed in vigorous resistance instead of passive submission. But Cuitláhuac was made leader of the Aztecs, and Moctezuma was henceforth ignored. Daily fighting, with heroic sallies from their fortress, netted the harassed Spaniards nothing, and it was seen that a retreat, if possible, must be effected.

But to get out was not so easy as to get in. Cuitláhuac and his followers had resolved upon their extermination. The city was connected with the mainland only by narrow causeways. These were closely watched and strongly defended. They were cut by numerous canals, and the bridges were gone. But the menaced Spaniards, leaving such treasure behind as cupidity would permit, essayed an escape on the night of June 30, forever famous as the Noche Triste, the Sad Night. While moving stealthily along the causeway, they were discovered. Amid beat of war drum and enemy shouts they found, at the second gap in the causeway, that their only portable bridge could not be brought up because it had caught fast in the mud at the first crossing. There they were all but overwhelmed by numbers, struck down by native weapons, or drowned in the lake. Horses, men, and treasure all seemed lost. Those who could, saved themselves over the bodies of the fallen. At Popotla, the enemy having desisted from pursuit, Cortés gathered the remnant of his forces and, legend says, sat down to weep under the ahuehuete tree which still marks the historic spot.

It was the purpose of the leader to fall back upon his allies, the Tlascalans. First, it was necessary to defeat the Aztec enemy in the valley of Otumba, where myriads of plumed warriors disputed the path. Fortunately the leader of the native hosts was killed and the mighty army dispersed. Cortés reëntered Tlascala, spent the autumn in recuperation and building brigantines to fight the Aztecs on their lake, and in subjecting all allies of the empire who offered resistance. Finally preparation for a new attack upon the capital was complete. The host of allies following the Spaniards numbered many thousands. On the borders of the lake the forces were divided, parts being placed under Alvarado, Sandoval, and Cristóbal de Olid. Cortés commanded the brigantines. The struggle nevertheless lasted for eighty-five days of bitter siege warfare. The Aztecs, under Quauhtémoc, for Cuitláhuac had died of the smallpox imported by a negro slave of Narváez, fought desperately, without food or water, amid the destruction of their city and the pestilential stench of the bodies of their fallen companions. "Tear down our walls," they shouted to the Tlascalans, "for you will build them up again, either for the Spaniards if they defeat us, or else for us if we win " At last, with only a remnant of their proud city standing, their leader attempted flight in a canoe. Apprehended and brought before Cortés he begged the latter, if tradition is faithful, to take with his dagger the life he had not been able to lose for his country.

The ancient capital was rebuilt while Cortés stayed at the nearby village of Coyoacán. A new city dedicated to Charles V was erected on the former seat of Aztec might. Round about it sprang up, in a few brief years, an empire unsurpassed in wealth, greater in area and richer potentially by far than the Holy Roman Empire from which Charles could not divorce his thought and attention. The foundations of New Spain were now about to be laid.

Even before his power had been established in Tenochtitlán, before the death of Moctezuma, Cortés had sent several expeditions throughout the surrounding country under guidance of the tlacatecuhtli's agents, to find gold mines. Effort to find a better site for a harbor than Vera Cruz led to the sending of Juan Velázquez de León to make a settlement on the Coatzacoalcos River. Rodrigo Rangel, with a group of followers, went to Chiantla to lay out a royal plantation, which was probably shortlived. The siege of Mexico interrupted the first efforts at expansion, but shortly the second Spanish city was set up in Tepeaca province and called Segura de la Frontera. This establishment was made shortly after the Noche Triste. Mexico itself was the third establishment, and Medellín, founded in 1521 in the present state of Vera Cruz by Gonzalo de Sandoval, the fourth. The desire of Cortés to find the "dubious strait" which, piercing the continent, should lead to the Spice Islands, induced him to send two expeditions to explore the coast of the South Sea, one reaching the region of Colima and the other that of

Tehuantepec. Another force, which set out about the same time as that of Sandoval, overran the present states of Puebla and Oaxaca during 1522. In the same year Sandoval founded a city, Espíritu Santo, on the Coatzacoalcos. Meanwhile, Álvarez Chico and Alonzo de Ávalos respectively, went to Zacatula and Colima. Chico was unsuccessful, but Ávalos explored a part of Jalisco, conquering the Provinces of Ávalos, as the region was long called. Alvarado was unsuccessful in efforts to make establishments in Tututepec, the present state of Oaxaca.

About the close of 1522 or the beginning of 1523, Cortés went himself to Pánuco, defeated the Huastecas, and founded San Esteban del Puerto (today Pánuco). This was for years the northeastern outpost of New Spain. Inland it reached westward from Pánuco to Meztitlán, in the northern part of the states of Mexico and Vera Cruz. Colima, with a Spanish garrison was set up by Sandoval in 1523. In December of the same year Pedro de Alvarado overran Oaxaca, Tehuantepec, and Soconusco, thence advancing into Guatemala, which soon became his separate captaincy-general. In the same month, Diego de Godoy subjected much of Chiapas.

On January 11, 1524, Cristóbal de Olid left Vera Cruz with five ships to effect a settlement in Honduras. At the same time Diego de Hurtado with three vessels began the Cortesian exploration of the eastern coast in search of the strait. Olid, touching Cuba on his journey, was induced by Velázquez partisans and his own ambition to desert the cause of Cortés, and attempt independence. Francisco de las Casas was sent by sea to chastise him, and Cortés, fearful that suitable results might not be achieved, himself undertook his famous journey overland to Honduras in October, 1524. This journey cost the conqueror innumerable fatigues, did little to promote the conquest, and besmirched his name with the foul murder of a group of Aztec chiefs, including Quauhtémoc, who were brutally hung under suspicion of treachery while being carried on the march as hostages. When Cortés, having passed through the swamps of southern Mexico and the mountains of northern Central America, finally reached Honduras, he found that Olid had been captured and had met his death at the hands of Francisco de las Casas. During his absence, his own enemies in Mexico did their best to undo the constructive work Cortés had left unfinished behind him; the colony was torn with bickerings, and soon came Luis Ponce de León, royal investigator, armed with a commission to succeed Cortés and place him on trial. Though Ponce de León soon died, his successors and the enemies of Cortés were able to cause so much perturbation that the work of discovery and conquest was for a time retarded. One minor expedition under Francisco Cortés, nephew of the conqueror, did overrun Jalisco again in 1526, but effected no settlement or discovery of consequence.

In 1527 Captain Diego de Mazariegos, under orders of Cortés, marched against the province of Chiapas and conquered the Chiapanecs; there he founded in March the settlement of Villareal. In 1529 it took the name of Villaviciosa, and in 1531 that of San Cristóbal de los Llanos; as San Cristóbal it is now known.

The conquest of Yucatan and the island of Cozumel was undertaken in 1527 by Don Francisco de Montejo, who, sent to Spain by Cortés on a mission brought from there the forces which began the enterprise as a part of the program of Cortés. The adelantado Montejo was driven out of the country by the Maya Indians in a very few years, and the conquest of the peninsula was not effected until 1547 when the son of Montejo, also named Francisco, completed the pacification of that area. Civil government and religious institutions had been established before that time.

The determination of Cortés to conquer the territory of Mexico was secondary to his will to find the strait that had since the time of Columbus been believed to communicate with the western or South Sea and lead the way to the fabulous empires of the Orient, then considered to be near at hand to the west coast of Mexico, such being the common error regarding the size of the earth. The various explorers sent out by Cortés to the Atlantic and Pacific seaboards brought no news of a strait, but once he found himself in possession of the west coast, he ordered two caravels and two brigantines built, the first for the high seas, and the latter for coastwise reconnaissance. Materials were carried two hundred leagues overland from the Gulf of Mexico for the purpose. The storehouse burned just after all these necessaries had been collected in it, and they had to be replaced by importations from Castile. Vessels procured on the Atlantic coast, two caravels and two brigantines, were sent to run the coast from Florida to Newfoundland. Nothing is known of their voyage.

When finally the brigantines on the South Sea were ready to explore the coast from Zacatula to Panamá, they were burned. To replace them, new vessels were begun at Tehuantepec under Captain Francisco Maldonado. In the same year Cortés, despairing of justice in New Spain, was obliged to go to Spain to counteract the jealousy and persecution of his enemies. Returning triumphant over them in 1530 with more than four hundred new followers for his maritime expeditions, he spent the next year in getting together a new fleet. This was put under command of his cousin Diego Hurtado de Mendoza and sailed from Acapulco, June 30, 1532, to discover the islands of the South Sea and the west coast of New Spain. After running the Jalisco and Culiacán coasts the fleet made a port in twenty-seven degrees north latitude, where the Spaniards found no provisions. The crews were becoming mutinous, so Hurtado took the best seamen and went on to make further discoveries. He and his party were all lost at sea. The remaining expeditionaries reached Culiacán and sent twenty men inland for provisions, but, coming into the territory of Jalisco, then under the bitter enemy of Cortés, Nuño de Guzmán, they were cast into prison. The remaining men on the ship were wrecked near Jalisco and all but three were killed by the Indians. These survivors reached Aguatlán in Jalisco, but Guzmán seized all the remnants of their ship and equipment, and refused to restore anything to Cortés.

The undaunted leader thereupon hastened the completion

of vessels which were under construction at Tehuantepec. He equipped two; upon the *Concepción* was Captain Diego Becerra, with Fortún Ximénez as chief pilot. The *San Lázaro* was commanded by Hernando de Grijalva. They were to search for and succor Hurtado if possible. They sailed from Santiago in north latitude 16° 30′, on October 30, 1533. The vessels became separated almost at once. The *San Lázaro* reached 20° 21′ north latitude, but returned south to Acapulco, and subsequently explored the Tehuantepec coast. Diego Becerra, commander of the *Concepción*, was murdered by his pilot, Fortún Ximénez. The latter then sailed to Santa Cruz on the Lower California coast, where he and twenty-two others perished at the hands of the Indians. The vessel returned to the coast of Jalisco, where Guzmán seized everything. Cortés made a plea to the audiencia, then judicial head of New Spain, to recover his vessel. Guzmán ignored the order of the court, so Cortés determined to recover it himself and continue his discoveries at the same time.

For this purpose, he ordered three vessels, which had been built at Tehuantepec, to proceed to Chametla. From that place he sailed April 15, 1535, ere long reaching Santa Cruz, where Ximénez had been killed. Attempting to colonize there during months of arduous toil and privation, with loss of ships and cargoes from the mainland, Cortés was able to effect only a temporary hold upon the peninsula. In the same year he was able to provide Francisco Pizarro, bound upon the conquest of Peru, with two shiploads of supplies, but the treacherous waters of the Sea of Cortés, now called the Gulf of California, were too great an impediment to the colonization of the inhospitable California coast. At the order of Antonio de Mendoza, first viceroy of New Spain, who had arrived in 1535, the colonists were withdrawn from Santa Cruz.

But Cortés fitted out three more ships, and sent them out under Francisco de Ulloa in 1539. This activity was opposed by Mendoza and by the second audiencia as well, for this was after the return of Fray Marcos de Niza from his investigations of the lands described by Álvar Núñez Cabeza

de Vaca, who had crossed the continent with a remnant of
the Narváez expedition of 1528, reaching Culiacán in 1536.
Mendoza and the audiencia had no notion of seeing their
power diminished by allowing Cortés to discover and possess
a government on the periphery of the newly organized
viceroyalty of New Spain. Ulloa did, however, set sail,
making a voyage to the head of the Gulf of California and
up the outside coast as far as Cedros Island. From that
point one vessel returned to New Spain while Ulloa sailed
away on new discoveries, nothing later being known of him.

The net results of the voyages under orders of Cortés in
the South Sea were expensively disappointing to him. He
had discovered the peninsula of California and had reached
the head of the Gulf of the same name; he might have been
satisfied with this; but his mind was fired with the Fray
Marcos stories as strongly as was the mind of Mendoza the
viceroy. Cortés was sure that he had the right, by the
terms under which he held the title of captain-general, to
follow up the Fray Marcos stories. The bad feeling engendered between him and Mendoza over this last discovery was responsible for the judicial processes brought
against Cortés before the audiencia of New Spain. Hence
the unhappy conqueror, who had added to Charles' empire
the richest area of America, weary of the repeated failures
which destroyed his plans, decided to return again to Spain
to seek justice. There, with no recognition or attention,
worn out by futile solicitations for the indemnity he craved
for his enormous expenditures, he ended his days in Cas-
telleja de la Cuesta, near Seville, December 2, 1547. His
ambition, his astuteness, his audacity, his early success,
have given him the fame of Spain's greatest conqueror, as
Columbus and Magellan were her most illustrious navigators. His many crimes, ruthless and inexcusable, treacherous and murderous, were the common practices of his time;
in them he sank to the level of his day; in his daring, his
pertinacity, his genius for leadership, and in his total achievement, he rose far above any other Spaniard whose name is
written on the page of the American continental conquest.

CHAPTER IV

ESTABLISHMENT OF THE VICEROYALTY

THE expedition fitted out by Diego Velázquez, adelantado of Cuba, which sailed under Cortés and brought about the conquest of the empire of Moctezuma during the dramatic years 1519–21, had been organized under authority issued by the Jeronymite Fathers, Friar Luis de Figueroa and Friar Alonzo de Santo Domingo. These two men were the governing power in La Española at the time, they having been sent out from Spain with a third father, Bernardino Manzanedo, at the solicitation of Father Bartholomew de Las Casas to settle the troubles which had arisen with regard to the status of the encomiendas in that island, and to serve as a committee with authority in affairs which concerned the Indians.

Thus the legal filiation of the enterprise was, until the disagreement between Velázquez and Cortés, complete and regular. The instructions given to Cortés authorized him to proceed to the Yucatan coast and rescue certain marooned Spaniards believed to be existing there among the natives, shipwrecked men from the expeditions of Nicuesa, Córdova, and Grijalva. He was then to proceed over the routes taken by his predecessors, the last two named voyagers, and report upon his findings. He was not authorized to proceed with a conquest nor effect any settlement. Velázquez had furthermore, as was intimated in the preceding chapter, revoked the authority of Cortés to lead the expedition just before it left the island. Cortés therefore had no official status as a conqueror from that moment, although he certainly had some rights in equity as to disposition of the fleet because of his large investment, comprising his entire resources, in its equipment.

49

When, after their arrival at San Juan de Ulloa, Cortés and his personal adherents among the expeditionaries resolved upon a settlement and conquest, the color of legality was given to the changed character of the enterprise by the organization in April, 1519, of the municipality of Vera Cruz; the regidores or town trustees of this volunteer political entity immediately made their leader captain-general and justicia mayor (chief justice) of the conquest. The Emperor Charles V, King of Spain, was apprised of this action, and his confirmation thereof was sought by the first of Cortés' letters to his ruler, upon whose clemency he threw himself in his insubordination against Velázquez.

His attempt was at first unsuccessful. In August, 1521, Cristóbal de Tapia came, authorized by Bishop Fonseca, arch-enemy of Cortés as he had been of Columbus, to take the rebel prisoner. Tapia was prevented from executing his commission by the town councils of Vera Cruz, the recently founded Tepeaca (Segura de la Frontera), Mexico, and Medellín. These bodies united in a junta for the purpose—in which they succeeded—of persuading Tapia to go away leaving Cortés in power.

In October, 1522, Cortés was named by the Emperor governor and captain-general of New Spain in reward for his marvelous conquest and his magnificent gifts. His insubordination was thus forgiven and his status legalized. At the same time the royal power was affirmed by the appointment of treasury officers who were to attend to the national interests. These were Rodrigo de Albornoz as accountant, Gonzalo de Salazar as administrator, Alonzo de Estrada as treasurer, and Pedro Almíndez Chirinos as inspector or royal marker of gold and silver. When in 1524 Cortés, solicitous for the integrity of Cristóbal de Olid, followed the latter into Honduras, he left in charge at Mexico Alonzo de Estrada, with the licentiate Alonzo de Zuazo as his judicial adviser. In 1525 the town council of Mexico added Rodrigo de Albornoz to this governing committee. Bitter quarrels among them resulted in serious ruptures; Salazar and Chirinos were put in wooden cages and exposed to popular derision by the friends of Cortés, in resentment of their procedure in the matter of the bestowal of encomiendas. Cortés, returning from Honduras unexpectedly as from the grave in 1526, named Albornoz and Estrada as his lieutenants in government. But in that same year came Luis Ponce de León, armed with a royal commission to supersede Cortés and bring him to trial for his administrative acts. Ponce's sudden death, so sudden that Cortés has never been wholly exonerated of responsibility for it, left in control a second new governor and investigator, Martín de Aguilar, inquisitor from Santo Domingo, an old man who ruled nine months and in turn also died. In March, 1527, Alonzo de Estrada, servant of the opposition to Cortés, obliged the friends of the latter to give up such share in the government as they held. The great conqueror himself, under the cloud of the official investigation, yet uncompleted, of his conduct, spent his time away from the capital, in Coyoacán and Tezcoco, and, finally despairing of justice from his peers, voyaged to Spain in 1528 to make a personal appeal to the Emperor, as has been previously noted.

During the period 1522–28 the town council of Mexico held its regular meetings in the residence of Cortés at Coyoacán, hence it is obvious that his influence over that body must have been materially felt throughout that time. But in 1528 a turn in the affairs of New Spain was given by the arrival of a judicial and administrative body, the audiencia, formed for the mainland colony as one had previously been established at Santo Domingo, and modeled largely on the same courts long existing in Valladolid and Granada.

The first audiencia of New Spain, which assumed control in the year named, was headed by Nuño de Guzmán, who had been governor of Pánuco and had there come into conflict with the Cortés party in 1527. The other members of the audiencia were Ortiz de Matienzo, Diego Delgadillo, Alonzo de Parada, and Francisco Maldonado. Parada and Maldonado soon died, and the functions of general government were exercised by the three remaining.

The deeds of Nuño de Guzmán as head of government

were so perversive of good order, and so bitter was the out-cry against him, that Archbishop Zumárraga of Mexico made a serious representation against him to Charles V. The Emperor, leaving Spain about that time to attend to his ambitions in Germany, left the affairs of New Spain in the hands of the Queen, Doña María, and the latter, influenced by the communication from Zumárraga, resolved to appoint a new audiencia. These new judges and governors were to make a formal judicial inquiry into the official activities of their predecessors, and send them to Spain with their trial records, if the complaints against them should be substan-tiated. It was in anticipation of the advent of this inquest that Guzmán, deciding that his safety lay in absence, went westward for the conquest of Nueva Galicia and brought about the foundation of Compostela, the later Guadalajara.

The second audiencia, which assumed control in 1530, had for its president Sebastián Ramírez de Fuenleal, bishop of Santo Domingo, and president of the insular audiencia, who already had achieved a reputation for probity and efficiency in the administrative work which he had done in La Es-pañola. The other judges or oidores of this audiencia were chosen by Bishop Fonseca of Badajoz. They were Juan de Salmerón, Alonzo Maldonado, Francisco Ceinos, and last, but most noteworthy, Vasco de Quiroga, later bishop of Michoacán and in that region still superior today in reputa-tion to the great Las Casas as friend and apostle of the Indians.

The audiencia was to carry on the executive government and also administer justice; with it was to come Cortés, successful as to newly bestowed titles at least, to serve as captain-general. The new audiencia made its solemn entry into Mexico City in 1531, and took up its residence in the house of Cortés. Soon after, Fuenleal arrived from Santo Domingo, and governed New Spain in ad interim capacity pending the coming of a viceroy as president of the audiencia until 1535. His control was beneficent and peaceful for the colony, torn as it had been by the dissensions among the encomenderos and enemies of Cortés during the unhappy

years which ensued immediately after the fall of Tenochtitlán. Fuenleal was a wise governor whose interesting work
has received all too scant recognition from historians. His
rule established justice where only bickerings had preceded.
He was responsible for founding the city of Puebla de los
Angeles, for constructing a part of the City of Mexico, for
the building of many sadly needed bridges and roads, and
for the framing of regulations for the incipient civilization
of the colony.

In 1528, when Doña María had resolved upon the establishment of the audiencia of New Spain, she had also determined
to inaugurate in the New World another modified Spanish
governmental institution which had proved successful in
the management of the great empire of Charles. This was
the establishment of the office of the viceroy. Such a scheme
had indeed been used by the doges of Venice in their Oriental
trading stations, by the Portuguese, their successors in
maritime colonies in the same area, by the kings of Aragon
in Sardinia and Sicily, and by Charles V in Naples. The
monarchs of Castile had also frequently used the title for
rulers of dependent areas.

The adoption of the viceroyalty in New Spain was induced
by the difficulties which had attended the adjustment of the
encomienda system of exploiting the Indians and the quarrels
that had accompanied every attempt at regulating the status
of the conquerors and first settlers. Cortés, his lieutenants,
the audiencia, all had alike shown themselves powerless to
affirm the royal dominion and will in these interminable
broils. But these men were of and among the adventurers
themselves. They had been partisans, were without rank or
prestige, and were, except Cortés, personally unknown to
their royal master. The crown felt the need of a personal
representative removed in spirit from the acerbities of the
conquest, whose category and prestige as its personal representative would aid efficiency and whose loyalty would be
beyond cavil. In the last named quality Cortés was considered deficient.

Doña María made the offer of the new position to the

Conde de Oropesa, and next to the Mariscal Fromenta; each in turn refused an honor so remote and so hazardous. Next Manuel Benavides was approached, but he demanded too large a salary for the exchequer to meet, and the final choice fell upon Antonio de Mendoza, the Conde de Tendilla. The choice and acceptance occurred in 1528, but, due to delays caused by necessary arrangements of his personal affairs, Mendoza did not depart for the field of his labors until 1535.

It was his task to carry forward the consolidation of the royal power which had been begun by Fuenleal. A serious impediment in the way of the consummation of this ideal was the presence of Cortés in the new viceroyalty in the position of captain-general. He might naturally have been thought of as a suitable recipient of the new office, but his reputation for insubordination against Velázquez, and the suspicion that he had been implicated in plots looking toward the independence of New Spain, combined perhaps with his power of astute manipulation of the wills of his numerous associates in arms for his own advantage, had caused him to be overlooked when the office was seeking the man. He was, however, left undisturbed for the time in his captaincy-general, partly because he had a prescriptive right in it, and partly no doubt because of the hope, still cherished, that through his ambition other great realms might yet be added to the Spanish crown.

The qualities needed in the viceroy were prestige and loyalty. Mendoza belonged to the military order of Santiago, had been a successful ambassador to Rome, was a cousin of the archbishop of Seville and cardinal of Spain, and a relative of the royal house. He was appointed April 17, 1535, as viceroy and president of the audiencia, with a salary of three thousand ducats in each capacity and two thousand for his viceroyal guard. Probably his combined annual perquisites had the purchasing value of about $75,000 of present day American money. No stated term of office was specified; from the character of his duties, as will be shown, it was evidently intended that his period of ser-

vice should be a long one, perhaps for life, as it practically
turned out to be.

The character of the new office may be gathered from the
nature of the royal instructions to Mendoza.   There was
already an audiencia in the country, and a captain-general,
but there was no explicit distribution of the functions of
government, no idea of scientific colonial control, and no
suitable tradition to follow.   The king, as absolute ruler of
Spain, was the fountain of law and justice; within New Spain
his viceroy was to be the impersonation of the same autocratic policy, subject to the limitations of personal loyalty
and meticulous advice or direction through orders of the
Council of the Indies or advice of the audiencia.   His presidency of the audiencia gave him the control of its administrative deliberations and general knowledge of its legal
processes, though he was not permitted to vote in judicial
decisions, he not being a jurisconsult.   He was to advise with
the court in administrative affairs, but was not bound to
follow its counsel.   He was also made acting captain-general,
with power to assume the corresponding functions if need
should arise.   In ecclesiastical matters the prelates were to
be consulted and reverenced; the viceroy was to report to
the king at once concerning all religious needs.   The king's
prerogative in church patronage was to be safeguarded;
ecclesiastical courts were to have no powers over laymen,
but ecclesiastical immunity was to be preserved; scandalous
living in parishes or convents was to be prevented.   No
papal bull or brief was to be published except when issued
through the Council of the Indies.

The non-spiritual purpose of the colony, that is the
creation of wealth for the crown, was to be met by increasing the revenues.   Hidden treasures were to be sought,
the tribute from the Indians increased if possible, and the
alcabala (sales tax) imposed upon them if this should be
thought feasible.   All industries that might promote wealth
were to be encouraged solicitously among natives and
Spaniards alike.   The royal treasury officers were to be
watched carefully, and their collections paid into the treasury.

The defence of the kingdom was to be provided for by the erection of suitable forts. The Indians were to be rendered as harmless as possible from the military point of view by being prevented from learning to make or to bear arms.

The interests of the conquerors were to be conserved by maintaining their rights to the land. The viceroy was authorized to sell land to them and others, but he was instructed to prevent its falling into mortmain, the curse of Spain, and, in spite of these early and oft-repeated orders, of Spanish America as well. The grants of encomiendas were to be made the object of a special inquiry and report.

Such were the precepts under which Mendoza set forth upon his mission. It was anticipated that added instructions and orders would from time to time be issued, but the viceroy was expected to act, in all practical issues which might arise, as he conceived the king himself would do if actually present in person.

The viceroy arrived in October, 1535, and assumed control. Very shortly afterward, Fuenleal and two other members of the audiencia returned to Spain. They had worthily prepared the way for Mendoza. But his task was onerous because of the diversity of the regions he was to rule, the clashing interests of the first conquerors against the new settlers, and the spirit of restlessness and insubordination which was engendered in the hearts of everyone by distance from Spain.

Naturally, the public safety demanded immediate attention. Arms were scarce among the Spaniards, and their negro slaves, imported for sugarmill work and other tasks, knowing this weakness, soon plotted the destruction of their masters. Mendoza, learning of the danger, removed it by seizing the conspirators and executing them. The Indians had been aware of the plot. A military muster incident to this menace showed that Mexico City then possessed less than 500 well armed horsemen, and about as many foot soldiers. Others were scattered about in mines, on farms, and engaged in conquests. The threatened insurrection of the negroes suggested restriction of their importation for the sake of the preservation of the colony, for their number was already great enough to be hazardous, there being more negroes, not counting mulattoes, than there were Spaniards in New Spain by the middle of the century.

A more serious problem was the relationship between the viceroy and Cortés. The latter had been recognized as captain-general by the second audiencia, but had been ordered by that body to obtain its approval for all his activities. This engendered bitter animosities, especially when it became increasingly evident that the power of the captain-general had become, with the successive reorganizations of the government, more fictitious than real. Even in the military affairs incident to an Indian uprising in the years 1530 and 1531, Cortés had been thwarted by the audiencia in the normal affairs of raising, disciplining, and directing the armed forces needed to save the colony. A moot point of conflict was the royal grant to him of a huge marquisate in the valley of Oaxaca and overlordship of some 23,000 Indians. His territories were considered so great as to be a menace to the consolidation of the power of the central authority, and the number of his tributaries was believed to be vastly in excess of the terms of the royal grant. Repeated efforts to count them having proven futile, Mendoza, acting under his original royal instructions, attempted an adjustment, thereby causing the beginning of a sensitiveness between the two men which was increased during the succeeding years.

Some previous account has been given of the South Sea explorations by Cortés, and of the difficulties which, added to those imposed by nature, were placed in his way by Nuño de Guzmán and the second audiencia. Into these mischances and thwartings Mendoza injected his own act also when he induced the withdrawal of the colony attempted by Cortés at La Paz, Lower California. The viceroy himself in 1537 asked permission to conduct discoveries. It was not long before punctilios of procedure arose between Cortés and Mendoza, and when, in 1539, Friar Marcos de Niza's account of the cities of Cíbola, first hinted at by Álvar Núñez

Cabeza de Vaca and his remnant of the Narváez expedition, set all New Spain by the ears with hope of sudden undreamed of wealth, the question of superior right in conquests became acute. When Cortés dispatched his last sea expedition under Francisco de Ulloa, the viceroy seized the remaining ships which Cortés had at Tehuantepec and attempted to guard the northwest coast of New Spain to prevent Ulloa from using the ports. The adherents of the marquis were imprisoned and tortured, and his prestige and power were entirely destroyed. Hence, even while Ulloa was absent upon his voyage, Cortés went in 1540 to Spain once more, to plead in vain a cause that was lost, and to die, a broken and disappointed man, in 1547. De Soto, Guzmán, and Alvarado, all bent upon northern quests, were still to meet disappointment, failure, and death in pursuit of the ambition which had animated the great conqueror, and Francisco de Coronado, agent of Mendoza, after wandering through the great northwest in search of the wealth and glory promised, was to return to New Spain to experience in his turn the viceroyal displeasure.

It has been stated that Nuño de Guzmán, upon the advent of the second audiencia, had gone into Jalisco and Sinaloa in 1529, and had effected a conquest over territory which came to be known as Nueva Galicia. In northern Sinaloa he founded Culiacán in 1531. But his rule was so atrocious that Diego Pérez de la Torre was in 1536 sent by the king to supersede him and bring him to judgment. De la Torre, though a beneficent ruler, was mortally wounded in 1538 in a battle with the natives of Tonalá, and Mendoza placed Coronado in his government.

This leader was in Mexico City at the time. Through him Mendoza was determined to make discoveries and conquests. Proceeding to Guadalajara in November, early in 1540 he set out with a party of over two hundred Spaniards, a thousand Indian allies, and thousands of livestock for remounts and provisions, for Culiacán, prepared to explore far inland. From that point he advanced ahead of his expedition with picked men, conquering the Zuñi villages, sending parties to the Moqui Indians, to the Colorado River, and Lower California, and fixing his headquarters at Tiguex near the Río Grande Valley. Hearing of a fabulous kingdom, Gran Quivira, which promised the wealth he had as yet missed, Coronado marched in 1541 to its location in eastern Kansas, only to find it a cluster of Indian tepees. He returned to Mexico in 1542, broken in prestige. The most important result of his great exploration was to bring back actual knowledge of the northwest, particularly of the semi-civilized Indians of New Mexico. In the area occupied by these sedentary tribes New Spain was to establish, later in the century, and to make permanent in the following one, its northernmost spread previous to the settlement of Upper California in the last third of the eighteenth century. But from Mendoza's viewpoint the expedition was an enormously expensive failure in attempted expansion.

Similar efforts by sea were equally unproductive of tangible results. During the Coronado expedition Hernando de Alarcón, attempting to accompany and aid the land party, ascended the Gulf of California and the Río Colorado for some eighty leagues, with no permanent result save the excellent Del Castillo map of the peninsula. This was about the same time that Francisco de Ulloa completed the navigation of the Gulf and sailed up the outside coast to Cedros Island and Cabo del Engaño.

While efforts at expansion northward by sea and land were proving failures, the tenure of already conquered territory was proving difficult because of Indian revolts.

The removal of so many Spaniards from Nueva Galicia upon Coronado's expedition, combined with the brutalities inflicted upon the Indians by the remaining encomenderos, brought about discontent, outrages, and finally open insurrection. Cristóbal de Oñate, left in charge of the province, was unable to quell the uprising, which in 1541 became general. Tenamaxtli, leader of Indians who fortified the rocky cliffs of Mixtón, Nochistlán, and other towns, was preparing annihilation for all the Spaniards. Defeats in many engagements and revolts as far north as Culiacán determined Oñate to appeal to Mendoza for aid. Pedro de Alvarado, bent upon Spice Island discoveries, and diverted therefrom by the Niza stories of Cíbola, had reached Navidad on the West Coast with his fleet from Guatemala in 1540. Coming to the aid of Oñate, he made a rash assault upon the fortress of Nochistlán, was put to flight with his men, and crushed to death by a horse which fell upon him through the terrorized awkwardness of his secretary companion. Further fighting resulted in the siege of Guadalajara and its imminent peril of massacre.

Mendoza, now realizing that the Indians aimed at destruction of all the Spaniards in North America, raised a force of 450 Spaniards and about 30,000 Tlascalans and Aztecs, the allies being hazardously allowed to have firearms. Tenamaxtli had over a hundred thousand warriors, in strongly defended cliff fortresses. After numerous assaults upon them, ending with the taking of Nochistlán and Mixtón, the war ended. It had needed all the resources of New Spain to prevent a fatal issue.

After the cessation of these hostilities, commonly called the Mixtón War, Mendoza had time to revert to his ideas of expansion. Possessing two of Pedro de Alvarado's vessels, he sent them in June 1542, under Juan Rodríguez Cabrillo, a Portuguese, to extend the coastal discovery made by Ulloa. The expedition, intended to pursue the search for the phantom continental strait, discovered San Diego Bay, the islands of the Santa Barbara Channel, and, attaining the latitude of 38° 31′ north, returned to the Channel Islands, where Cabrillo died from injuries sustained in a fall. His pilot, Ferrelo, returning northward, reached a latitude which he estimated at 44° north, but which was probably 42° 30′. The inefficiency of the search for a strait is seen when it is noted that both leaders had missed both Monterey and San Francisco bays. No practical benefit was then realized from this arduous voyage.

To Mendoza's initiative was also due the voyage begun in 1542 by Ruy López de Villalobos to the Philippines in search of La Especería, or the Spice Islands, wherein the Portuguese

were making fortunes. The ill success of the voyage, survivors of which made their way around Africa to Spain years
later, was another example of the misfortune which attended
Mendoza's efforts to make good his opportunity to expand
the realm on lines suggested by the rumors of wealth which
had animated Cortés. Where that doughty leader had failed
there was scant chance for the viceroy's lieutenants.

During this same period one other notable attempt at
expansion which was not part of Mendoza's program was
under way. This was Hernando de Soto's ill-fated struggle,
begun in 1539 from Cuba, to find a great empire in the Gulf
region of the present United States. De Soto died in 1542,
and the tragic remnant of his party, led by Moscoso to
Pánuco from the Mississippi, was kindly befriended by the
viceroy when it reached Mexico City, but perhaps fortunately
for him it added nothing to his official cares of governing new
areas. About this time viceroys and oidores were prohibited
by royal order from making discoveries. After all, the
great contribution of the first viceroy was not in discovery or
conquest, but in perfecting the machinery of internal administration whereby the hold of Spain upon North America
was established.

The most important affair which engaged his attention
was the regulation of relations between the conquering
Spaniards and their Indian subjects. Cortés had rewarded
his followers by giving them Indians to exploit under the
system of encomiendas which had been forced upon Columbus in La Española. To each conqueror were given groups
of Indians who were to be exploited, clothed, fed, and taught
Christianity. The system, as legally conceived, was ideal.
The Indians were not held in legal slavery, and, by the
grants, which were intended at first to expire with the life of
the recipient, it was quite possible and evidently intended
that they should attain to a condition of individual vassalage
under the king approximating in political privileges and
economic opportunity the status of the average Spanish
subject. Probably no more humane theory for the assimilation of a backward people has ever been conceived.

But in actuality the encomienda system prevented rather than fostered Indian development. The arduous tasks of field and mine, the separation from home and family entailed by mining work, the rigor of the exploitation in most of its aspects, combined with the incapacity of the Indian to profit by the inculcation of Christian precepts and the amenities of Spanish civilization, made his condition one of abject slavery. The strict orders of royalty imposing humane treatment were ignored or disobeyed in the quest for wealth. The two phases of the conquest, exploitation and proselyting, were diametrically opposed to each other, and it is not surprising that the less practical of the two should suffer. The incessant urge for wealth which drove the colonists to excesses of ruthlessness was augmented by the kingly demand for added profits from the colonial enterprise, always for the sake of the royal treasury at home.

Bartholomew de Las Casas had inveighed against the system while still an encomendero in Cuba. Becoming a Dominican, he carried his campaign to court, and, after vicissitudes needless to recount here, achieved the passage of the famous ordinances of 1542 and 1543 known as the New Laws.

These laws were an attempt to place the Indian upon an entirely new legal status. It had long been legal to make real slaves of Indians who were caught in open warfare against the Spaniards. All such were to be set free, but with the unhappy proviso that owners who could establish legal title to slaves might retain them. No longer might any be newly enslaved, even if taken in rebellion, as formerly. More crushingly revolutionary from the colonists' standpoint were the provisions which did away with inheritance of encomiendas, a legal custom which had received royal sanction. Furthermore, no new encomiendas were to be granted under any consideration, and churchmen and royal officers were to be deprived of their encomiendas.

There were other features of these New Laws which prescribed changes in the methods of making discoveries and reduced governors to subordinate relations with the audiencias. The laws providing all the changes enumerated were to be translated into the principal Indian tongues, and promulgated throughout the American settlements generally. These provisions were all unpopular enough, but the special point of conflict was over the economic question of the permanency of the encomiendas. Before the laws were published their purport became known, and they were met generally throughout America by storms of protest and by acts of violence. The colonization had grown up on the establishment of legally vested rights in the exploitation of the bodies of the natives. If these rights were to be molested, the economic fabric of the new settlements would be ruined, for lands and mines would be of no service without native labor.

The crown realized that this revolutionary program would require delicate handling. To enforce it in New Spain, Francisco Tello de Sandoval, a member of the Council of the Indies, was sent to assist Mendoza. Sandoval was, unfortunately, also authorized to take the residencias of all the crown officers in the viceroyalty, including the members of the audiencia and the viceroy. This power to examine their official conduct and refer charges against them to the Council of the Indies naturally predisposed the ruling class against him. Especially was the feeling bitter when the purport of the New Laws became known. The encomenderos met Sandoval when he landed at Vera Cruz in 1544, and vainly tried to persuade him not to proclaim the laws. They were published in Mexico City on March 24 of that year.

Even the religious orders were against the new legislation, for they, no less than the encomenderos, were beneficiaries of the system in vogue. Even Archbishop Zumárraga held an encomienda himself. It was argued by the Dominicans that Indians on encomiendas were better treated than those in the king's own towns (ports and chief towns were reserved to him, for the sake of the tribute) where the corregidores (governors) who represented the kingly authority were more harsh than the encomenderos. No effective voice was raised in favor of the proposed changes. Mendoza and Sandoval, bowing before the storm, sent envoys to Spain to plead against the laws. Their arguments were so effective that they succeeded, in 1545, in securing postponement of application of the obnoxious measures, though Las Casas made a brave fight for his ideals. The plan was too idealistic for the age, and the exploitation system was too well grounded, for reform to meet success. Mendoza did wisely to postpone it. Charles V, knowing the Spaniards, could not afford to fight them on the issue, for his demands for revenue were always pressing. In the other Spanish American possessions wherever less tactful authorities attempted to enforce the changes proposed, disorder and in some cases open insurrection followed. New Spain would have offered a like sample of loyalty to self interest.

Among the many misfortunes inevitably incident to the clash of two civilizations achieved under diametrically opposite ideals of social organization, religious faith, and political aspirations, to which the Indians were the prey during these early formative years, none were more destructive than the frequent scourges of epidemic diseases which smote the land with devastating fury. Such an epidemic, caused by the introduction of smallpox upon the occasion of the arrival of the anti-Cortés expedition under Narváez, had wrought havoc among the Aztecs and was a contributory cause of their defeat. Other scourges had frequently devastated the Indian population even before the arrival of Cortés. During the term of Mendoza appeared another terrible disease, said by some writers to have been hitherto unknown, and by others to have made frequent ravages in pre-Columbian America. It was called by the Aztecs matlazáhuatl; modern opinion inclines to the idea that it was a form of influenza. The Indians believed that it was caused by a comet, by eruption of volcanoes, or other supernatural phenomena. The Spaniards themselves were almost as superstitious regarding the origin of disease. Whatever may have been its origin, it carried off huge numbers of the natives in the space of six months, and called for all the efficacy of Archbishop Zumárraga's prayers and the valiant prophylactic energies of the viceroy, royal officers, and the religious of all orders. The disease stayed its course before complete annihilation came, but made frequent inroads upon the native population in subsequent years. The Spanish population escaped its ravages. This would indicate that the malady was one to which the Europeans already had an immunity, or that it was caused by under-nourishment and unaccustomed toil.

The work of conserving the health of the population always fell in large measure upon the church. Its various orders were especially well adapted to such labors, and private beneficence often aided them where the hand of the government was ineffectual because the wealth of the land, collected in taxes, was poured into the Spanish treasury with a more lavish hand than into improvement of the colony. The hospitals maintained by the religious orders were practically the only institutions adapted for the alleviation of suffering until the organization of the Hospital Real de Indios, established in 1540 by the absorption of an institution already existing in Mexico City. This hospital was endowed with the income from an encomienda, and supported by a tax of half a real (two and one-half cents) annually from each Indian tributary. By the end of the eighteenth century there were nine government controlled hospitals in the capital besides several private ones. They were either in the hands of religious orders or supported by the benevolence of wealthy members of the church.

The coming of Sandoval as a royal visitor-general to examine the viceroyalty and hear complaints against public officials was in keeping with an old Aragonese legal custom. It had been introduced into Castile, and from there spread into La Española and throughout America as the occupation progressed. The visitor-general could bring to trial for malfeasance such officers as were designated by royal instructions, hearing accusations against them and sending transcripts of testimony and his findings to the Council of the Indies for definitive sentence. Theoretically it was an admirable contrivance for renovating the entire political fabric, as its prototype the episcopal visitation was intended to do in ecclesiastical affairs; but as a matter of fact it developed into a dubious expedient because the visitor-general was usually a new man in the viceroyalty, and his mission, directed against the entire ruling class, served to align all self-interested officials against him for the purpose of nullifying his efforts. Especially was this true when large numbers of officials were already corrupt. To offset this opposition the evidence taken by the visitor was collected secretly, accused officials being denied the right of knowing who were their accusers and what were the exact charges made against them. This inquisitorial character of the visitation made it an unpopular device, against which all means were considered legitimate. Especially difficult was the situation created between viceroy and visitor, because the viceroy was expected to facilitate the visitor's work while conscious that he was himself presumably the object of a secret investigation. As the chief executive officer, he had naturally acquired a large number of enemies, who would inevitably seek to injure him, while the special powers of the visitor tended to make the latter autocratic and overbearing.

Francisco Tello de Sandoval and Mendoza enjoyed pleasant relations for a time, but official attrition had its inevitable result. Mendoza resented the fact that Sandoval became practically governor during the period of taking the residencia of the viceroy and members of the audiencia. Sandoval had announced when he reached Vera Cruz that he was now ranking officer, and would, as he had a right, remove Mendoza to Spain should conditions warrant. The clergy, influential, and with interests akin to those of the viceroy, seem to have feared that this might happen, and wrote to the king asserting that such a step would be a serious blow to the country. Indeed, Mendoza had succeeded in winning the hearts of many by his efforts to establish the peace and prosperity of the realm. True, these efforts had inured chiefly to the benefit of the upper class Spaniards, but the clergy averred that he was no less popular with the Indians.

The residencia of Mendoza and other officers was taken in 1545. None of the charges preferred against the viceroy were sustained. Accusations in plenty were brought by Cortés, who alleged that Mendoza had been at fault in his conduct during the Mixtón War, that he had illegally engaged in expeditions of discovery, had sold Indian towns, allowed his official family to be corrupt, had misappropriated funds, smuggled, and committed other official misdeeds often alleged and frequently proven against succeeding viceroys. Whatever the merits of these accusations, Cortés had an obvious grudge, and his star was then in the descendant, while Mendoza was a relative of the royal house and a useful, competent lieutenant. He could act with severity, even cruelty, upon occasion, but he could also act with caution or assurance, as the case might require.

The visitor does not seem to have accomplished much beyond deferring promulgation of the New Laws. That he had not made a case against Mendoza did not reflect to his discredit, nor was the viceroy's attitude against him taken seriously enough to void his mission. He did attempt, having concluded his judicial labors, to call together the bishops of the several sees of New Spain for the purpose of outlining an ecclesiastical policy. From this conference the astute Mendoza secured the absence of the troublesome Las Casas, who was on his way to attend, by detaining him outside the city. Las Casas in turn excommunicated the viceroy and audiencia for having ordered the hands cut off an ecclesiastic of Oaxaca. The move caused little excitement. Sandoval tried to please Las Casas by introducing before the prelates of Guatemala, Oaxaca, Michoacán, Chiapas, Mexico, and perhaps Puebla assembled in the conference, the discussion of the relations between the encomenderos and the Indians, but Mendoza removed the topic from the purview of the assembly by declaring it not an ecclesiastic one. Las Casas later succeeded in getting a resolution passed by the lower clergy declaring unlawful the enslavement of Indians. As technical slavery was not prevalent, the dictum of the clergy could have little practical effect, though it was published widespread in the native tongues. Sandoval returned in a short time to Spain, Mendoza went on ruling for another five years, and the condition of the viceroyalty steadily improved under his rule.

A viceroy was not only expected to determine broad administrative policies, but to take care of the smallest details of government. Mendoza brought running water into the capital, improved Vera Cruz, and began a policy of fortifying the interior of the country against Indian and negro uprisings. He fomented wool production, establishing the grazers' court and guild, the Mesta, at the behest of four wealthy sheep raisers of the capital. He encouraged the teaching of trades to Indians, and the gremial legislation of the time permitted their entrance into some of the lower branches of the manual crafts. He attempted to regulate and limit the making and sale of pulque which had become a curse in Mexico even before the conquest, and continues so until now.

Colonization was encouraged by giving bonuses for marriage; men who would take Spanish girls to wife were given offices as corregidores, in which position they were overseers of Indians not gathered on encomiendas but left in the king's towns. Measures to improve various colonial activities resulted in general prosperity which went on with little check, though frequent disorders occurred, and more than once there were fears of uprisings against the dominant race. Forced labor, in the royal towns under corregidores as well as on encomiendas, was the cause of the greatest discontent. Under it the supply of workers gradually lessened, and search for more toilers began another expansion, as it had once done from the larger Caribbean Islands.

Querétaro, northward of the Aztec area, some 167 miles above Mexico City, had been conquered in 1531, and was settled by Indian allies. There is a quaint story that the wily Otomis here, anticipating failure of bows and arrows against Spanish armor, proposed a fist fight with the Spaniards to settle the issue of their conquest. The challenge was accepted, the Otomis were worsted in an all-day round, and abided by the result. Some authors give this event as occurring in 1522, others as in 1531, but actual occupation began in 1550, when Querétaro was held as a buffer province against the wild Indians of the north, known in the contemporary annals as Chichimecas.

The western area of the viceroyalty, known as Nueva Galicia, continued to be a sparsely settled country for a long time after the Mixtón War. In 1548 it was, because of its remoteness, given an audiencia situated at Compostela. This new court ruled all Nueva Galicia, Colima, Zacatula, and the country known as the Ávalos towns or provinces in modern Jalisco. Shortly afterward, the capital was placed at Guadalajara, and the audiencia moved thither. Relations between this court and that of Mexico were for a long time undetermined, and some hostility grew out of the attempts of each to extend its jurisdiction. The president of the Guadalajara court was usually a military ruler, not a judge, and he was actually subordinate to the viceroy in administrative affairs. In fact he was little other than military governor of a province. The growth of Nueva Galicia during the period of Mendoza was due principally to mining development, though the area soon became and is now a leading agricultural one.

Zacatecas was discovered and developed by prospectors who went out from Nueva Galicia. This marvelous silver-bearing region was penetrated as early as 1530 by one Captain Chirinos, but few if any other entries were made until 1546. It had been the haven to which retired the unsubdued residue of Indians who had been driven out of the Guadalajara region during the Mixtón War, and from it they had continued to make raids upon the Spanish frontier. The town councils of Nueva Galicia in 1543 asked permission to subdue them, but were ordered by viceroy and king to reduce them peacefully. In 1546 Juan de Tolosa advanced to the foot of La Bufa, a mountain crowned by a curious crescent-shaped ridge of solid protruding rock which dominates a wide horizon beyond the city of Zacatecas. He had a group of Franciscans and a band of Juchipil Indians as allies. After more than a year of the pacifying process, Tolosa was joined by Cristóbal de Oñate, Diego de Ibarra, and Baltazar Treviño de Bañuelos. These men all became famous as wealthy miners and prospectors. The city of Zacatecas was founded in 1548, in the midst of a great mining rush which rivalled "the days of '49," three hundred years later in California. In a few years half a dozen large mining towns appeared, among them Fresnillo and Sombrerete. Nueva Galicia suffered from depopulation as the wave advanced; Zacatecas grew steadily in importance as a mining center; it has been unrivalled save by Guanajuato, to the south, where the ore deposits are even more fabulously rich. This region proved the greatest success as a wealth producer since the fall of Tenochtitlán. From it, after the turn of the century, the settlement advanced into the Durango and Sinaloa regions. It may also be said that with the advance into the northern mining region, beginning in 1543, the character of the conquest took on a new form. The area of the sedentary tribes had now been definitely passed beyond. Town, convent, and farm were to be replaced by the institution of mining camps, missions, and great grazing ranches, on which cultivation of cereals and other foodstuffs marked pace with the advance of mining interests.

About the close of 1548, Mendoza began to long to return to his native Spain. His health had suffered during fourteen years of unremitting administration of the Emperor's largest and most profitable American kingdom. He needed rest, and he needed to look after his personal interests at home. It was hoped that his son Francisco might be designated as his successor, but instead Luis de Velasco was named in 1549. The reins of office were transferred to him at Cholula in 1550. The old viceroy delivered to the new one a memoir of his rule, with valuable recommendations as to policy. This feature of a report of general conditions upon the transfer of administrative power became legally customary and permanent in Spanish America.

Mendoza had proven a valuable royal representative. In a day when executive clemency was the exception, he had usually refrained from the acts of brutality which sullied the names of too many conquistadores. He had calmed the bickering strifes inherited from the days of Cortés. He had advanced the conquest into productive regions. He had avoided disruption within, quelling numerous revolts successfully. The amenities of Spanish civilization had come in the shape of churches, convents, hospitals, schools and crafts. The revenues had been increased. Commerce, industry, agriculture had prospered. Religion had been fostered. The codification of the colonial laws had been begun. The Indians had, true, continued to suffer, and it is not evident that Mendoza had developed an impressionable conscience regarding the welfare of the exploited race. But he had represented the kingly office in a manner so satisfactory that his services could not be spared. Peru, potentially as great in wealth as New Spain, was still in the throes of strife between contending factions, strife more bitter and more devastating than New Spain had ever felt. If Mendoza had succeeded here, might he not put an end to the Peruvian muddle? If he would do so, he might go there and try his skill as moderator; if he preferred to stay in Mexico, Velasco was to be sent to Peru. But Mendoza chose Peru, and left Mexico, to take charge of his new post at Lima in September, 1551. After nine brief months of service there death claimed him before his new viceroyalty was thoroughly quieted.

CHAPTER V

THE AGE OF PHILIP II IN NEW SPAIN

THE half century following the advent of Velasco finds an historical unity in the reign of Philip II. Called to assist in managing American affairs several years before the abdication of his father, though he did not ascend the throne until 1556, Philip, ruling Spain until 1598 as no monarch did before or has done after, gave to the viceroyalty only in less degree than to the Peninsula an epoch distinctive in political government, territorial expansion, and religious ideals. Each of these phases of endeavor was to receive, during the term of the second viceroy, from 1550 to 1564, an impetus which was to characterize the rest of the cycle, carrying the viceroyalty into the seventeenth century on a wave of expansive greatness which was to break and recede in proportion as the later Hapsburgs dissipated the power which had belonged to Charles V and the glory that was sought and largely won by Philip.

Luis de Velasco was a member of the family of the Constable of Castile, a Knight of Santiago, and, like his predecessor Mendoza, a relative of [the royal house. Industrious, patient, affable, efficient, he was a suitable subject in whom to repose the great responsibility of governing the immense realm that had been reduced to a permanently organized colony by the first viceroy.

His instructions from the king, issued as he left Spain to assume his New World duties, give an excellent idea of American affairs and policies as they were conceived in Spain.

One of the most notable features of these instructions was the declaration of the policy to be pursued in dealing with the Indians. It was the will of the king that definite steps should now be taken toward emancipating the Indian slaves—a problem that had been postponed at the instance of Mendoza and the visitor Sandoval. In 1551 it was ordered that women captured in war, males made prisoners when under fourteen years of age, and men held in slavery by persons who could not show that these slaves had been taken in open warfare, should be set at liberty forthwith and made free vassals. Against this program there was the same rage of opposition from the Spanish masters as had arisen under Mendoza in 1544. The economic basis of the colony, the distaste of the conquerors for work, coupled with the ineptitude of the natives for a free system of labor, made it seem imperative that the Indians should be held to forced toil for direct personal masters. But the power of the monarch in New Spain was now stronger than it had been when the agitation of Las Casas prompted the enunciation of the New Laws. The idea of actual slavery was abhorrent to the mind of the Spanish government, and there was still a more potent reason yet; the Indian as a free vassal would pay tribute directly into the royal treasury, whereas in slavery he would contribute chiefly to his master's prosperity. Hence, the orders of the king were speedily made effective to the extent of setting free one hundred and fifty thousand men slaves and a large number of women and children. For this act of interested humanity Velasco became known as "The Emancipator." It is apparent from the relatively small number of manumissions under this order that no extensive change was made in the status of Indians held in encomienda. Only those who had been seized and held as slaves, usually branded with marking irons as such, without grant of authority from the king to hold them, were apparently included under this legislation. The change of status of so few natives made little difference in the labor system, and it is unfortunate that no information has come down to us concerning the ultimate fate of these particular individuals who were liberated, but it is not likely that they continued long as free persons, for their own ill preparation for self-directed industry, coupled with

the well known propensity of the Spaniards for obtaining
Indian labor without payment of wages, make it improbable
that the slaves set free could have been materially benefited.

The young prince, Philip, issued a law in the same year,
1551, providing that the viceroy and members of the audiencias must keep no Indians except upon payment of just
wages. Personal service was to be discontinued as a means
of paying tribute, and this tax was thereafter to be paid in
money, the Indians preferring that method. As Mendoza
had recommended, slaves held in the capital were not to be
removed, as they might there obtain their freedom with
greater ease than in the provinces. Burden bearing by
natives was also to be discontinued, a regulation which has
never had any marked influence in reducing the brutalizing
practice of using the lower class laborers as beasts of burden,
despite the enormous number of draft animals which have
been raised in Mexico. Necessary regulations were also
made to prevent the native chiefs from maltreating their
people by cruel and unnecessarily brutal forms of punishment. To insure proper payment of wages due to Indian
laborers, it was ordered in 1557 that the chieftains should no
longer be intrusted with disbursements of wages, but that
paying-off should be done by the parish priests. It is thus
evident that the native organization of society had been
adapted to their own uses by the Spaniards, and that the
system was working undue hardship upon the lower levels
of the native group. As a matter of fact, the chieftains,
many of whom had arisen to that dignity simply by assumption of prerogative, or had been thrust into responsibility
by the conquering Spaniard, were the hardest of task masters.
In a few years after the invasion, as many as one fourth of
the natives, says Bancroft, had assumed or attained this
ascendancy. They had become possessed of large proportions of the productive lands, had imposed severe tasks
upon their less fortunate fellow vassals, and were exploiting
them by collecting high rents in addition to the annual
tribute.

Not only did Indian laborers serve their chiefs thus, but

they had to perform many duties described as personal service, such as gathering fire-wood and forage for animals. Everyone in the social scale above them exacted some form of personal service, from conqueror or priest to the king. Public services, such as building government edifices, or the like, were rendered by them gratuitously. When the population decreased, new tribute rolls showing the diminution were prepared for official use, but the old exactions were kept up, and the collectors pocketed the surplus. Cortés had suggested that these frauds could be obviated by apportioning the land and taxing property instead of making per capita levies of tribute, but the attempt when made in 1558 was defeated by giving to the Indians the poorest of the lands, upon which their natural indolence soon proved too discouraging. Finally, the crown had to resort to compulsion to make the Indians work enough to produce any surplus over their own meager requirements.

The enforcement of ameliorative measures among the Indians was intrusted to Spanish official visitors, some of whom were members of the audiencia; the most important visitor under Velasco was Diego Ramírez; he had also the task of notifying the encomenderos that their encomiendas might be inherited by one heir, but that after the second generation these holdings should revert to the king, that is, that Indians on encomiendas should in two generations become free vassals. This process of attempting to raise the Indians to a status of economic independence was soon defeated by the extension of the right of inheritance of encomiendas to several generations. Not until the first quarter of the seventeenth century did the encomiendas begin to lapse to the king upon the death of the owners, and the system continued in vogue still another century.

It is notorious that the Indians profited little by these or by the many kindred regulations. They were brutally exploited by the dominant race, and driven to find solace in their inveterate vices of sensuality, drunkenness, and gambling. They returned the harassments of their superiors by engaging them in interminable litigation whenever

possible, usually over dispossessals of land. The work of
assimilating the dependent population, a difficult task at
best, was hindered both by the natural instinct of the
Spanish colonists to enrich themselves as rapidly as possible
and by the impractical character of the idealistic legislation
passed in their favor. Not only was it impossible to find a
sufficient number of Spaniards whose self interest normally
prompted them to humane treatment of their wards, but the
judicial redress provided for the Indians was seized upon
by them, or by Spanish officials charged with their protection, to bring on endless litigation which created an unhappy
mental attitude between the races—an attitude which lies
at the base of the racial differences of modern times, retard-
ing the real formation of a national spirit.

Already the cleavage of society into the two sharp groups
of dominators and dominated had created great economic
disparities. The economically elect became the frequent
prey of the economically derelict. The viceroyalty began
to be infested by bands of highway robbers, disinherited or
vicious wanderers who frequented the trails leading into the
chief cities and ports, trails traversed by rich pack-trains
laden with precious metals from the mines or merchandise
for Spaniards at home or within the viceroyalty. Life and
property became so seriously menaced that an energetic
remedy was demanded. It was found in the extension to
New Spain of the Santa Hermandad, a peninsular police
institution which had served Ferdinand and Isabella in such
good stead in establishing the public peace of their realms.
The functions of the Hermandad were by Velasco reposed
in the two alcaldes of the Mesta, the grazers' guild or court
with special jurisdiction in New Spain erected as an adjunct
of the town council of Mexico City. The alcaldes de mesta
continued to be named annually throughout the colonial
period; the Santa Hermandad, initiated in 1552, became in
1722 the greatly feared court of La Acordada, the captains
of which dedicated their energies to the protection of the
roads with such vigor that their very names became syn-
onyms of summary justice.

Of signal importance in the annals of New Spain was the inauguration in 1553 of the royal and pontifical University of Mexico. Educational activities, accompanying the turmoil and stress of the early years of conquest, seem an odd contrast, but there had by now come into existence a second generation of colonists, whose mental development could not be satisfied unless a higher institution of learning should be provided. Naturally it was the religious element that gave the first impetus, and it was that interest that was chiefly to be served. Clericals from European universities filled most of the chairs for many years, the university providing from time to time the added courses which made it a normal medieval institution. The royal cédula authorizing the erection of the university was issued September 25, 1551; the Papal confirmation was granted by Paul IV in 1555; under these basic laws and later ordinances the institution served the people of Mexico as a legally organized body until the time of Maximilian. Upon the occasion of its inauguration the university was honored by the attendance of the viceroy and audiencia at classes every day for a week, one class only being held daily for the sake of prolonging the ceremony and demonstrating the importance of the event. The sister American university, that of San Marcos, at Lima, Peru, was temporarily closed in 1921, but is now again functioning in something of its ancient form. The University of Mexico was reorganized as the National University in 1910, with a preparatory school and professional faculties of law, medicine, dentistry, and art.

During the year 1553 torrential rains in the Valley of Mexico demonstrated that the capital, rebuilt by Cortés on the site of ancient Tenochtitlán, had been unfortunately located for purposes of drainage. In three days' rainfall, coming after a prolonged drought, the streets of the city were so generally inundated that recourse to canoes for traffic was universal. The viceroy himself donned working clothes and labored a day at the head of great bands of laborers on canals and dikes as an example of energy to his associates. During the remainder of the effort to prepare Mexico City against recurrence of the flood he personally directed the many groups of natives employed. The inundation had been unusually heavy because the dikes of Indian times, constructed to keep the waters of the upper lakes from flooding Lake Tezcoco, which were destroyed by Cortés in his maneuvers against Tenochtitlán, had never been restored. It is indeed remarkable that Cortés and his companions had permitted the rebuilding of Tenochtitlán. There was no longer the need for the lake as a means of defense that had animated the Aztecs in their choice of a location, and a higher spot would have been more sanitary and freer from arduous effort. Attempts during the early colonial period to procure the removal of the capital to a more hygienic region proved unavailing because real estate interests had become too powerful to permit the losses such a move would have occasioned. At the beginning of the next century, in 1607, the drainage of the valley was begun by Enrico Martín, a Portuguese engineer, who built a tunnel by which the flood waters of the plateau lakes were carried off to the Gulf by way of the Tula and Pánuco rivers. The tunnel, constructed at inordinate cost in lives of thousands of Indians, was subsequently changed to an open cut, now called the Cut of Nochistongo or the Huehuetoca Canal. Successive works on this construction continued through the centuries, until its final completion in the late years of the "reign" of President Porfirio Díaz.

The rule of Luis de Velasco I was marked by effort to extend the power of the Spanish arms into areas which had been explored during the preceding half century. The first expansion came in parts immediately adjacent to the center of New Spain, while the greater and more spectacular attempts were made in remoter northern regions.

Those settlements near at hand were planted as defenses against the frontier Indians. The unsubdued bands of the north, called Chichimecas by the Spaniards, had developed guerrilla warfare against the convoyed trains which connected the northern mines with the capital. In 1554 a strongly guarded train was practically annihilated, the disaster coupled with similar misfortunes resulting in the establishment as military colonies of the villas of San Felipe Itzlahuaca and San Miguel el Grande, as way stations protecting the route to the mines.

The Durango region, then known as Chichametla, or land of the Chichimecas, was brought under the conquest by Francisco de Ibarra, a nephew of the Diego de Ibarra who had married a daughter of the viceroy. The Ibarra expedition was sent out in 1562 "to explore the lands seen by Francisco de Coronado" and find locations for mines and settlements, the hope being that another discovery as rich as that of Zacatecas, with which the Ibarras had been associated, might result. Ibarra, at his own expense, following the customary practice, led into the north a large expedition of Spaniards, Indians, and negro slaves. His discoveries resulted in the establishment of rich mining centers at Durango, Nombre de Dios, Indé, and elsewhere in the new territory, to which the name Nueva Vizcaya was given. Into it came almost as great a mining rush as that which had preceded in Zacatecas. The city of Durango was founded in 1563 by Alonzo Pacheco, serving under Ibarra. Shortly after this, in 1564, Ibarra crossed the western sierras and founded San Juan in the present state of Sinaloa. This establishment lay within the prior discoveries of Nuño de Guzmán and his captains. Ibarra also occupied the territory of Nueva Galicia from San Juan to Culiacán, and between Culiacán and Compostela. He included the port of Chametla, where there were valuable salt works which he took in the name of the crown. Ibarra became a notable overlord in this new country, where he was governor and lieutenant-general of the viceroy. This great "Kingdom of Nueva Vizcaya," practically the area of modern Durango and Chihuahua, was an important addition to the viceroyalty; the Ibarra conquests west of the sierras were soon separated from the Ibarra holdings. The San Juan establishment nearly caused warlike hostilities between Nueva Galicia and Nueva Vizcaya, but they were happily averted by Diego

Ibarra, and the San Juan area, for a time governed by the viceroy, finally became part of Nueva Vizcaya.

Desire to strengthen maritime communication between Vera Cruz and Spain led to numerous attempts to conquer northern territory on the Atlantic. In 1553 the treasure fleet lost all save three hundred persons out of one thousand on the reefs of Florida. The survivors who reached land were practically destroyed by Indian hostilities and privations. This loss induced the king to order the conquest of Florida, a land thought to be immensely rich in mineral deposits. In 1559 Velasco, obedient but dubious, sent upon this conquest Tristán de Luna at the head of five hundred soldiers and one thousand Indian allies, to conquer and colonize at Santa Elena on the Atlantic Coast of the Florida country. The expedition landed first at Santa María de Filipinas, later called Pensacola, but was ill-starred from lack of a good base support, Indian hostility, hunger and disease. When De Luna was replaced by Ángel Villafañe, the new leader attempted to carry the disheartened expeditionaries around to Santa Elena, but storms at sea, added to discord and discouragement, brought the Santa Elena attempt to an end, and a weak garrison left at Pensacola was also withdrawn. Florida, without great riches, and protected by inhospitable shores and savage denizens, seemed unworthy of the sacrifices it had entailed, wherefore royal orders were issued in 1561 to the effect that its conquest be abandoned.

But sea warfare against Spain's rich treasure fleets, first waged in the eastern Atlantic, had now been transferred to waters adjacent to the American coast. Furthermore, the French, anticipating the English, began to use America as a refuge for religious dissidents. Jean Ribault, leading a Huguenot colony to Port Royal, South Carolina, began the movement, which it became necessary for the Spaniards to thwart. The French were annihilated in 1565 by Menéndez de Avilés, who in the same year founded St. Augustine. Menéndez, as adelantado of this new territory, and working from Cuba rather than from New Spain, established a number of other posts on the Atlantic or Florida coast within the present bounds of South Carolina and Georgia, and made efforts, though unsuccessful ones, to effect the geographical union of his territory with that of New Spain. The northernmost establishment was made at a mission, temporarily held, on Chesapeake Bay. Indian hostility prevented the success of numerous Jesuit and Franciscan missions which dotted the coast between 1566 and 1593, and later. The great day of the Florida enterprise was before the death of Menéndez in 1574. He had before that secured the extension of his adelantamiento southwestward to the Pánuco region, but the Florida area never did, in his time or later, become an integral part of the viceroyalty of New Spain. Menéndez was famous as the organizer and first commander of the Armada de Barlovento, or Windward Island Fleet, which for many years served as a detached naval guard, often successfully, but too often with scant support from either the viceroys or the Spanish kings, against the constant raids of pirates and buccaneers upon the rich Spanish shipping and the coast towns of Central America and Mexico.

The "far flung battle line" had reached the Philippine Islands in 1542 under López de Villalobos; expansion thither halted thereafter until Portugal's spice trade aroused emulation of that country's successes, and it now became Velasco's duty to proceed with the occupation of that remote quarter. Miguel Gómez de Legaspi with four vessels, in which were six Augustinian friars led by Andrés de Urdaneta for a spiritual conquest, sailed from Navidad in Colima in 1564 with forces and colonists, to found in 1571 the City of Manila, soon thereafter Spain's rich entrepôt for a wide and prosperous Asiatic commerce. The terrible Pacific voyage was rendered less disastrous to lives and shipping by the discovery of the Great Circle route eastward to the California coast and southward to Acapulco, where the Manila galleons for centuries after unloaded their rich cargoes of Asiatic silks, and set sail with the "cargoes of friars and silver pesos" bound for the Manila end of the voyage. Legaspi before his death in 1572 had effected a rapid and comparatively bloodless conquest of several of the larger islands of the archipelago by bringing the native chieftains into semi-feudal relations with himself and the king of Spain. During this same half century the valiant conquerors planned to extend from the islands to Japan and the Chinese mainland both the Roman Catholic faith and the power of the monarch, but the limit of Spain's wonderful expansive thrust had now been reached. There was a period, from 1549, when Francisco Xavier arrived in the country on a Portuguese ship, to the early years of the next century, during which Christianity, preached by Jesuit fathers, made notable progress in Japan, so that Catholicism has continued to exist until the present day in the field of those early labors; but the Japanese, realizing that proselyting was a preliminary step to temporal conquest, drove the Jesuits out and effectually checked the Spanish pretensions. In 1614 Christianity was proscribed and the ban was not lifted until 1873. Solicited permission to secure a foothold in China was forbidden by the cautious Philip II, who realized that the limit of Spain's power of expansion had been attained.

The viceroy had succeeded in checking numerous abuses in the relationship between Spaniards and Indians; but while lowered tributes, abolition of personal service, and other ameliorations of living conditions benefited the Indians meagerly, the Spaniards were discontented because their own wishes were not entirely met. The audiencia, with power of review of judicial cases, was able to set aside many viceroyal decrees, and delay justice to the Indians. The rapidly growing half-breed population, the mestizos, encouraged the Indians to enter into prolonged land litigation, making themselves so obnoxious that Velasco took measures to expel them, and the Spaniards as well, from the Indian towns, in which they exerted a corrupting influence. The negroes, now numbering 20,000, were again a menace to internal peace; they greatly outnumbered the entire Spanish population, and it was feared they might upon occasion rise against the established authority, as they had done in the time of Mendoza. The Spanish population had moreover

received a large admixture of vagrants from Spain. Having
no land, no official capacity, no legitimate economic status,
they resorted to informal exploitation of the natives. Their
influence continued for many years to be bad. The Spanish
conquerors and first settlers had not yet been confirmed in
their encomiendas, and were naturally restive with anxiety
over their prospective fortunes. Velasco proposed to grant
them their encomiendas; but to give them no jurisdictional
powers thereon and to tax them for the benefit of the Indians.
This policy was opposed by members of the audiencia, whose
economic interests aligned them with the conquerors instead
of with the viceroy. The natural result was conflict between
the two highest powers in the land, and a successful effort
by the oidores to undermine Velasco's influence at court and
limit his powers. Their representations that his health was
bad and his judgment variable, won a decree specifying that
the viceroy should not in the future act without the consent
of the audiencia. The natural consequence was endless
confusion and disheartening delays in administrative affairs.

Seeking vindication, the viceroy had recourse to a request
for a visitor to be sent to review his government. The request was granted, and a jurisconsult named Valderrama
was sent. He arrived in mid-August, 1563. It was his
duty to require the audiencia judges to desist from conquests
and commercial business, matters in which they had in-
sistently disobeyed the king. The visitor was able to effect
some reforms; he removed some incompetent oidores,
doubled the tribute to two pesos, checked dishonesty in the
treasury, and attempted reforms in the method of bestowing
corregimientos and in determining the official responsibility
of the oidores and the viceroy. Naturally, conflict between
the latter and Valderrama was caused by this intervention
in the supreme affairs of government. The quarrel might
have become a severe one, as it too frequently did when
viceroy and visitor were at loggerheads, had it not been cut
short on the last day of July, 1564, by the death of Velasco.
The second viceroy was buried with pomp in the church of
Santo Domingo, with the grateful memory of the people of

New Spain, especially the Indians, among whom he was called the Father of his Country. He died a poor man.

According to the king's previous instructions providing for such an emergency, the audiencia now assumed control, under the title of audiencia gobernadora. The visitation of that body was still incomplete, however, hence Valderrama the visitor was in practical control. That astute official was evidently provident for his own future, for it was not long before the Council of Mexico City urged that no viceroy, with costly salary and retinue, be sent to New Spain, but that Valderrama be made governor and that Martín Cortés, the second marquis del Valle, who had arrived from Spain some time before, be made captain-general. This suggestion, which looked toward the benefit of the encomenderos and smacked of autonomy, of course went unanswered.

Perhaps it might have been the wisest thing to have followed the suggestion, for the audiencia, once free from limitations, embarked upon a rule of marked incompetence. The turbulent Spaniards began to indulge in street fights and feuds over trifles of punctilio which were participated in by the dashing and irrepressible young Cortés. At such a juncture news arrived that the king had decided against the permanency of the encomienda system.

The encomenderos began to talk of resistance by force. They were led by the Ávila brothers. While they plotted they were spied upon and reports of their conspiracy were carried to the audiencia. Their project was alleged to be the proclamation of Cortés as king of New Spain, to seek his confirmation in that title from the towns and from the pope, and to open New Spain's commerce to the world. The young Cortés received the proposal as a joke, but at a party given at the christening of his twin sons he foolishly allowed himself to impersonate his father at the famous entry into Tenochtitlán, while one of the Ávilas, in the rôle of Moctezuma, received mock royal homage.

Then it was planned to slay the oidores, the visitor, the brother and son of Velasco, and other enemies. The whole kingdom was to be seized, and Spanish rule obliterated. The aid of France was to be sought in trade and economic affairs. But Cortés hesitated. During his vacillation Alonzo de Ávila fell ill, and the plot languished, largely because Valderrama, who had heard the story from Cortés, refused to consider the matter seriously. But when Valderrama returned to Spain the audiencia, inimical to Cortés, began a self-interested investigation. While it was in progress renewed rumors that the encomiendas were doomed brought on fresh activity for open rebellion. The audiencia, gathering courage from necessity, arrested Cortés and several other suspected persons. The Ávila brothers were promptly beheaded, to the horror of the disapproving community.

At this juncture came a new viceroy, Gastón de Peralta, on October 19, 1566. He speedily formed an opinion that there had been no real conspiracy against Spain. He wrote to the king that the audiencia had been needlessly severe, and when the court endeavored to expedite the trials of the remaining culprits he naturally resented such action, as he had previously ordered the proceedings stopped. The oidores accused the viceroy of favoring the conspiracy, sent charges against him to the king, and prevented his reports on affairs from being transmitted to Spain. Since no official report came to his hands to refute the accusations, Philip sent out three investigators, jueces pesquisidores, to take the government from Peralta and send him to Spain for trial.

One of these men, Jarava, died on the voyage. The leader, Alonzo Muñoz, with Luis Carrillo, arrived in October, 1567. Muñoz inaugurated a reign of terror. Prodigal with arrests, swift of judgment, and vindictive in executions, he tortured Cortés, hanged and quartered several other encomenderos, and filled the jails with suspects. Many were fined and exiled, even the viceroy was tried, but sentence was referred to the king. The people were desperate. They smuggled to Spain a report of the tyrant's atrocities, and the king, irate, sent judges to return the pesquisidores to Spain. There was jubilation in Mexico when they left. Curiously enough, they departed on the same ship that carried the deposed viceroy. Carrillo had the good fortune to die of apoplexy while on the way to Havana. Muñoz, arrived at court, was coolly received, and died on the day of his arrival, probably from chagrin. New Spain had been freed from conspiracy, if such indeed had existed. The power of the king was supreme within the land; it was now time to turn to defense of the colonies from enemies from the outside.

The English nation, retarded in its process of expansion by internal strife during the opening period of American discovery, had been deterred from engaging in New World conquests by the commercial failure of the Cabot voyages and by the long Wars of the Roses and did not become an aspirant for the riches of the new hemisphere until maritime enterprise became quickened during the reign of Elizabeth. The first opportunity for success came with the opening of the slave trade. In 1530 William Hawkins traded a cargo of negroes on the Brazilian coast. In 1562 his son John Hawkins brought a cargo of "black ivory" from Guinea to sell at La Española, receiving colonial products in exchange. A second time he ventured, under royal patronage, with like gains in the West Indies. In 1567 his third enterprise, Francis Drake his cousin being his second in command, brought him with nine vessels to seek refuge from storm, as he alleged, in the dangerous port of San Juan de Ulloa, at Vera Cruz. But while there he seized the island of Los Sacrificios and fortified his position, merely, he said, as a matter of form until he could effect needed repairs to his vessels. He had made an agreement with the audiencia whereby he should receive the desired help if he made no further hostile demonstration, when suddenly his plans were upset by the arrival in the port of thirteen Spanish vessels, one of them bearing the fourth viceroy, Martín Enríquez (1568–1580). The Spaniards agreed to leave Hawkins unmolested until his repairs should be made if he would refrain from firing on them as they entered. Hawkins consented, but the viceroy once inside attacked the Englishman, who was obliged to flee with only two ships. Much booty fell to the Spaniards. Of those who escaped on the two vessels about one hundred Englishmen who landed at Pánuco rather than venture a voyage on the overcrowded ships, arrived in Mexico and were imprisoned or sent to Spain. It is said that his ill fortune at Vera Cruz animated the future activities of Francis Drake, who felt impelled to obtain compensation for the losses his cousin Hawkins had sustained at the hands of Enríquez. Drake's later piratical expedition of 1578, in which he raided the entire Pacific Coast, his frequent sackings of Spanish American ports and his marauding in the harbor of Cádiz, probably more than amply repaid the early loss.

Enríquez, arrived in his viceroyalty, turned his attention toward securing his frontiers and his coasts. Armed troops were organized and placed at Vera Cruz, the Isla del Carmen, Acapulco, and San Blas. An expedition against the northern Indians, the Chichimecas, was successful, and to restrain them, forts or presidios were established at Ajuelos, Portezuelo, San Felipe, Jerez, and Celaya. These fortifications proving insufficient to stop disastrous Indian raids, blockhouses were built, stronger escorts were provided for treasure trains, and even portable towers for defense were constructed to use as modern armored cars are employed. Even so the remedy was inadequate, and Indian warfare became a permanent feature of the frontier.

Enríquez was transferred to Peru in 1580, after a rule of twelve years. During this period some thought was given to reorganizing the government of New Spain. The Council of the Indies recommended that the viceroyal term should be limited to twelve years, and the terms of lesser officials to six. The system of appointing corregidores should be superseded by use of alcaldes mayores, twelve of whom should be appointed to make annual inspections of all the towns, to see that the local authorities duly performed their functions. This may have been the origin of the custom of permitting new viceroys to nominate twelve alcaldes mayores. The corregidores were continued however, both officers serving practically the same purposes in the economic and political systems, as supposed guardians of agriculture and protectors of local peace.

Enríquez had found the viceroy's position onerous. Everyone brought his troubles to him for settlement. He had to attend to all his work himself, dependents being untrustworthy. His duties as head of government were combined with those of head of the church as a political body. His tasks were so engrossing and so exacting, and complaints at decisions were so numerous, that he felt that holding public office in Mexico was for an honest man only a misfortune. He had done fairly well however. Though not a great viceroy, he was a successful administrator. One of his wisest policies was that of utilizing creoles in positions of governmental responsibility. He believed in their integrity and efficiency and recommended that his policy should be continued. Had his advice been consistently followed, the native-born Americans in Mexico might have built up groups of families in which an established tradition of government service would have obviated the manifestations of incompetency which have all too often characterized public administration during the independence epoch.

The excellent judgment which had governed the choice of individuals for the position of viceroy of New Spain was now to suffer a relapse in the selection of the fifth of the line. Lorenzo Suárez de Mendoza y Figueroa, count of La Coruña, though possessing high personal qualities, a relative of the first viceroy, a soldier of reputation, affable, frank, and generous, had the negative virtues which ill fitted him for the high responsibilities which he assumed on October 4, 1580. His advanced years, his mild manners, leniency, and lack of energy, made him no match for the avaricious officials who surrounded him with flattery, deception, and self-interested dissimulation. The regulations which had fettered Velasco, making his judgment subservient to that of the audiencia, still crippled administrative efficiency, and the practice of permitting notaries and scriveners to resell their offices directly to the highest bidders, merely paying one-third of the price received into the royal treasury, created a set of subordinate officers not readily amenable to discipline and not of the character which would have best represented the royal interests.

As a result, the public administration entered upon a period of fiscal corruption and judicial venality. The viceroy was impotent to check the tide of dishonesty, and realized that his only recourse was the dubious one of calling for another visitor-general. The time was ripe for strenuous measures. The wealth of the colony, though it had grown amazingly through development of stockraising and mining, was not great enough to satisfy the rapacity of the white conquerors. Fray Gerónimo de Mendieta, the ecclesiastical historian, had early addressed the viceroy, saying: "It is very necessary that a much different purpose and aim from that which has been followed during these times should now be sought. We must not consider gold or silver or temporal interests as our principal quest, but the conversion and protection and increase of these natives . . . for the insatiable covetousness of our Spaniards wherever they go makes us like the leech, sucking the lifeblood of all those whom we reach, especially of these poor Indians, who are powerless to resist."

The remedy chosen was to send a visitor, as Suárez had requested. He did not come, however, until some time after the viceroy had gone to his untroubled grave in June, 1582. There was a brief interregnum under an incompetent and insignificant audiencia gobernadora until 1584, when the duties of visitor were confided to the Archbishop of Mexico.

This man, Pedro de Moya y Contreras, was austere and uncompromising. Armed with unusual power, being the first incumbent in the newly established Inquisition as well as visitor-general, he proceeded quietly with his investigation of the corruption of the audiencia, and then reported his findings to King Philip. In reply the monarch designated Moya y Contreras viceroy, thus combining in one person the four highest offices in the colony. Now in complete power, he removed many delinquent officers and fined others; some were promptly hanged. Honest men were placed in positions of responsibility, and as a result the collections of taxes increased so notably that the viceroy was able to send to Spain 300,000 ducats of silver and 11,000 marks of gold, whereas previous exportations of these metals had been insignificant.

But complaints of too much viceroyal efficiency began to reach the ear of the ever suspicious Philip. As a result of charges of incapacity to govern, of disobedience to the king, of concubinage, of being proud, vicious, and inhuman, he was removed from the viceroyal functions, but placed again as visitor; in this work he quarreled with the new viceroy over ecclesiastical affairs and the visitations of the oidores. He was recalled to Spain and made president of the Council of the Indies, a signal honor which indicated that his American experiences had fitted him for higher service.

The seventh viceroy, Álvaro Manrique de Zúñiga, marquis of Villamanrique, was hailed with joy in Mexico on October 18, 1585. His comparatively brief term of four years was marked by the advent of Francis Drake and John Cavendish in Pacific waters. , The rich Manila galleon *Santa Ana*, seven hundred tons burden, bound for Acapulco from Manila, carrying 122,000 pesos in gold and much Chinese silk, fell prey to Cavendish off the bay of San Bernabé, Lower California, in November, 1587. Blame for carelessness concerning protection for the Asiatic trade fell upon the viceroy, who was unfortunate in many other situations. He removed a judge of the audiencia of Guadalajara because that official had, contrary to a law enunciated in 1575, married a wife from a family which lived within his jurisdiction. Strife arose, even clash of arms threatened. Bitter recriminations reached the king, but the trouble was temporarily patched up. Villamanrique, though he had shown enterprise in renewing northern explorations along the California coast, had accumulated many enemies; he had to bear the brunt of general discontent bred by a widespread and violent epidemic, by an earthquake at Mexico, and sundry other mishaps to the disgruntled colony. Again complaints were launched against him, and he was removed to make way for a successor bearing the illustrious name of the great second viceroy. Before he left New Spain Villamanrique was tried by a judge of residencia, Bishop Romano of Tlascala, and found guilty of many charges, the most serious being that of having allowed undue appropriations of royal funds. The deposed viceroy was fined nearly all his possessions, and left the realm in sorrow and poverty with his afflicted wife and the body of his daughter, who had died during the epidemic. His property was not fully restored to his heirs until after his death in a Franciscan convent in Spain.

Luis de Velasco II (1590–1595), the eighth viceroy, entered the capital on January 25, 1590. He was an old resident, having been in the viceroyalty with his father and after; he had taken an active part in quelling the troubles incident to the Ávila-Cortés conspiracy, and had been a member of the town councils of Cempoalla and Mexico; in short, he knew his kingdom. He was one of the colony; able, intelligent, loyal to duty, honest instinctively, he added lustre to the name his father had made famous.

He believed in the saving grace of work, and to the end of its accomplishment reopened extensive woolen and cotton factories which Mendoza had initiated, but which had since been idle. Employment was thus provided for hundreds. He beautified the capital, strengthened the defences of Vera Cruz, and successfully defended the northern frontiers. This was accomplished by wise reception of Chichimeca warriors who came to propose cessation of their hostile raids in exchange for annual supplies of cattle and clothes. This near-tribute to savage hordes was granted upon their acceptance of Christian Indian families sent among them to assimilate the wild bands to civilized life. The Tlascaltecs, four hundred families strong, were sent to found such colonies as San Luis de la Paz, to which Franciscan and Jesuit missionaries ministered. Efforts to induce the Otomis of the northern forests to settle in towns were unsuccessful, and the dubious policy of forcing them to sedentary life was left to the injustice of a later régime.

During the term of the viceroy Moya y Contreras the

necessity of holding the Pacific Coast under better control
had become a matter of policy because of the activity of
Englishmen and Dutchmen in western waters. Cavendish
and Drake had opened up the way into the Pacific, and were
emulated by Dutch freebooters before the end of the century.
Moya y Contreras ordered one of the generals of the Manila
galleon, Francisco de Gali, to search on the California coast
as he returned from the Orient, to see if he could not find a
strait or a tenable point which might be fortified. Villamanrique had been uncertain as to the advantages to be
derived from northern maritime explorations, but the second
Velasco, with characteristic energy, resumed the project in
1595, ordering Sebastián Rodríguez Cermenho to explore
the coast carefully when he should return from Manila with
his annual galleon. The unhappy wreck of Cermenho's
vessel in Drake's Bay, with the loss of the cargo, impressed
the point that merchant vessels could not safely engage in
exploring an unknown coast, hence it was determined to
reconnoitre the shoreline with light craft adapted to such a
purpose, unencumbered with a precious cargo, which would
be put at hazard by close-in coastal explorations. The project was delayed for a time by a change in the viceroyal office.

The ninth viceroy, Gaspar de Zúñiga y Acevedo (1595–
1603), took up the proposed northern discovery in 1596 by
sending out Sebastián Vizcaíno. This Pacific navigator, who
had been on the galleon *Santa Ana* when Cavendish took it,
made a settlement at La Paz in Lower California, intending
to engage in a monopolistic pearl trade. His venture failing
in 1597, he was sought for in 1599 when royal orders came
again to find a California port for the homing galleons.
His expedition went forth from Acapulco in 1602, covering
the waters explored previously by Cabrillo and Ferrelo, and
reaching two degrees above Cape Mendocino. As a result,
an excellent chart of the Pacific Coast was made by this
expedition, which is especially distinguished for having
entered and named the port of Monterey, a body of water
which had no doubt been previously seen by Cermenho, and
was to become the objective of the late eighteenth century

explorations which led to the occupation of Upper California. As Drake, de Gali, and Cermenho had done before him, Vizcaíno missed the present San Francisco Bay. The fact that this great inland sea was undiscovered by so many experienced navigators has given rise to the suggestion that their failure was due to the nonexistence of the bay during the sixteenth century. Geological experts give scant credence to the hypothesis of so recent an upheaval as to have created this great body of water since the time of those explorations.

It seemed as though a desirable port had been found, and that its occupation, which was planned, would at least be carried into effect. But the measure was laid aside because of a will-o-the-wisp romance like so many of those which had urged other Spaniards to heroic endeavor. Stories became current that the islands Rica de Oro and Rica de Plata, somewhere in the Pacific, would not only furnish a better port and a shorter route from Manila, but would yield untold store of precious metals. Accordingly the Monterey project was held in abeyance and Vizcaíno in the year 1611 led an ill-fated expedition in search of these fabulous islets. His journey led him to Japan as ambassador from the viceroy Velasco, and into unending troubles which cost him his reputation and brought no results. This was the only time that New Spain ever had ambassadorial representation before a foreign court.

The close of the century came with no net gain to Pacific Coast expansion save some knowledge of the coast line, which soon fell back into the haze of forgetfulness. The prime reason was that the galleons, after sighting the California coast, had no need of a port for refuge or repair, as the southward voyage was quickly completed with fair winds from the vicinity of Cape Mendocino to Acapulco.

Interior expansion was attended with better fortune under Zúñiga, better known as the Count of Monterey. In 1581 the Spaniards again penetrated into the famed regions of the Pueblo Indians of New Mexico; renewed interest in the conquest of those towns, even of reaching the notorious but unlocated kingdom of Gran Quivira and the equally distracting and mythical Strait of Anián led to northern expeditions by Castaño de Sosa in 1590, by Leiva and Humaña in 1593. It was not until 1598, however, that Juan de Oñate, son of that Cristóbal Oñate who had fallen victim to the fury of the visitor Muñoz, left Nueva Vizcaya to establish connections with the Pueblo country by way of El Paso, effecting a temporary colony at San Juan in the Río Grande valley and securing a tenuous hold on the New Mexico country, which was made firmer by the establishment of Sante Fe in 1609. At about the turn of the century Oñate's lieutenants explored the Colorado River to the Gulf of California and penetrated eastward into Kansas.

This northward thrust by Oñate was simultaneous with the expansion of New Spain in the northeast. Luis de Carabajal had secured a grant to the territory of Nuevo León in 1579, under Viceroy Enríquez. This area lay between Nueva Vizcaya and Nueva Galicia on the west and the Gulf coast on the east. Carabajal used Guzmán's old base at Pánuco, advancing westward over the route which the lieutenants of Cortés had explored. In 1583 he laid the foundations of León, now named Cerralvo. The settlements of San Luis, near the site of the present Monterrey, and Nueva Almadén, near the later Monclova, marked the areas of occupation. The leading industry of this conquest was slave catching; it engaged the activities of several hundred conquerors, who attempted to modify the encomienda and mission systems of handling the natives by collecting them in congregas, under color of giving the Indians better care than they would receive in encomiendas. The congrega was but an added name for forced labor, and failed. Abuses committed in its name led to the persecution of the Carabajal family by the court of the Inquisition. The alleged crime was heresy, for the Carabajals were Portuguese Jews. Their destruction by the iron hearted Tribunal Suprema de la Inquisición is one of the most pitiful stories of sixteenth century Christian barbarism in New Spain.

In résumé, it may be said that the close of the century saw

the great areas of the conquest blocked out. The great push outward had now practically spent itself. In the seventeenth and eighteenth centuries added areas were to be annexed, chiefly as outposts for the defense of what had been won during the great days of Philip II. With the passing of that zealous monarch was to ensue a period of consolidation, of frontier initiative, and then of decay and retrogression, to be followed just before the eve of emancipation by a soul-stirring reanimation under Charles III of the House of Bourbon. While the sixteenth century was an age of discovery, conquest, and occupation, it was no less an age of the development of the spiritual and intellectual forces of the viceroyalty, the chief agency of which was the church.

CHAPTER VI

THE papal bulls under which the Spanish monarchs undertook the occupation and subjugation of the western world amounted in essence to the establishment of a contractual relation between themselves and the papacy whereby the latter bestowed the sovereignty in consideration of the obligation assumed by Spain to Christianize the native population. Fulfillment of the terms was more than willingly undertaken. The conquest thus partook of two characters, temporal and spiritual. It would be difficult to decide which aspect of the problem was entered into, at first, with the greater zest and enthusiasm. Throughout the sixteenth century at least the Spaniards were as zealous in proselyting as they were avid for conquest and riches. The church was no whit behind the lusty conquistadores in improving its opportunities. And though religion and morals, religion and humanitarianism, were sharply divorced in the minds of the military campaigners, they were strongly united in the minds and purposes of the sovereigns, and their spiritual agents the churchmen were imbued with the same principles. The idealism of the church was eminently practical for its age; it strove for wide and prompt conversions; the fathers even coveted the oft received crown of martyrdom at the hands of the savages in their all too scantily appreciated apostolates.

The conquest of Mexico fell into the hands of a man of peculiarly intense piety. Cortés was a highly religious man, with a heart softened by moral and humanitarian considerations when self-interest did not impose opposite attitudes. Cruel in his persecution of the conquered Aztec nobles who scantily rewarded his demand for gold, heartless toward his enemies, ruthless in eliminating undesirable associates, the great conqueror felt that he was ordained of heaven to accomplish the spread of holy religion; he even cherished the belief that his military successes were achieved because of the sacred motto, "The Holy Cross is our banner, and under it we shall conquer," under which he essayed his great enterprise. He even proclaimed the spiritual conquest to be the primary motive of his campaigns, and declared that without it his temporal conquests would be unjust.

Hence it is not strange that he took prompt means to further the cause of Christianity. No sooner had Tenochtitlán fallen than he began to seek from Spain the spiritual assistants needed to carry on the labor of conversions for which his army chaplains had been inadequate. He recognized that more churchmen would not only work for the salvation of souls, but that they would aid admirably in the necessary exploitation of native labor on which the Spanish colonial system was to be built.

During the siege of Tenochtitlán there were present five ecclesiastics, Fathers Olmedo, Juan Díaz, Juan de León, Juan Díaz de Guevara, and the Franciscan Pedro Melgarejo de Urrea. Of these the most conspicuous were Olmedo and Díaz. In April 1521, Pope Leo X issued a bull permitting two Franciscans to enter New Spain and practice their religion with episcopal powers. Various causes prevented their coming, but in May of 1522 all the mendicant orders were authorized to undertake religious work in America, and were invested with all ecclesiastical powers not requiring episcopal rank. With that action formal governmental proselyting began.

The work of Christianizing the Indians and ministering to the conquerors was thus confided first to the mendicant orders. These were those bodies of men who operated in communities under a vow of poverty and chastity similar to that under which the Benedictine order had been organized.

The Franciscans were the first of the mendicant orders to arrive in New Spain under the papal permission. Three fathers of the order came from Ghent, reaching Vera Cruz at the end of August, 1522. They were Juan de Tecto, Juan de Ayora, and Pedro de Gante. The latter was an illegitimate relative of Charles V. Repairing to old Tezcoco, seat of the fallen throne of Nezahualcoyotl and Nezahualpilli, these holy and humble men began there the work of spreading the gospel, ignorant as they were of the language and customs of the Indians. In May 1524 twelve new brothers came, led by Father Martín de Valencia, to establish the Custodia del Santo Evangelio, the beginning of the Franciscan province. Reaching San Juan de Ulloa, these twelve apostles marched barefoot toward Mexico City. It was on this march that one of them, Father Toribio de Benavente, accepted the soubriquet Motolinía, applied to him by the Indians because of his poverty and lameness. Father Motolinía became famous in New Spain as a zealous Christian, a humane friend of the Indians, and an earnest and observing student of their native culture.

The conquerors, led by Cortés himself, reverently kissed the robes of these saintly men when they reached the capital, displaying a humility which had its intended deep effect on the Indians. The influence of the friars was sedulously courted because of their power as representatives of the church, but more practically because their hold over the Indians would tend to make the latter better vassals and laborers. Then too it was advisable to stand well with the friars, for their reports to the king's ministers might bring great good or evil. Cortés submitted, upon a staged occasion, to being flogged by a friar for non-attendance at mass, that his example might quiet the complaints of natives who had received similar treatment.

The Custodia del Santo Evangelio, established July 2, 1524, was divided into four districts, Mexico, Tezcoco, Huejotzingo, and Tlascala. There were then seventeen Franciscans; four were placed in each district, and Father Valencia remained in the capital as a fifth member and director. In each district convents were soon built, hospitals and schools springing up beside them.

The first school, begun by Father Gante, contained facilities for instructing a thousand children. They learned prayers and religious exercises, with gradual advancement into the mysteries of Spanish civilization through the avenues of reading, writing, drawing, and music, while practical utility for future church building was sought by training boys as carpenters, bricklayers, and masons. Soon churches began to be erected without Spanish overseers. The friar was a most successful handyman. Spanish weavers, saddle-makers, and other artisans soon found their selfish monopolies broken by the zealous copying of their apt Indian imitators. The Aztec culture, could it have been taken in hand solely by the missionaries of the faith, might have advanced rapidly to the stage attained by the Spaniards. The missionaries speedily acquired the native tongues, and began teaching the adult Aztecs. Then came baptism of imperfectly instructed converts. Father Gante said that he and one of his companions baptized by wholesale, often inducting as many as fourteen thousand Indians a day into the rites of the church. No doubt it was complaisance and curiosity, joined with political cupidity, which led such great multitudes to accept the sprinkled sacrament, rather than genuine conception of the religious principle involved. Indeed it was more than suspected that many of the natives underwent the ceremony again and again, either to please the missionaries or in the superstitious belief that they would receive some mysterious recurrent benefit from the repetition of the ceremony.

It soon became necessary for the missionaries to harmonize individual practices into a policy in the matters of conversions, marriages, and other essentials of the formal practice of Christianity by the natives. This necessity led to the holding in 1526 of a council of friars and jurisconsults which has been termed the first synod of the church in New Spain. Through it some uniformity was attained, and principles were laid down.

It was the practice during these early years to effect conversions through native helpers, who, becoming adept, performed baptisms without Spanish supervision. It must be

confessed that conversions did not eliminate heathen practices entirely, but these were gradually relegated to remote
places or carried on secretly by the expedient of hiding the
heathen gods about the Christian altars. Eradication of
heathenism was effected by destruction of Aztec temples
and images. These Franciscans boasted that in seven years
they demolished five hundred temples and twenty thousand
images. The modern world would be grateful if they had not
been so zealous.

The Catholic form of Christianity made a vivid appeal to
the Indians through the charm of mystery, the attraction
of the pomp of ritualistic ceremonials, and the promptings
of obvious advantage to be obtained by conforming with the
desires of the invaders. The category of the friars, their
saintliness and benignity, markedly contrasting with the
rough exterior and demeanor of the lay conquerors, served
also as attractions. Work had to be performed for the
fathers, but it was less exacting than that demanded by the
encomenderos.

The second of the regular orders which took up work in
New Spain was that of the Dominicans. Like the Franciscans they had been for some time established in the insular
settlements. Under their vicar-general Tomás Ortiz they
came to Vera Cruz in 1526 at the same time that Luis Ponce
de León came out to try Cortés and supersede him in the
government. In 1528 a few more Dominicans arrived; it
was not long before twenty of them were collaborating with
the Franciscans.

Dominicans and Franciscans worked harmoniously together during the period of their earliest contacts. Several
Franciscan districts were almost immediately turned over
to the Dominicans, and the two orders made common cause
against the abuses committed by the audiencia. It was not
long, however, before the ancient antipathies between the
two orders were renewed, the difficulty arising from
agreements as to methods whereby conversions were to be
effected. The Franciscans were the more militant of the
two groups, and held the dominant position among Spaniards

and Indians alike.   The Dominicans had still a sphere of influence to develop.

They rapidly built for themselves imposing convents; that of Santo Domingo in Mexico was the chief of them.   They also erected establishments at Puebla, Vera Cruz, and Coatzacoalcos, spreading soon into Pánuco, Oaxaca, and Guatemala, the convent at Antequera being established in 1529.   They established their Provincia de Santiago de Mexico in 1532.

Like the Franciscans, the Dominicans took matters of politics and government into their pulpits and made themselves active opponents of the abuses committed by the governing classes.   The Franciscans were notably missionaries to the poor; their early labors among the children of the Indians and the slaves of the early Spaniards were characteristic of their services to mankind.   The Dominicans, on the other hand, were of a more aristocratic category.   They made their appeal to the upper strata of society and were important in the councils of the country through voices like those of Las Casas the Apostle of the Indians, Montesinos his companion, and Pedro de Córdova.

The third of the religious orders to enter New Spain was that of the Order of Mercy or the Mercedarians, who were brought out by Cortés upon his return from Spain in 1530. They were led by Fray Juan de Leguizamo, who was confessor to the family of Cortés.   There was also in the retinue of the captain-general at this time a number of nuns of the Order of Concepción.   They rapidly attained a notable membership among the aristocratic young women of the colony.   The Mercedarians who came with Cortés made their way into Guatemala, and did not establish convents in New Spain proper until 1589.

While Franciscans and Dominicans were spreading their influence over the kingdom, came the Augustinians.   Fray Francisco de la Cruz, with six companions, arrived in 1533. They began their labors in the territories of Tlapán, Chilapán, and elsewhere.   Five of them were placed outside of Mexico City while the other two organized means for their support. The crowning monument to their effort in the capital is their great monastery, now occupied as the Biblioteca Nacional. By 1536 eleven friars of this order were in the colony. Their province, organized in 1543, was named the Province of Michoacán. In it a convent, established in Tiripitío, became one of the early universities of New Spain in which the conventional faculties were organized. Not only on the plateau, but in the tierra caliente of the southern shore, the Augustinians carried on their labors. In 1596 they had seventy-six monasteries; early in the seventeenth century they erected part of them into a second province.

Latest of the important missionary societies which entered New Spain was the notable Society or Company of Jesus, the Order of the Jesuits, not a mendicant order. After their inception under Ignatius Loyola as a force to counteract the Lutheran Reformation, they entered the New World as an added agency for the propagation of the faith, establishing missions in Havana and Florida before their arrival in New Spain in 1572. In Florida they had served as the zealous coadjutors of Pedro Menéndez de Avilés, who attempted to hold the Atlantic coast and the peninsula as a measure of colonial defence against the French Huguenots and the sea rovers who menaced Spanish shipping. Their field in Florida proving unsatisfactory because of the intractable disposition of the Indians, those missions spread along the Georgia and Florida coast had been discontinued with the consent of the king. Numerous efforts before 1572 had been made to bring the Jesuits into New Spain, and when they arrived they were enthusiastically received. Twelve of them, under Dr. Pedro Sánchez, reached Vera Cruz on September 9.

Jesuit activity was first directed toward education of young Spanish gentlemen, the Indians being then cared for by the mendicant orders. Dr. Sánchez therefore founded colleges in several cities, hoping to improve moral and spiritual conditions. This was a welcome service, for the Spaniards had hitherto missed the advantages of the normal education of their times. The first college was that of San Pedro y San Pablo in Mexico City. It was remarkably successful and influential through a large part of the colonial epoch. The building of the Jesuit church called the Casa Profesa marked the increase of the influence of this order. Its erection was opposed by the mendicant orders, but their opposition, which resulted in a lawsuit, was finally overcome by decision of a court of justice in favor of the Jesuits in 1595.

In 1576 new Jesuit priests arrived from Europe, and the Society was further increased by native and Spanish colonists who joined from time to time. It became one of the most powerful organizations in New Spain, as it was elsewhere. The Jesuits soon began missions to the Indians as well as service for the Spaniards. They entered this work in Nueva Galicia in 1574, in Oaxaca in 1575, in Michoacán soon after 1573, in Vera Cruz in 1578, in Puebla in 1580, and in the Philippines in 1585. During the seventeenth century they were the pioneers of the conquest of Lower California and the Mexican northwest.

Other orders of lesser importance during the sixteenth century were those of La Caridad and San Hipólito. The founder of La Caridad was Bernardino Álvarez, who had been a private soldier in New Spain. This order founded hospitals in Oaxtepec, Jalapa, Perote, and Puebla before the turn of the century. The Carmelites arrived in 1585. They devoted themselves to instructing the natives. Their province, San Alberto, was founded in 1588. The Benedictines came in 1589 and founded the monastery of Monserrate in Mexico City.

None of the orders excelled the Franciscans in missionary activities. Their province was expanded before the end of the century into three, Mexico, Michoacán, or San Pedro y San Pablo, and Yucatan or San José. They received large and regular alms from natives and Spaniards, in the form of land, labor, and other services. For the first forty years they had no allowance from the king, subsisting on pious gifts alone. But in the course of time they received regular treasury subsidies. This was particularly true after they advanced into areas of scant white population. Many of them were martyred in their frontier missions, but they continued their ministrations throughout the entire colonial epoch, being second only in political and social influence to the Jesuits. In 1580 or 1581 the Barefoot Franciscans established their province, San Diego de Alcalá. They built a number of convents in the larger cities, but never became as conspicuous in missionary work as the first Franciscans.

At the end of the century the Dominicans possessed two provinces, Santiago de Mexico with forty-eight monasteries and San Hipólito de Oaxaca with twenty-one. Many of their distinguished men, such as Juan López Castellanos, and Hernando de la Paz, left names as distinguished as the Franciscan Bernardino de Sahagún or his earlier mentioned confrères.

The very numerous foundations of these and other orders manifest the importance of their services to the dual conquest. The conspicuous service rendered by the regulars was in the mission field. The mission as an institution came into vogue as soon as the conquest had spread beyond the area of the sedentary tribes. It was a clerical modification of the encomienda system. In it the asperities of the attrition of the two races were modified, so that it became the institution par excellence for the spread of Spanish civilization. The fathers, two in number, usually, in each mission, taught religion, agriculture, handicrafts, and self-government, to a small band of more or less willing neophytes. They depended for protection and escort upon a small detachment of soldiers, the influence of whom on the Indians was habitually so bad that the fathers were fain to do without it. But the mission as a frontier post needed guards, and as a subsidized colonial outpost was rarely left without a semblance of military protection. The missions were established as temporary agencies for the civilization of the natives, and were expected to be turned over to the secular church at the end of their utility, which was supposedly to be outgrown in ten years' time. The system of education employed did not tend to accelerate the self-reliance of the Indians, however, and the orders found it painful to relinquish their investments at the end of the period, so that there was usually a running fight between the regulars and the seculars on the matter of such transfer, or secularization, as it was called. But the net influence of the regulars in their work with the Indians was to bring to the indigenous population the highest type of civilization which Spain possessed. With their ideals of labor, service, and preparation for the other world, they did their utmost to pass on the light of civilization with a benignity, a charity, and an energy which was worthy of a higher success than was attained.

While the regulars were first in the field of the spiritual conquest, the secular organization or arm of the church was not long in entering the new colony. It is of course understood that the secular church was organized with its headship in the pope, as were the bodies of regulars. While the latter had their generals and provincials as superior officers, the seculars were led by their bishops and archbishops. Within the settled areas they occupied the same territory as the regulars. They served the Spaniards especially, though as the missions were secularized the districts or doctrinas of the latter were turned into parishes, with the parish priests or curas in charge.

The episcopal organization of the secular church in New Spain may be said to have begun with the appointment of a bishop for the little island of Cozumel, off the coast of Yucatan, as soon as Grijalva's voyage became known in Spain. In 1526 this bishopric was extended to include Tabasco, Vera Cruz, and Tlascala; Father Julián Garcés, the appointee, who was a Dominican friar, took charge of his see in 1527. Another bishopric, for Mexico City and environs, was created in the same year and bestowed upon Fray Juan de Zumárraga, who was sent to New Spain with the first audiencia in 1528.

Zumárraga wrote his name large upon the early pages of

New Spain's history. Zealous and austere, he was a suitable person in whom to repose the office of Protector of the Indians, a position already made famous by the conscientious and vehement Bartholomew de Las Casas of Chiapas. But Zumárraga found amelioration of the condition of the indigenes a thankless and difficult task. His vociferations against the excesses of judges and conquerors brought about curtailment of his powers as Protector, and his restless energy found vent in orgies of destruction of the relics of Aztec religion and history which had eluded thus far the alert eyes of his confrères. Anthropology and history have been sadly handicapped by the fervid zeal of this archenemy of the "works of the devil" which might have served as keys to the story of pre-Cortesian man on the American continent. And yet this earnest man laid deep and sure the foundations of the secular church in New Spain.

The progress made by the church during the early years of the conquest was not so rapid as it should have been, because of the fact that the teachings inculcated by the friars and the secular clergy were practically ignored by the Spanish residents, and the natives were not slow in observing that very little attention was paid to the clergymen by their superiors. Hence they followed the example of the laymen, being induced to that course of action by their natural proclivities of heathenism and indifference. The Great Zumárraga made genuine and wholesome efforts to improve the status of the natives, but his efforts served rather to make him the object of obloquy than of gratitude. Being called to Spain in 1532 to give advice concerning the proper method of handling the indigenous population, he was able to make his voice heard on this subject. His powers were at that time extended to allow him to examine the methods of tribute collection, and the audiencia was ordered to assist him in his labors. In 1534 he returned to Mexico and there began his active labors as bishop. In 1530 the first parochial church was raised to the rank of a cathedral. After about four decades the building of the present great cathedral of

Mexico City was begun. It was not ready for utilization, however, until 1626.

Episcopal organization was taken in hand in 1531 by members of the second audiencia. The old episcopal jurisdictions first established, particularly that of Tlascala, were found to have been unwisely selected. Many parts of this bishopric were as much as one hundred and sixty leagues from the episcopal town, and the customary bishop's visitation was therefore a practical impossibility. Hence it was urged that a reorganization of the bishopric should be taken in hand and that the metropolitan see of Mexico should be restricted in area. In 1532 these suggestions were adopted. The bishopric of Tlascala was restricted in area and the town of Puebla was included in it. Sebastián Ramírez de Fuenleal, whose episcopal experiences in Santo Domingo rendered him a useful adviser in his position as president of this audiencia, also recommended that the four bishoprics of New Spain should be increased in number as speedily as possible and that Mexico should be raised to the rank of a metropolitan church at once. In 1534 therefore New Spain was divided into four bishoprics with the names of Mexico, Michoacán, Tlascala and Oaxaca. All these dioceses were to be limited to fifteen leagues radius with the cathedral town in the center. The intervening spaces were to be equally divided. The obvious inconvenience of these subdivisions was soon manifest in numerous boundary disputes. In 1535 the bishopric of Oaxaca was established under the leadership of Juan López de Zárate, a Dominican, and Antequera was made the cathedral town. In 1536 the bishopric of Michoacán was established, the see being at Tzintzuntzán. The distinguished oidor of the second audiencia, Vasco de Quiroga, was made the first bishop of Michoacán. He was offered this position before he had taken his holy orders and was rapidly raised through the successive ranks so that he might occupy the bishopric. He was consecrated in 1538, but did not fully organize his diocese until 1554. During their early years, the bishoprics of Tlascala and Michoacán were subject to the jurisdiction of the archbishop of Seville, as was that of Mexico, until its organization as an archi-episcopacy.

The organized efforts of the church, after the establishment of the bishoprics and the organization of the provinces of the regulars, began to have a more durable character than the conversions which had been previously effected. Beginning about 1530, we may speak of the spiritual conquest as having come into a stage of advancement which had durable effects. Proselyting was effected by shrewd appeal to racial consciousness. One of the early legends of this time is concerned with the miraculous apparition of the Virgin Mary to a poor Indian, named Juan Diego, who presented himself before Bishop Zumárraga, stating that he had been delegated by the Virgin to request that a temple be erected in her honor on the hill of Tepeyac, just a few leagues from the center of Mexico City. In token of his authority to transmit this message, Juan Diego, bearing flowers plucked from the rock-bare hill on which the Virgin appeared to him, went into the presence of the bishop and flung out the folds of his mantle showing that the miraculous blossoms had left upon the coarse cloth a perfect painting of the Blessed Virgin. This miracle brought about the prompt establishment of a chapel at Guadalupe in 1532. The manifestation of the Virgin Mary as patroness of the Indian population was a clever device whereby the bishop gave impetus to the campaign of conversions amongst the indigenes. Certain it is that after this apparition, idolatry rapidly declined. The Virgin of Guadalupe has continued since that day to be extremely popular in Mexico and Spanish America generally, being venerated still as the patroness of the poor and lowly. Her statue is a representation of a gentle-faced Indian woman. Under her banner, Hidalgo led his rabble hordes to the early victories of the Revolution, and under the protection of her shrine grows up the tradition of spiritual unity amongst the commonalty of Mexico today. Frequent investigations of the alleged miraculous painting have failed to establish any other than the mysterious origin claimed for it by the early ecclesiastics.

NUESTRA SEÑORA DE GUADALUPE
(From the original of the miraculous appearance in 1531, as reproduced in
M. Cuevas, *Historia de la iglesia en México*)

The rapidity with which conversions were carried on is attested by the records of Fray Toribio de Benavente Motolinía. From 1524 to 1539, he claims that in the City of Mexico and environs more than a million children and adults were baptized, a million round about Tezcoco and three millions in Michoacán. These were harvests of souls by Franciscans only. Some sixty friars were engaged in it. Undoubtedly the good father meant by these figures that very, very many Indians were baptized.

Archbishop Zumárraga died just before the close of the term of the great viceroy Mendoza. His place was filled on June 13, 1551, by Fray Alonzo de Montúfar. This notable man was a prominent Dominican and an officer of the Inquisition. He came to New Spain bringing ten Franciscans and ten members of his own order for the purpose of adding to the benefits which were to be bestowed upon the Indian population. His interest in the friars was not of sufficient force to prevent the jealousies which had previously characterized the relations between these two mendicant orders from continuing.

His archiepiscopacy was also marked by a serious clash of interests between the seculars and the regulars. The regulars, arriving first in New Spain, had gradually spread throughout the conquered territory; everywhere they had assumed not only full charge of all religious work, but they also took upon themselves the functions of civil officers. In the early stages of the occupation this was a meritorious, even a necessary thing to do. When the seculars arrived upon the scene they often found that the regulars had absorbed all the opportunities for religious and political service in very large areas, many of which were the best locations within the viceroyalty. As the secular organization became widespread and important the ascendancy of the Franciscans, the Dominicans, and the Augustinians was looked upon as an encroachment upon the normal field of operation of the secular arm. The dissension grew with time into bitter feuds, in which the clergy on one side and the friars on the other indulged in uncharitable recriminations. The subjects of the disputes were involved very largely in the matters of the collection of tribute, tithes, and the administering of the sacraments. The bitterest controversy arose over the collection of the tithes. The secular church required the payment of tithes to the bishops by all inhabitants, Indians and whites alike. The regulars, not objecting specifically to the collection of tithes from the Indians, did consider that the payment of the entire revenue to the bishops deprived them of a reasonable income from their services under a license from the pope. The question resulted in a long drawn out battle. The friars were also aggressive with regard to their political preferments. In the Indian towns they not only controlled the municipal government but interfered in the collection of tribute as well. They struggled to maintain the political control by the device of concealing the number of tribute-paying Indians. In fact the friars opposed proper counting of the Indians and went so far as to exempt all natives who served in convents and churches from the payment. During the viceroyal term of the second Velasco, in 1564, the battle between the two branches of the church was waged with disgraceful bitterness. The partisans of the regulars, foremost among whom was the Franciscan Gerónimo de Mendieta, attributed the ills of the country to the transfer to the seculars, by bishops and oidores, of the privileges of the friars, whom he considered, rather naturally, to be in the right. His invectives against all public officials, except Velasco, in fact against all others who were not friars, rather clouded the value of his testimony. He reported the friars as having lost interest in their work because of the animosity displayed against them by their opponents.

As a matter of fact the position of the regulars was indeed hard. The archbishops and bishops refused steadfastly to ordain regulars for services as priests, so that the number of effective clericals in the field was becoming very much reduced. The king espoused the cause of the regulars in this particular and ordered that friars should be ordained as parish priests when they should be found necessary. The regulars also complained that those of them who were ordained were excluded from the privilege of administering the sacraments and were limited to celebration of the mass and the instruction of the Indians. This restriction of their opportunities they felt lowered their prestige among the natives. In 1557 the religious orders were at the request of King Philip granted, through a bull issued by Pope Pius, the privilege of administering the sacraments in the Indian towns.

The influence of the ecclesiastics is perhaps most conspicuously demonstrated by the frequent public disorders, which, like that of 1569, characterized the clash between the adherents of the opposing factions. It was not an uncommon thing to find the rabble of society so zealous to espouse the cause of their religious adviser that they indulged in stone throwing and fights in the streets in order to show their predilections. In these emergencies the powers of the viceroy were taxed to the utmost because of the delicacy of handling the reverend fathers involved in the difficulty. The privileges of administering the sacraments, however, were denied to the friars by royal order. This action in 1583 was superseded in 1585 by a royal decree granting the friars who were acting as parish priests the privileges of administering the sacraments to both Indians and Spaniards alike. This decree was temporary, pending the final decision later rendered.

In 1555 archbishop Montúfar convoked the first Mexican church council, which was attended by the four bishops, the viceroy, the audiencia, and other officers. The declarations and rules adopted by this council were for the purpose of facilitating conversion of the natives, defending them from abuses in collection of the tribute, and of reforming the manner of living of the clergy, as well as systematizing the church administration. In 1565 the second council was called, its deliberations being very largely concerned with the recognition of the obligations imposed upon the church by the Council of Trent in 1563.

Montúfar passed from his earthly labors on March 7, 1572, leaving a reputation for earnestness and for efficiency second only to that of the great Zumárraga. Prior to his death the distinguished Pedro de Moya y Contreras had been made coadjutor.

It was during the concluding years of Montúfar's life that the Inquisition was established in New Spain. Prior to this time there had been only temporary representatives of this institution, a number of whom were members of the Dominican order. These occasional representatives had conducted the processes of the Inquisition without great severity or malignancy. In 1571 a regular inquisitorial court was established in Mexico City under Moya y Contreras. This tribunal had jurisdiction over all Catholics who were accused of heresy and schism. Foreigners and Protestants who might come within the viceroyalty through shipwreck or other cause were also subject to it. The Indians were humanely excluded from its operations, which were deemed too severe to be employed against such tender converts. The Inquisition was specifically charged with vigilance against the intrusion of Moors, Jews, and New Christians. Its first auto de fe occurred in 1574, when sixty-three victims were punished, five of whom were burned. In 1575 another public exhibition took place and between that year and 1593 seven more occurred. In 1596 the tenth auto de fe of the century occurred. It was a great and solemn occasion, set upon the day of the Feast of the Immaculate Conception. For the purpose of viewing it, seats and benches were arranged before the quemadera or bonfire in the form of an amphitheater. The viceroy with his official suite, the archbishop and bishops witnessed the punishment of sixty-seven penitents who were brought from the dungeon and led in procession to the scene of execution of sentence.

The installation of the Court of the Inquisition shows either that a large amount of heresy had developed or else that an enormous amount of personal spite and vindictiveness was vented by the class in power. Many of the victims of the Holy Office were amongst the Portuguese settlers, who were persecuted for political rather than religious reasons. The small population of Mexico City could hardly have furnished within thirty years over 2,000 persons who had committed crimes against religion. It was a symptom of the political and religious status of the country that such a court could flourish in an atmosphere where the greatest occupation of mankind might well have been the subjugation of nature, and the development of a normal Christian state.

The third Provincial Council for New Spain was convoked in the City of Mexico in 1585 by Archbishop Moya y Contreras. It sat for a period of about six months. The chief activities were the enactment of a code of church discipline, the framing of a new catechism, and the establishment of rules calculated to smooth the way for contacts between civil and ecclesiastical powers. The chapters of the two preceding councils were embodied with those of this Third Council, in order that the pontifical sanction thereto, which had been omitted from the prior church councils, might be secured for all three. The enforcement of the decrees passed by the council was authorized by the king in 1591, and the viceroy added his local sanction shortly afterward.

At the close of the century there were in New Spain no less than four hundred convents belonging to the several orders, and about four hundred parishes in charge of secular clergymen; that is to say, there were no less than eight hundred centers for the administration of the sacrament and the inculcation of the precepts of Christianity. Aside from these centers many lesser ones existed, called visitations, in which at least occasional opportunities for Christian education were offered. The number of bishoprics had then increased to six, Yucatan and Nueva Galicia having been created in 1541 and 1544 respectively.

The study of the form and organization of the church is barren unless a clear idea is formed of the very great part which religion and the church played in the minds of the people from king to lowest laborer. It must be remembered that most of the processes of life, social, economic, moral, and political, were in the hands of the clericals. Education, public morals, charity, beneficence in general, practically all intellectuality and artistic expression, were controlled by it. In the parishes the priest was the chief arbiter of destinies. The bishops and archbishops were frequently called upon to assume civil offices, and in their ecclesiastical capacities they were of no less influence. Business, that is merchandising, and agriculture, were often engaged in by them. And in warfare against the savages there was seldom wanting the friar or the priest to urge to added conquest or offer spiritual consolation. In brief, scarcely any phase of life was outside the purview of the religious organization. The power of the church survived the decline of the political power during the seventeenth century, becoming the great problem of the twentieth.

CHAPTER VII

THE colonization of New Spain presents an interesting study in a governmental and social policy of race admixtures, with results far reaching in effect. Not often has a dominant nation set out to absorb a dependent race as a direct feature of colonial policy. The Spanish method was in sharp contrast with the English one in America a century later. The Englishman made no effort to absorb the Indian. His progress in dominating the continent was effected by excluding the natives deliberately from areas which he immediately coveted. The characteristic method was to make treaties with the Indians by which they relinquished certain tracts contiguous to established white settlements. When these had been occupied by white settlers, aggressions began by the pioneer whites on lands not yet ceded. Habitually the Indian was thrust westward beyond the white horizon, often in utter violation of treaty stipulations, in an obedience to a racial land-hunger which obsessed the pioneers with the force of instinct.

In New Spain the process was quite different. The Spanish colonization here was begun amongst a people of sedentary habits, endowed with many of the attributes of a well developed civilization, but with a political and social organization which rendered them an easy prey to their conquerors. It has often been pointed out that the so-called Confederacy of the Aztecs speedily fell before the onslaughts of Cortés because of internal dissensions and because their governmental and religious practices, inculcated under hierarchical and tribal tyrannies, had bred deep in their natures facility for submission. An equally potent factor was their ineptitude for change of habitat, their

115

incapacity for running away to the unconquered wilderness and beginning anew. No other desirable habitat existed. For them there was no alternative to submission. Furthermore, the Spaniard distinctly desired their presence. No attempt, as a matter of state policy, was made to drive them out. Their rapid destruction was wanton yet not understood waste of a precious natural resource. Quite the opposite course was intended. Their love of home suited the plan of the exploiter, who had no mind to engage in physical toil. They were allotted among the conquerors in parcels of fifty or more men, and made to work for their new masters on farms and in mines, in a system of encomiendas by which they gave daily physical service in exchange for scant food and clothing and some effort to effect their souls' salvation.

Over this submissive indigenous population the European Spaniard ruled as he listed and lusted. The Peninsulars, early falling into two distinct groups called Conquerors and First Settlers, blended in time into an upper stratum of society to which was applied the invidious soubriquet gachupín. This word, derived from an Indian one meaning a spur, characterized the ruling class as would have the application of the phrase "the man on horseback." These gachupines normally controlled all important government offices, all the higher ecclesiastical preferences, and nearly all social distinctions. Among them were the leaders of conquering expeditions, grantees of huge mining and agricultural estates, the chief merchants, the viceroys, governors, judges of audiencias and many lower courts, archbishops, bishops, and many of the priests and friars. New Spain existed for them, and they for their superiors in Spain. Numerically weak, they felt the danger of their position as exploiters, and strove to maintain their superiority by a polity of suspicion and emphasized exclusiveness. They feared uprisings and revolts, and sought to forfend them by prohibiting Indians from possessing firearms or riding on horseback, and by other repressive laws.

Their careful attitude toward the Indians, who were

thus held in subjection in ways compatible with the tenuous character of the Spanish hold upon them, was reflected in their attitude toward their own full-blood white sons. It was steadfastly believed and solemnly asserted that occidental skies, climate and surroundings, bred in the American-born Spaniard an unsubstantial character which incapacitated him for faithful political service and made him a menace to continued Spanish domination. Indeed, though character did not cause the defect, the economic system and the political policy did their best to promote disaffection. Such incidents as the Ávila-Cortés conspiracy were the direct effects of economic determinism rather than of inherent alienation of mind and heart or climatic deterioration of character. The creoles, as these American sons of Spaniards were called, were no doubt endowed with all the intellectual powers and native energy of their more favored fathers. But nearly all avenues of social aspiration were closed to them. Only limited opportunities for positions in church, state, or army, fell to their lot. They did, however, become possessors of minor political distinctions. Many of their Spanish born fathers purchased for them in the beginning positions as regidores or town councilmen. These positions being hereditary, the whole fabric of municipal organization came in a few generations to be in the hands of the creoles. This distinction might in time have bred contentment had it not been the steadfast policy to nullify the municipal power by subjecting it to the central control of the viceroy. The creoles developed, as a consequence of scant opportunity, a spirit of odium toward their fathers, and were ready, when opportunity came, to be the foremost in endeavoring to shake off allegiance to Spain.

A still more difficult class of society was the half-breed or mestizo group. These racial unfortunates were the product of illicit relationships between Spanish adventurers and Indian women, and of the policy of the government, which favored licit unions of the two races. The half-breed population grew from the first amazingly. One of the first cares of the viceroy Mendoza was to make provision for foundling children, who were already numbered by thousands in the wake of the conquering bands of Spaniards which overran New Spain. For them he founded the orphanage and school of San Juan Letrán, in which instruction began in 1553. The ancient edifice still stands on the street of the same name. By a curious coincidence, or perhaps from a grim viceroyal sense of humor, the endowment for this school was derived from sales of stray cattle which had wandered from the branded herds of their owners.

The mestizo population was less favored than either the creole or the native group, though it should have received all the careful attention which the dominant race could bestow. It has often been asserted that the half-breed is endowed with all the vices of both progenitors but with the virtues of neither. Such an hypothesis neglects the factors of social environment which are as potent as heredity. Modern scientific thought rejects the theory of inherent inferiority of mixed races. If the mestizo element of New Spain had sprung from the better group of Spaniards uniformly, and if it had found the paths of political and social aspiration open from the beginning, its share in the history of the land would doubtless have been far other than it has been. But nowhere in the world, then or now, has the foundling outcast or the half-breed had equal opportunity. The mestizos during the sixteenth century found service in exploring expeditions, in menial occupations in households and convents, and in minor trades. They were much more close to the Indian than to the Spanish population. Without land grants or mines, commerce, or positions of responsibility in church or state, they naturally became a deterrent to progress. Those of them whose mothers were of noble Indian families usually continued to possess the social category which had belonged to their forbears before the conquest, but they were relatively few in number. The mestizo population had to await the coming of independence before it found opportunity to express itself; after the removal of the Spanish governing class, the dominant creoles were slow to admit them to positions of power. They shared meagerly in the benefits of the independence movement, but their chance came with the Wars of the Reform in the middle of the nineteenth century. Since that time they have been an increasingly dominant influence. The progress of the mestizo type has been the cause and effect of the three great revolutionary movements which have marked the trend of Mexican history during the past century and a quarter.

The indigenes of the Mexican area had never become amalgamated into a people during the dominance of their own rulers. The so-called Aztec Confederacy was only some seventy-five years old at the time of the advent of the Spaniards. At its best and greatest it was merely a superimposed political control, the permanence of which was continually menaced by jealousies among the three tribal groups of the hegemony, and by the disaffection of the dominated allies. The constant attrition of peoples who warred for victims for human sacrifices in religious ceremonies or for the exaction of burdensome tributes tended constantly toward social and political disintegration in spite of consanguinity and linquistic affinities.

Where these similarities of culture were less marked, that is, north of the northern limits of the Aztec domination, the conditions which prevented homogeneity were practically unsurmountable. Nomadic life and tribal wars were the deterrents. The tradition of "Aztec" origins cherished by certain of the northern Indians today is merely an historical fiction, and such notable groups as the Yaquis and Mayos of Sonora and Sinaloa, or the Tarahumaras of Durango, remain even yet integral groups alien in spirit and interest from the body of the nation, Indian or mestizo. All over the country, in less numerous groups than those mentioned, existed and still exist many tribes speaking Indian languages and dialects instead of Spanish, touched only in slight degree by centuries of white domination. Their native cultures have been repressed, but they have not assimilated the habit of thought or the form of culture brought in by the invaders.

The Spaniards of the sixteenth century maintained toward these heterogeneous peoples the attitudes initiated with the beginnings of exploration and discovery. The Spanish errand was one of exploitation and conversion to Christianity. The points of closest contact between the races were thus religious and economic. The theory adopted by the Spanish government for legal control of the relations between the races was that the Indian was a child, the ward of the crown, and that the laws must be so framed as to protect him in this condition while he remained in it. It is not true, as is frequently stated, that the Indian was originally expected to remain in a *perpetual* state of wardship. The termination of that condition was contemplated both under the lay system of economic exploitation, the encomienda, and under the system of religious instruction, the mission. In actual practice however, each system kept him practically under the bonds of wardship. Neither the encomendero nor the missionary was willing to relinquish his institutional advantage as a means of exploitation, nor did the Indians as a race demonstrate aptitudes warranting essential change in the spirit of either method of treatment.

Another erroneous assumption is that all the Indians were placed on encomiendas or were attached to convents or missions. Disregarding the wild Indians, who were always numerous in the northern wastes and in the mountains and forests of the sedentary area, there were large numbers of "free" Indians who were not under either of these agencies. These were the Indians in the seaports and principal cities of inland districts, in both of which they were direct tributaries of the king, and not of encomenderos. Their lot, under the royal corregidores, was not, however, essentially better, and was possibly worse in certain instances, than that of the Indians controlled by encomenderos.

The encomienda system began in La Española under the government of Columbus; it was rapidly transported, with non-essential variations chiefly consisting of varying periods of servitude, to all parts of Spanish America. By its simple formula grants of right to the toil of groups of Indians,

under the direct supervision of their chiefs, were made by
leaders of conquering expeditions to deserving conquerors
and first settlers. The formula ran: "Unto you, so-and-so,
are commended so many Indians under such and such a
chief, and you are to instruct them in the things of our Holy
Catholic Faith." With such an informal unilateral contract,
it is not strange that the prescribed religious instruction
consisted almost entirely of adult baptism, which was
strenuously opposed by most of the religious, and that the
consideration consisted of unremitting toil with scant
supplies of clothing and food. All the historians agree that
the condition of the Indians on encomiendas was brutalizing,
but it may be doubted whether it was much worse than that
of European peasants of the same epoch.

This condition was intended to be only temporary. That
is to say, the encomienda was not at first intended to become
a prescriptive right of the possessor. Cortés, wiser than his
generation, earnestly desired to avoid the implantation of the
encomienda system within the area of his early conquest,
because he recognized the fact that the sedentary population
of the Plateau of Anáhuac had reached a stage of culture
wherein it would be profitable to the Spanish crown if left
in a "free" condition. But the spirit of his time was against
such a generous plan. He only yielded under pressure to the
demands of his followers for Indians to use on encomiendas,
for they could not otherwise have utilized their conquests,
being without other laborers and having no will to work
themselves.

The grants of Indians were made originally for the life of
the grantee only. It was evidently the expectation that
within the one generation provided for, the Indians so controlled would advance from the condition of glebe serfs,
wherein they would require such tutelage, to one of normal
vassalage to the king. That they failed to do so was because
their masters had no intention that they should rise, and
because the system of exploitation of Indian labor demanded
the perpetuity of the encomienda. Thus during the sixteenth
century, in spite of the royal policy, grants of encomiendas

were extended successively to two, three, and even to four lives or generations of legal heirs. Not until 1612 and 1620 was legislation promulgated which provided that lapsed encomiendas should not be regranted, but should become crown—that is state—property, meaning that the Indians so taken over should become free laborers under the supervision of corregidores, though still paying the annual tribute of one or two pesos as the peculiar badge of their vassalage. Spanish vassals did not pay this tax. The payment of the tribute thus became one of the chief instruments for the perpetuation of the stratified caste form of Spanish American society.

If the encomienda was intended as a mere stage in the improvement of the condition of the Indian, in still more emphatic measure was the mission looked upon as an institution for temporary education in citizenship. Normally, an Indian individual granted to a conqueror in encomienda might not expect to survive his master. But it was the theory of the government that when a mission was established, its neophytes would become sufficiently educated within a term of ten years, both in religion and understanding of the processes of civil life, to assume independently the functions of citizenship within their social stratum. That is, after ten years the missions were to be secularized. Secularization meant that the ministration of the regular order of religious which had control of a mission would cease, and that the Indians in it would come under the control of the secular church with a parish priest for their spiritual guide. The natives so released would not then be regranted to any one in encomienda, but would assume civil status as free men, working for wages or on their own communal lands. They would have passed from a purely tribal organization to a municipal one in which they would choose their officers annually, as did their Spanish superiors.

Needless to say, such a consummation was impossible. The regular orders uniformly fought secularization, as much in the interest of the Indians as for their own vested rights. The Indians were incapable of such rapid advancement, and it is to be doubted whether those who were secularized were at all improved by their new status. Indeed, reports on their condition during the eighteenth century indicate that their towns were mere mockeries of the institutions they were intended to become, and that they were vicious in character, lacking morals, industry, and intelligence. Where the missions were planted among the nomadic or semi-nomadic Indians of the northern reaches, the characteristic process was one of diminution of the number of neophytes, and the growth of dissensions between natives and religious, or the gradual decay of the missions.

The effects of the theory of the wardship of the natives are curiously evidenced in the legislation of the century. The Indian was not allowed to have individual title to land. His holdings were communal from time immemorial. If he possessed property, he was not allowed to sell it to a Spaniard unless he worsted the latter in the bargain. Lands left vacant or abandoned by Indians reverted to the crown, and might not be taken up by encomenderos. Essentially, the habitual legislation regarding Indian lands gave them only possessory rights; they were not allowed to alienate communal lands at all, though as a matter of fact they showed scant inclination to do so. For their especial protection, after the audiencias had become clogged with more important judicial business, there was created a court for Indian litigation, the Juzgado de Indios, served by special practitioners known as protectors of the Indians. These persons were paid salaries derived from a tax of half a *real* (five cents) per annum collected from the Indians in connection with and in addition to the annual tribute, to which was added a half *real* for maintenance of a special Indian hospital. The Indian was unhappily prone to litigation, and was frequently incited to it by his protectors, who hoped to gain by causing the natives to bring suit against large land holders for real or fancied encroachments on their tribal lands. Thus the system intended to preserve them from needless court actions was perverted to accentuate their natural penchant for litigious proceedings. The effect was to make them more suspicious of their white superiors, more truculent in their attitudes, and more unstable in their relations with the dominant race.

No doubt the happiest Indians in New Spain, aside from those who continued untrammeled pagan lives remote from mine, farm, and mission, were those in the latter institutions. There they were better fed and clothed than elsewhere, even though their toils were arduous and their compensation largely spiritual in a cult they could little understand. They were encouraged to practice manual arts, lead virtuous lives and respect religion and the state. Their nominal leaders were still their native chiefs, now invested with the cane of the alcalde. To be locked into their quarters at night, caught and flogged when they ran away, prevented from continuing polygamous relations or from indulging in unbridled license, ceremonial or otherwise, were incidents in a civilizing process which frowned upon and vainly attempted to eradicate the rites and practises of heathenism.

The system of using the chiefs of tribes, either in free towns under the priests, or in missions under the friars, as the natural leaders of their fellows, developed the use of caciquismo, chief-rule, as the most undesirable feature of the racial contacts. Not only was the Indian exploited for the sake of the Spaniard, whether missionary or encomendero, but he had this burden of supporting the white man merely superimposed upon the weight he had sustained for his native overlords in the days of his heathenism.

The admixture of the races through illicit relations continued and has continued as an ever present social difficulty in New Spain. In spite of this rapid amalgamation, however, the tendency has not been to develop a cohesive group of half-breeds in which the national spirit becomes highly developed. In the sixteenth century conspiracy looking toward independence, frequently initiated, was inevitably a failure, because of the fact that the racial groups or mixtures had no capacity for amalgamation. It was not until after the close of the colonial epoch that anything like a spirit of homogeneity appeared amongst the people of Mexico.

The interesting phenomenon of the admixture of these races was recognized contemporarily in New Spain by the invention of names to designate the various racial combinations. Notice has already been made of the mestizos and mulattoes, but the Spaniards noted the differentiations down to the nineteenth degree of blood mixture. For instance, the offspring of a mestizo and a Spanish woman was known as a castizo; the offspring of a mulatto and a Spanish woman was called a morisco. The "throw back" familiar to our own frontier parlance in the United States was also known in Mexico under the cognate designation of "salta atrás." The "salta atrás" was one born in a white family but having the dark complexion which indicated that somewhere in his ancestry there was a strain of negro blood. The "chino" a word which still lingers in the phraseology of certain western parts of the United States, was the offspring of the "throw back" and an Indian woman, that is to say, that he had somewhere a streak of negro blood. This is manifested in the popular alternate definition of the word chino as "curly." Other curious racial admixtures were those known as lobos (wolves), zambos, and coyotes. These various designations indicate that the complexities of interracial unions were soon too great even for the capacity of a vocabulary as rich as the Spanish, and the social distinctions described by these designations were gradually eliminated, the lower group of society coming to be known generally as "los pardos y demás castas—the dark ones and other castes."

Obviously the dominant characteristics transmitted to all these groups were Spanish. The society of Hispanic America, however much authors may argue to the contrary, is essentially Hispañolized, that is to say, the social organization, the recognition of social groups or, in these later years, the more evident revulsion of feeling against socially and politically privileged groups, is inherently and characteristically Spanish in type. Governmental forms, judicial formulæ, language, and race feeling, are all more or less conformed to the Spanish norms. The trend of the development has, of course, been toward the creation of a dominant mestizo group, as has already been said in this chapter. It was the rise of the mestizo group which precipitated the wars of independence, the reforms of Juárez, and the revolutions of the second decade of the twentieth century.

The advent of the negro into the continental area of Spanish America followed immediately upon the heels of the Cortesian conquest. Very shortly after the occupation of New Spain sugar raising became one of the most profitable industries of the area, and it was the success of this industry which necessitated the importation of negro slaves. It was mostly in the low lying regions of the tierra caliente that sugar farming proved profitable, and in those regions the negro was largely utilized. Practically every bishopric in New Spain contained more blacks than whites before 1575. In agriculture, negro labor was of greater utility than that of the Indian. The black man could perform in a day six times as much work as an Indian, and did not suffer from punishment or privation as did the more delicately constituted native. However, the Spanish law looked upon the institution of actual legal slavery with something of a spirit of abhorrence, and it was easy for the negro in New Spain to achieve his liberty by purchase or by manumission much more readily than in English America. Furthermore, the importation of negro slaves was unpopular amongst the settlers because of the fact that from the time of Mendoza until later years there was a constant tendency on the part of the negroes to rise against their Spanish masters, and the latter always entertained a wholesome fear of large groups of negroes, so that their number was held somewhat in check by these considerations. The negro was an unhappy admixture in New Spain. As a rule the vicious traits inherited from savage life in Africa made him gravitate toward the native population, and it was not infrequently that he became a renegade and mischief maker amongst the wild mountain Indians who were not under Spanish control. Today the negro population seems largely to have been absorbed or to have disappeared.

Over such divergent racial groups the authority of the king of Spain was established and extended by the development of a political system adapted from Spanish conditions to those of the New World with a remarkable degree of success. The territory of New Spain included practically all of the North American conquests within one general political unit. In 1534 the beginnings of political differentiation were indicated when four provinces were created. The first one was the province of Michoacán, lying southwest of the capital, Mexico; the second was the province of Mexico, north and east of Michoacán; the third was the province of Coatzacoalcos, along the gulf coast, and fourth, the province of the Mixtecas, which lay inland from Coatzacoalcos, and between Michoacán and the modern state of Chiapas. These provinces roughly conformed with the centers of the earliest conquests, and were merely designations of areas without any regular boundaries. There is, indeed, no information as to how these provinces were governed. In fact, that matter is of only momentary interest, because they were very shortly superseded by a more permanent organization. It will be remembered that Nueva Galicia on the west and Pánuco, to the north, were at the same time considered separate governments. Pánuco soon lost its separate identity, and Nueva Galicia fell to secondary importance as a separate area.

The judicial organization of the country developed in 1527 with the organization of the audiencia for New Spain. This supreme court, authorized in 1527 and organized in 1528, presided over the area of what was called New Spain proper, that is, the provinces of Michoacán, Mexico, Coatzacoalcos and Mixtecas, with the addition of Yucatan, Cozumel and Tabasco, and along the gulf coast, including Pánuco, to the Cape of Florida. On the South Sea or Pacific side this audiencia had jurisdiction between the areas given to the audiencias of Guatemala and Nueva Galicia. Both of these last named audiencias were organized many years after the audiencia of New Spain, that of Guatemala being established in 1543, when it was called the Audiencia de los Confines. The establishment of this jurisdiction withdrew the area of Central America from the control of the central court of New Spain. The audiencia of Guadalajara, established in 1548, removed from the control of the audiencia of New Spain the provinces of Nueva Galicia, Culiacán, Copalá, Colima, and Zacatula. No specific boundary seems to have been drawn between these two audiencias, and as a matter of fact, no definitely workable arrangement was made for the differentiation of their jurisdictions. In the course of time, however, the audiencia of New Spain dominated the larger part of the viceroyalty, and the spread of the jurisdiction of the audiencia of Guadalajara, at first rapid during the sixteenth century, was checked by the extension of the authority of the greater court and by the prestige of the viceroy. The first audiencia, that of Santo Domingo for the insular area and Venezuela, had little direct contact with New Spain after the establishment of the viceroyalty.

Apparently the establishment of the audiencias superseded the organization of the four provinces above mentioned. Within each of these audiencias there were placed, as the conquest advanced, many local governors known as corregidores and alcaldes mayores, or sometimes as governors. These local governors were appointed by the king from nominations made to him by the viceroy, after the institution of the latter office in 1535. They had direct official connection with the chief municipalities within their areas, serving as the officers of the central government as checks upon the local government. In certain of the larger areas the direct connection of the governor with municipal organization was not so conspicuous a characteristic as was his relation to the entire area. Such men as Francisco de Ibarra and Luis de Carabajal were governors and lieutenant-generals of the viceroys, with influence over widely extended areas, while such men as Francisco de Montejo, the adelantado of Yucatan, were practically independent of the viceroy as long as they needed no assistance from him. The president of the audiencia of Nueva Galicia or Guadalajara was nominally subject to the viceroy in matters of defense and tax collection, and it was only in judicial administration that the presidency of Nueva Galicia was essentially separate from the viceroyalty as a whole.

The distinction between provinces, corregimientos and alcaldías mayores was not marked. Some of the corregimientos were of as great area and importance as were certain of the provinces. In general, however, it may be said that the corregimientos and alcaldías mayores were subdivisions of the provinces. The alcaldías mayores and the corregimientos were, as has been intimated, situated in chief cities of important areas, and bore the name of the chief town. The ecclesiastical jurisdiction of bishoprics and parishes was organized alongside of the civil organization, and the legal documents of the colonial epoch carefully indicate both jurisdictions when localities are mentioned.

Within their areas the governors or corregidores or alcaldes mayores were practically autocratic, the municipal organization with which they were connected exercising a diminishing power as the century progressed. The organization of the Spanish towns provided for regidores, usually five or more in number in the lesser towns, and numbering from eight to twelve in Mexico City. These ayuntamientos or town councils were in charge of municipal improvements, police, and the handling of municipal revenues. A part of the regidores were perpetual, their offices having been purchased for them or by them, and the elective regidores were chosen annually by the perpetual regidores. Annually the regidores elected from their number two alcaldes ordinarios who had charge of judicial affairs for the municipality. The Indian towns affected a similar type of organization, but the actual management of municipal affairs was very largely, if not entirely, in the hands of the friars or the parish priests.

The power of the audiencias limited that of the viceroy in matters of administration, and that of the towns in judicial affairs. The judges of this court, sitting as advisers to the viceroy, began to limit his freedom, as has been seen, during the term of the second Velasco. Their power over the towns came about through their being appointed as regional visitors. They went about their districts to review affairs of justice, and managed thus to absorb the functions of the municipal judges or alcaldes ordinarios. They served also as assessors and equalizers of taxes, fixing the rates of tributes and of prices of commodities. As a superior court of justice, the audiencia heard all cases on appeal from the municipal courts. It was also a court of first instance in matters outside of municipal control. Appeals went from the audiencias to the Council of the Indies, which was the ultimate judicial authority.

The tax collector was ever at the elbow of the Spanish-American vassal. Financial matters were the prime interest of the viceroy. His business was to see that the royal revenues were increased to the highest amount possible and that large sums were dispatched to Spain. In 1554 he was given a financial board, the junta superior de real hacienda. The junta was composed of the viceroy, the senior judge of the audiencia, the *fiscal* or state's attorney, and the three treasury officials of Mexico City. The superintendence of this junta was, except for a brief period, in the hands of the Council of the Indies.

As in Mexico City, so there were in all other important towns the three treasury officials or oficiales reales. They were supervised in the provincial towns by the governors. They were really central officers of the crown, and not local officers. They were obliged to live in a royal establishment, called the casa real, and in an office in this house they kept a huge iron box, called the royal coffer, or caja real. Each officer had an individual key to an individual lock on this box, and when money was to be put in or taken out, all three had to be present in person, each to undo his particular lock. This was to prevent peculation. Other restrictions limited their engaging in gainful business or marrying into families of influential officers. It was so carefully planned that no one might steal, that the system broke down, and peculation was probably worse because of the royal suspicion.

The treasury officials collected all the taxes, bought and sold goods for the royal account, tried cases involving non-payment of dues, and for a time sat as members of the local town councils or cabildos. It was their business to send moneys collected to Mexico City, where they were put into the viceroyal treasury and thence the surplus over expenses was sent to Spain. These treasury officials were really customs officers; they were as numerous as are tax collectors in modern countries, and had much closer contacts than these with the everyday life of the people.

The category of treasury officials was practically as high as that of the provincial governors. In the sixteenth century they exercised a great deal of power, each group having absolute jurisdiction in affairs of revenues within its district. Early in the seventeenth century the audiencia, and the Court of Accounts, tribunal de cuentas, took over a large share of the jurisdiction and practically all of the accounting. This centralizing measure had the effect of locating more power in the capital.

One of the earliest regular taxes was the tribute collected from the Indians. It was paid partly in personal services, and usually ranged from one to two pesos a year. Negroes paid the tribute also, usually at double the Indian rate. Soon taxes were levied on the colonists in every department of their activities. By the end of the colonial epoch the different kinds of taxes collected numbered over sixty. The average annual revenue from 1522 to 1804 was 6,830,986 pesos, but in the later years the annual treasury receipts were over twenty millions.

The Spanish miners paid the crown a quinto or fifth on all metals mined. The "fifth" was the name always applied to this tax, though it soon became only a tenth. Late in the eighteenth century the gold impost was made three percent, and the impost on silver eleven percent. One of the most famous and most hated taxes was the alcabala or sales tax. Its collection began in 1575. It was levied on every thing salable, whether movable or immovable, except a few very common commodities which were reached in other ways. It was begun as a two percent ad valorem tax; in the eighteenth century it was at times as high as fourteen percent during the exigencies of war. The Indians were exempt from this tax. Churches and churchmen did not have to pay it except when they engaged in gainful commerce. They frequently used this immunity to defraud the government, especially in the cacao trade from Guatemala. The collection of the tax was an essential to every sale, and titles to land were imperfect without accompanying certificates of its payment. Early figures for its yield are incomplete. Between 1780 and 1789 it produced 34,022,552 pesos in the entire viceroyalty.

Other taxes which increased the revenues and the burdens of the colonists included the peage or transportation tax, which was supposedly used for maintenance of roads. Commerce was assessed an ad valorem import and export tax, called the almojarifazgo, begun in 1522 at seven and one-half percent. It was paid on goods on entering or leaving Spain and again on the same goods on entering or leaving American ports. Though the proportions paid at each end varied, the total collection was usually fifteen percent ad valorem. The impost netted strangely little income. From the Vera Cruz customhouse the collections between 1785 and 1791 amounted to 3,185,192 pesos. Duties were habitually avoided when possible. The Vera Cruz officials and the merchants during the latter part of the eighteenth century had a graft ring organized which had perfected means of avoiding most of the imposts due. Their organization was familiarly called the "Vera Cruz Pig," and a greedy porker it was.

Not only were there scores of taxes to be collected, often several of them to be gathered and accounted for separately on the same items, but there were other sources of revenue from government monopolies of industries, and from sales of offices. The crown maintained the policy of permitting industries to expand under immunity from taxation for a brief period followed by levy of a tax as soon as a given enterprise could support one. Either the royal officials collected the tax, in which case it was said to be administered by the crown; or the tax was farmed to an individual, when it was said to be leased or in arrendamiento, or it was intrusted to an important town or cabecera, in which case it was said to be in encabezamiento. The most profitable taxes were usually administered directly by the crown officers. During the Hapsburg régime the system of farming out the taxes was more and more commonly resorted to, as it produced the annual revenue in advance of collection. This was an apparent advantage to the impecunious royal treasury.

But when for any reason the government profit from any activity seemed especially sure and certain, or when in the nature of the case the production and sale of a commodity could be controlled by the state, it was likely to be declared a government monopoly. Salt, gunpowder, tobacco, and quicksilver were such monopolies, and could be produced and sold only by government agents. Quicksilver, so essential in mining, was monopolized in 1559; gunpowder began to be put under restrictions in 1571, and salt in 1580. The greatest of all was the tobacco monopoly, not established until 1764, after which time it yielded over three million pesos of revenue every year for nearly half a century. Other monopolies were those on "snow"—ice brought from the mountains and sold in Mexico City for refreshment, on stamped paper for all legal documents, on playing-cards and on cock-fighting. Revenues were also collected on alcoholic beverages.

The Bulls of the Crusade, preached in Spain every year, were preached in New Spain every two years, beginning in the early 1530's. These Bulls were sold to Indians and whites alike, at prices to suit the economic status of the purchaser. Under these Bulls, which were really indulgences, the purchasers were granted immunities from moral punishment for derelictions, or permission to eat forbidden foods during Lent. The Bulls were supposedly purchased voluntarily, but a good deal of suggestion accompanied their proffering. The receipts were used for pious purposes.

The mint, established as a leased enterprise in 1535, paid revenues on all moneys coined. About one-third of the silver mined in the world came from Mexico, and passed through the mint at the capital. At the close of the viceroyal period it paid over a million pesos' profit annually. It was characteristic of the tedium with which administration was perfected that the mint did not come to be directly controlled by the government until the lease of the original contractors was purchased in 1730 and the new organization perfected in 1733. The duties paid on precious metals were the assay tax, the duty on gold, the fifth on silver, the jewellers' tax, and the seigniorage duty. It is remarkable to note that although the reason and purpose for the existence of the Spanish American colonies, even surpassing the motives of the spiritual conquest after the cooling of the ardor of the sixteenth century propagandists and conquerors, was to seek direct and unceasing enrichment of the royal treasury, yet the organization and management of that great department or phase of government was far from perfect or on the whole even successful. It was not until 1673 that the treasury was free from deficits, and again in 1716 it was spoken of as a bankrupt institution, by which only the most urgent of its debts could be paid. Even after the wide and deep reforms following the reorganization of the administration of the viceroyalty in the reign of Charles III, the public treasury was found empty in 1794. The exigencies of the government in Europe demanded every peso, and when the troublous times of the wars of independence came on, the patience of loyal vassals was exhausted by repeated demands for forced loans, a practice hallowed by long observance by all the kings of Spain.

In recapitulation, it may be said that the social and political organization of New Spain, the mould in which Spanish civilization in America was set, was practically completed during the century of the great conquests. After the first inspired thrust of the imperial arms almost around the whole world in those years, when the two twin ambitions of proselyting and geographical expansion were satiated, there was little further genuine growth in New Spain until the eighteenth century. The next hundred years were spent in consolidating and maintaining the advantages gained.

There was a society formed then, of an advanced race

superimposed upon and exploiting a dependent one. Amalgamation, at first rapid, was not intelligently pursued nor managed so as to bring into effect the intention of the benevolent spirit of the conquest. This was because the character of the conquest involved conscious and premeditated divergences of purpose, contradictions of aim. A governing class of Spanish laymen and clericals, seeking to dominate and exploit the dependent race, could not reconcile self interest with the spiritual, moral, or temporal advancement of its wards. The practical and temporal side of the undertaking won against the spiritual, the altruistic one. The white man sought the advantages of conquest and domination, or, and ever increasingly so, the immunities of clerical influence and seclusion, without taking the red man essentially into his organization, as his beneficent laws demanded. Caste was the result, an abyss between exploiter and exploited, between American and European; rigidity of social forms which meant the cleavage of the two elements along geographical lines at the moment of opportunity.

It was a wonderful thing that Spain held her American dominions during her period of decay, disintegration, and political decrepitude of the seventeenth century. The elements by which she survived the loss of kingly rulers, her Portuguese empire, and her naval supremacy, were the immunity created by distance from Europe, the ignorance of her competitors concerning the real condition and strength of the colonies, and the remnants of frontier initiative which remained in the aspirations of her far-flung colonials. The seventeenth century is interesting as a period of survivals of form and spirit, and of the mellowing of the amenities of the transported civilization of which Spain was the author. New Spain established her place as the greatest Spanish colony.

CHAPTER VIII

THROUGHOUT the closing years of the sixteenth century New Spain expanded with remarkable rapidity along the northern frontier. The territory of New Mexico, conquered at the close of that century (1598–1602) by Juan de Oñate, had as its center Santa Fe, founded in 1609 by Oñate's successor, and remained the outpost of the Spanish colonization in North America down to the year 1680. In that year a general revolt of the Pueblo Indians because of the rigorous treatment to which they were subjected by the encomenderos and religious, drove out the Spanish settlers and for a decade and a half New Mexico rejected Spanish domination. In 1690 the reconquest began, being completed by 1696. This remote territory, however, was not a strong part of the viceroyalty, being barely held against the inroads of the neighboring nomadic tribes; in the latter part of the seventeenth century it became the object of the interest of western traders of the French and English nations. During the early part of the century it was the center from which expeditions were sent out to the Gulf of California and to various parts of the Northwest.

The Provinces of Sonora and Sinaloa, originally part of Nueva Vizcaya, were united under a single governor or alcalde mayor. In this territory, lying along the Gulf of California, the gradual expansion during the century was largely due to Jesuit activities. This order had taken upon itself the spiritual virility which in the sixteenth century had distinguished the Franciscans. Jesuit work began at the close of the sixteenth century in Sinaloa, and passed successively into the valleys of the western rivers, the Fuerte, the Mayo, the Yaqui, and the Sonora. The frequent uprisings

136

within Sonora and Sinaloa, and the frequent reconquests through Jesuit zeal, show that the spiritual domination was in a state of ebb and flux. By 1700 the missionary entradas had extended to the line of the Colorado River, which at the close of the seventeenth century marked the ultimate reach of the northwestern frontier. Mining and agriculture had brought in several hundred families of mixed and Spanish blood.

In Texas the Spanish occupation was due to the rumors of inroads there by the French. La Salle made his expedition to Texas in 1684, but his attempted colonization was shortly doomed. Within a few years the Spanish sent eleven expeditions into the territory, through which they finally became satisfied that the rumored French occupation was without living reality. Missions in eastern Texas were founded on the Neches River in 1690, but were abandoned three years later. The country, however, had become known to the viceroyal authorities by the activities which had been organized to drive out the French. De León and Massanet had made their expeditions into this territory, amongst others, and the Bay of Santa María (Pensacola), a weak outpost of Spain on the Gulf, was fortified in 1698 to hold the area from the aggressions of both the English and the French. Shortly after the turn of the century, in 1716, eastern Texas was again occupied by missions, and from that date went on the permanent occupation of the country through Franciscan missionary enterprise.

Farther north, on the Pacific slope, Nueva California was yet an indeterminate province. The voyages of Vizcaíno, beginning in the late sixteenth century and extending into the early years of the seventeenth, had resulted in no further definite tenure of this coast though efforts to explore it by homing Manila galleons were made, and it remained beyond the realm of Spanish activities until the last third of the eighteenth century. As a matter of fact, the entire northern frontier was less definitely delimited than it had been during the sixteenth century. Baja California, on the other hand, received increasing attention during the trend of the seventeenth century. From the date of the first voyage by Fortún Ximénez in 1533, there were no less than eight recorded voyages during the sixteenth century which brought this area to attention. Two or three of them were by foreign intruders. During the seventeenth century, beginning with the voyage for Tomás Cardona by Juan de Iturbi in 1615, more than a dozen official efforts were made to establish the Spanish authority in Baja California, and very many unauthorized expeditions sought the riches of the Gulf pearl beds. Most of these efforts were carried on by the alcaldes mayores who had charge of the province of Sonora and Sinaloa, their object being to establish settlements on the peninsular coast for the purpose of gathering pearls. The continuous efforts of the pearl seekers were unsuccessful, however, and it was rather a Jesuit expansion than a civil one which brought the peninsula under the Spanish flag. The Jesuits, being given exclusive colonizing rights in Baja California, with the privilege of excluding lay Spaniards, made this territory a Jesuit republic similar to the Paraguayan area held by them during the seventeenth and eighteeenth centuries in South America, and it was not until their expulsion in 1767 that Baja California really became a political member of the viceroyalty of New Spain.

Practically the entire northern frontier, through this century, was disputed by the Indians; raids on mining camps, missions, and farms, were a distinguishing characteristic of the period. Many of the most promising properties which had been developed were during this period completely destroyed by the savages of the north. In the Kingdom of Nuevo León, which had been settled by the Carabajal family, the peculiar method adopted for exploitation of the Indians was responsible for serious outbreaks in the year 1692. The Indians, under the congrega system, were placed in the hands of a Spanish lay conqueror, who utilized them for purposes of exploitation, but was supposed, because of his natural piety and of his special obligation, to contribute to their spiritual welfare in a much more efficacious way than the encomenderos had done. The system was odious to Indians and religious alike for obvious reasons.

More important than the provincial subdivisions were those of the two audiencias, Nueva Galicia and Mexico. The audiencia of Mexico had an administrative area containing thirty alcaldías mayores and eighteen corregimientos; the audiencia of Nueva Galicia contained twenty-three alcaldías mayores and forty-five corregimientos. Each of these local administrative units, the alcaldías mayores and the corregimientos, being practically identical in form and organization, depended upon the authority of the viceroy more directly than upon the provincial governors. The province of Tlascala was presided over by a governor; the captaincy-general of Yucatan had a governor and captain-general appointed by the king; New Mexico was under the control of a governor; Nueva Vizcaya had a governor and captain-general, this office depending upon the viceroy, with nineteen alcaldías under him. The audiencia of Guadalajara, otherwise known as the Presidency of Nueva Galicia, was ruled by the president of the audiencia, from which officer it derived its name of presidency. Hence we see that the internal administration of New Spain had developed an amorphous group of local units, provinces and presidencies, with no uniform system. Over these local officers the viceroy exercised the authority vested in him by his instructions, and by the growing code of the Laws of the Indies, but he was in large measure limited by the audiencia of Mexico in his administration. The system, as it developed, allowed the viceroy intervention in many minute phases of local government, particularly in the capital and larger cities, so that the process of administration was always meddlesome and slow. During the century there were frequent conflicts between the civil and the ecclesiastical powers. The authority of the church, which had been great in the days of the actual conquest, led that organization to consider itself of momentous consequence in all affairs of administrative nature wherein it had opportunity of intervention. The quarrelsome character of the relations between the viceroy and the ecclesiastical power was conditioned very largely upon the fact that during the seventeenth century the custom grew of assigning to the archbishop ad interim appointment as viceroy when vacancies occurred in the chief administrative office.   During the sixteenth century the succession had more frequently devolved upon the audiencia.

The large cities of the viceroyalty during this period were those of Mexico, Puebla, and Guadalajara.   In the city of Mexico itself there were some 8,000 Spaniards.   The census reports made showed that there were about 30,000 houses in the city, including those occupied by the Indians.   The old dividing line between the areas used by the native and the foreign populations, known as the traza, had become obliterated with the passage of time, and the two elements of the population had become intermingled.   Many Indians were now living in the courtyards of the Spanish houses, and had become directly dependent upon the foreign element. Until the rise of the cities of British America in the eighteenth century, Mexico was the largest centre of population on the American continent, and all that there was of religious and political government, trade and commerce, mining activity, and agriculture, centered in that metropolitan community.

The progress of agriculture during this century was slow, as it had been during the preceding one.   This was due to the lack of laborers which has characterized the agricultural activity of Mexico from time immemorial.   Development of enormous estates, the latifundios, was in great measure responsible for this characteristic of agricultural employment.   Equally potent was the almost universal system of forced labor.   A large number of the encomiendas still existed, though legislation had begun to limit their number, since they now reverted to the royal crown when their ownership by Spanish grantees lapsed.   The encomienda as an institution was also coming to be characterized by better treatment of the Indians than had prevailed during the century of the great conquest, because more humane sentiments now animated the hearts of the Spaniards than formerly. To some extent this may have been due to the influence of the growing group of mestizos, who were coming to take their places in the lower ranks of the clergy and of the civil government. The new immigrants amongst the Spaniards, moreover, no longer felt themselves to be like the conquerors of old, but like settlers who had their way to win in the western wilderness.

Agriculture came to be finally on a more stable basis, as the wheat crop had become acclimated in New Spain and as the immigrants became actual farmers. Early attempts to develop this cereal had resulted in frequent failures, so that it was a considerable time before the Spanish population was able to subsist upon other food than the native maize. The century was also marked by the extension of the cultivation of the maguey plant for the production of pulque. The maguey plant (the century plant) grows readily without much tilling and from its juice is manufactured the fermented liquor, pulque, which was in general use amongst the Aztecan civilizations before the arrival of the Spaniards. This liquor, being very cheap, and highly intoxicating when consumed in large quantities, has long been the principal source of inebriety among the lower classes; before the conquest its use came to constitute a regional vice which had a deleterious influence upon the population, and a disastrous one upon the economic situation. The church made repeated and valiant efforts to destroy this industry and habit, but was unable to effect its will in spite of frequent excommunications of those who engaged in the production of the liquor. The wide extent of good agricultural lands which had become dedicated to maguey growing, both for the production of pulque and tequila or mezcal, a distilled native brandy, removed from cultivation a large amount of land which should have been dedicated to the production of cereals. The frequent failures of cereal crops—it being considered normal that three out of five crops prove a failure in Mexico— have resulted from earliest times in serious food shortages which have retarded the development of the population. The efforts of the Spanish government to overcome this difficulty by establishment of granaries (depósitos) was only partially successful.

Another rural industry which had been introduced by Hernán Cortés and fomented eagerly by the early Spanish monarchs, the production of silk, was definitely stamped out in 1679 by a royal order which commanded the destruction of the silk worms and mulberry trees which had at that time become widely extended over the southern part of the viceroyalty. It was the influence of Andalusian silk growers which brought about this short sighted destruction. Another crop of importance was the cochineal, an insect produced on the cactus in the territories of Oaxaca and Yucatan for the manufacture of the so-called "vegetable" dye; it was a source of great income to Spaniards and Indians alike. Vegetable wax, corn, beans, squash and tobacco were also widely produced.

The mining industry was the object of practically all the entradas made during the sixteenth century into the frontier. The main object of search was silver. The laws of Charles V and Philip II for owning and working mines protected discoverers in their tenure of mines, and gave them great economic advantages. The mineral regions of Nueva Galicia, Michoacán and Oaxaca were the scenes of the earliest developments of mining, which gradually expanded into the northwest during the seventeenth century. The industry received enormous impetus in 1557 by the discovery of the quicksilver process at Pachuca in that year. Immediately upon the realization that here was another opportunity for added taxation, the sale of quicksilver to miners became a government monopoly in 1559, and produced of itself an enormous revenue for the crown. The patio process of mining was the direct result of the discovery of amalgamation by quicksilver and was responsible for the utilization of ores that had hitherto not proved amenable to the more primitive salt treatments. Legislation protecting the mineral industry was not codified until 1680, when the mining laws formed a large part of the Laws of the Indies compiled in that year by order of Charles II and published in 1681. The special

protection given to miners had a peculiar effect upon the
social organization of the viceroyalty, in that it made for
great riches held by a small minority of society, to the great
disadvantage of the less provident masses. The disproportionate wealth thus made possible was a source of sharper
cleavage between the privileged and non-privileged groups
than would have existed had small miners been encouraged
to the same extent that the large operators were protected.
When the miners' guild was given the pronounced government protection afforded by the legislation of 1782 known
as the Ordenanza de Minería, the price of quicksilver was
reduced to the extent that it became available for smaller
operators. But the gravity of this social problem remains
as a heritage to the Mexican Republic of today. It has been
one of the serious conditions which has militated against the
formation of a people with a national instinct and homogeneous feeling. The social and political problem is rendered
doubly acute because many mine owners are absentees or
even foreigners.

The situation with regard to commerce during the seventeenth century was anomalous. It would normally be expected that the trade between Spain and New Spain would
have been greater than the commerce between New Spain
and Manila, but the reverse was true. The Asiatic trade
carried on by the annual passage of a galleon across the
Pacific brought more wealth into circulation in New Spain
than did the entire Atlantic trade. This was in some degree
due to the fact that during a large part of the epoch under
consideration commerce between Acapulco and Lima had
government sanction, and a large proportion of the merchandise brought from the Orient found its way into Peru
as well as into New Spain. The Asiatic commerce was composed very largely of materials gathered at Manila, the great
Oriental entrepôt for the products of China and India.
These found ready sale in both the great Spanish viceroyalties. The wealth produced by this commerce became the
object of the cupidity of the European nations which were
competitors with Spain, and during this century there were

frequent piratical expeditions, led by the Dutch and English in particular, for the purpose of seizing the Manila galleons. Another reason for the decadence of the Atlantic trade during the same period was caused by this same fierce informal warfare against the Spanish, chiefly by the same European nations. The annual dispatch of commercial fleets from Spain, one of them to Cartagena and Porto Bello on the northern coast of Nueva Granada, and the other to Vera Cruz, in New Spain, was frequently interrupted by this informal warfare and by the vicissitudes of the Spanish monarchy in Europe. The exclusive policy under which Spain admitted only her own vessels to her colonial ports, and the excessive protective duties which she levied upon her own exports, further militated against her own commercial dominance. The Spanish colonists found it possible to purchase European manufactures more cheaply from the Dutch and the English than from their own merchants, and their officials were susceptible to the corrupting influences of foreigners who sought to introduce their goods with tacit sanction for a price. The contraband trade of the seventeenth century was exceeded only by that of the eighteenth century. In 1646 customhouses were established both at the ports of Acapulco and Vera Cruz for the control of commerce. Up until that time export and import duties had been collected by treasury officials only. After the organization of the customhouses, a more regular and efficient collection of duties had the effect of increasing, rather than decreasing, the amount of contraband trade. A high protective tariff and a strictly exclusive policy required a more perfect system of vigilance than was possible at that epoch, owing to the difficulty of surveillance of the coast without the help of steam navigation. The seventeenth century was the heyday of the pirates and filibusters who infested both shores of New Spain.

Conditions of labor in New Spain were very largely determined by the character of the conquest and the existence of a large body of forced laborers, though not all of the Indian population was reduced to that condition. In the cities, particularly in Mexico City, there came to be developed a system of free labor which was conditioned by the existence of the medieval trade guild, which was transferred to America with the inception of the conquest. The general characteristics of these guilds were not unlike those of their European prototypes. There was a graduated system of instruction of apprentices through a long period, characterized by much abuse of the apprenticeship. Advance into the higher ranks of the guilds depended upon the production of a masterpiece, and the membership was limited in much the same way as it was in Europe. The guild system effectually debarred much of the Indian population from lucrative participation in many of the so-called technical occupations, though they might in many of these organizations perform the rougher labors connected with manufacture. The period of the formation of the guilds was almost exclusively within the sixteenth century, but certain organizations were perfected also during the seventeenth century. Negro slaves, as well as Indians, were denied membership in them. There were no less than one hundred such organizations within the City of Mexico, with others in the chief provincial towns, and they were very sharply under municipal control. Each of the guilds had its religious counterpart in a brotherhood, cofradía, which made it amenable to religious as well as civil control and susceptible of taxation for the support of the church, as well as of the municipal government. Conspicuous amongst the larger guilds were those of the silk growers and manufacturers, saddle makers, hatters, weavers, candle makers and pottery makers. The pottery makers of Puebla during the epoch reached a perfection and enjoyed a renown equal to that of the best Spanish workmen.

The growth of the royal treasury in New Spain was, like that of Spain, casual rather than systematic. There never was a studied, orderly plan of finance, nor any question of interchange between the policy of protection and free trade. The imposition of taxes depended directly upon the immediate necessities of the crown, and changes were effected very largely through the influence of Spanish merchants, who adhered closely to the theory that the colony existed for the benefit of the mother land, and that no industry should be allowed to thrive in the colony which in any way limited peninsular business. Such changes might, and did often, either make or ruin an entire industry, or bring prosperity or disaster to a whole province. This adventitious policy was not due to ignorance, because during the seventeenth century no less than seven fairly complete censuses of the viceroyalty were made, and the conditions of business and industry were not unknown to the crown, but the policy of favoritism first to one group, and then another, was that which animated legislation.

Compared with some of their illustrious predecessors of the sixteenth century, the viceroys of the seventeenth hardly measured up to the standard set during the reign of Charles V. Yet the chief royal representative was always of political significance, even if negatively.

The tenth viceroy, Juan de Mendoza, marquis of Montesclaros (1603–1607) was transferred to Peru, being succeeded by Luis de Velasco II, eighth viceroy, who for a second time ruled ably, his term extending from 1607 to 1611. His government was notable for the completion of the drainage of the lacustrine district of the plateau, the quelling of a notable negro revolt near Orizaba, and the embassage of Sebastián Vizcaíno to Japan coupled with his quest for the fabled islands Rica de Oro and Rica de Plata. Velasco's successor, Friar García Guerra, archbishop of Mexico, ruled from June, 1611, to February, 1612, when he died. A brief interregnum of the audiencia gobernadora was followed by the period of the marquis of Guadalcázar (1612–1621). During his rule a Tepehuane revolt in Nueva Vizcaya was quelled, Nayarit was conquered, and Baja California was claimed again for Spain by Tomás de Cardona, a redoubtable pearl fisher.

Guadalcázar's successor, the marquis of Gelves (1621–24) was distinguished as a most signal failure in this important office. His difficulties arose over an attempt to deny the right of asylum to a criminal, claimed by the archbishop as

amenable to the ecclesiastical courts. His rash acts incited
mob violence, his palace was burned, and he himself narrowly
escaped with his life. The clerical authorities, equally at
fault, were deposed along with other culpable civil officers by
the new viceroy, the marquis of Cerralvo (1624–1635). This
man's relatively long term was marked chiefly by his modest
claim made to Philip IV (1629) that no one "since Cortés
had served his King so well in many years as he himself had
in five." His successor the marquis of Cadereita (1635–
1640) spent his energies repelling Dutch pirates and in fore-
fending a threatened uprising of creoles and mestizos who
desired independence by recommending that New Spain
should be allowed representation in the Cortes, a procedure
that was not, unhappily, followed.

The seventeenth viceroy, the duke of Escalona, Diego
López Pacheco (1640–42), was the first grandee of Spain to
serve in this office in New Spain. His brief rule was marked
by a bitter struggle between the Jesuits of Puebla and the
bishop, Juan de Palafox, over episcopal licenses to Jesuits
for parochial duties. The viceroy sided with the Jesuits,
and was moreover thought to be partial to the Portuguese
independence from Spain, then being accomplished; con-
sequently he was superseded by Palafox (1642) who held
concurrently the offices of viceroy, bishop of Puebla, visitor-
general, and inquisitor-general. He declined the archbishop-
ric, which was proffered in an excess of royal confidence.
His quarrel with the Jesuits brought his retirement from
political office; he returned to Spain and died some years
later in poverty and comparative neglect.

The term of the count of Salvatierra (1642–48) was marked
by nothing more significant than the voyage of admiral
Pedro Porter y Casanate to Lower California, which ended
in failure in 1648. The viceroyalty was now at a low social
and political ebb, reflecting the decline of Spain's European
power, and harassed by continuous demands for money,
which ere this had been obtained by the device of selling
titles of nobility to American vassals. Dutch and Portuguese wars in Europe had their counterpart in New Spain in

Indian revolts and piratical raids along the shores of both oceans.

A single exception to the policy of appointing the archbishop of Mexico viceroy ad interim was made when, Salvatierra being promoted to Peru, the bishop of Yucatan, Marcos de Torres y Rueda, with the title of governor only, was given the supreme command during 1648–9. Then for fifteen months the audiencia gobernadora held sway, until the count of Alba de Liste (1650–1653) arrived. Border warfare, pirate raids, and forced loans to the king engrossed his administrative powers. His successor, the duke of Alburquerque (1653–60), was exceptional in that an attack was made on his life in the cathedral by an insane soldier who was promptly hanged. Juan de Leiva, count of Leiva, twenty-third viceroy (1660–1664), unpopular because of his vanity and his quarrels with the archbishop, withheld knowledge of the appointment of the latter to succeed him until the fact was discovered by the accident of letters taken from a shipwreck. . The archbishop, Diego Osorio, ruled from June to September, 1664, his tenure being characterized by unwonted energy and efficiency.

The marquis of Mancera (1664–73), gained distinction by reforming the collection of taxes and enforcing honest administration of the royal treasury. He paid up the public debts which he had inherited, sent valuable subsidies to Cuba and the Philippines for imperial defense, and was still able to provide the king with four million pesos. During his term the English, whose American colonies had been augmented by seizure of Jamaica in 1655, acquired treaty recognition in 1670 of their legal possession of the hitherto unrenounced Atlantic seaboard down to the Savannah river. In internal affairs Mancera's rule was signalized by the completion of the great cathedral of Mexico, which had been begun in 1573. His resignation was deeply regretted by the Mexicans. His successor, Pedro Nuño Colón de Portugal, a descendant of Christopher Columbus, was an old man who died after only five days in office. Following him, Archbishop Payo Enríquez (1673–1680), a descendant of Cortés by the female line, ruled beneficently in matters relative to the capital city alone, which might have been as effectively cared for by an efficient corregidor.

The marquis de la Laguna (1680–86) was in charge of the government during the Pueblo revolt in New Mexico, the piracies of Agramont, who sacked Vera Cruz, and of the English, who sacked Campeche. The captaincy-general was for the most of these seventeenth century viceroys as important as their civil command. The count of Monclova (1686–88), "he of the silver arm" left his name to a frontier town in Coahuila, in the colonization of which he was active. The count of Galve (1688–96) narrowly escaped death in a corn riot which arose during a famine in 1692. He was in power during the period of the expected dissolution of the Spanish monarchy, yet his rule was marked by the feeble enterprises which resulted in the temporary mission-occupation of Texas and the erection of a colony at Pensacola, Florida. Both establishments were to ward off French territorial aggression.

In 1696 Galve was succeeded for a few months by Juan de Ortega Montañes, bishop of Yucatan, who was soon followed by the count of Moctezuma (1696–1701); the wife of the latter was a third grandniece of Moctezuma the Great. His administrative activities were directed against bandits. It was reserved to a descendant of the famous Aztec emperor to see the humiliation of the proud Hapsburg line in the impotence and final dissolution of the imbecile Charles II, and at the same time to witness the accession to power of Philip V, first of the Bourbons, a dynasty whose puissance fell only a little short of restoring to Spain much of the grandeur of the age of Philip.

CHAPTER IX

THE REFINEMENTS OF COLONIAL LIFE

It is an Anglo-Saxon tradition that the Spanish occupation of America was one long nightmare of swashbuckling conquest, ruthless destruction of barbarous aborigines, and religious fanaticism and bickerings. The "superiority complex" of the English-speaking peoples as above the Spanish-speaking nations had its beginnings in the national jealousies which accompanied the Elizabethan tradition. It was perpetuated by the commercial rivalry and the friction incident to the colonial expansion of the seventeenth and eighteenth centuries. Especially during the latter cycle the British nation alleged that the decline of the Spanish colonial institution was the result of narrow religious prejudice and exclusive commercial restrictions and monopolies, and was ample justification for an aggressive campaign of commercial infiltration which sought economic and political advantage as the ultimate aim. The Spanish Americans themselves in their wars of independence sought by all means to disparage their own civilization in their accusations against their fatherland. In our own generation the habit of the sentiment of excellence has fed upon the causes and incidents of the Spanish-American War, the political instability of Central and South American republics, the protracted revolution in Mexico, and the economic conflict which has developed in the wake of the nationalistic legislation under the Constitution of 1917, which seeks to recuperate economic autonomy for the Mexican Republic.

While some of these unhappy contrasts in the two civilizations are obvious, it must be remembered that to be historically fair they should not be made indiscriminately as to epochs. Spanish-American civilization of the colonial period must be contrasted, if justly, only with English-American colonial culture. When this is done, disparities are minimized and discrepancies are found to be less important than popular tradition makes them.

For three hundred years Spain was the chief agency in the transmission to America of European culture. Her work in that field deserves warm praise for its depth, breadth, and permanency. The refinements of colonial life which accompanied the conquest were inferior to those of no other colonial agency, they approached closely the excellencies then manifested in European culture itself. They were visible in the developments of education, literature, painting and sculpture, music and the drama, in architecture, and in social amenities which continue today the happy characteristics of the nations politically descended from the second greatest American colonial power.

Enthusiasm for education characterized the earliest establishment of the Spaniards in Mexico. Mention has already been made of the beginnings of school work by the Franciscan monks immediately after their arrival. Wherever the priests went, a school was soon established for instruction of natives or education of clericals who were already at work or for those who were soon to take holy orders. From these schools and colleges sprang the great colonial universities, of which, including that of Mexico already referred to, there were seven in Spanish America before the seventeenth century closed. Hundreds of degrees were conferred in them upon graduates in laws and theology long before the first continental English settlement was founded.

In 1536 the Franciscans opened the famous college of Santa Cruz de Tlaltelolco for Indian boys under the shadow of their convent. Instruction was given in reading, writing, Latin grammar, rhetoric, philosophy, music, and Mexican medicine. No instruction in theology or jurisprudence was offered. The enterprise began with seventy students, and had the enthusiastic and material support of the viceroy. Among the famous teachers were Fray García de Cisneros, Fray Andrés de Olivos, a great linguist, Fray Juan Focher, doctor of laws from the University of Paris, and Fray Bernardino de Sahagún, the distinguished historian and writer on Mexican ethnology.

Father Gante's school of a thousand boys and the boy foundlings' school, San Juan Letrán, have been alluded to. The city council also established a number of elementary schools for boys, and several Spaniards opened private schools in their homes, not infrequently assisted by crown stipends. A female foundlings' school, where sewing, embroidering, and the Christian doctrine were made instruments for training young women for the responsibilities of matrimony, was among these early institutions. Agitation began for the founding of the university in 1539, and a school of theology which granted degrees was established by the Augustinians at Tiripitío in 1543. It was later consolidated with the University of Mexico.

The university continued to exert great social and intellectual influence throughout the colonial epoch. The instruction was of course scholastic, in keeping with the universal custom of the times. The fees for matriculation were not excessive, placing the institution within reach of most of the Spanish inhabitants. Degrees came to be heavily expensive toward the end of the colonial period, however, and graduates were usually obliged to seek a well-to-do patron in order to find money wherewith to meet the heavy costs of the doctoral degree. The investiture was accomplished by public oral examinations, and professorships were conferred competitively in the same way, as they still are. The government of the institution was medieval, being in the hands of the students, alumni, and professors who constituted the cloister. The rector, elected annually by the cloister, wielded civil and criminal jurisdiction over the institution, and was a personage of much political and social prestige. Nearly thirty thousand bachelor's degrees were conferred between 1553 and 1775, and a fair proportion of master's degrees. About one thousand doctoral degrees were granted during the same period. The graduates occupied many of the most important positions in the religious and political organizations of the viceroyalty. A second university was founded at Guadalajara in 1791.

The existence of this great university of Mexico gave the creoles of New Spain educational facilities far superior to those enjoyed by their pioneer fathers, who were for the most part of inferior birth and breeding. The intellectual life of the institution was by no means confined to the routine courses offered, for the students were active in smuggling in contraband books by French philosophers, especially those by Jean Jacques Rousseau. The social philosophy thus inculcated fed the aspirations of the American born Spaniards, and served to hasten the independence movement when it came.

In the provinces the Jesuits were conspicuous educators. They began a college in Zacatecas in 1616, and at Guadalajara in 1659. These were both important. Another was founded in San Luis Potosí in 1623. Another was erected in Querétaro some years later. The colleges at Valladolid and Pátzcuaro were among their first institutions. In Mexico city their college of San Pedro y San Pablo, incorporated in 1618 with that of San Ildefonso, was one of the most influential schools in the country, rivalling the university itself. They had similar institutions at Pueblo, Tepotzotlán, and elsewhere. At their expulsion in 1767 they had twenty-three colleges and several seminaries in different provinces. Several of these were taken over by the Franciscans upon the expulsion. The other orders also conducted numerous schools and colleges, but the Jesuit influence was supreme in education.

Most of these institutions were conducted for students of white blood. The most popular courses were those which led to the church or the law. The medical course at the university was hardly as frequently studied, doubtless because of the custom of considering disease as a dispensation of providence and a resigned trust in simple remedies and unskilled practitioners. Mathematics and the sciences were confined to the few, as they were in other countries. This in spite of the habitual friendly interest of many of the viceroys. Yet scientific thought in New Spain was as advanced as it was in Europe. Now and then a short intelligence like that of the viceroy Branciforte held the opinion that the catechism was enough of instruction for the people.

Education of Indians was not entirely neglected, though their intellectual emancipation was hardly a policy of government. There was little reason for any great expenditure of energy in educating a class of society the place of which was intended to be perpetually at the base of the social pyramid. The Indians were adept in manual skill, and they cleverly took advantage of all the instruction they obtained in industrial arts and crafts. In the region of Michoacán industrial instruction given under the auspices of Bishop Vasco Quiroga developed along community lines. In each of numerous villages that notable prelate taught a specific craft to the entire population, so that for many years each town was distinguished for its unique product of some single artefact. This regional idiosyncrasy in production still persists in many parts of the Republic even where there is no essential reason for it except tradition.

The friars, and often the priests, gave instruction to pupils of all ranks of society in reading, writing, and in vocal and instrumental music. There was some teaching of Latin, drawing, and painting, and occasionally teachers of mechanical arts could be found. Foreign mechanics were encouraged to immigrate upon occasions. There came a time when the policy of educating the lower classes was looked upon with general disfavor, and even the white children received all their instruction in schools provided by private philanthropy and in private academies conducted by laymen. In such schools algebra and geography were added to the curricula. The well-to-do managed frequently to send their sons to Spain for education.

In 1783 royal decrees urged the establishment of primary schools, and a few such institutions were undertaken. The viceroy Azanza was engaged in 1800 in an undertaking for advancing primary education. Just before the close of the eighteenth century there was a remarkable revival in the teaching of the theoretical and the concrete sciences and in the industrial and fine arts. This wave of enthusiasm gave New Spain high standing among cultured communities until the social disorganization incident to the wars of independence made educational efforts impossible.

The wide world of new nature opened to the European mind with the discovery and occupation of the Western Hemisphere brought about the foundations of the modern natural sciences. In this work Spanish savants were the pioneers. The flora of New Spain was studied by the Spaniard Sessé and two native collaborators, Mociño and Echeverría. Their findings were incorporated in the monumental work on the fauna, flora, and minerals of New Spain by Dr. Hernández, *Nova plantarum animalium et mineralium mexicanæ historia*, published at Rome in 1651.

The school of mines established in 1783 in Mexico City gave a remarkably practical course of studies. It was founded and conducted by the great metallurgist José Fausto Elhuyar. Andrés del Río, his associate, published the then best Spanish treatise on mineralogy. About the same time the distinguished Antonio de Alzate, for whom the modern scientific society of Mexico is named, was publishing his encyclopedic articles on a wide range of scientific and philosophical subjects in the *Gacetas de Literatura*. Alzate deserves a place among the founders of the modern natural sciences for his mordant criticisms of the old orthodox and unscientific ideas which Darwin, Huxley, Wallace, and Spencer fought at a later date in England.

Alzate was an astronomer of no mean ability, while Cárdenas y León, and León y Gama, his associates, were also notable in this field. The first was a skilful geodesist, and Gama was a scientific student of Mexican antiquities. These men were accomplished in almost as many diverse fields as the notable Carlos Sigüenza y Góngora of the seventeenth century, who wrote authoritatively on many subjects from comets to political virtues.

It is perhaps strange that the Royal Academy of Beaux Arts should not have been founded until 1773. This institution provided free instruction in architecture, sculpture, and painting. It was and is open to everyone, and has always been an object of great national interest and pride. Perhaps the tardiness of the foundation was due to the widespread existence of painters, Spanish and native, in the viceroyalty, whose teaching obviated need of such an institution.

Painting in Mexico was, among the aborigines, devoted to chronological records or astronomical observations, mingled with theogony. The Toltecs, Acolhuas, and Aztecs all used it for historical records. If we could read all the paintings accurately we should know much more about primitive American culture than we do know. The tonalamatl of the Aztecs were a sort of almanac or calendar. Other paintings contained the horoscopes of children, the dogmas of religion, or records of land ownership. Religious pictographs were full of secret symbolism, with horrible monsters representing ideas retained in the arcana of the priestcraft, unintelligible to the laity.

The work was done on skins filled with clay, on thick paper from the maguey or century plant, or on a palm fibre called icxotl. The writings were rolled like papyrus books. Brilliant vegetable dyes were used. The artists lacked knowledge of perspective and light and shade, hence the products were deformed and disproportionate. There is nothing else like them extant, for it must be remembered that hieroglyphs and symbols, when used to express ideas, demanded natural representations in which exact delineation was sacrificed to dexterity and speed in production. Hence art, painting as art, not as writing, did not arise in Mexico, but was brought in by the Spaniards. This of course does not apply to the Mayas and the early people of Teotihuacán, who really painted mural decorations. Primitive mural designs have been uncovered at Atzcapotzalco, and also at Chichen Itza.

History has it that Father Pedro de Gante first taught painting and sculpture to the Indians. The Dominicans taught both arts in their conventual schools before 1537. The work done was probably mere imitation of pictures and statues brought from Italy, Flanders, and Spain. The object sought was not artistic culture, but media for religious instruction. The pupils were very adept, especially in painting, but it was many years before the painting of Mexico, that is, the work of white artists characterized by the designation of The Old School, came to be recognized as having individuality.

The first Spanish painter in New Spain, Rodrigo de Cifuentes, of mediocre ability, came in 1523, and achieved scant distinction except for his early arrival. Another artist, Alonzo Vázquez, is also accredited to the sixteenth century. The works of both men have disappeared save one; there is, in the National Museum a painting by Cifuentes of Cortés rendering thanks to San Hipólito for the conquest of Mexico. Vázquez was described as being "as skilful in drawing as Michael Angelo, and as happy in coloring as Titian." He is given credit for introducing the work of the Seville school into New Spain. Three Indians, Andrés de Aquino, Juan de la Cruz, and a certain Rúa, all mentioned by Bernal Díaz and Torquemada, have been noticed by Nicolás León as belonging to the same century. None of their work is extant. Of course mediocre painting was widespread throughout the century, but no other creditable names among artists of the Old Mexican School belong to the epoch.

During the seventeenth century there were at least twenty-six painters of sufficient merit to warrant notice by Antonio F. Villa, whose authority is here followed. The first of these was Baltazar Chávez or Echave, called El Viejo because there was a second artist by the same name. Several of his subjects, all religious of course, are still preserved in the Academy of San Carlos. He has, like Sebastián de Arteaga, been erroneously called the first artist in New Spain.

That the work of these and of later Mexican artists influenced by the Seville school was meritorious artistically is evidenced by the opinions of numerous foreign critics, and by the fact that the French, during the Intervention, carried many of them away to Europe. Their paintings are characterized by a softness and smoothness apparently inspired by the gentle atmosphere of New Spain. They manifest a purpose of aiding the spiritual conquest by sympathetic representation of the principles inculcated by the missionary fathers. They show intimacy with sacred history and legend, the tender mysticism, piety and extasy of the days of early religious enthusiasm. In profane or mythological subjects the Christian virtues shine through without the slightest intimation of immodesty. They transport the contemplator to the simple days of the Spanish pioneers. Their compositions are well coördinated, with warm tints and happy contrasts in coloring, and excellently modeled. Above all, the most marvelous thing is the fecundity of the school, which is so prodigious that it evidences great freedom of execution. The characteristic faults are carelessness in the drawing of certain accessories, monotony in backgrounds, and uniformity of draperies.

During the eighteenth century the number of artists grew until the total for the three hundred years of the colonial domination reached one hundred and fifty worthwhile painters. Five or six of them attained undisputed reputations, as for instance Miguel Cabrera, Juan Rodríguez Xuares, Sebastián de Arteaga, José Alcíbar, and Francisco Eduardo Tresguerras.

The latter artist, who was born in 1745 and died in 1833, closed the epoch of the Old Mexican School. When Rafael Jimeno y Planes of Valencia took charge of the Academy of San Carlos, he attempted to introduce the baroque style, but without success. Modern painting follows the composite French, Italian, and Spanish style introduced by Peregrín Clavé and perpetuated by his Mexican successor Pina.

Not so distinguished artistically, but yet characteristic of the race and the nation, is Mexican music. We know that the Aztecs were lovers of beauty in flowers and song, for they show the same characteristic today. But we know really very little about the pre-Cortesian music. There are a few

Aztec musical instruments in the National Museum, the character of which indicates that instrumental music was probably as barbarous and unlovely as the ceremonies which it embellished. The Aztecs used various percussion and wind instruments which were incapable of producing pleasing harmonies, and were undoubtedly used for the purpose of producing rythmic effects for religious dances. They lent themselves readily to the business of "evoking the most vivid scenes of ferocity illuminated by the glare of sacrificial fires, colored by the blood of expiatory victims, vibrant with the terrified howlings of mystical insanity and destructive frenzy carried into paroxysms. The music which accompanied such episodes must have been lugubrious, Macaberesque and completely incoherent, as were the passions which elicited it." (Herrera y Ogazón.)

Side by side with this music of grotesque ceremonial fervor, there existed among the primitive Mexicans beautiful poetic fancies which might in time have developed a high standard of culture. A few of their religious ceremonies were full of the beauty and romantic enchantment which only spring from sincerity and deep feeling. The symbolic and propitiatory dances of the Tarahumaras, the Tepehuanes and the Coras, suggest something of the Hellenic religious ceremonials. The Tarascans of Michoacán had developed a comparatively high degree of pleasing expression in their songs. One of these, says Herrera y Ogazón, called the tzoptizhaue, contained the identical theme used by Beethoven in the scherzo of his Seventh Symphony. Another when harmonized, was used in a collection of modern school songs. Neither of them exhibit any trace of either Italian or Spanish influence.

Probably there survives some slight primitive influence in the popular songs of Mexico, though just how much is not possible to know in the absence of unadulterated primitive specimens. Most of the modern popular music is European, not Spanish alone, for there is a perceptible Italian influence. With the Spanish domination Mexican music suffered incessant modification if not the total eclipse of complete decadence. Probably the native music, with the rapidity of the conquest, was quite silenced, and when it revived it assumed the foreign style of composition.

The mestizos, quick, talkative, full of fun and happy-go-lucky, developed a happy medium between the sadness of the Indian and the vivacity of the Spaniard. Many of them have an amazing facility in metrical improvisation and a marvelous readiness in satire and mordant humor. The melancholy Indian blood combined with the Spanish is capable of producing really moving lyrical effusions and songs which are not infrequently noteworthy samples of poetical expression. Those who are familiar with the curious examples of improvised versification so common among the rancheros and common people of the interior have often expressed their wonder at the keenness of the wit and the astounding facility of their metrical improvisation. Couplets fly from mouth to mouth without a moment's hesitation, the rhymes abound in challenges, insinuations, reminiscences, picaresque *mots*, political allusions—graced by rich coloring and languidly amorous plaints. They go on all day, disputing in verse form, or interchanging amicable rhymed opinions, without the slightest fatigue or symptom of impoverishment of words or imagination. All this in the midst of total absence of any form of culture.

In the older Spanish society, prohibition of books and other fearsomenesses of political policies bred a state of obscurantism and backwardness. There is no danger that any musical enthusiast, searching the unknown depths of colonial documentation, will ever discover a great musical masterpiece of the epoch. It is evident that none was created.

Comedies were presented in the viceroy's palace, and sacred dramatic compositions in the convents, as early as the first decade after the conquest. In the palace the opera by Manuel Zumaya, "La Parténope," was presented about 1711. In the Coliseum of the Hospital Real de Indios very mediocre plays were given until the edifice burned in 1722. A new theatre was then built, in which the first company ever in the capital began to perform. It gave comedies, dances of various kinds, popular songs, medleys, olios, and even operas. The operas were wearisome things, such as "The Foolish Virgin and the Wise One," "The Brute of Babylon," "Prudence in Girlhood," and the like. The tonadillas or topical songs, always popular, showed a more vivacious repertory, while the seguidillas (songs with dancing) were even saucily piquant.

The performances began early and lasted until near midnight, with much time out for chats, cigarettes, and confections. Favorite performers were showered with gold, silver, or even jewelry, and often were invited to parties after the show to accept gifts from admirers.

In 1786 the orchestra of the Coliseum contained five violins, a viol, a violincello, two oboes, and two trumpets. In those good old days the musicians had a variety of duties. Miguel Gálvez, who played the 'cello, had to teach two new songs every month, keep the sheet music in repair, and supply the bass viol. José Ortega had to play the violin and call the musicians to practice.

The viceroy Bernardo de Gálvez showed great interest in this theatre, and provided it with many material improvements. His untimely death came before any improvement in performances occurred. As a matter of fact there was no musical growth under the viceroys. Possibly convents and wealthy homes had clavicords on which the music of the epoch could be played by white-fingered women, and the guitar no doubt found its use in humbler surroundings, but their record does not exist. It was an epoch distinguished by literary rather than by musical production. Literary competition, in the form of public contests for prizes, gave occasion for great public festivals at which interminable compositions with scant merit were read to assembled multitudes of holiday makers. The whole musical capacity of the people flowed into extremely poor verse.

The first formal opera sung in Mexico was "The Barber of Seville," by Paesiello, in December, 1806. It was a pronounced success, demonstrating the capacity of Mexican audiences for appreciation, and paid a handsome profit. A remonstrant in the *Diario de México* urged that the Coliseum ought to present more material of the same class, instead of the old mediocre stuff. There were two new native operas, many poets and composers of music for sainetes and the new and characteristic tonadillas of the country, and unless they were given, the programs would never be as attractive as they should be. But by that time New Spain was ripe for revolution, and in it the theatre disappeared for the time being. The only other musical agency was the church.

Colonial architecture presents a more pleasing picture. The first buildings which Cortés and his companions created on the débris of Tenochtitlán were rough fortress homes, devoid of architectural beauty, surmounted with turrets and battlements for defense. Andalusian patios admirably served this purpose, as well as affording light, health, and cheer. Open galleries often surmounted the upper story and in most cases the owner's arms were escutcheoned over the main entrance.

None of them exist today. But it is known that the house of Cortés covered the immense area lying between the modern streets Monte de Piedad, Francisco I. Madero, Isabel la Católica, and Tacuba, equal to several present city blocks. Its second story was an open gallery, there were strong turrets at the corners, and the sides showed elaborate columns and arcades. It was burned in 1636, and rebuilt on an altered plan. The National Pawn Shop or Monte de Piedad now occupies the most important part of it.

Existing sixteenth century houses have plain façades lacking entablatures and cornices, for which are substituted simple brick weather-mouldings. The flat surfaces of the exterior walls are usually covered with elaborate stucco relief-work and scrollwork. Angels, crowns, monograms, and vases are used for border ornamentation. There are several such homes still standing in what is now the poorer quarter of the city.

Baroque architecture in the seventeenth century, and churrigueresque in the eighteenth, softened the aspect of

the city as time passed.   Native artisans imparted to buildings a primitive dignity and elegance.   Nearly all the houses
were built of tezontle and chiluca.   Tezontle is a crimson
porous volcanic stone which was largely employed for plain
surfaces; chiluca being gray, made excellent border work,
the combination of the two giving a picturesque effect enhanced when glazed colored tiles were added, as was often
the case.   Sometimes religious designs were carved on the
plain surfaces.

Eighteenth century architecture was remarkable for the
importance given to composition of doorways, and corner
houses were elaborately decorated on both fronts.   Sometimes carved serpents taken from the old Aztec temple or its
enclosure were used.   Huge gargoyles in the shape of stone
cannon projected from the cornices of houses whose owners
ranked as captain-generals.   This was true of the old house
now Number 30 Calle Pino Suárez, which was a favorite
rendezvous of the aristocracy when owned by the counts of
Santiago Calimaya.

The turrets on the old manorial residences are relics of
the sixteenth century style in bastions.   Niches containing
statues were much used for corner ornaments.   Surfaces
were often carved in one of the two leading styles already
mentioned.   Important military officers, oidores, and other
magnates were allowed to have battlements on top of their
houses.   Some eminent personages used breastworks of
inverted arches between pilasters surmounted with neat
pinnacles.

The most luxurious tile-walled house, known as the casa
de azulejos, still standing and in use, was built by an eighteenth century scion of the condes del Valle de Orizaba.
The blue and white glazed tiles on the exterior were no doubt
made at Puebla, city famous for glazers.   Tiles were used
profusely throughout the building.   It has an immense court
now serving as a popular restaurant.   Down the street is the
present Hotel Iturbide, built as a residence by the count of
San Mateo de Valparaíso.   This was the tallest of the colonial
residences; it had life-size statues over the main entrance,

and a gallery around the top story. It has the only colonial façade which was properly designed architecturally. From this great house Iturbide went to be crowned emperor in 1821.

The interiors of these houses have the inevitable patios, filled with plants potted or set in open spaces in the tiled floors. The patio presents a pleasing contrast to the forbidding exteriors. None of the rooms in the houses have the amplitude suggested by the proportions of the patios, but they provide seclusion and a certain amount of comfort, if the temperature does not fall too low. The colonial style commends itself to the visitor better than does the ornate modern-style home of the Porfirian period, in which ostentation seems to be an effect sought quite as much as is freedom from the possible inroads of the mob or the adept ratero or sneak-thief of the streets.

The primitive churches and convents of colonial Mexico City were typical of those built in the provincial cities and towns. In the capital they were more numerous relatively, but not, with few exceptions, more elaborate. Their architecture is as a general thing rough and plain, with very thick flat walls. The roof of San Nicolacito consists of planks laid on beams and covered with brickwork and gravel; the interior shows bare walls and a floor of rough planks and bricks. Nearly all have one simple belfry on one side of the entrance. All of them have lost the old adobe walls with inverted arches which formerly surrounded the churchyards.

Types of the Mexican baroque architecture are the famous churches Santo Domingo, San Hipólito, San Agustín, and La Profesa, and half a dozen others built during the seventeenth century. Most have a single nave, others are in the shape of a Roman cross. They display arches meeting in curved triangles, surmounted by a cupola. Doorways and façades are highly ornamented. A variety of columns is used, between which are floridly decorated niches for saints. Opposite the entrance there is usually a large window or bas-relief in a rich frame. Various orders of architecture are employed in the ensemble. The square belfries into which are let curved or pyramidal openings, and the cupolas which crown the towers, give these churches very pleasing lines. The doors are of fine woods, with good panelling and metal studs. The naves are barrel-arched, with branch vaults to the side windows. A few of these churches, like La Encarnación, show Arabic influence. Usually the domes and towers are covered with glazed tiling.

The churrigueresque churches, chiefly of the eighteenth century, like San Francisco, differ from the baroque style only in ornamentation. Most have only one nave, while a few have transepts. The interior walls are profusely decorated with reredos which cover all available space. Crowded in are gilded pilasters, columns in various modifications and capitals in fanciful variations of Corinthian order. Statues of saints are omnipresent. The towers and façades are highly ornamented in carved stone. All the wall surfaces, frames of doors and windows, are ornate in keeping with the façades. Glazed tile domes and the fanciful profusion of the ornamentation produce a most charming ensemble.

The Mexican renaissance in church architecture is marked by the preponderance of horizontal lines, absent in the preceding styles. In buildings like San Pablo and Jesús María the main entrance is formed by a semicircular arch set on brackets. The Doric order prevails. The most salient feature of this style is the cupola resting on a drum of striking proportions and tasteful decoration. Most of these churches show great mastery of proportion and harmony. They depart from primitive plans, having been designed with consummate architectural skill. The designing of the naves makes the transepts the dominating features of the buildings. Of course the domes are the most striking external parts.

The great cathedral of the capital is the masterpiece of Mexican colonial art. Though it was a growth of three centuries, during which architects of diverse schools worked on it, the conception of the original architect was closely adhered to. The mannerisms of the baroque style of the seventeenth century, and the over-ornamentation of the later churrigueresque modes, have alike been kept out. The edifice presents unity of conception demonstrated in the strength of the structure and the purity of its style. The first Mexican church was finished by the Franciscans in 1525. Then came the principal church of the city, which was begun in the same year on what is now the southeast angle of the present atrium of the cathedral. The tawdry edifice was constituted the first cathedral in 1534 by Archbishop Zumárraga, then still in Toledo. During ensuing years attempts to enlarge and improve it were thwarted by quarrels between the secular and the regular clergy, so that the reconstruction of this edifice was not complete until 1584.

Meantime the new cathedral edifice had been begun in 1573. Its foundations were laid on the site once occupied by a part of the main Aztec temple. By 1625 five chapels, the sacristy, and several vestibules were completed. Thousands of Indians, managed through interpreters, were used on it. In 1656 and 1667 dedications of important parts completed were celebrated.

During the first part of the eighteenth century work on the exterior was long suspended. Possibly this is why there is so little of the churrigueresque ornamentation on the exterior. Inside, the new style was lavishly used. There still remain, however, retables in the old style of the Spanish renaissance or baroque. The main altar today is in neither style, it having been "restored" in 1850 in extremely poor taste.

The Sagrario, standing beside and as a part of the general ensemble, was dedicated in 1768. It is the most notable example of the Mexican churrigueresque. Its exuberance of imagination is overwhelming, but the construction is architecturally questionable. In 1788 the completion of the great pile was determined upon, and the finished work was realized in 1813. In its history it epitomizes almost the whole span of the colonial story of Mexico. The majestic building is the largest, oldest, and by many persons thought to be the most beautiful church edifice in North America. So well is it built, though on the ancient lake bed, that it suffers little from earthquake. There was a tradition once among the simple-hearted faithful that this was because it was suspended on chains from heaven. It dominates the old Zócalo or modern Plaza de la Constitución with imposing grandeur.

Mexico City had its own printing press in 1535, and deserves credit for possession of that instrument of culture a hundred and forty years before the irascible old Governor Berkeley could ejaculate to Providence his gratitude over the illiteracy of the settlers of the Old Dominion. Reflecting the spirit of the epoch, this old press turned out for its initial imprint a translation from the Latin version of the Greek work of St. John Climacus the Hermit. It was called the *Escala espiritual para llegar al cielo*. The "way to heaven" was the theme of most of the books printed in Mexico during the first half of the sixteenth century. Nearly eighty religious works of that epoch and imprint still exist. They were published in Latin, Spanish, and in Aztec, Tarascan, and other native tongues.

Other presses were later installed in Puebla, Guadalajara, and Vera Cruz. In the capital there were six of them in 1761, but by 1800 these had been reduced to three only. Printers were only permitted to work under government licenses, and the Inquisition limited the character of the works which might be printed at all. The effect of the strict surveillance which this court exercised over importation of books, in an effort to exclude works of heretical character, and even books containing accounts of the Indies, was to induce a great deal of smuggling of philosophical works. This smuggling was indulged in by the clergy.

The first periodical of New Spain was the *Mercurio Volante* or "Flying Mercury" edited by the famous savant Carlos Sigüenza. It began in 1693, and reached four volumes. Prior to that time small occasional sheets had been published when the flotas arrived. They contained nothing save lists of appointments, accounts of current events of no political significance, government orders, and the like. They were sedulously kept free from expressions of opinion. The *Gaceta de México*, begun in 1728, was published every month until 1739. In 1789 it reappeared with more frequent issues, and ran on to 1805. In 1772 the *Mercurio Volante*, revived, began to print a small amount of scientific and literary material. In 1805 the *Diario de México*, with light literature and political articles, began publication and continued some years. The queer papers which came out during the Revolution of Independence, are, like those mentioned above, preserved in facsimile or originals in the Bancroft and other libraries. While they are of extremely great value as materials for social and political history, their style as news sheets would not command very high respect today.

Collections of books worthy of the distinctive name of libraries were gathered at the convents in the chief towns of the provinces of the regular orders. Of course they were mostly religious books. Cords of them are now stacked, uncatalogued and unlamented, in the attic of the Biblioteca Nacional, whither they were gathered when the orders were abolished as an incident of the War of the Reform. The secular church also had a great many good libraries. But the restrictions on importations and the church censorship on publication gave everything printed a religious tinge, which was after all only a reflex of the times. The people who could read were very few, and they wanted religious works. Franciscan authors alone published four hundred such works. Those who could not read played cards or diverted themselves otherwise. There was scant night light to do anything by.

The Indians themselves produced a number of notable books, not remarkable for originality, but better than might have been expected when so few Indians had leisure for any culture. They adapted their knowledge to the Spanish alphabet and the Spanish language. These writings, such as remain in the so-called form of Codices in the great libraries of the world, are crude, but are precious monuments to the power of the Aztecs and Mayas to construct rudimentary narrative history and skilful scientific records of astronomical observations. Many of these precious documents are now in the National Museum of Mexico. Others are in

Rome, Berlin, and London. They have been used and studied by scores of Mexican and foreign students, and the works written about them number well into the hundreds.

After the Spaniards came, there were several Indians who desired to perpetuate their native history. Three Tezcocans, Fernando Pimentel, Antonio Pimentel, and Fernando de Alva, all bearing too the name of their great forbear Ixtlilxochitl, wrote about the Acolhuans of their city Tezcoco. Juan and Antonio Tovar, father and son, wrote the history of the lake region, Tezózomoc that of the southwestern region, and Chimalpain and Pomar wrote on kindred topics. Several others might be mentioned. They constitute the best available material on the native culture. Modern historians and archæologists are constantly endeavoring to interpret their stories and harmonize them with facts ascertained from cultural remains in an effort to amplify our knowledge of the ancient and fascinating American cultures.

The non-religious works of Spanish writers who participated in the conquest form the most important part of the literature of early New Spain. Hernán Cortés himself wrote five intensely interesting letters to Charles V about his exploits, in which he strove manfully to do himself ample justice. These long letters have all been published in English, and, while they were not of course an important part of what sixteenth century people in New Spain would have called literature, they are certainly that today for us, and Americans everywhere are coming to know the pleasure of finding out what was said in them. The same is true of that wonderfully intriguing book by. old Captain Bernal Díaz del Castillo, *The True History of the Conquest of New Spain*. Bernal Díaz, when he was eighty years old, wrote his reminiscences in this book to show that Gómara's account of the Cortesian exploits had put the emphasis on the wrong person. Modern readers who want something fresh, with the charm of a gentle old conqueror's pardonable self-conceit and generosity to his humble companions in arms, will not overlook Maudslay's translation of the *True History*.

Similar writings are those of Father Toribio Benavente

or Motolinía, who garrulled about the Indian primitive culture, in his *Historia de los Indios de Nueva España*, not yet translated, and those of Father Mendieta, whose *Historia eclesiástica indiana* is more general and better than the many chronicles of the provinces of the regular orders. Father Juan Torquemada's *Monarquía indiana*, Father Vetancourt's *Teatro mexicano* and Father Beaumont's *Crónica de Michoacán* are works yet closed to the modern reader of English for lack of translation. They reveal their times in just as interesting and just as important writings for their epoch as did the Venerable Bede, Gregory of Tours, and other chroniclers of medieval Europe for theirs.

At the end of the eighteenth century a Jesuit school of writers produced a number of important works on early Mexican history. While they lack the charm of the impression given by the writings of actual participants in stirring scenes and events portrayed, they also are devoid of the tedious constructions and meandering style of some of the early writers. These were the historians Alegre, Clavigero, Andrés Cavo, and Mariano Veytia. They were all creoles.

Poetry, during colonial days was, with all courtesy to the worshipers of its muses, rather a sorry form of literature. It was perpetrated by hundreds of well-meaning people. At university functions, at literary contests, which were entered into with the avidity of modern days of political jubilation, the contestants were permitted, even encouraged, to read metrical compositions the length of which was their most enduring bid for immortality. Among the real poets stands preëminent the name of the nun Sor Juana Inés de la Cruz. Her numerous works, though produced during a period of literary decadence, show that she had great philosophical and critical power. She is famed as the one woman of the colonial epoch in New Spain who achieved enduring poetical reputation. Her Peninsular contemporaries bestowed upon her the complimentary designation of the Tenth Muse.

CHAPTER X

DURING the dominance of the Hapsburgs (1516–1700) Spain gradually lost her European ascendancy as a result of a number of causes internal as well as external. The proud empire of Charles I (1516–1556) dropped to pieces under his successors, largely because the European ambitions of that monarch had drained the country of men and money. The wealth of the Indies, poured into the vortex of European politics, was inadequate to the demands made upon it. A cumbersome and inquisitorial system of taxation hampered industrial growth. Other causes contributed. Among them may be mentioned the ideal of a religious unification of the state which brought about the expulsion of the industrial classes and numerous religious persecutions. This policy had been begun even before the unification of Spain, and was revived under Ferdinand and Isabella. The Jews in large numbers were expelled in 1492 because they were not assimilable. Many thousand Moslems in 1502 were also driven out because they refused to become Catholics. The ideal of religious unity became an obsession with the great Charles which he passed on to his son and successor.

The policies of Philip II (1556–1598) both at home and abroad sought the enhancement of the power of Spain and the church, but inevitably hastened the process of disintegration. He continued to discriminate against the Moslems, expelling many of them in 1570; his son in 1609 drove more of these people, upon whom the industrial wealth of the nation depended, out of the country. The effect was to reduce the economic status of Spain and seriously to limit her revenues. Political ambitions resulting in costly wars for the sake of Spanish prestige and the protection of Catholicism, the expenditure of treasure and blood in the exploration and conquest of the New World, and a rigidly exclusive commercial policy which drove overseas trade into the hands of the English and the Dutch, were all serious causes of the depletion of Spanish wealth and virility. Impoverishment came also from the fact that a great flow of precious metals to the Peninsula from the New World brought about a notable rise of prices of commodities which seriously injured those parts of the population which did not participate in New World subjugation. The failure of Spain to develop commerce and manufactures, combined with her exclusive trade policy, threw her own cities into the camps of her economic enemies to such an extent that the protective barrier became almost completely broken down before the dynasty ended.

Under the successors of Philip, the advancing decay was hastened by the cumulative effects of the policies just named, combined with favoritism, selfishness, and incompetence in administration. The Hapsburgs after Philip II reigned but did not rule. Their favorites governed for them without broad or foresighted policies, seeking personal advantages not consonant with the interests of the empire. The ultimate degree of degradation was reached during the closing days of the reign of Charles II (1665–1700), a poor bewitched creature who had to be watched to keep him from hanging himself with his bedclothes, while a pro-French party and a pro-Austrian party at court disputed and connived over the succession to his heirless throne. During the century both the French and the English had snatched away much colonial trade, and had established themselves on the smaller islands of the West Indies. While Charles was drivelling toward his unhappy end the master of Europe, Louis XIV, had busily grasped many of Spain's fairest provinces in a series of aggressive wars, finally desisting from his enterprise of dismembering the wretched empire when it began to seem possible to secure the whole of it, metropole and colonies alike, by placing upon the throne of Spain a member of his own house.

This purpose seemed achieved when Charles II bequeathed his throne to the young duke of Anjou, grandson of Louis, who ascended the Spanish throne in 1701 as Philip V, first of the Spanish House of Bourbon. The prize was a meager one, and dearly bought. The discomfited Austrian party inaugurated the War of the Spanish Succession, setting Europe against France and Spain for thirteen years. The struggle ended only when the Austrian aspirant to the Spanish throne became head of the Holy Roman Empire. Philip was obliged to limit his ambitions by agreeing that the crowns of Spain and France should never be united. This preserved that Balance of Power which the enemies of Louis had fought for from the beginning.

If Spain had been economically and politically sound, the struggle might have seemed justified. But Spain was at the ebb tide of her misery. Catalonia and Aragon were rebellious. In the loyal area the Spanish army, once the terror of Europe, was reduced to a body of only 20,000 men without prestige on the battlefield. The fleet, which once had threatened to overwhelm England, consisted of only twenty ineffective vessels. Much of the carrying trade, and most of its protection, was cared for by the French marine. The public treasury was empty. The population, numbering now only some six millions, lived in misery in a land in which there were no roads, no commerce, no agriculture, no industry. Society was dominated by an ignorant, haughty aristocracy and a fanatical clergy over whom the influence of an idiot king had been nil. This stagnant condition had gradually extended to the colonial world, where the accession of Philip V was acknowledged with a stolidity sharply contrasting with the hostility which was to mark the attempt of Napoleon a century later to establish another French dynasty over the Spanish world.

To reorganize and rehabilitate this decayed Hapsburg monarchy became the task of the new Bourbon régime. It was to be undertaken with French benignant absolutism as the model and French imperial aggrandizement as the ultimate aim. Philip attacked the problem with energy, and did much, under French tutelage, to effect the desired end. He centralized the government of Spain and of the colonial home offices, assimilating their organization to the French model, utilizing the French system of intendants, bringing administration and collection of revenue under crown management, abolishing the disastrous Hapsburg policy of tax farming. He also inaugurated the recuperation of the army and navy. His reforms would have been more effective had the increased revenue not been consumed in bootless European wars. The assistance of the French during the War of the Spanish Succession had been obtained at cost of concessions in the famous Asiento Treaty by which France engaged in American commerce and slave trading. That privilege passed to the English in 1713, after which date England's aggressions upon Spanish commerce were a continuous and potent cause of economic disaster.

Even so, Philip V was able to leave to his successor, Ferdinand VI (1746–1759), a kingdom in which resurgent energy had done much, and an international situation in which he was able to observe a precarious but successful neutrality. Thirteen years of peace, badly needed, marked a golden age for Spain, preparing the means and the atmosphere adapted to the majestic effort of Ferdinand's successor to place his kingdom on a parity with any other in Europe.

Charles III (1759–1788) possessed rare qualities which his predecessors had lacked; he it was who renewed the regenerative policies begun by Philip V. He merits a place among the greatest of Europe's benevolent despots. With the meager resources at his command, and in spite of the changing political conceptions of an age which was to produce a French Revolution a scant year after his death, he gave to Spain an administration which all but restored her to her ancient prestige; he almost made a success of his colonial world, even when the ideals of colonization were undergoing radical processes of change which are today altering the political destinies of mankind.

Unfortunately for Spain, the rise of England as a colonial

power during the seventeenth and eighteenth centuries saw
its apogee during the reign of Charles III. The English
aggression on Spanish commerce had brought about in 1739
the "War of Jenkins' Ear" because of Spanish reprisals; this
struggle merged into the War of the Austrian Succession,
which resulted in still greater commercial advantages to
England. At no time were sentiments of cordiality existent
between England and Spain during this epoch. The cause
was the inevitable clash of the two greatest colonial powers
of modern times. Not only did conflict arise over navigation
of the high seas; England impeded Spanish fishing rights off
Newfoundland, she established logwood camps in Honduras,
and continued to hold Gibraltar and Minorca, all offenses to
Spanish pride and menaces to her imperial entity. When
England refused Spain's proffered mediation in the Seven
Years' War (1756–1763) Charles III cast his lot with the
French, and signed in 1761 and 1762 the two treaties which
constituted the Family Pact or Bourbon System. By these
treaties, the first forming a defensive and the second an
offensive alliance, Spain's fortunes were once more identified
with those of France. The war justified current and later
criticism of the Pact. Spain at the Treaty of Paris lost all
her territory in North America east of the Mississippi, the
Newfoundland fishing rights, the exclusive usufruct of
Honduras, and the right to determine the outcome of admiralty suits for British seizures of Spanish vessels in prior
peace times. Moreover, France, driven from the North
American continent, gave Louisiana to Spain, giving the
weaker nation a frontier abutting on English territory and
binding Spain perforce thereby to continue her alliance with
France. This alliance was disappointing to Spain, the reason being that France shamelessly deserted her ally when
for reasons of self-interest she expected to profit thereby.
Such an occasion arose when in 1770 Spanish forces
drove the English out of the Falkland or Maluine Islands
when the latter power had seized them, though they were
acknowledged Spanish territory. The English threatened
war, and Spain accepted the challenge, expecting French

aid. When this was not forthcoming, Spain suffered the humiliation of having to surrender the islands, though she recovered them a few years later.

This humiliation was aggravated when England espoused the cause of Portugal in her boundary dispute with Spain over possession of the post of Sacramento, on the Río de la Plata. England was prevented from rendering material assistance to the perfidious Portuguese minister Pombal in this affair because she was then in deep trouble with her American colonies. When the Portuguese king died in 1777, María Victoria, sister of Charles III, became regent of Portugal. Pombal was dismissed, and the rapprochement between Spain and Portugal became one of Charles' greatest successes. This made it possible for him to listen, though with misgivings, to suggestions from France to follow that country's lead in giving aid to the British American colonies in their War of Independence. Spain was even more in favor of aggressive action for a time than was France, being largely influenced by the dispute with Portugal. From 1776 on, Spain aided the North American revolutionists by furnishing secretly arms, munitions, and money. France held off from formal aid to the Americans until 1778, when she espoused their winning cause without apprising Spain, as she should have done under the Family Pact. Now determined to act independently, Charles offered mediation, which England rejected. Repeated suggestions for an arrangement also failing, Spain, her vessels having been repeatedly attacked by the British, declared war in June, 1779, renewing her alliance with France. The military part which Spain played in this war, aside from the campaigns of Bernardo de Gálvez in Florida and the lower Mississippi Valley, was comparatively negligible. When peace came in 1783, the reward to Spain, aside from pleasure at the discomfiture of an ancient enemy, consisted in her recovery of Florida and Minorca and a time limit on logwood cutting by the British in Honduras. On the other hand, Spain restored the Bahama Islands, which her fleet had captured, to England; she had, moreover, been an unwilling abettor of the cause of independence and democracy in America. In less than another generation the fruits of this policy were to be reaped in the loss of her entire continental empire.

Scantily successful in his foreign policy, Charles was great in internal reforms of the whole empire. The system of administration which had proved effective in Spain was extended to the colonies. A general survey of conditions in Spanish America was undertaken following the revelations of weakness there disclosed by the reports of Jorge Juan and Antonio de Ulloa upon conditions in South America in the 1740's. Following their voyage, and adopting the recommendations of Bernardo Ward and José Campillo y Cosío, a number of visitor-generals were sent to the several viceroyalties and captaincies-general during the ensuing years. Among these the most famous were the visitation of New Spain by José de Gálvez and that of Peru by his understudy, José de Areche.

The result of the visitation by Gálvez is particularly significant, as he was made minister of the Indies at its close, and his measures were largely responsible for the reconstructive policy pursued elsewhere in the colonial empire. The burden of his reforms was directed toward efficiency of administration for the purpose of increasing revenues in preparation for expected war with England. His two greatest reform measures were the establishment of the intendant system throughout Spanish America, and the abandonment of the government's commercial monopoly for a system of restricted free trade. The intendant system was established in Mexico in 1786. It divided the viceroyalty into twelve intendancies and three provinces; over each intendancy a governor-intendant ruled, with sub-delegates for assistants who replaced the old corregidores and alcaldes mayores. The intendants and their subordinates were expected to relieve the viceroy of many of the burdensome details of his great office, and to assist him in the collection of revenues, the administration of justice, and the economic features of government. They were chosen from among Spanish born subjects, since these were supposedly more efficient than the creoles and mestizos who had served as local administrative officers. The intendants were also charged with military control of their areas.

The organization of the intendancies in New Spain left intact the establishment of a commandancy-general in the frontier provinces which had been effected in 1776 as recommended by Gálvez in 1768. It had been proposed in 1760 to erect the audiencia of Guadalajara into a new viceroyalty, but the idea of the commandancy prevailed as more practical and economical. The two Californias, Sinaloa, Sonora, Nueva Vizcaya, Coahuila, Texas, and New Mexico were included in it at first, and Nuevo León and Nuevo Santander were later added. The commandant was independent of the viceroy, but might call upon him for aid. His duty was to erect his territory into a buffer state against English, Russian, or French aggressions, and to observe an adequate Indian policy toward the hostile tribes who dwelt within and near his dominion. It was a new viceroyalty in embryo.

The commercial reform known as the establishment of free trade was a tentative measure whereby for a period of ten years the principal import and export duties on overseas commerce were remitted. The practice of sending out huge convoyed fleets of merchant vessels was discontinued, and individual ships were allowed to sail without naval protection. Free trade between the Spanish colonies was also allowed. The measure went into effect first in the least important of the colonies, being gradually extended to the great viceroyalties. The effect was to break the monopolies hitherto enjoyed by large merchants who had conducted great fairs at Vera Cruz, where they had controlled prices and distribution of goods at will, often to the serious injury of the public. The great fortunes which had been engaged in mercantile business were removed to the interior and engaged in agriculture and mining, to the decided benefit of those industries. Many small merchants entered the importing and exporting field. Many new small fortunes were made, and a general era of

prosperity was begun. Before the free trade scheme could
be perfectly worked out, the recurrence of European wars
demanded even more money than the greater volume of
taxation had produced, and before the close of the century
all the old taxes had been reimposed. The New World
possessions had had only a breathing space from ruinous
taxation, but this had taught its lesson.

Other reforms enacted under the influence of Gálvez
were the centralization of the collection of taxes, the imposition of the tobacco and other monopolies, and the reduction of peculation and other dubious practices among the
customs officers at Acapulco, Vera Cruz, and Mexico City.
But more conspicuous were his measures for expansion and
defense of the realm.

The expansion of New Spain, we have seen, was greatest
during the sixteenth century. During the seventeenth
century there was little advance that was not the direct
outcome of frontier initiative rather than of strength and
well-ordered policy of the central government. Before
that century had ended the reverse tide had set in. The
northern frontier of New Spain had been advanced into wild
Indian territory, where Apaches and Comanches disputed
white supremacy. Lesser tribes also menaced. The secular struggle was at its height when Gálvez came. By
his efforts, determined though scantily successful war was
waged on the Indians of all the frontier, chiefly in Sonora,
Sinaloa, and Chihuahua. In 1772 the irregularly located
frontier presidios were redistributed and arranged in a
form of boundary line conforming to the limits of actual occupation reaching at regular intervals from the western
coast to the Gulf of Mexico, primarily for the purpose of
keeping the Indians in check. This reform had been in
contemplation for many years, but privileged border settlers had used influence to postpone its completion.

There was another motive for reorganization in fear of
foreign aggression. The Pacific had ceased to be thought
a comfortable Spanish lake since 1742, when Lord Anson
had sailed across it and taken a galleon and her secret chart.

The Dutch and French had also menaced Spanish isolation there. In 1741 Vitus Behring for Russia discovered Behring Strait, and started the Northwest fur trade. The Spaniards believed the Russians would soon spread in this activity from the Aleutian Islands down the whole mainland coast. To forefend this encroachment, Gálvez revived the long forgotten plan to occupy Monterey Bay in California. In 1769 expeditions from Baja California occupied San Diego in Upper California, and Monterey Bay in 1770. Soon a number of missions in a chain along the coast were established. San Francisco was occupied and fortified in 1776. California had been made Spanish only as a matter of defense. It was then proposed to establish land communications with the new colony, for which purpose settlements were made on the Río Colorado near Yuma. These were soon destroyed by the fierce Yuma Indians, and the main contact with the northern coast was for long thereafter by way of the sea.

The Western coast indeed loomed conspicuously important after the occupation of Upper California. Rumors that the English were at last to pierce through the northern part of the continent by the long unfound Strait of Anián, and that the Russians were planning expeditions down the coast, led to action to hold the remote new frontier. Juan Pérez was accordingly sent northward to take formal possession up to 60° north latitude. His farthest north was 55°, but he explored Nootka Sound, important internationally a few years later. He was shortly followed by Heceta and Bodega y Quadra, who, sailing in 1775, discovered the coast to 49° and 58° respectively. In 1779, incited by James Cook's famous voyage to the same waters in 1776 in search of the northern passage, Arteaga reached 60°, but Spanish tenure of the extreme northwest was postponed for a time by the American Revolution.

After that conflict had ended, news that the Russians had occupied Unalaska and Nootka called for resumption of Spanish activity. In 1788 Esteban Martínez and Gonzalo López de Haro visited the coast, finding Russians established near Cape Grenville, and learning of their other settlements, including Unalaska. The contacts of Russians and Spaniards on this occasion were amicable, but in 1789 Martínez was again sent north to occupy Nootka, which his nation claimed priority in discovering. He was also to prevent foreign occupation. Finding English ships there, he seized them; England threatened war, and Spain, again denied support under the Family Pact, for France was then ruled by the Assembly, had to yield the British the right to trade and found establishments on the Pacific north of the Spanish settlements. This agreement, in 1790, marked the beginning of Spain's retrogression in North America; it occurred at the very time and place of her greatest expansion.

The attempt to hold Nootka and the Northwest Coast was accompanied by other measures intended to acquire control of the seaways of America. The Falkland incident has already been noticed. Another effort was that made to occupy Tahiti in 1772-6, by Domingo Boenechea and others under orders from Peru, also to anticipate the English. Still another defensive measure was the establishment of the viceroyalty of La Plata in 1776, as a means of controlling eastern South America against the Portuguese and English. Shortly thereafter, exploration of the southern Argentine in the 1780's by Basilio Villarino, and settlements on the southern coast by Antonio de Biedma, made the southern part of the continent more secure, as early expeditions had done on the Brazilian frontier. The establishment of the southern viceroyalty had had its counterpart in northern South America in 1739, when the viceroyalty of Nueva Granada was definitively established that Spain might better cope with Dutch smugglers of Venezuela and the Caribbean. That defensive measure was accompanied by the foundation of Commercial Trading Companies as offensive weapons. The Caracas Company and the Santo Domingo Company were examples of this sort of merchant coastguard organization which proved fairly effective.

Thus from Nootka, San Francisco, and the frontier presidial line which marked the bounds of the military comandancia general on the north, in the Caribbean, the Falklands, and Tahiti, Spain tried to forge a ring of defenses about her American empire to keep out the enemy. To man all these defenses, an expedient of dangerous purport was the creation for the first time of a large colonial army. Native Americans were made officers and soldiers of a great colonial militia which fought the Indians on the frontiers, manned the presidial strongholds, and put down incipient revolts in the provinces. By this policy a colonial military tradition was created, and the Spanish Americans learned that they were the equals of Spaniards on the battlefield if nowhere else. Spain was confronted by the dilemma of losing her colonies to England or of training the colonists to fight for their own independence. They were confident, in a military sense, of their power when the issue of conflict came, and the process of imperial disintegration was merely postponed; Spanish America was lost to the colonists instead of to England.

In New Spain itself this century of Bourbon rule which has been briefly sketched was begun during the viceroyal term of the count of Moctezuma. Suspected of being unfriendly to the new French dynasty, he was very promptly recalled. He was succeeded by Archbishop Montañes (1701-2), who thus appeared a second time as viceroy, ruling for only thirteen months. During that period he dispatched to Spain a treasure fleet under French and Spanish convoy. The fleet was overhauled by the allied enemies of Louis XIV off Vigo, Spain, and in a disastrous fight on October 22, 1703, the entire fleet and its cargo of 50,000,000 pesos and 2000 persons were lost. This blow was followed by charges of malfeasance, under which Montañes was removed.

He was succeeded by the duke of Alburquerque (1702-11) second viceroy with that title. At this time it was expected that the War of the Spanish Succession would be carried into America, and great military preparations were made against foreign attack on Vera Cruz. These were the times when Captain William Dampier appeared in the South Sea

(1704), Captain Clipperton captured vessels at Realejo on the east coast, Captain Woodes Rogers rescued Alexander Selkirk from Juan Fernández Island in the South Sea (1709) and, raiding Mexico's west coast, failed only to capture the longed-for treasure ship from Manila. Thus Alburquerque's administration was much concerned with defending the coasts of his territory and fighting the pirates. In 1710 he established the important Tribunal de la Acordada for the purpose of driving out bandits whose depredations had gone beyond the power of the Santa Hermandad to quell. A characteristic change came during the period of Alburquerque. He was very much influenced by French ideas in civilization and under him came about the change from the old style Spanish clothing which had characterized the Hapsburg dynasty, because of his adoption of the modern French dress, which was introduced with the advent of Philip V.

In 1711 he was succeeded by Fernando de Alencastre, better known as the duke of Linares. Linares found New Spain in a condition of great moral and material decadence, as he says in his famous Instrucción to his successor. He averred that corruption and libertinage had not only come to have baleful influence upon the common people but that these vices had invaded the sanctuaries of God and of justice. Linares finished his rule in August 1716, but continued to reside in Mexico until his death in August of the following year.

His successor was Baltasar de Zúñiga, marquis of Valero. The most notable incident of external relations which ocurred during the period of Valero was the expulsion of the English logwood cutters from the Island of Carmen in Tabasco. The English retired to Belize and Jamaica, returning later with troops to retake the Island of Carmen, but the Spanish governor, Andrade, succeeded in defending it. The logwood question remained a bone of contention throughout the century.

In 1722 Zúñiga was succeeded by Juan de Acuña, marquis of Casafuerte, who was a creole born in Lima. This American viceroy, thirty-seventh of the line, continued in power until his death in March, 1734, his term being the longest one during the eighteenth century. During this period the Spanish discovered the English colony of Belize. They also sent an expedition to eastern Texas in 1720–22, under the marquis of San Miguel de Aguayo, by which the abandoned missions were reëstablished and the growth of the province assured. Casafuerte's rule was marked by the publication of the *Gaceta de México* and the *Mercurio de México*. He is one of the few viceroys who are buried in New Spain.

His successor was Juan Antonio de Vizarrón Eguiarreta, archbishop of Mexico, who began to govern May 16, 1734. This viceroy was credited with having sent more treasure to Spain than any of his predecessors and that without oppressing the people or diminishing the reserve held in Mexico for government uses. The march of internal history in the viceroyalty was disturbed in 1735 by a general uprising of the negroes near Córdoba because of the circulation of a rumor that the king of Spain had declared all slaves free. A force of six hundred Spaniards was needed to overcome the revolt. In 1736 a recurrence of the terrible epidemic known as matlazáhuatl, which had destroyed two million natives in 1576, caused great loss among the population. When Vizarrón retired in 1740 from the viceroyalty he resumed his position as archbishop of Mexico, in which he continued until his death in 1747.

The thirty-ninth viceroy, Pedro de Castro, duque de la Conquista (1740–1741), started to New Spain on a Dutch ship in order to avoid English war vessels in the vicinity of Porto Bello, rather a sad commentary on the efficiency of the Spanish navy. He was so nearly caught by the enemy that he had to make his escape in a slower vessel, leaving his credentials behind. The Spanish colonial possessions were at this time the object of attacks by the English general Oglethorpe, founder of Georgia as a buffer colony, who bombarded San Agustín, Florida. Admiral Vernon had captured Porto Bello and had destroyed the castle of San Lorenzo at the Chagre, and now threatened San Juan de Ulloa and Vera Cruz. The viceroy had gone to fortify Vera

Cruz against the enemy, when he became violently ill and returned to Mexico City to die August 22, 1741. This viceroy, like Casafuerte, was born in America, and is one of the few American viceroys of the colonial period.

The term of the fortieth viceroy of New Spain, Pedro Cebrián y Agustín, count of Fuenclara (1742–1746), was marked by a most serious blow to Spanish monopoly of the Pacific Ocean through the loss of the treasure ship *Covadonga* to Lord Anson in Philippine waters in 1743. Such a great disaster reacted against the prestige of the viceroy; war conditions within Europe seriously disturbed New Spain, causing scarcity of European supplies and a period of high prices. Fuenclara's rule continued until ill health forced him to resign.

Juan Francisco de Güemes y Horcasitas, count of Revilla Gigedo (1746–1755), was advanced to the viceroyalty from the position of captain-general of Cuba. The same policy was frequently observed in the appointment of viceroys of New Spain after this time. Güemes y Horcasitas was noted for having made his position as viceroy serve as a financial asset in speculative commercial enterprises, and was humorously called "Don Juan Tobago" because of his lucrative but illicit participation in the Havana tobacco trade. Yet he commanded respect because of his personal courage and because of his effective control over the affairs of state. In spite of his enormous personal gains he was able to increase the government revenues. He is also well known for his generous protection of the Escandón family which settled Nuevo Santander.

Agustín de Ahumada, marqués de las Amarillas (1755–1760), a soldier who had won fame in the Italian wars, devoted his time to attempts to correct the abuses of administration which had grown up in New Spain and gave his life in this service, dying in Mexico City, February 6, 1760. In contrast to Revilla Gigedo, Amarillas was so poor at the end of his administration that his widow had to be furnished with funds to return to Spain.

Again the governor of Havana was given the viceroyal

office when Francisco Cagigal de la Vega ruled for a few months during 1760. His successor, the forty-fourth viceroy, Joaquín Monserrat, marquis of Cruíllas, came in the same year and ruled until 1766, witnessing the inauguration in New Spain of the reform policy of Charles III, which made the Spanish empire again a first rate European power. In the development of the policy, however, Cruíllas bore very little part because of his conflict with the great visitor-general, José de Gálvez, who procured his removal and obtained the appointment of Carlos Francisco de Croix, marquis of Croix (1766–1771). Cruíllas had in fact begun the reorganization of the general defenses of New Spain and these were carried further under the active care of Croix, who was dominated by Gálvez. The epoch is marked by the personal intervention of the visitor-general in every detail of the viceroyal government. Indeed Croix was chosen for his characteristic of punctual obedience to the orders of the king and for his genial disposition, two factors which gave to Gálvez a predominance which no other visitor-general had enjoyed. This period was marked by the occupation of Alta California and the reconquest of the north-western frontier.

Croix's successor, Antonio María Bucareli (1771–1779), a lieutenant-general with disinguished ancestors and personal glories won in European campaigns, had also served as governor and captain-general of Cuba. In 1777 Bucareli's compensation was advanced 20,000 pesos, making the vice-royal salary 80,000 pesos with a purchasing value of something like from $160,000 to $200,000 of American money at its current value in 1922. Bucareli was one of the most popular viceroys of New Spain. His efforts were given to the organization of military forces and coast defenses, to the maintenance of the colonial efforts begun by Gálvez and Croix in California, and to the general care of the treasury, administration of justice and the reform of public instruction. Bucareli was an opponent of many of the reforms in public administration suggested by José de Gálvez; his attitude is, no doubt, largely responsible for the tardy initia-

José Burgaleta. Drainage Map, Valley of Mexico, 1774

tion of the system of intendancies in New Spain which Gálvez had urged from 1768 onward. Bucareli died of pleurisy in April 1779, much to the sorrow of the inhabitants for he had become known as the viceroy beloved for the peace of his realm. His body lies beneath the floor of the church of Guadalupe, where it is trampled daily by hundreds of the descendants of his Indian subjects.

The anticipatory provision for his successor known as the pliego de mortaja or provisional emergency appointment designated as his successor ad interim "the president of Guatemala." The incumbent in the presidency of Guatemala was Martín de Mayorga. An order of the Spanish government removed Mayorga and designated Matías de Gálvez, brother of José, as president of Guatemala; but the order appointing him reached the capital of Guatemala some time after the announcement that the "president of Guatemala" was to become viceroy of New Spain. Therefore Mayorga instead of Gálvez was inadvertently made viceroy, a circumstance which brought him the ill-will of José de Gálvez, then minister of the Indies, and greatly detracted from the value of his viceroyal period (1779–1783). He was a faithful and efficient public servant, though he was constantly snubbed by the minister, and mysteriously died on board ship while enroute to Spain and practically within sight of Cádiz.

Matías de Gálvez now came into possession of the office which his brother had coveted for him. Matías was at heart the plain farmer which he had been in his youth, and liked to talk about his experiences as a tiller of the soil. He was an old man without particular capacity for the position which was thrust upon him and happily died in the fall of 1784. His appointment served to postpone the progress of the reforms which an abler man might have carried out with vigor.

He was succeeded by his son Bernardo (1785–1786), a young man who had barely escaped annihilation in the Apache warfare on the Texas frontier in the 70's, to win glory in the brilliant campaign of the American Revolution which he conducted in the Mississippi Valley for Spain as an ally of the United States. The young and affable Gálvez became unusually popular with the people, at the same time falling under suspicion because his reconstruction of the castle of Chapultepec had the appearance of attempting to make it serve as a citadel from which it was thought he was planning the secession of New Spain from the monarchy. The young viceroy passed away in October 1786, after a short illness.

The fiftieth viceroy, Alonso Núñez de Haro y Peralta, archbishop of Mexico, served from May to August 1787 as a brief ad interim appointee whose influence as viceroy was practically nil. His successor, Manuel Antonio Flórez (1787), was the first of the viceroys to hold office under the reduced powers provided for in the Ordinance of the Intendants, which was promulgated for New Spain in 1786. By this legislation the financial duties of the viceroy were delegated to a superintendent of the treasury so that the great position once held by Mendoza and Velasco had now come to be merely a formal presidency of the supreme court and a showy control of the military organization as captain-general. The ill success of the scheme which made the viceroy a nonentity brought about a reversion to the prior system after the death of Gálvez in 1787. Flórez was engaged in making campaigns against the northern Indians in 1788–1789 and in efforts to defend the coast of California from San Blas to Acapulco. Ill health obliged him to petition for removal in 1788. The following year he was succeeded by the second count of Revilla Gigedo, who became the greatest of the eighteenth century viceroys (1789–1794).

The greatness of Revilla Gigedo's character and of his conception of the viceroyal office is shown in the remarkable Instrucción which he left to his successor. No contemporary document of the colonial period compares in breadth of view and understanding of Spanish colonial governmental machinery with this remarkable résumé. Revilla Gigedo's superb energy was displayed in the purification which he administered in the internal life of the city of Mexico, the material cleansing and beautification which he superintended and the remarkable vigor with which he undertook to accomplish vast reforms in the offices of the viceroy. The greatest contribution which Revilla Gigedo made in this last named interest was more in the nature of the vigor and enthusiasm with which he assisted in the installation of the system of intendancies than in the actual change effected. At the same time the public revenues were raised to the highest figure ever reached in colonial times.

So statesmanlike a viceroy as was this man could hardly expect to survive the changes which were then occurring in the Spanish court. The great Charles III had died on December 14, 1788, and his weak son, Charles IV, was now in control of the empire. The son was the antithesis of all that his father had been. His insight into governmental policies was less masterful than that of his capable though somewhat eccentric viceroy. The son had scant conception of the meaning of the policies which his father had inaugurated but could see clearly the enormous expenditures which the reorganized government of New Spain was entailing. Hence it was not unexpected that the central government should begin to observe a selfish and shortsighted policy in regard to these reforms and to place all obstacles possible in the way. If a man of Revilla Gigedo's type could have been viceroy at the time of the ineffective rule of Martín Mayorga and the two Gálvezes, father and son, New Spain might have enjoyed greater prosperity during the closing years of her colonial government.

The fifty-third viceroy, the marquis of Branciforte (1794-98), inaugurated an administration which was in strong contrast to that of Revilla Gigedo. He was proud and vain, and unpopular because of his selfishness and his more than suspected dishonesty. He was a fit representative in New Spain of the court as it existed at that time at Madrid, being a creature of Godoy, Prince of Peace, and favorite of Queen María Luisa. A storm of war which was beginning to break in Europe between Spain and France on the one hand and Spain and Great Britain on the other occupied this incompetent viceroy during the greater part of his period.

His successor, the fifty-fourth viceroy, Don Miguel José de Azanza (1798–1800), had been for a long time in the American service. He was one of the under-secretaries of José de Gálvez in 1767, and had been imprisoned by that visitor-general for circulating a truthful report while in Sonora that the latter was temporarily insane. Azanza was perhaps the best viceroy that Charles IV sent to New Spain. He reduced the armaments which Branciforte had undertaken to maintain for protection of the viceroyalty, and endeavored to reduce public expenditures as much as he could and still preserve the security of the realm. He was succeeded by Félix Berenguer de Marquina (1800–1803) the least esteemed of the Bourbon viceroys.

The days of great rulers in New Spain were now ended. Seven mediocre men were still to rule during the next twenty years. Twenty-two chief executives had been required to span the century; half a dozen or more of them had been exceptionally strong as administrators, and only one or two of them had been conspicuously unfit for their tasks. But the position of viceroy had become too great a burden for one man to carry. Internal administration under the close tutelage of the Spanish court had grown impossible. Moreover the growth of New Spain in population, resources, and developed wealth, had but just preceded the widely spreading changes of the late eighteenth century in the conception of proper political relationship between parent country and colonies. The transmission of European culture to America was not yet a completed process, but the best possible results from the transmission of European form and spirit of benevolent despotism had now been reached. Henceforth there was to be readjustment and readaptation of political forms to meet new social ideals. America was beginning to come into her own. Added to the menace of foreign aggressions was the storm of internal dissatisfaction which was now breaking in the Spanish American colonies. A plot against the Spaniards had been organized under the leadership of one Juan Guerrero even during the time of Branciforte. Guerrero was only the mouthpiece of certain Europeans who desired to foment disloyalty. While Guerrero and his friends were being tried for their treachery another plot in Mexico City, called the Machete conspiracy, about the end of 1799 occupied the attention of Azanza. Neither of these plots was of sufficient seriousness to menace the safety of the realm but they indicated rather the trend of opinion during those days.

CHAPTER XI

IT is an error to suppose that New Spain and the other Spanish colonies were so moved by centuries of misgovernment that they sprang to arms simultaneously to effect separation from the fatherland. In fact the movement for independence was rather conditioned upon political events in Spain than upon general desire in Spanish America for separation. Those events and the conditions out of which they sprang merely furnished the occasion for the general resort to arms. But justification for the movement by its participants was based on the centuries old colonial policy which Spain had pursued. Much the same policies had been followed by England in her colonies though with less rigidity of monopolistic exclusiveness and with less destructive rivalries; that great competing colonial power had lost her American possessions through a movement which derived its inspiration from the new social theories evolved by the French school of political thinkers during the late eighteenth century. The success of the American Revolution animated the French struggle for liberty, fraternity, and equality, and the current set in motion finally swept Spanish America into the great stream of political events and economic developments which at last changed the whole trend of modern colonial theory.

The inhabitants of New Spain really had a great deal of which to complain. They were far away from their king, whose will, however benevolent, was interpreted by a viceroy who acted upon the theory declared by the marquis of Croix, that the subject was "born to obey and be silent." Such an atmosphere stifled political thought; political activity was still-born. The courts, from top to bottom, were dilatory, corrupt, and incompetent. Executives everywhere curried favor with the privileged classes in government and church circles. The church, as well as the government, reserved its highest favors for the Spanish born. Business was in the hands of the Peninsulars.

Commerce was weighted with a complex multitude of import and export duties. The Cádiz trade was still monopolistic, in spite of the liberal legislation of 1778. Even so, a very large part of the profits on American trade went to French and English factories. Goods bought within the restricted trade avenues were very expensive, because of high freight costs, delays in port, and the greed of merchants, who literally sought to make a fortune from the proceeds of the first vessel they sent to Vera Cruz. There was scant domestic commerce because of the irregularity and scarcity of the food crops and colonial exports. This in turn was due to lack of governmental intelligence in encouraging cereal crops by liberal export privileges, and to the idleness of the Indians, who were encouraged to sloth by the policy of protecting them as wards. The hated alcabala tax, high freight rates, and scarcity of mules for transportation purposes over ill-kept roads, added to the trammels which kept prosperity away. Trading privileges with immunity from duty payment enjoyed by officers of the royal navy kept the regular merchants in uncertainty as to conditions of the market, and rendered profits from sales uncertain.

Religion offered little relief to society in an outworn spirituality, an antiquated education, a decrepit and ill-directed charity. There was no circulation of ideas; there was no participation in affairs of state; municipal autonomy was long dead. The new army gave to the creole aristocracy a few ludicrous military titles which superseded the hunt for resonant but meaningless titles of nobility. Taxation and monopoly sapped the country for expenses of administration and subsidies for defence of other colonies which were operated at a loss. Government officials labored under loads of restrictive regulations on their authority.   Hence the well-intentioned system, which sought to prevent dishonesty and oppression, actually promoted the unhappy conditions it was intended to make impossible. The viceroys, who were for the most part persons of high character and capacity, were prevented from effective administration of their offices by the multiplicity of their duties, by unending ceremonials, by being required to spend four to six hours daily merely signing official papers which they had not time to read, and by the constant necessity of receiving the opinions of their subordinate advisers.   When to this interminable array of routine was added social ambition or speculative investment or peculation, the office of viceroy was generally a highly inefficient one.   Lesser administrative positions suffered comparably in the same ways, their chief inherent defect being lack of authority.

If the man in the street had little opportunity to offer these constructive criticisms of the chief administrative office, most of the vassals of the Spanish king had opportunity to judge of the ineffectiveness of the judicial system.   Judgeships were salable and transferable; responsibility was thus hard to fix; graft in law cases was prevalent, even customary.   Not only were judicial offices sold, but it was possible to procure decisions, or failure to decide, for a price.   The viceroys were too busy sending money to Spain to correct evils in justice. In the lower courts the alcaldes mayores were often set aside by the audiencia judges who tried Indian cases in the Juzgado de Indios, and there was continual disorder and delay in the dockets.   The judicial system was indeed a lack of system, it never having had a real reorganization during the entire colonial epoch.

Failure of administration and break-down of justice were accompaniments of racial embitterments through preference to Spanish born vassals in all political and social employments.   The constant drainage of funds to Spain by continually added taxes, collected in most annoying fashion, was creating unrest and dissatisfaction.   The economic domination of the church as chief mortgagee of productive real estate was irksome to all souls imbued with the pregnant philosophy of the epoch. The intellectual stagnation bred by long years of the *Index Expurgatorius*, which forbade all questionable literature, and the moral laxity caused by the practice of fawning for privileges before an absolute autocracy instead of establishing equal rights for all men, were the essential causes of the alienation which was rapidly growing to the breaking point between colonial and peninsular Spaniards. Hipólito Villarroel of Mexico bared the condition of the body politic in his *"Political Ills of New Spain";* the City Council of Mexico protested, but little political change would have come of it all, had it not been for the dry rot of the Spanish throne and the Peninsular ambitions of Napoleon Bonaparte.

The reign of Charles III had been marked by numerous internal reforms calculated to reïnforce the external policy of checking the menace of England's growing colonial power. It has been shown how reforms, diplomacy, and statesmanlike policies had tended to knit the Spanish colonial world together to that end. Spain rose again to the rank of a first-rate power. But under Charles IV (1788-1808) the epoch of reform closed abruptly, and the characteristic international relations concerned France rather than England.

The new king began his reign under the auspices of wise ministers, who had already begun, however, to recede from their liberal internal policies in view of the propagation in Spain of the ideas of the French Revolution. In this policy Spain became involved, when the Nootka affair, to which allusion has already been made, renewed the traditional hostility to England. In the midst of these difficulties, Charles espoused the cause of Louis XVI of France, who had been obliged in 1791 to accept the limitations imposed upon him by the revolutionary constitution. When a French agent persuaded Charles that his opposition to the radical powers in France was injuring Louis instead of helping him, Floridablanca was removed from the prime ministry and Aranda supplanted him. This meant temporarily that more friendly relations would prevail, but Aranda was driven by the progress of the revolution to oppose it. He was in turn removed and Manuel Godoy, paramour of María Luisa, the Spanish queen, was made foreign minister. He succeeded in defending Louis to the extent of bringing the Convention to declare war upon Spain in 1793. This indecisive struggle was concluded by the Treaty of Basle in 1795. By it Spain lost her final half of Santo Domingo, and gave the French some trading privileges in the Peninsula.

The Peace of Basle enraged England, which had been Spain's lukewarm ally. England had not fought very earnestly in the war, and after the peace she continued to lord it over Spanish shipping. She encouraged the Spanish Americans to seek independence, and she insulted the Spanish ambassador in London. Charles IV therefore newly allied himself with France and declared a war against England which brought nothing save loss of the island of Trinidad. The hope had been that the French republic would fail and a Spanish Bourbon might be put on a new French throne.

While the scheming Godoy was hoping for some such eventuality, Napoleon Bonaparte overthrew the French Directory in 1799, and began to use Spain according to the established French custom. In 1800 he arranged a treaty agreeing to enlarge the Bourbon duchy of Parma in return for retrocession of Louisiana, and he fomented war between Spain and Portugal in 1801.

In this war Godoy coerced Portugal into refusing her ports to English vessels in return for Spain's guarantee of her territorial integrity. From this time on Napoleon distrusted Godoy. He browbeat Spain, forcing her into war with England (1804), selling Louisiana contrary to his promise, and obliging Godoy to seek England again as an ally (1805). When Napoleon had defeated his northern enemies at Austerlitz (1805) and Jena (1806) he was ready after the Peace of Tilsit (1807) to hear what Godoy had meant by calling on the Spanish people for military action

against an unnamed foreign enemy. It was evident that
Napoleon had determined now to destroy once for all the
Spanish Bourbons.

This he could do by enlisting Godoy's cupidity for a
share in a proposed partition of Portugal. When the French
army had taken that country (1807) it became manifest
that Napoleon's promises were faithless, but his troops
poured into Spain. Charles was too terrified to fight him,
and, after failing to slip away to America, as the Portuguese
ruler had done, he suddenly abdicated the throne of Spain
on March 19, 1808. His popular son became king as Ferdinand VII.

The accession of Ferdinand displeased Napoleon for he
had planned to put one of his own brothers on the Spanish
throne. Charles IV wished to recover his throne to save
Godoy, who had been imprisoned, and gave himself into
Napoleon's hands to effect this. Then Napoleon forced
Ferdinand to meet him in French territory, at Bayonne,
whither Charles was also induced to go. There the royal
Spanish family indulged in mutual recriminations in the
presence of Napoleon, who induced both supine aspirants to
his favor and the throne of their own nation to abdicate,
after which he proclaimed his brother Joseph Bonaparte
king of Spain upon the unwilling acceptance of the latter
by the Council of Castile.

The Spanish people idolized Ferdinand, considering him
the virtuous victim of Godoy, and wanted him for their
king. But the French army was possessed of Madrid, where
it had already clashed with the populace. In a battle on
May 2, glorious in Spanish annals, the kingless country
began a war which was taken up by all parts of Spain and
conducted with such tenacity that it served as the beginning
of the weakening of Napoleon's hold upon Europe. Napoleon
had had much experience in fighting professional armies,
but none in opposing the will of an entire national populace.
By falling unexpectedly upon his lines of communications
and suddenly disappearing, by never presenting a front
against Napoleon's perfect troops and tactics, the Spanish

guerrillas were able to make the tenure of the Peninsula a costly effort until formal aid by the English could come. The disintegrated nation split up into its local provinces, each conducting its own warfare and owning control by none save its own junta. Joseph Bonaparte was a king without a country.

In Mexico the news of these events was received with varying emotions. There was great rejoicing at the removal of the hated Godoy and the accession of Ferdinand VII, for that unprincipled reprobate was considered a perfect prince who was the victim of the immoral king and queen and the favorite Godoy. Among the Spaniards in Mexico only the viceroy José de Iturrigaray (1803–1808) was moved with apprehension, for he had lost in the removal of Godoy his protector and friend. When it became known that Ferdinand had in turn abdicated, Iturrigaray regained a degree of composure for it then seemed likely that he might continue to rule New Spain and even gradually increase his authority because of the confusion in the fatherland.

But when the news came that Joseph Bonaparte was in Madrid trouble began. Though there had been frequent revolts in New Spain against the home government these had not been participated in by the privileged upper, dominant classes. They were essentially loyal. The audiencia, sitting administratively as the real acuerdo, voted to notify Spain that no obedience would be rendered to Napoleon's officers. Iturrigaray on the other hand wanted to play for time, thinking that a turn of affairs might improve his political prospects.

Into this situation there entered a new element. The city council or ayuntamiento of Mexico, composed of course of creoles, proposed that a demonstration of loyalty to Ferdinand should be publicly rendered, in which the Spanish abdications should be declared null, but that, since there was no rightful king, the sovereignty should be declared to reside in the viceroyalty and its various classes; this sovereignty was to be exercised by the audiencia, the ayuntamiento, and other courts and governing bodies, who should return it to the legitimate sovereign of Spain when he might be set at liberty. The City of Mexico, as representative of the viceroyalty, would sustain the Bourbons, but invited the viceroy to continue to rule provisionally, refraining from acknowledging the Bonaparte king.

The viceroy was naturally flattered at this mark of respect from the native white American element, but when he referred the business to the audiencia, which was composed of Peninsular Spaniards, the judges were shocked at the ayuntamiento's sudden assumption of importance and at the idea implicated in the suggestion for a provisional government. To the audiencia it seemed only natural that government should go on as usual, hence it politely urged the ayuntamiento not to concern itself further with affairs outside its purview. "The audiencia and the viceroy will not hesitate to call upon you when your help is needed."

Here was a vital recrudescence of the long established class antipathy between the European and the American Spaniards. The former began to fear that the members of the ayuntamiento were plotting for independence, and demanded that the viceroy punish them. The creoles were sure the European-born audiencia members and their adherents were striving to keep Spain and America united regardless of dynastic problems, just as had been done during the War of the Spanish Succession when the Bourbon rule began. The temper of the colonials was far from acquiescence in a change of dynasty. Meantime, the provincial cities of New Spain began to elect representatives to sit in a general junta for the viceroyalty, as the ayuntamiento had suggested. The creole attitude, widely spread, was that the Spanish junta might represent Spain, but that the people of New Spain should have their own junta, coördinate with the Spanish junta and independent of it, each of them equally representing the imprisoned King Ferdinand until the hoped for day of his happy release.

To the viceroy and his friends it seemed unthinkable that the disunited Spaniards could defeat the mighty Napoleon.

Iturrigaray betrayed this opinion from time to time, and his obvious expectation induced the creoles to begin to plan for immediate independence. Such a step demanded a rapid education of the people away from monarchical ideas; this could be fostered through formation of a national junta composed of the various municipal authorities of the provinces. Iturrigaray favored this idea, thinking that such a junta, being merely consultative, would be under his control. He even began to hope that events would move toward his nomination as the first king of an independent New Spain. In spite of the opposition of the real acuerdo, he fostered the convocation of a general junta, and it met in August, 1808. Here the ayuntamiento pressed for the organization of a provisional government with popular sovereignty (under Ferdinand in prison) but the audiencia was able to defeat the proposal, as the Spaniards feared the American Spaniards, the Indians, and the idea of popular control in any form. As a matter of fact, so far as externals were concerned, the audiencia had much the best of the argument.

The viceroy's private ambitions led him to believe that espousal of the popular side would bring the most complete success for him. He therefore clutched at superior control, declared that all officers should continue as formerly, and, when representatives of the Junta of Seville, then supreme in the unconquered part of Spain, came to seek allegiance and assistance, he discouraged recognizing them. The Spanish element in a second general junta which the viceroy called succeeded in forcing a vote to acknowledge the Seville Junta in war and treasury affairs. But they were now convinced that Iturrigaray was an extreme separatist; they were disgusted with his apings of royalty, angered at his bids for popularity, and determined to get rid of him. On September 15, a group of Spaniards, led by Yermo, surprised the viceroy in his palace at night, put him in prison, and named in his place an old general, Pedro de Garibay.

Garibay was the nominal head of the viceroyalty only until July 19, 1809. He was put into the position without any official Peninsular sanction, of course, by the Spanish

party in the hope that the removal of Iturrigaray and his
subsequent banishment would check the popular movement.
The creoles, desiring the power exercised by the people of
Spain, entered into a conflict with the Spaniards which was
embittered by three centuries of political and social repression. Poor old Garibay, seventy-nine years of age, was no
match for the situation. He had come to new Spain in 1764
with General Villalba when Charles III began to form a
militia. He had only a military experience, knew nothing
of civil administration, was a complaisant, easy going old
gentleman, and was beginning to show signs of decrepitude!
These were the real reasons why the audiencia, which exercised the genuine power, had chosen him.

He began his rule by requesting all subjects who were
loyal to Ferdinand to wear a badge declaring their adhesion
to the monarch. The next step was the reorganization of the
army and the withdrawal from Jalapa of detachments
stationed there, for it was feared they might be used to
isolate the viceroyal government in the event that the independence party would take the field and win them over.
Revolutionary ideas were indeed growing rapidly. The
Spaniards, by the coup in which they seized the power and
set up Garibay, had reduced the respect in which the viceroyal person and office had been held; they had given the
creoles a good object lesson. Following the methods of the
French Revolutionists, the radical party began to organize
secret societies. The Caballeros Racionales, or Rational
Gentlemen, formed dissident bodies at Vera Cruz, Jalapa,
and in the capital. They had proven successful in influencing
Iturrigaray by flattery while he was viceroy, and they hoped
for similar operations with Garibay. The emissaries of
Napoleon were in the country, endeavoring to distract the
loyalty of the people. There began a campaign of boyish
tricks; people posted lampoons and pasquinades on public
walls; the face of the sovereign on coins was mutilated;
seditious papers were circulated, and no one could be caught
to be punished. The news of defeats to the juntas of Spain
brought joy to the hearts of the Mexicans, who turned deaf

ears on the viceroy's appeals to them for moral and financial support for the juntas.

The once great Spanish nation was indeed in a sorry plight. In New Spain there was such confusion of political thought that there was little surprise when an Aztec proposed that he be recognized as heir of Moctezuma and king of New Spain. From Brazil the sister of the imprisoned Spanish king wrote to the audiencia of Mexico urging that her young son Dom Pedro should be recognized as lieutenant of the king of Spain in Mexico. To this motherly solicitude the judges were only formally polite, without giving encouragement. Then the Junta Central in Spain wrote that Napoleon was planning to send Charles IV to rule in New Spain in the same way as the king of Portugal had gone to Brazil. Garibay ordered that he should not be permitted to land, but no attempt was made to send him.

The old viceroy was so decrepit mentally that his Spanish supporters repented their choice of him. He did not even make a good figurehead. The judges of the audiencia feared to designate a successor, so the Junta Central of Spain, which had been recognized as supreme by New Spain in March, 1809, was appealed to. That body followed the traditional policy of the old monarchy by naming the archbishop of Mexico.

Francisco Xavier de Lizana y Beaumont (July 1809 to May 1810) proved as unsatisfactory to the loyalists as had Garibay. He soon began to favor the creole party, let himself be influenced by the Caballeros Racionales, and in many ways supported the independence party unwittingly. At the same time he was zealous in getting funds to send to Spain to fight the usurper. He continued in power an obnoxious court, called the junta de seguridad, or Committee of Safety, which Garibay had organized to try persons charged with sedition or insurrection. So active were its members, and so bitter was the creole feeling against them, that plans began to be laid in the capital to circumvent their efforts.

While this was going on in the capital, the provincial

city of Valladolid (now Morelia) was the scene of revolt with separatist intention. The revolt was led by José María Obesa and Fray Vicente de Santa María. They planned to carry the whole intendancy of Guanajuato with them into open rebellion. The movement was to begin in December, 1809; it was expected that the Indians would rise to the number of eighteen or twenty thousand, provided they be freed from the tribute, which was contemplated. Unfortunately for the conspirators, one of their number disclosed his knowledge of the plan to the intendant, who began to scatter punishments with a vigorous hand until stayed by the viceroy, who attached little importance to the actual conspiracy, but feared the popular effect of reprisals. The Valladolid revolt was the beginning of armed resistance to Spanish sovereignty in New Spain. Only nine months later, in the same intendancy of Guanajuato, the cry of liberty was to be raised at the little village of Dolores by a radical parish priest, Father Miguel Hidalgo.

Meantime in Spain things were going badly for the loyalists. They had been assisted by the campaign of the Duke of Wellington, but when the British army retired into Portugal, the French forces began to defeat the Spanish patriots. The Junta Central, which had sat first at Aranjuez and then at Seville in 1809, had to flee at last to the Island of León in the Bay of Cádiz. The popular government was now crowded entirely off the mainland. It had become so unpopular that its members determined to resign, which they did on January 29, 1810, after having created a Regency of five men to carry on. The Regency voted to convoke the ancient Spanish Cortes, which had long been in abeyance.

In the condition in which Spain then was, it was extremely difficult to convoke this old popular assembly, but after many delays it finally met, its notable characteristic being that the American colonies were represented in it, though inadequately both as regards number and quality of delegates. The struggle of the Spaniards against a foreign usurper had almost taught them to recognize the equality with the Peninsula of the overseas colonies. On January 22,

1809, the Junta Central had in principle recognized the American possessions as integral parts of the Spanish nation. Representation. of the colonies in the Cortes was grudgingly provided for. Each viceroy and independent governor was to be allowed to choose one representative for each government in Spanish America. This plan would have provided so scant representation that the number was raised to twenty-eight, to admit one representative from each district instead of each "government." But many of the twenty-eight permissible delegates were never elected. Most of those who were chosen never went, being afraid of the dangerous sea voyage or the political hazard. Finally, New Spain was represented by seven substitutes chosen because they were Mexicans living in Spain at the time. They met with the Cortes on the Island of León on September 24, 1810. There they joined in presenting to that body a statement of the grievances of the American colonies. If these grievances had been liberally considered and removed, a basis might have been formed for holding the empire together a little longer, but the time was not ripe for such action.

Meantime, Spanish authority and ideas of loyalty to a headless kingdom were beginning to wane in New Spain. The endless process of sending millions of pesos to fight the ever victorious French was having a wearing effect. The merchants, who were standing the chief strain of these contributions, begged for a change in government. The Junta Central decided to try another old monarchical device, and gave the audiencia of Mexico control of affairs. But the regente, Catani, was continually at loggerheads with the senior judge, Aguirre, so that there was stagnation in administration. A general feeling of dissatisfaction was augmented by the skimpy representation allotted to Mexico in the imperial Cortes. To mend matters, the Junta Central now sent out another viceroy, Francisco Xavier Venegas (September, 1810 to March, 1813).

He was no better than his recent makeshift predecessors. His first important act was to summon for consultation the

several civil and military bodies which existed in the capital.
To them assembled he read a statement of the condition of
affairs in Spain, adding the usual appeal for funds to fight
the Napoleonic usurper. He then committed a faux pas
which showed that though a Spaniard, he had faint appreciation of the Spanish temperament. He finished his appeal
for money by announcing a list of newly created titles of
nobility. It included, of course, many persons who had
assisted in deposing Iturrigaray. This naturally offended
many Mexicans who inferred that the Peninsulars thought
loyalty could be purchased and others who felt that Iturrigaray should not have been deposed. The result was that
the new viceroy's overtures, instead of assisting to weld the
popular parties in both hemispheres, drove the Mexicans in
large numbers to join the insurrectionary movement then
already in the field under Hidalgo, the priest of Dolores.

CHAPTER XII

"EL GRITO DE DOLORES"

MEXICO owes her first genuine flame-burst of independence to the group of creole conspirators who operated in the center of the country after the failure of the movement at Valladolid. In the same intendancy of Guanajuato, at Querétaro, meetings of a revolutionary group were held during 1810 for the purpose of planning measures of rebellion. The leading spirit in this group was the parish priest of the village of Dolores, Father Miguel Hidalgo y Costilla.

This man was born May 8, 1753, of a respectable creole family. In 1770 he received the bachelor's degree from the University of Mexico. Returning to his native Valladolid, he lectured for a time in the College of San Nicolás on philosophy and theology. He was ordained to the priesthood in 1778, and later became rector of the college. It is possibly no mere coincidence that the first hero of Mexican independence should come out of Valladolid. There in 1767 had burst a preliminary flame of insubordination among the Indians, led by the native Indian governor of Pátzcuaro, Pedro de Soria Villaroel, also known as Armola. When José de Gálvez was making his provincial tour in that year, over four hundred Indians were imprisoned for following Soria in a movement for independence which comprised the inhabitants of one hundred and thirteen Indian villages. Of the Indians caught, Gálvez condemned three to death, including Pedro de Soria. Their heads were set on pikes over their homes. Twenty-four others received two hundred stripes each, twenty were imprisoned for life, and twenty-nine were banished. The young student Hidalgo, then fourteen or fifteen years of age, must have been profoundly impressed by this efficiently bloodthirsty reprisal, even

THE IDEALIZED HIDALGO. THE SPIRIT OF 1810

though he may not have been an eyewitness of it. So also may Morelos, likewise a native of this region, though at the time a mere child in arms, have gathered some early impression of the ruthlessness of this sample of Spanish repression of his fellow countrymen, a sample of a form of retribution too commonly enforced throughout the days of the viceroyal régime. More recently, the unsuccessful attempt at rebellion in this city mentioned previously, had had its widening effect on the minds of all the inhabitants.

Hidalgo had served in numerous parochial charges after filling the rectorship of San Nicolás. In 1785 he was priest at Colima, and in 1793 he held the same position at San Felipe. But he left parochial duties in 1800, having fallen under the suspicion of the Inquisition, before the court of which he was accused of heretical teachings. It was alleged that he was guilty of gambling and profligacy; worse, he had read prohibited books, from which he had taught Jansenist doctrines. He had become imbued with the ideals of the French Revolution—was an "afrancesado." This early case against him had been dismissed because of lack of dependable evidence, but the testimony against him was preserved and later used, as will appear.

In 1803, his brother, who was parish priest at Dolores, died, and Miguel received the very desirable living. There he was able to make a beginning of labors for the social and economic uplift of the natives, in which he was deeply interested. He taught his parishioners to engage in the outlawed silk industry, and had them plant the forbidden vine and olive tree, which Spain reserved as a Peninsular monopoly. Naturally he gained a great ascendancy over the simple country people by his disinterested love and fatherly advice. Of his political ideas they probably had very scant knowledge.

In 1805 he paid a visit to Mexico, where he began to hear of the political difficulties in which the viceroy Iturrigaray was already becoming involved over the expropriations of church lands under royal orders issued in 1804. There also his activity in the silk and wine industries became known, and the civil authorities sent agents to root out his trees and vines. The Inquisition reopened its case against him for teaching heresies. In 1807 and again in 1809 witnesses appeared against him, but the once famous tribunal was no longer powerful, and his case was not pressed. Its records show that he was during those years profoundly influenced by French thought. He was forever discussing matters of the faith which had long been considered as settled. He had the reputation of being a very liberal, unorthodox man and priest.

His associates were of like liberal tendencies. Liberalism throve better in provincial cities, among the creoles, than it did among the official Spanish class in the capital. The desire for equal political and economic rights was growing among the creoles, who found but limited opportunity in the professions of the law, the church, and the army. Probably four-fifths of the native clergy were independentists; they saw and were exasperated at the privileges of the Spaniards, especially of those who held the higher and better paid positions in the church.

The licentiate Primo Verdad, syndic of the ayuntamiento of Mexico, proto-martyr of independence, who was chained in a dungeon and left to die alone of starvation, was the typical creole lawyer of the separatists. Ignacio Allende, later companion in arms of Hidalgo, was of the military type of revolutionist. He is reputed to have been the organizer of that *literary and social* club in Querétaro which became the center of the independence conspiracy. This group included the corregidor of Querétaro, Miguel Domínguez, and his wife, Josefa María Ortiz. Other members were the licentiate Parra, at whose home the society often met, Altamirano, Laso, Dr. Iturriaga, Captain Juan Aldama of the Queen's Regiment, and Captain Joaquín Arias of the Regiment of Celaya. With this group, through Captain Allende, Hidalgo was in communication at the time of the fall of Iturrigaray. He joined the literary society shortly after in 1808, and thereafter was its leading spirit.

The general plan of the conspiracy of Querétaro was to seize the Spaniards of the important towns of the intendancy of Guanajuato, and then raise the banner of independence. It was not intended to do them unnecessary violence, but their property was to be confiscated to form a public treasury. If resistance appeared, Allende was to be generalissimo of the military forces. A government composed of a senate representing the provinces and ruling in the name of King Ferdinand was to be selected. Having planned thus far, the society then set to work to enlist the support of neighboring towns, naming December 8 as the time for the uprising, which was to take place in the midst of the great annual fair at San Juan de los Lagos.

But the plot became known to the Spanish authorities as early as August 11. A postal clerk, Mariano Galván, told of it to his superior, who reported it to the oidor Aguirre in Mexico. Hidalgo himself made efforts to win over the infantry battalion stationed at Guanajuato, and its officers betrayed the project to their superiors. The government remained strangely inactive in the face of this information; the authorities merely watched and waited, though Captain Arias of Querétaro also turned traitor to the literary society, and Dr. Iturriaga, at the door of death, divulged the plan in his last confession. Finally the corregidor, Domínguez, was forced on September 13, to arrest one Epigmenio González at Querétaro, in whose house the literary society had stored a large quantity of arms and ammunition prepared at its sessions. Doña Josefa gave warning to Captain Allende of the arrest of González, but very promptly she and the corregidor were placed in confinement, though they were soon set at liberty, Aguirre and his associates contemptuously refusing to attach importance to the plot or the connection of the corregidor with it.

As soon as Allende was apprised of these arrests, he sped at once to Hidalgo at Dolores with the news, in a long ride on the night of September 15 which had something of the elements of Paul Revere's midnight excursion in it. Waking the priest, he told the story of the imminent danger confronting the conspiracy. The answer of Hidalgo was prompt and decisive: "Action must be taken at once, there is no time to be lost; we shall yet see the oppressor's yoke broken, and the fragments scattered on the ground."

The news of impending crisis spread rapidly. Hidalgo summoned the workmen of a little porcelain factory of his; with a few followers they went and arrested the Spanish priest, Father Bustamante, and the Spanish sacristan. Then the venerable Hidalgo raised the battle cry of Dolores: "Viva Nuestra Señora de Guadalupe, viva la Independencia;" Long live Our Lady of Guadalupe; long live Independence. The little band of his followers, some sixteen or twenty persons all told, then set out for the jail, where they set the prisoners free. About dawn of September 16 Hidalgo rang the bell of the little church to announce the new movement. Every year now the scenes of this night are celebrated throughout the Republic. At the capital the President sounds the tocsin of liberty while the assembled multitude in the Zócalo launches the battle cry of freedom.

That battle cry, invoking the Virgin of Guadalupe, patroness of the Indian population, unfortunately made its appeal to the worst spirit of racial hatred. Through it the hatred of six million Americans was launched against some sixty thousand Spanish oppressors. Through it, Hidalgo rapidly gathered about him a rabble of some four thousand Indians. With them he at once took up the march to San Miguel, twenty miles away, to procure a royal store of arms and ammunition. On the road, as they were foraging, they stopped at Atotonilco, where they seized a banner of the Virgin of Guadalupe and immediately adopted it as the emblem of the new crusade. Arrived at San Miguel they were there joined by Allende's regiment. Here, after a near quarrel with Allende for the military preference, Hidalgo was chosen commander, and on the eighteenth of September the rebel horde set out for its new objective, the strategic town of Celaya. That point was easily taken, but the patriot hosts, increased by hope of booty to the number of 50,000 Indians, were ill restrained from pillaging the place.

It was here decided that the next move should be made against the capital of the intendancy, Guanajuato, as a

preliminary to advancing against the central government
at Mexico City. This meant a march of fifty miles to the
northwest. On September 28 Hidalgo sent to the intendant,
Riaño, a demand for the immediate surrender of the city,
with a promise of humane treatment to all. The Spanish
official, knowing better than to confide in a promise impossible to keep, answered declaring his determination to defend
the city to the last. He gathered the Spanish population
into a great stone building, the public granary, called there
the Alhóndiga de Granaditas. In that stronghold he believed he could hold out for a week if need be, until help
could come from Mexico under General Calleja.

The Alhóndiga was a good fortress, but it was surrounded
by near hills, from which the insurgents invested it. Early
in the fighting the intendant was shot to death, and while
his subordinates quarreled over which of them should succeed to the command the mob outside set fire to the wooden
door. Gaining entrance, Hidalgo's Indians killed all the
Spaniards, even those who had surrendered. They then
seized five million pesos which Riaño had brought thither
for safety, and burst forth to spread throughout the city,
sacking and burning and murdering as they went. For four
hours the fury went on unchecked. The penalties for
barbarity which Hidalgo and Allende attempted to impose
had no effect until the lust for blood was ended, and over six
hundred of the inhabitants had been butchered. Among the
attacking forces fully two thousand Indians lost their lives,
besides casualties among the regular rebel soldiery.

On the following day, Hidalgo set about establishing an
insurrectionary government. The town council was reorganized, being constituted of creoles who favored the
cause of independence. A mint was started for coining
money, and a foundry, which proved ineffective, was inaugurated for the purpose of supplying the revolutionists
with much needed cannon. A feeble attempt was made to
begin military instruction and enforce discipline. The great
movement for independence had begun, but its leaders were
ignorant of their own purposes or the most effective methods

of securing them. The guiding spirit was not trained in military affairs or statecraft, and the force in the field was animated by no constructive ideal. Its aim was lust and destruction. This was the beginning of a struggle that was to continue with varying fortunes for a period of ten years.

The disaster at Guanajuato finally convinced the new viceroy Venegas that the danger to Spanish domination, which had been so repeatedly threatened throughout colonial history and so often reasserted without serious menace, was now real and definite. New Spain was ill-prepared to cope with such an insurrection. Under Iturrigaray the native army had been widely scattered; there were no Spanish troops in the country. As the revolution proceeded Spanish regiments were brought over, but on the whole the conflict was between Mexicans who found their place on one side or the other. The loyal army was composed largely of mestizos officered by creoles. The revolutionists numbered many of the same social groups, but their fighting force was more largely Indian than was the loyal army. Venegas at once sent troops to hold Querétaro, San Luis Potosí, and other northern towns, while the capital was fortified and garrisoned. Rewards were offered for the heads of Hidalgo, Allende, and Aldama, and they were excommunicated, while the old case before the Inquisition against the cura of Dolores was once more revived. These means kept the capital and other large cities loyal, for in general the creoles and mestizos, as well as the Spaniards, knew that they had reason to fear the vindictive hatred of Hidalgo's Indian followers.

In the meantime Hidalgo had easily taken Guadalajara, where he continued to work for the construction of an independent government. He issued a call for the organization of a congress to pass laws for the insurgent districts. He proclaimed the emancipation of slaves, and announced the cessation of the hated tribute tax, a move imitated by the viceroyal government in an attempt to reduce Hidalgo's hold on the lower classes. He ordered the restoration of their lands to the Indians of the intendancy of Guanajuato, organized a provincial government, and appointed municipal alcaldes and other officers. For himself he assumed the modest title of "Captain-general of America," and called upon the populace to support him. Many creoles declined, preferring to remain "loyal to Ferdinand VII," though no action against that much overrated royal prisoner had been proposed.

Hidalgo knew that the viceroy's forces under General Calleja were gathering at San Luis Potosí and Querétaro, so he left Guadalajara and moved to Valladolid, taking it without resistance, though the church faction was hostile. Here discipline was enforced upon the Indians, some military training was given them, and, with 200,000 pesos of private funds, a march upon Mexico City was planned with the largest insurrectionary force yet gathered. It now numbered 80,000 men. Their march was intercepted near Toluca by General Trujillo, commanding a trained army of 7000 men. At a hill called the Monte de las Cruces, from the crosses there set to commemorate many previous violent deaths, Trujillo found himself surrounded and nearly defeated. Being hard pressed, he called for a parley. Three conferences were successively held before Trujillo thought he had the insurgents in a disadvantageous position. Deeming his opportunity come, he suddenly violated the truce, and turned his guns upon the enemy. Surrounded again, and obliged to cut his way back to Mexico, harassed by avenging pursuers, he claimed to have won a great victory. Hidalgo's forces retained the field, though at severe cost. Allende urged an immediate descent upon the capital; Hidalgo opposed. Over this issue began a quarrel between the two which continued to the end. Allende was piqued that his military training did not meet with deference from the inspirational but inexperienced priest.

A rapid movement at this time upon Mexico might have ended the revolution, though it would have meant certain massacre in the city. The viceroy was frightened enough to plan flight to Vera Cruz, but delayed. On November first Hidalgo sent commissioners to treat with Venegas, but the latter ordered them out of the city on pain of being shot as traitors. Hidalgo was in a difficult position. His troops of 80,000 men were really a small proportion of a total population of six million people. His army was ill disciplined, his best military leader was Allende. He knew Calleja was coming southward from San Luis Potosí, and, fearing to be caught between two hostile armies, planned to move away toward Querétaro, which he thought he could hold.

The defense of the loyal interests was practically in the hands of General Calleja. He raised an army of seven thousand men, with which he intercepted the patriot forces at Aculco. Aldama and Allende had grown fiercely jealous of the military power confided in their idealistic priestly leader, who was now being deserted, in the traditional fashion, by the rabble which had been drawn to the expectant cause by the prospect of looting Mexico City. The moment having arrived when the opposing forces were about to confront each other, the revolutionists made a slight feint to cover an inevitable retreat, in which they lost all their cannon, ammunition, and a quantity of supplies. Calleja reported a wonderful victory, asseverating that he had pursued and slain hundreds of the rebels. It was thought in the capital that he had ended the insurrectionary movement. He had indeed driven Hidalgo's forces to Celaya and saved Querétaro.

But revolt lived in many guerrilla bands from San Luis Potosí to the Pacific shores. While Allende led the patriot army to Guanajuato, Hidalgo repaired to Valladolid to manufacture arms and raise new troops. Nueva Galicia was rebel country, in which Torres and Mercado seized San Blas and Guadalajara. In the latter place Hidalgo again made his base. Zacatecas and San Luis Potosí were also insurrectionary. In the south Morelos was beginning to meet small successes. But Allende, who had entered Guanajuato on November 13, was dislodged on the twenty-third, and Calleja's forces indulged in a retributive massacre of creoles and mestizos because they had killed some of the prisoners which Hidalgo had left there. After this butchery, Calleja reorganized the province upon a loyalist basis.

He then proceeded to move against the insurrectionists at Guadalajara. There Hidalgo was extremely popular. He had been joined by a number of patriots who assisted him to organize a government. He appointed a minister of grace and justice, José María Chico, and named for his secretary-general another prominent fighter, Ignacio López Rayón, of whom we shall hear again. It was also planned to establish a national government with the reorganization of the royal audiencia upon a native American basis. An emissary to the United States was appointed in the person of Pascasio Ortiz de Letona, who was instructed to arrange a treaty of alliance and commerce, but he was captured on his way to Vera Cruz and poisoned himself to avoid the terrible death which he knew awaited him.

In military preparation for the coming struggle with Calleja, Hidalgo transported forty-four cannon from San Blas, and manufactured hand-grenades and rockets, for small arms were very scarce. His adherents meantime were adding Sonora and Sinaloa to the patriot area, though that gain was only temporary. Nuevo Santander and Coahuila were also added to the revolutionary territory. Even Texas declared for independence in January 1811.

Meantime Allende had in December again joined Hidalgo at Guadalajara. The army, now once more at its maximum number of 80,000, was gradually improved by discipline, by supplies of hand grenades, and by elimination of hangers on. When it seemed as though success might come to the defenders of the city, a deplorable conflict of opinion came up again between Hidalgo and Allende. The former believed that all the troops available should be used at one stroke against Calleja when he should arrive, while the latter held that the proper method would be to depend upon successive waves of attack by detachments. Hidalgo won his point, and the entire patriot forces moved out of Guadalajara to meet the approaching Calleja, who was leading only 6000 troops, but well disciplined ones, to retake the city.

The opposing forces met on the banks of the Lerma at the Puente de Calderón, some twelve leagues outside the city. On January 17, 1811, the fighting commenced. The royalist troops were all but defeated, when a strange occurrence turned the tide of battle. A Spanish bomb exploded a patriot ammunition wagon, and the flames spread to the dry grass of the field which constituted Hidalgo's position. The patriots were stampeded by the smoke and flames, and fled precipitately, making their way toward Zacatecas, pursued by the victorious royalists. Six hours' fighting had decided the whole issue of the Hidalgo movement.

While on the retreat toward Zacatecas, the insurgent officers compelled Hidalgo to surrender his military control to Allende. Henceforth, though his magnetic character was useful in holding adherents, his voice was not heard in military councils, and he was treated practically as a prisoner. Nevertheless he continued loyal to the cause he had originated. Perhaps no other course was open to him. And yet he was a superb loser.

Allende's decision was to continue the retreat beyond Zacatecas, which was threatened by Calleja, to Saltillo. As he pressed northward with only some 5000 men, the royalists rapidly occupied Zacatecas and San Luis Potosí. Farther northward, thought the insurgents, lay rebellious provinces, and beyond them the United States, friend of freedom and home of revolution. There help would surely be found. But Ignacio Aldama and Father Juan Salazar, sent to Texas in advance for help, found there a counter-revolution in full swing. They were caught, taken to Monclova, and shot.

Meanwhile the fleeing rebels were working across Coahuila northward. Now came the opportunity for treachery. A creole lieutenant-colonel, Ignacio Elizondo, disgruntled because he had not been given the preferment in rank which he craved, now turned traitor to the revolution and deserted it. Allende was at Saltillo with the forces, expecting to move on to Texas. Elizondo determined to intercept and capture them at the wells called Acatita de Baján, at which they were due to arrive on February 21. Allende had no suspicion of treachery, and his forces were straggling badly. As they came up to the wells, the successive groups of insurgents fell into Elizondo's hands with almost no resistance. After Hidalgo himself was taken, a short engagement dissolved the remainder of the straggling forces.

The cura, Allende, Jiménez, and several others, were sent for military trial to Chihuahua, which was the capital of the comandancia general in which the treacherous capture had occurred. The march to Chihuahua was over two hundred miles of desert, with its attendant hardships. At that city Allende, Jiménez, and some others were shot in the back as traitors, sentenced by a military tribunal. Hidalgo, being a priest, had to endure more tedious formalities. First he had to be degraded from the priesthood and then given over to the secular law. On July 31 he was led forth to meet the firing squad. Courageous, thoughtful, he forgave his executioners, distributed sweetmeats to the soldiers, asked them to aim at his heart, and waited. After two volleys and a coup de grace the great spirit of the revolution went to its Maker. The heads of Hidalgo, Allende, Jiménez, and Aldama were hung in iron cages at the corners of the Alhóndiga de Granaditas at Guanajuato to warn rebels of their proper expectation at the hands of Spain.

The rebellion led by these men might have succeeded under better military leadership than Hidalgo's but it had flashed into being because of the personal influence and aspiration of that man alone. True, he had raised and used a mob which was incited by lust and vengeance. He had failed to prevent murder of many Spaniards; he had, among his military indiscretions, been vacillating and indecisive in action; he had depended on undrilled troops and had rejected the best military advice available. Morally he was not a very good man, judged even by the standard of his times. But those times had afforded him many bloody examples, many vicious comparisons. His generation smarted under an accumulated tradition of abuse and grievance at a time when political ideals were changing all over the European world. That generation produced no greater or more constructive program than his. To it he gave his services unselfishly when the time for action came. and he suffered serenely at the end, when "the last full measure of devotion" was exacted.

Mexican historians have not indulged in over-fulsome praise of Hidalgo or his movement. Dr. Mora, Lorenzo Zavala, and of course the pro-Spanish Lucas Alamán, all condemned him, the latter most severely, for having instigated a bloody racial conflict without any plan or object of constructive character. If the plotters of Querétaro had remained undiscovered a little longer, and had enlisted the better classes, who were ripening for revolt, success might have been attained.

Undoubtedly the creoles in Mexico City planned to call Ferdinand or some other Bourbon to a throne in New Spain. The patriots, Licentiate Verdad and Father Melchor Talamantes, early martyrs of separatism, had in 1805 drawn up plans for social and political reorganization which included reforms in church and state of far-reaching import. They were thoroughly Roman Catholic and thoroughly monarchistic, even absolutist. Even though proposed by creoles, their movement met some encouragement from the stable class of society. The common opinion in the colony was that the Napoleonic movement in the Peninsula must surely win. That prospect was not very welcome to the clericals, for Napoleon in 1809 suppressed the Council of Castile, feudal rights, the Inquisition, and two-thirds of the convents. He was sure to impose upon Spain his concordat of 1802 with the pope whereby alienation of church lands was legalized and their private status after sale confirmed. The clergy of New Spain would preferably have joined with the creoles or the Indians rather than have accepted Napoleon's French revolutionary heresies.

The dominant merchant class had similar motives for desiring separation. They knew that Napoleon would probably destroy their monopolies by opening colonial ports to the commerce of France. Separation would serve to prevent this destruction of their special privileges. In 1810 the French were everywhere victorious in Spain, and it looked as though a few months more would see their complete triumph. With this prospect looming, the merchants and clericals, stout opponents of creole supremacy, but stouter protagonists of their own privileges, must soon have been forced to make common cause with the creole separatists. Hence it was more than a personal tragedy that the conspiracy in Querétaro was prematurely discovered and its members suddenly obliged to choose between the scaffold and open revolt. It was a most inopportune event.

The plan at that moment, and for some time afterward, was to surround the Bourbon prince, who should come to take the throne, with a new aristocracy composed entirely of creoles. If Spaniards cared to remain they were to be reduced to plebian status. It was the first principle of this, as of all social revolutions, that the ins should be put out, and the outs in. With their long theocratic and absolutist training, it is not surprising that the creoles should have had little desire for a revolution beyond this point, nor marvelous that they should have hesitated at frank enunciation of their aim. To have called upon the Indians to make a mere substitution of one master for another would have been the acme of political simplicity. Hence they directed their campaign merely against all Spaniards, saying that the whole remaining population was to be considered as no longer stratified according to the old formulæ, but that all were to be considered as simple free Americans, equal in political power and economic privilege. This would create adhesion to the cause of getting rid of king log; king stork must bide his time. In so far as opportunity came, as has already been pointed out, Hidalgo took occasion to organize governments and propose laws. It must be remembered that his control was of far too short duration for him to effect much in the way of a well modeled plan. Hidalgo was dead before the Spanish Constitution of 1812 was proclaimed in New Spain. That instrument marked a great forward stride in the Spanish American revolutions. After its enunciation had broken the shackles of royalty and conserva-

tism which bound the minds of the people, after their idealized king had become a mere dethroned mortal, a pawn in
the hands of the conqueror of Europe, they could talk about
independence, but not till then. The time for a declaration
of such a principle was not to come until Morelos, with his
Constitution of Apatzingán, could declare that Mexico
should be free and independent. Hidalgo's movement is
not to be blamed for the omission. The Hidalgo plan,
published in Valladolid in December 1810, proves that he
sought not mere popular vengeance, anarchy, but that he
wanted to create a strong government.

The bloodthirsty character of Hidalgo's movement has
also frequently been pointed out and execrated. But if he
had adhered strictly to the rules of "civilized warfare,"
what would have been the result? In the first place, civilized warfare is a myth today. Countless instances prior to
the European cataclysm prove it. Respect for private
property had never been so strong under the Spanish legal
system as it is under Teutonic conceptions. With the autocratic system developed under the Hapsburgs and Bourbons, tenure of property was essentially based on royal
favor, on privilege, rather than on sacred contractual rights.
Confiscations at the royal behest were of frequent occurrence.
Grants of land were institutionally designated as favors—
mercedes. Hence spoliation of acquired rights has never
created the social shock in Spanish American countries which
it causes in English American communities. Moreover, it
was the very unevenness of the distribution of property
which gave the greatest animus to the insurrectionary
movement. Removal of the Spaniards from their position of
economic superiority was the immediate spring to action.
Little wonder that the despoiled Indian, his long-suppressed
mestizo half-brother, and the ambitious creole, should strike
blindly and unreasonably at the institution which synthe-
sized and cemented their inferiority. If the revolutionists
had respected Spanish property rights there would have been
no revolution.

The independentists necessarily depended upon guerrilla

warfare for success. There were several disciplined regiments which espoused the revolution, it is true; but they had no opportunity to import or manufacture suitable arms, they had scant number of leaders, and they had no easy way of sending money out of the country to purchase munitions. Guerrilla warfare meant lack of central authority, lack of discipline, lack of coördination in movements, lack of knowledge of what had been gained or lost. Furthermore the warfare waged against them was carried on very largely by native Mexican troops. These troops were, in conformity with long tradition, guilty of fierce retributive punishments inflicted upon the rebels. Quarter in battle and respect for the lives of captured enemies were not characteristics of the form of warfare waged by the viceroy's forces. It would have been absurd to expect the insurgents to wage more humane warfare than their opponents under the circumstances. The war was needlessly cruel, bloodthirsty, and relentlessly bitter on both sides, but very little blame can be attached to the name of Hidalgo for that reason. "Mueran los gachupines"—Death to Spaniards— was a battle cry which sprang from a social situation, not from the bigotry of one single patriot leader.

Hidalgo himself was at the head of the revolution only four short months, from the night of the Grito until the defeat at the Puente de Calderón. During that time he was not guilty of a proved act of incendiarism, nor were crimes against women committed by him or his military associates. Cases of sacking of towns were exceedingly rare. Plunder of haciendas of stock and foodstuffs was of course habitual, and theft of money and valuables was held legitimate warfare. But neither extortion nor forced loans were indulged in.

Popular esteem for Hidalgo fluctuated with his military successes. He was naturally blamed for the failures of Aldama and Allende, but for these posterity readily forgives him. The most serious charge brought against him is that after his capture he retracted his insurrectionary policy, and craved forgiveness from the government. Mexican writers differ radically on the question whether the written **retraction** attributed to Hidalgo is genuine or not, but the truth seems to be that in the final hour Hidalgo weakened and abjured the Revolution, admonishing his old companions to submit to Spain. The advice carried very little weight.

CHAPTER XIII

THE EPOCH OF MORELOS

THE executions of the insurgent leaders and some thirty of their companions in arms by no means stopped the independence movement. It was merely left for a time headless. But some one has well said, "Revolutions never go backward." This one, with Hidalgo the soul of it gone, now assumed a new form and character. Instead of an Indian insurrection against Spanish overlords, it became a military struggle for freedom. There was no revolutionary government for a time, and no recognized head of operations. Just before Allende had set out toward the United States on his last march he had issued orders to Ignacio López Rayón at Saltillo to lead forces into the center of the country, but Allende was of course not expecting arrest and execution, and his commission to Rayón did not contemplate the latter's assumption of the supreme command. Nor did Rayón's companions in arms choose to consider him their leader until his superior military skill caused him to emerge for a time as the most commanding figure.

In each of the insurrectionary provinces local commanders acted independently under prevailing handicaps of scant funds and uncoördinated plans. Hence the gains that were made were often only temporary and without ultimate objective. Far too often, indeed, the revolutionists were mere bandits and criminals, making use of the disturbed condition of the interior of the country to further their own rapacious ends. Even so, at the end of 1811, they held the rural parts of the provinces of Guanajuato, Jalisco, Michoacán, and Zacatecas, and large parts of Puebla, Vera Cruz, San Luis Potosí, and Mexico. They fought by guerrilla methods, which gave them a marked

advantage over the formally organized and well armed
government troops. The latter were able, through organization and abundant supplies, to hold all the important cities of the interior, and, what was more important,
to keep control of the seaports. This of course prevented
insurgent contact with the other revolted parts of Spanish
America or possible foreign encouragement.

Ignacio López Rayón, who had had merely a legal instead
of a military training, obeyed the orders given him by
Allende with notable brilliancy. He fought a successful
engagement with enemy forces at the pass of Piñones,
and surprised the royalists by retaking Zacatecas, which
they thought was sufficiently well garrisoned to prevent
such a contretemps. The Spaniards were surprised to see
that a mere attorney could perform such a feat, and after
it maintain the most rigid discipline, protecting Spanish
lives and property in that ancient mining town. Finally
obliged to abandon this point, Rayón proceeded southward to Zitácuaro, on the edge of the tierra caliente in
Michoacán, where he fortified himself in a remarkable
series of defensive works which excited great admiration.
He ran a moat around the entire town, by means of which
he obtained a water supply and could at the same time
flood all approaches to his positions. Behind the moat
he built a double stockade, and inside an artillery foundry.

Here also he began the organization of a new revolutionary
government, installing a body with the resounding title of
the "National Supreme Junta of America for the conser-
vation of the rights of Ferdinand VII, the defense of holy
religion, and the indemnification and liberty of our op-
pressed fatherland." The Junta was chosen by the principal landowners and inhabitants of Zitácuaro, under the
best available semblance of an election. There were three
members of the Junta, the intention being to increase
the number to five later. Their chief function as announced
was to preserve the rights of the king and of the church.
Their program was thus decidedly reactionary, but it must
be remembered that there had yet been given no public

voice to the widespread desire for political separation from Spain, and certainly there was no desire anywhere to break connection with the Roman church. In accord with practically all shades of opinion in New Spain, this body was determined to prevent the viceroyalty from recognizing the Bonaparte rule.

The Junta failed in its purpose of uniting the insurgents under one banner because of internal quarrels, and because Morelos, the other prominent insurrectionist, held off from its domination, he being an out and out independentist. Perhaps his aloofness was due to the fact that the Zitácuaro movement had been from the start none of his own. Rayón stood merely for a National Junta, coördinate with the Spanish Peninsular body, for the cessation of appropriations to help the Spanish cause, and for other measures short of absolute separation.

But any insurgent government had to be put down by force, thought the viceroy. Hence he sent General Calleja against it. After numerous delays and subsidiary engagements, the chief royalist general invested Zitácuaro early in January of 1812. Rayón had had all sorts of difficulties with the National Junta, and worse ones with his subordinates. After a short resistance to Calleja's cannonading of his defenses, his forces were put to flight in disorder, and the Junta fled to Sultepec, where it established itself anew. Zitácuaro was sacked and burned and the inhabitants exiled. Though Rayón continued to serve the revolution, his military importance was never great again.

The outstanding figure of the revolution for the next four years was to be the priest José María Morelos y Pavón. He was a mestizo, born in 1765 near Apatzingán. The son of a carpenter, he had been in his youth a muleteer on the trails between Acapulco and Mexico City over which the silks of India brought on the galleons were carried to market. Educated in Hidalgo's College of San Nicolás at Valladolid, he had there been a servitor as late as his thirtieth year, after which he received holy orders. He attached himself to Hidalgo's forces near Valladolid shortly after the fall of Guanajuato, asking a chaplaincy. But he was persuaded to take a more militant share in the enterprise, and was sent to carry the revolution into his own southern coast country. To seize Acapulco was to be his chief object, for the insurgents had vital need of a seaport.

Like Hidalgo, Morelos began his career with only a handful, some twenty-five, it is said, of men. In October 1810 he began operations in Guerrero; when he captured Chilapa in the following August he had a force of fifteen hundred well armed and well disciplined men. His second campaign began in February, 1812, when he had gathered over three thousand followers and moved with them upon Cuautla, about fifty miles distant from Mexico City, upon which he planned to advance, as Hidalgo had done before him. His forces were here soon raised to five thousand.

The viceroyal general, Calleja, being determined to defeat this army, advanced upon it from the direction of Chalco, and began his attack on February 19, 1812. Being unsuccessful, he called a council of war, at which it was decided to besiege the town. The insurgents had to withstand bombardments, loss of water-supply, and finally blockade of all food supplies. When the royalists were also reduced by sickness, and proximity of the rainy season made them fear the further protraction of the enterprise, Calleja sent the starving insurgents a general pardon if they would lay down their arms.

Its apparent acceptance was only a ruse under which evacuation of the post began under cover of darkness in the early morning of May 2, 1812. Soon however, the movement was discovered by the enemy, and the quick loss of several hundred men led Morelos to order his followers to disperse. He himself, in flight, was overtaken and nearly captured near Zacatepec. The noncombatants of Cuautla were promiscuously butchered by Calleja's harrying troops. The victorious royalists returned to Mexico, and Morelos again to Cuautla to rehabilitate his forces. Shortly thereafter he began his third and most brilliant campaign. In August he made his headquarters at Tehuacán, where he planned to make expeditions into Oaxaca and against Orizaba and Vera Cruz on the coast while still remaining close to the capital and in position to attack it upon favorable opportunity.

While the immortal defense of Cuautla was in progress, some headway had been made in revolutionary affairs in Spain itself. It will be remembered that the Junta of Seville had been driven to the Island of León in 1809 where it had resigned the government into the hands of a Regency of five members, which in turn convoked a national Cortes which met at León September 24, 1810. In this Cortes seven Mexicans who were then residing in Spain sat as substitute representatives of New Spain.

The American delegates to the Cortes on December 16 presented to it for consideration the aspirations of the people of Spanish America, as they understood them. Their demands were made under eleven points. (1) They demanded equality with Spain in representation in the Cortes for the American realms, on a population basis. This the Cortes rejected, alleging fear of the Indian populations. (2) Their demand that agriculture, manufacturing, and the mechanical trades should be freed from all restrictions, was accepted without debate. But their proposals (3) that commerce should be absolutely free, whether carried in Spanish or foreign bottoms, (4) that free trade should be granted between America and Asia as well, and (5) that all restrictions of this kind should be immediately abolished, all brought forth the warmest discussion, as a result of which it was decided to take no action until the advice of the American commercial and governmental bodies could be ascertained. The pretension (6) that all government monopolies should be abolished, with compensation in special duties on all monopolized articles freed, was also postponed, the only lucrative monopoly then being that of tobacco. The suggestion (7) that the working of American quicksilver mines should be made free was adopted without debate, as was the proposal (8) that all Americans, whether Indian or white, were to be given the same political rights as Spaniards. But when it came to granting (9) that at least half the offices in the several kingdoms should be given to natives, postponement was again taken. The same action was taken upon the proposal (10) to create a nominating board to control the equitable distribution of political offices. The eleventh point, which called for the reëstablishment of the Jesuit order, was almost unanimously rejected; many of the American delegates themselves opposed it, though a generation earlier the marquis of Croix had said of the Jesuits, when they were expelled from all Spanish America, that they absolutely controlled the minds and hearts of the Mexican people.

Such were the aims with which the American delegates entered the Cortes which was on March 18, 1812, to enunciate the famous Spanish Constitution of that year, a constitution destined to become a model for most of the revolutionary countries of Europe which set themselves shortly to the undoing of the old powers of absolutism. The salient features of this new constitution may be briefly set forth. It declared: that the sovereignty should henceforth reside in the nation; that Catholicism should be the established religion; that the government should be an hereditary monarchy; that the powers of government should be segregated into functions legislative, executive, and judicial; that representation in the Cortes should be proportionate to population; that municipal offices should be no longer hereditary, but annually elective; that each province should have a chief appointed by the crown and advised by a council, which should control the municipalities; that freedom of the press should prevail.

If this constitution could have been promulgated two or three years earlier, it might have been more successful; but it was now behind the growing desires of the American revolutionists. Furthermore, the promulgation was issued in a niggardly spirit, and its provisions were only in operation a short time. After it reached New Spain it was discussed at length by Venegas the viceroy, his real acuerdo, and several corporate government bodies, and published by edict on September 28, 1812. It was hailed with joy by the people, who gladly took oath of allegiance to it in the hope that it would do away with the ancient despotism which had held the colony in its sway. Even mulattoes in the army, who were denied the boon of citizenship by the instrument, took the oath to obey it with apparent gratification. Following the promulgation, there became manifest a desire to make all things new in so far as nomenclature could effect desirable change. The old Plaza Mayor, or Zócalo, became the Plaza de la Constitución, the word "nacional" was substituted in names of buildings for the older word "real"—royal. Coats of arms of royalty on the façades of buildings were in many places destroyed. The jails were visited, and many prisoners, not including insurgents against the Spanish popular government, were set at liberty in an effusion of idealistic reconstruction.

These were the externals and accidentals of the change, but much had been done essentially as well. First, there had come a division of the civil and military power, until then vested in the viceroy alone. The audiencia, hitherto a council to the viceroy when sitting as the real acuerdo, became now merely a supreme court. The amazing network of special courts of privilege, such as the ecclesiastical courts, the consulados, the mesta, the protomedicato, the Acordada, the Inquisition, and others of like limited class application, were to go out of existence and be replaced by a system of justice in which all the subjects of the monarch were to be equal before the law. The provincial deputations were to assume larger functions, and the municipalities were to become living members of the political organism by grant of authority to elect their town councils. The ordinary courts of first instance were to replace the Junta de Seguridad, or Committee of Safety which the viceroyal government had created to check political dissidence, taking a leaf from the experience of the French Revolutionary Convention. But perhaps the most important change, certainly the one which brought the new régime into the most prompt and sharp disrepute among the conservatives, was the provision for freedom of the press. The plan of establishing elective town councils was likewise a measure which caused much apprehension among the ranks of the privileged.

Indeed, the viceroy was so fearful to give rein to the press that he delayed the proclamation whereby its full liberty was to be secured. All the authorities feared the measure, and opposed it successfully until its promulgation was forced upon the viceroy by Miguel Ramos Arizpe. This Coahuiltecan represented Mexico in the Cortes of León which framed the Constitution; he knew that the freedom of the press was being held back, and insisted that the measure be made known. It was proclaimed on October 5, 1812. The wisdom of the viceroy was shown by the immediate result. The new liberty was used as license, the press became an agency for promulgating revolutionary ideas and for insulting officials with an abandon of vituperation which could be of no benefit to anyone. Freedom of political expression was formally withdrawn just two months later, wisely enough as things were.

The effect of the new Constitution was quite the opposite of what might naturally have been expected. Instead of quelling revolution, it made royalist success quite impossible, because of the freedom of the press. Such trenchant writers as Fernández Lizardi, who styled himself El Pensador Mexicano (the Mexican Thinker) and published a periodical bearing the same name, launched criticisms of the government so violent in tone that the viceroy suspended the entire Constitution by executive decree. But the existence of the document and its temporary and partial enforcement had effected a complete change in the political organization of the Spanish empire. Now the colonies were political equals of Spain. They had acquired the rights of equality. These rights must be vouchsafed to them, otherwise political separation to vindicate them became politically logical. War to attain separation became the normal expectation. Hence, after the Constitution had been withdrawn it was only natural that Morelos should write, as he did, to Rayón on January 15, 1813, that no further proof was needed of the duplicity of Spain. On the other hand the Regency and the Cortes demanded that the Mexican rebels be defeated, as concessions enough had been made. Thus the liberal movement in Spain became antagonistic to the liberal party in New Spain.

There had been no suspension of hostilities between the viceroyal government and the insurgents. The royalist forces won successes in the interior, the insurgents in the east and south, but they had no great victories. Down in Oaxaca in the middle of 1812, Morelos relieved Huajuapán, which was holding out bravely under Trujano against a royalist siege. It was then that he established his base at Tehuacán, where he could command the road to the east coast and still be within striking distance of Mexico City as has been stated. His power to check commerce thus deprived the viceroy of the sinews of war, hence of power of initiative or resistance. Morelos was able to take Orizaba in October, then on November 25 he captured Oaxaca in his most brilliant engagement. Beginning his fourth campaign from that place on January 9, 1813, he set about the realization of his darling dream, the conquest of the port of Acapulco.

In February 1813, Venegas, who was old and infirm and weakwilled, and who had exasperated the Spanish element by many strenuous measures to raise funds for a war which had not been marked by successful results, was replaced as viceroy by his jealous enemy General Calleja. This leader had won successes, but was only moderately satisfactory to the Spaniards. As viceroy he had to resort to the unpopular forced loans which had destroyed his predecessor; he had to admit that he held only the chief towns and ports, while the countryside generally was insurgent. Morelos controlled southern Vera Cruz, Puebla, Oaxaca, Guerrero, the coast of the Gulf of Mexico north of Jalapa, the littoral of Michoacán, and Guanajuato. Many small leaders were acting independently in numerous localities, where they held the roads to the mines, cut off the royalist muletrains, and governed or misgoverned as opportunity and inclination indicated.

Most of these little leaders, acting without concerted plans, succumbed in turn before the successful movements of the new viceroy's forces. In this way, while Morelos was besieging Acapulco, which fell to him in April, 1813, Calleja succeeded in clearing the way for direct action against the most conspicuous and successful insurgent leader. The viceroy's cause was also aided by dissensions among the independentist group. The Junta, which Rayón had instituted, and which still survived in a prolonged attempt to control fighting men who paid it scant attention, had fallen into acute dissensions, and Morelos began to conceive the idea of controlling it to suit his own purposes. In this aim he was assisted by the fact that the three disagreeing members of the Junta each in turn appealed to him as the fourth member, to adjudicate their differences. He induced them to meet him in his own territory, at Chilpancingo, in September. There he revived the idea of drafting and proclaiming a constitution, for which purpose a congress would be necessary. This was no doubt a measure intended to counteract the effect of the re-promulgation of the Spanish Constitution of 1812 by viceroy Calleja early in the year. The Congress, installed on September 14, elected Morelos generalissimo with the powers of chief executive, and adopted a plan of organization which he had drafted. Under the control of Morelos the Congress assumed the legislative authority. No change was made in the judiciary, the courts in existence in insurgent territory not being molested.

One of the earliest and most important acts of the Congress was to issue a definitive declaration, on November 6, of independence from Spain and Ferdinand. It then adopted a number of the decrees of Morelos practically as a constitution. These decrees abolished all distinctions of race and color, including slavery and the tribute. Offices of church and state were declared open to everyone; debts to Europeans were declared cancelled as a confiscatory measure, and taxes were limited to excises, parochial fees, and tithes, all to bear equally on whites and reds without distinction. The Jesuits were to be restored for the sake of religious education. Half the population of each town was to be utilized in the warfare to achieve independence. This constitution or set of laws drawn at Chilpancingo was preliminary to the drafting of a republican constitution by the Congress, which sat in 1814 at the town of Apatzingán, from which place the instrument later derived its name.

During the remainder of the year 1813 several successes of the viceroy's armies reversed the situation which had confronted his government at its inception. In November Morelos undertook the recapture of Valladolid, but his forces were routed by Iturbide and fled to Puruarán, where they were again defeated. Matamoros, chief aide of Morelos, was captured and shot. This defeat marked the end of the military prestige of Morelos, and he soon gave up the supreme command. The Congress assumed control of the insurgent forces. Had it not been for a political reversal of form at this time in Spain, complete success might have attended the royalist program.

But the restoration of Ferdinand VII to the Spanish throne following a French defeat at Vitoria in 1813, and a promise of the English to leave Spain if he were restored, had brought about reaction. Ferdinand, enthroned in 1814, restored the old absolutism, softening the change by promising a new Cortes with American representation, then failing to keep the promise. His reactionary measures embittered the liberals, who now befriended the American insurgents in large numbers. Even certain members of the Spanish population of New Spain, notably at Vera Cruz, looked upon the changed political program with sullen disapproval. Ferdinand's restoration was only mildly celebrated in Mexico City on June 10.

During the preceding month the king, appreciating the unpopularity of his reactionary program, sought to propitiate public opinion by an apparent condescension to liberal ideals. He placed five creoles, mostly Mexicans, on the restored and reorganized Council of the Indies. The Indian population was relieved from paying tribute; this hated tax was becoming increasingly difficult to collect;

it had never produced royal income commensurate with the labor of collection and the ill-spirit which it engendered, and both sides during the wars of independence made virtue of necessity by decreeing its abolition. But with respect to other measures, Ferdinand showed his reactionary spirit by restoring to the audiencias of Mexico and Guadalajara their anterior administrative and advisory functions, and by establishing the network of special-privilege courts which had grown up like barnacles upon the fabric of Spanish society. Then, to restore completely the atmosphere of the good old days, the gallows, the whipping-post, and the Inquisition were given their ancient status and functions.

Evidently there could be no compromise with such a reactionary program. Even though the viceroy might check expression of sympathy with the liberal cause by prompt shooting, or by granting amnesty to rebels who had become irked by their fruitless campaigns, the fact remained that the best hope of the country now lay with the insurgents. Their most constructive act was to issue a new republican constitution, intended to replace the one which Ferdinand had withdrawn. This document was the famous Constitution of Apatzingán.

This early charter of Mexican liberty was signed at Apatzingán on October 22, 1814, by a Congress composed of eleven deputies protected by Morelos and Dr. Cos at the head of a fragmentary five hundred insurgent soldiers. Though it never had any vital force except within the actual camp of this tatterdemalion detachment, it stands as the expression of the constructive aspiration of the ultra-independentists, and as a monument to the incipient nationalism of Mexico.

The Constitution provided, characteristically, that the sole religion of the land should be the Roman Catholic. It should be borne in mind that this provision was an imposition upon no one; there was no demand yet for religious liberty of conscience. The sovereignty, held by the people, was declared to be vested in the Congress. The country, divided into seventeen provinces, was to be represented in this Congress and be governed by it and two other bodies to be called the Supreme Government and the Supreme Court. The Congress was to have one member from each province. Members were to be thirty years old, and none might be near relatives of others. Elections were to be indirect, and participated in by *all persons* over eighteen years of age. Electors were to be chosen by each parish, and parish electors were to choose partido (district) electors, thus making the final choice doubly indirect. The executive officers of Congress, the president and vice-president, were to be selected by lot by the seventeen deputies for the brief term of three months. The Congress was also to appoint the members of the Supreme Government and the Supreme Court, and of a special court erected upon the old Spanish ideal of fixing official responsibility, called a court of residencia; its functions were to be like those of the colonial visitor-general, but it was to be composed of seven judges, not one only. Congress was also to have intervention in international affairs through its power to name foreign representatives. It was the law maker and law promulgator. The Supreme Government, or executive (not those of the Congress), was to be composed of three persons, alternating in office every four months. They were to be equals in the presidency, and be chosen for a period of three years. Secretaries of war, treasury, and government, were to hold office four years. Offices of finance were to be managed on the familiar Spanish model, by an intendant general with an intendant for each province. The Supreme Court, of five members, was to be renovated by the retirement of its members successively at yearly periods, new judges being chosen by Congress. It was specified that the Congress should provide opportunely for suitable national representation on a population basis; when such representation should become possible, the Congress must surrender its powers to the people's chosen representatives.

It is apparent that the Constitution of Apatzingán was a combination of French ideals of nationality and equality, Spanish models of efficiency in fiscal matters and official responsibility, and insurgent apprehension over the prospects of working a pseudo-representative government, with a framework of inhibitions on the preponderance of any one man in the control of the mechanism of the state. And yet, with all its weaknesses incident to the time and the circumstances of its creation and the political inexperience of its sponsors, it demonstrated their faith in the ultimate triumph of their cause; it showed that their struggle was not dominated by mere personalities, in which a self-appointed leader launched hollow promises. In its declaration of personal rights it ratified the earlier ideals of Hidalgo, surpassing the noteworthy Constitution of 1812 in this respect, although its denial of freedom of conscience seems like a retrograde expression. Furthermore, this Constitution, though only of historical interest in so far as it concerns the development of the Mexican government, is an important human document in which is clearly set forth the interesting psychology of the Morelos group. These men were the first to enunciate unmistakably their aspiration for complete separation from Spain. Until 1814 the struggle had been conducted under the pretense of loyalty to Ferdinand and adherence to monarchical ideals. The crude framework for executive control set up by Morelos indicates his suspicion of the effectiveness of the substitute for a monarch, and yet his courageous determination to attempt the experiment. Himself willing to sacrifice his preponderance for sake of the prestige of civil institutions, he set a high mark of public service in Mexico which has never been lived up to in practical political life by any of his successors. The Constitution, as Emilio Rabasa wrote, is a "glorious monument witnessing the high character of Mexico's first statesmen."

The viceroyal government met the promulgation of this insurgent charter by ordering all copies found to be burned. All local governments were required to make reports of their disavowal of insurgent congressmen who assumed to represent them. The church and the Inquisition gladly entered the lists against it. Inevitably, the operation of the instrument was greatly restricted, both in area and in completeness among its direct adherents. Its effect as far as gaining new adherents was concerned was practically nil.

The armed struggle continued, with varying successes netting gains for the government. Ramón Rayón, successful for a time in maintaining Cóporo Hill north of Zitácuaro in Michoacán, on the road between Valladolid and Mexico City, was defeated while menacing the royalist lines to Querétaro at Jilotépec in May, 1815, and the government's communications with both Valladolid and Querétaro were reëstablished. In Michoacán Iturbide the future emperor planned an unauthorized pursuit of the insurgent Congress, in which he narrowly missed capturing it before it succeeded in fleeing from Ario to Uruapán. The chief seat of insurgent power was now in Puebla and Vera Cruz. Hence the members decided to make for Tehuacán, where their enemies were less numerous, their friends in better control, and the hilly country their best natural ally. Morelos was chosen to lead this migration, which was to pass through the Tecpan and Miztec provinces of the south.

Calleja's various detachments, apprised of the movement, determined to intercept it. The royalist leader did not realize that Morelos was a fallen hero of no military or political importance. When part of his forces, consisting in their entirety of about a thousand men, had succeeded in moving eastward as far as Tezmalaca, the viceroyal pursuers came upon them. The revolutionists endeavored to withstand the attack launched upon them by Concha, the royalist commander, but their right wing gave way, and when failure was evident, Morelos ordered Nicolás Bravo to retreat with the Congress to safety. His own sacrifice would halt the pursuit of the Spanish forces. Then, ordering his own detachment to disperse, he made his way with a solitary follower toward a neighboring hillside. Just before he ascended the hill he was overtaken by the royalist leader of the pursuing detachment, who turned out to be one of his own old lieutenants, Carranco, who had renounced the independentist cause. "It would seem, sir, that we know each other," was the dry and unembarrassed comment upon the situation made by Morelos.

The captured leader was taken to Mexico City, where he was placed on trial for insurrection. His defense was that he had made war upon the Spanish Cortes and not against the Spanish people; his attitude was that Mexico was independent, and that he had as a loyal son only defended her liberties. It was of no particular consequence what his defense might be; his doom had been sealed before his capture, and the formality of his trial was for the sake of appearances only. Since he had been given holy orders, it was necessary as it had been in the case of Hidalgo, to degrade him clerically before he might be turned over to the civil court. He was accordingly branded as a heretic by the Inquisition, after which he went through a public formality of reconciliation to the faith. His process was the last imposing ceremony held by this tribunal—the successful revolution happily swept it away in a few years more. The degradation ceremony was performed by the bishop of Puebla. Then, the government still fearing that public disorder might attend the execution of so notable a patriot, Morelos was taken from the capital to a nearby hamlet, San Cristóbal Ecatépec, where he was executed by a firing squad on December 22, 1815.

Thus ended the second period of the Revolution for Mexican Independence. In spite of ultimate failure this warrior-priest without military training who never commanded more than six thousand men in his own forces was the dominant spirit of the Revolution for nearly four years. He created an epoch. Under his influence the rabble horde which Hidalgo had led produced an army which, though never united in large numbers, was able by guerrilla methods to defeat the viceroy's campaigns of pacification although the royalist forces in garrisons and field numbered eighty thousand men.

He developed military genius through experience. He

was the first insurgent who dared to assume the offensive against the viceroyal troops, and the first to defeat them. His tactics and strategy won him great admiration. Without impulsiveness or inspiration, he planned calmly and executed with precision. Perhaps his genius for command was best shown in his ability to train officers. He it was who trained the Ávila and the Galeana brothers, Nicolás Bravo, Matamoros, Trujano, and Guerrero, all of whom gave good account of themselves in the field.

Lacking the inspirational character of Hidalgo, he compensated for that source of influence by military qualities of superior order; like his old chief he knew how to surrender his claim to domination for the good of his cause without bitterness. More practical than Hidalgo, he knew how to die with the calm conviction that his course had been correct. He left no recantation of his revolutionary declarations to dim the glory of his faith in a free Mexico. His name shines brightest in the constellation of those who struggled with him. It was an ironical fate which made one of his most vehement military opponents the agency through whom was to be achieved the independence for which he fought so well.

CHAPTER XIV

ITURBIDE AND THE FIRST EMPIRE

THE capture and execution of Morelos did not of itself have the potent effect upon the Revolution which the pro-Spanish party had anticipated. The reason, already pointed out, was that Morelos had fallen from his preëminence in the insurgent councils before he was captured. For a time the management of the Revolution was theoretically in the hands of the Congress. There were numerous bands of armed patriots all over the country, prepared to carry on under their regional leaders as they had previously done, without much deference to the ideas of that wandering and ill-agreed organization.

In all, these bands in 1816 mustered nearly 9000 armed fighters. There were two thousand at the strategic position of Tehuacán under Mier y Terán, who was now the logical military leader of the revolt. Under Vicente Guerrero in Mizteca were a thousand; under Guadalupe Victoria in Vera Cruz there were two thousand; Osorno near Querétaro was at the head of about a thousand; Torres, in the Bahío region of Guanajuato, commanded eight hundred men; the Rayón brothers, in Michoacán, controlled approximately fifteen hundred followers, while Galeana and other chieftains in Tecpan led five or six hundred. Thus the main bodies were in Vera Cruz and Puebla provinces. They were indifferently armed, possessed little or no artillery, and commanded scant funds, for which they depended largely on raids upon commerce; worse than all, they had meager coöperation, with no well outlined plan of campaign.

On the royalist side there were at least thirty thousand armed troops, half of whom were of the regular professional army. Six thousand held Vera Cruz, eight thousand were in

Puebla, forty-five hundred were in the lake region of Anáhuac, twenty-six hundred were in the southern provinces,
four thousand to the north of the capital in Querétaro and
San Luis Potosí, four thousand held the posts of the northern
Interior Provinces, and nearly a like number were about
Guadalajara and the remainder of Nueva Galicia. Besides
these formally organized troops there were many armed
civilians or militia who were utilized by the government for
purely local defense against rebel raids. The royalist forces
counted thus all told about eighty thousand men.

With such a force, strategically disposed throughout the
viceroyalty, it should have been an easy task for Calleja
to crush the rebellion. The condition of the patriots and
their dissensions also accrued to his advantage. The ambitions of Rosains, whose struggle for leadership led him to
fight the other revolutionary leaders, then finally to his
defeat and treacherous acceptance of pardon from the viceroy, darken the story of this period. The insurgent Congress, which Morelos had let himself be captured to save,
attempted to take upon itself the direction of military affairs,
a duty which it might logically have performed advanta-
geously if its members had not dissipated their energies in
petty bickerings among themselves. But when the Congress joined Mier y Terán at Tehuacán in November, and
attempted to interfere with his military plans that twenty-
year old but accomplished leader, impatient of non-professional control, dissolved the pseudo-representative delib-
erative body by force, and assumed the headship of military
activities about the middle of December. Thus ended the
ill-conceived plan of Morelos to establish a form of national
government. The change was bad for the revolutionary
cause, since the other leaders were little inclined to recognize Mier y Terán as their superior, and such cohesive force
as the Congress had exercised was now dissipated.

As a result, Calleja was able to defeat isolated bands one
after another. A number of leaders gradually disappeared.
Matamoros had been executed after his capture at the battle
of Puruarán in 1813; Francisco Rayón, brother of Ignacio,

was executed upon the same day as Morelos. Galeana, a veteran rebel, had been defeated and killed near Acapulco in June, 1813. The outstanding event of 1813 was the treachery of Rosains. Mier y Terán had a few successes, but was defeated in November, 1816, by General Samaniego. The most distinguished and successful of the patriot chieftains was Vicente Guerrero, who continually raided the convoy trains which passed along the Vera Cruz road bearing the merchandise and revenues of the Spanish colony.

Better success would have attended the movements of the viceroy's forces had his campaigns been marked by precision and coördination, had his officers possessed the character and training needful for proper subordination, or had they avoided costly blunders, harsh exactions, shameless peculation and outrages upon the people. There was also the psychological effect of the partial enforcement and prompt withdrawal of the Constitution of 1812, adding to the discontent of a population expectant of some benefit to be derived from a changed order of affairs. When in 1814 reactionary government came again into power in Spain with the restoration of Ferdinand VII, the disappointment of the many liberals who had looked to that over-appreciated ruler for assistance threw many supporters of the viceroyal government into the insurgent camps.

The restored king was not long in noting that Calleja had been made viceroy of New Spain by the Revolutionary Regency, or in substituting for him in that position an officer of his own choice, Juan Ruíz de Apodaca, who arrived at Vera Cruz about the end of August, 1816.

The choice was the wisest in many years, from the Spanish viewpoint. The new viceroy believed in active measures. He struck promptly at Mier y Terán, defeating him in January of 1817. Upon this defeat the brilliant young leader gave up his struggle for independence and retired to private life. He had hastily and probably needlessly surrendered the important stronghold of Tehuacán. By striking vicious blows at the most important insurgent leaders, and by a judicious admixture of pardons to those who could be induced to lay down their arms, Apodaca soon obtained control of Vera Cruz, Puebla, Mexico, Mizteca, and Tecpan. North of the capital only a few bands remained, the short campaign proving what could be done by decisive action and humane methods.

Had modern conditions in communications then existed, it is probable that a secondary flare-up which occurred in the Mexican Revolution at this time would never have taken place at all. This was the episode in which figured the young Spanish liberal, Francisco Javier Mina. This reckless adventurer was among the Navarrese who revolted in northern Spain in 1814 when Ferdinand VII recovered his throne. When the revolt proved unsuccessful and its leaders were driven out of the Peninsula, young Mina, already a great guerrilla leader though only nineteen years of age, sought refuge in England, where all enemies of Continental autocracy were being made welcome. In England he planned, as had Miranda before him, to carry revolution into the Spanish colonies in America.

In this enterprise he had English assistance. In May, 1816, he sailed from Liverpool in a small vessel in company with twelve chosen spirits who were to become officers in his military undertaking. Six of them were Spanish revolutionists, two were Englishmen, one was an American, and the others were Italians. The plan was to get to New Spain and join the insurgent forces in the field. But the serious military reverses which the Mexican patriots were at that time sustaining made it evident that such a plan would be bootless, so Mina turned toward the shores of the United States. He was able to recruit some American followers in the port of Baltimore and elsewhere, and to get possession of a few small ships, with which he managed to transport his forces to Galveston on the Gulf Coast. Thence he moved to Soto la Marina on the low shore of Tamaulipas, planning to work for the complete independence of New Spain, but in order to obtain the support of the Spanish element he told them that he was in favor of the restoration of the liberal Constitution of 1812.

From Soto la Marina Mina began to move his forces toward the insurgent area in Guanajuato. Before he left the coast he was deserted by a group of fifty Americans who, under Colonel Perry, had joined him in the United States. With his other followers he reached the region of San Juan de los Lagos in the intendancy of Guanajuato, and there gained a number of small and unimportant victories. Soon however the fortunes of battle changed, and defeats by the royalists were accompanied by quarrels among his adherents. Finally, after numerous vicissitudes, Mina was surprised and captured by the enemy at El Venadito on October 27, 1817, and executed by a firing squad in November. It was not long before the famous fort of Los Remedios, for a long time the stronghold of revolution in Guanajuato, was taken and its last defenders killed. This was on January 1, 1818.

The revolution was now at the lowest ebb of its fortunes. Ignacio Rayón was captured and imprisoned. Verdusco was granted amnesty, Licéaga was assassinated by a jealous subordinate. By 1819 Apodaca reported to his king that he would have no need of further reinforcements from Spain, but would be able to control the situation with the troops then at his disposal. There was practically only one group of dissidents still in the field, Vicente Guerrero in the southeast still having a few armed followers who were to figure in the final stage-play of emancipation. One other irreconcilable was still at large; Guadalupe Victoria, whose real name was Félix Fernández, had been at one time a chieftain to be reckoned with. Now a price was on his head, and he wandered hopeless, friendless, naked and alone, for a period of thirty months, a symbol of the hopelessness of the liberal cause, but no less the symbol of its undying aspiration. Victory under the banner of the Virgin of Guadalupe, the sentiment of his ambition, and of his romantic pseudonym, was never to come to the liberal revolution.

A complete volte-face was given to the character of the separatist movement in 1820. In March of that year

Colonel Riego's troops, about to embark for service against the insurgents of Buenos Aires, started a new revolt which obliged Ferdinand VII to restore the liberal Constitution of 1812. Rather than lose his kingdom entirely, Ferdinand favored losing it piecemeal by swearing reluctant adhesion to the liberal constitution with wide mental reservations. The sudden change to liberalism was received with varying emotions by the people of New Spain. The group to whom the change appeared particularly menacing was that of the upper clergy. These men had been sworn enemies of the radical Revolution from the first, for its success meant their undoing. Now it seemed that liberalism had triumphed in spite of them, in a quarter in which they would be powerless to defend themselves. The new liberal Cortes in Spain was showing its constructive hostility to the church by abolishing the Inquisition. It had also availed itself of the funds of the church in order to carry on the expenses of the liberal government and program, by seizing the tithes which belonged to the Spanish secular clergy. The menace to conservatism and religion could now be best met by open espousal of complete separation from liberal Spain.

On the other hand, the independence party in New Spain expected that Spanish liberalism triumphant would accomplish something for the New World parts of the empire. They hoped for the restoration of the free press, for popular elections, and for non-hereditary town councils. The revolt in Spain was a Masonic movement, and this gave encouragement to the Mexicans, many of whom belonged to the same order; in the army a number of the officers were Masons, Apodaca himself being one. These hopes seemed on the way to be realized when on May 3, 1820, the viceroy proclaimed the Constitution of 1812. For the third time in New Spain was government undertaken under this instrument. The various provisions of the new charter were put into force as rapidly as possible. All the elections for which it provided had taken place before the end of September.

Meantime the radical Cortes was developing a more

strongly anti-clerical campaign. The American deputies shared in responsibility for a program which included the suppression of the Jesuits, the cessation of all special privileges pertaining to the holy orders, and the sequestration of church property. It was evident that the movement would be made to apply in America, for the American deputies fostered it, and the Constitution and general laws were to apply everywhere in the empire. Hence it became imperative to separate immediately from the metropole if the clerical interests of Mexico were to continue in power there. The clergy was now obliged to espouse as its own the cause it had fought against for a decade—absolute separation from Spain. It was liberalism that they were fighting, not that they loved Spain less. Thus indirectly, and without desire or intent, the liberal recuperation in Spain drove conservative New Spain out of the empire.

To decide was to act. The higher clergy resolved to oppose the enforcement of the Constitution, and began to hold meetings in Mexico City to outline their campaign. A leading part was taken in it by Dr. Monteagudo, a canon of the cathedral of Mexico; he had been a member of the Yermo party of Spaniards who had deposed Iturrigaray in 1808. Among his adherents were the regente of the audiencia, the upper clergy of the capital generally, the inquisitor general, and a number of the Spanish residents. With the aid of the church funds and the backing of the respectable element of society the separatist movement had all it needed except a suitable military leader to conduct campaigns in the field.

Such a person was found in Agustín de Iturbide, a mestizo of Valladolid who was generally accepted as a creole. He had refused Hidalgo's invitation to join the Revolution, had been active, as we have seen, in the royalist campaigns against the insurgents about Guanajuato and in the pursuit and capture of Morelos. More recently he had fallen into disfavor for insubordination and personal irregularities. He was now on the retired list, short of funds, and ready to turn his hand to any enterprise that fitted his desires for wealth and position. He espoused the clerical plans with alacrity, nursing the hope that he might be allowed to make a demonstration of force in the very capital, which he hoped to make his own.

The separatists, however, induced him to begin the movement in the provinces, and for the success of his venture a palpable scheme for deceiving the viceroy into giving Iturbide command of some troops was concocted. Vicente Guerrero, working out of the southeast, was believed to be preparing to threaten Mexico City, and it was only natural for someone to ask to be put at the head of troops to oppose him. This Iturbide did, meeting prompt and unsuspecting acquiescence on the part of Apodaca. The constructive traitor set out from Mexico on November 20, 1820, at the head of a body of 2500 men; his purpose was not to fight, at least not to fight seriously, against Guerrero, but to win him over to a plan of general emancipation from Spain. He utilized his troops for a few unimportant skirmishes with those of Guerrero, perhaps with an idea of trying out his opponent's strength. Being unsuccessful in those minor engagements, Iturbide next decided to utilize his powers of diplomacy, inviting Guerrero into conferences with him, but he was not successful in sufficiently allaying the suspicions of the old insurgent warhorse until the month of February, when the two leaders met at Iguala to discuss Iturbide's proposals.

Out of the conferences so begun was evolved the notable agreement called the Plan de Iguala, which was phrased mostly by Iturbide himself, Guerrero acquiescing in its terms rather than suggesting them. The Plan provided a scheme whereby all the inhabitants of New Spain could unite, on a basis of mutual toleration, in establishing the political independence of the country. It was proclaimed to the country at large on February 24, 1821.

In its first provision it was similar to all plans of government which had been promulgated during the decade; that is, the Roman Catholic religion was to be the only tolerated one; New Spain was declared to be independent, and it was proposed that its governent should be a moderate constitutional monarchy. The throne was to be offered to Ferdinand VII, or, in case of his failure to accept it, to some other member of the reigning Spanish house, who should be designated by a Mexican Cortes. Pending the formation of this Cortes, a Junta, composed of members named in Iturbide's official report to the viceroy, was to provide for the organization of the Cortes, and govern the country until an emperor should arrive.

Equality of all races was recognized in a provision that any and all inhabitants were qualified to hold office. Property and personal rights were guaranteed, and the special privileges of the clericals were to be upheld. The main provisions of the Plan, guaranteeing (1) the Catholic religion and clerical privileges, (2) absolute independence and (3) racial equality, were designated the Three Guarantees, and the enforcement of them was intrusted to an army to be organized and led by Iturbide himself.

The proposed Plan was laid before Apodaca by the new Liberator, who offered the viceroy the presidency of the proposed Junta; but Apodaca refused, took measures to oppose the movement, and declared Iturbide an outlaw. Even so, it is suspected that he had been earlier implicated in the clerical plan. At first, the conservative element favored a restoration of the old constitutional government, and Iturbide's Plan was left with scant support owing to activities of the Masonic order. Half of the army of the Three Guarantees melted away. But for delay by the viceroy in striking against Iturbide the latter would have been lost. He succeeded, however, in uniting his own and Guerrero's forces at Teloloapán, where the two leaders outlined a plan of campaign. Guerrero was to fight in the south, and Iturbide in Guanajuato.

As the latter moved northward with his forces, a number of royalist commanders proclaimed for him. The greatest early accretion was that of Anastasio Bustamante's troops, which brought the Trigarante forces up to six thousand men. From that time on the new cause was bound to win.

Soon Guanajuato, Valladolid, Toluca, Querétaro, Puebla, Durango, Zacatecas, and Oaxaca had gone over to it. The clever appeal of the Plan to all classes upon a "safe and sane" program offered security to life and property, equal political opportunity, and independence. There was no such prospect to be hoped for from Spain.

Apodaca, who had guided the country through nearly five years of storm, and had all but restored tranquility and Spanish power, found himself unable to stem the flood and was forced to resign because of his alleged lukewarmness against Iturbide. The Masonic element in the capital, utilizing their military members, went to the viceroyal palace and obliged him to surrender his powers to Major General Novella, who reluctantly assumed them on July 6, 1821. Novella ruled less than a month, for on the thirtieth there came from Spain the last of the long line of viceroys, Juan O'Donojú.

This officer, who had held high military command in Andalusia, was a Mason of high standing who probably received his appointment through the activity of Ramos Arizpe, the "Comanche" representative from Coahuila in the Cortes of León. It was generally believed that O'Donojú had really come out to aid in effecting the independence of Mexico, but his activities toward that end necessarily awaited the course adopted by the Spanish Cortes. He began his viceroyal rule in the city of Vera Cruz, from which place he was unable to advance into the interior because of the armed Mexican forces which lay between the port and the capital. At Vera Cruz he began to hold intercourse with Iturbide, and with Antonio López de Santa Anna, who, as commander of that port city, here came upon the pages of the history of his country in his first important rôle.

Iturbide granted the viceroy permission to advance out of pestilential Vera Cruz as far as the healthier air of Córdoba, where, on August 24, 1821, the two signed the Treaty of Córdoba, a document which practically incorporated the Plan de Iguala, but varied from it by providing that in case of default of Spanish aspirants to the Mexican throne, the crown should be given to "such person as the Imperial Cortes may designate." The way was thus left open for choice of someone outside the royal Spanish house. The Treaty also guaranteed liberty of the press, provided for eliminating speedily all Spanish troops yet in the country, and specified that the Army of the Three Guarantees should at once enter and control the City of Mexico. Thus Iturbide was well advanced toward his ambitions ultimately to seize the royal power; once in possession of the capital, which he occupied on September 27, he was acclaimed by the populace as "El Libertador." There he moved forward with plans for organizing a government, forming a Regency of which he himself became president, O'Donojú being also a member. The other members were reactionaries, in the choice of whom Iturbide neglected the old revolutionists who had insured his success. He was an aristocrat who heartily disdained the rabble which Hidalgo had led and the untrained military leaders schooled by Morelos. This early showing of his hand against the liberal group was ere long to reap difficulties for him, though his path was for the time cleared by the death on October 8 of O'Donojú. The vacancy so created in the Regency Iturbide was obliged to fill by the appointment of the bishop of Puebla. At the same time he did himself the favor to have his title made generalissimo, and his salary set at 125,000 pesos a year. For the purpose of establishing his control more firmly, he caused the Regency to convoke a Committee of Notables, whose duty it should be to convoke a Constitutional Congress. The Committee of Notables had not been chosen with perfect astuteness, for within it there developed a spirit of opposition to the Plan and the Treaty and to Iturbide himself. Several of the one-time revolutionists began to talk about organizing a republic. They actually planned to seize Iturbide and establish a representative government; for this purpose they held meetings at the Querétaro home of Hidalgo's old friend Don Miguel Domínguez; but their designs became known, and they

DOÑA JOSEFA ORTIZ DE DOMÍNGUEZ
Statue at Querétaro

reaped the reward of being clapped into jail for their activities, though they were soon released.

The Treaty of Córdoba prescribed that the Constitutional or Constituent Congress should be chosen by the method provided in the Constitution of 1812. But Iturbide had known how to serve himself better than that, by inducing the Notables to call for the election of deputies to Congress by social classes. Thus it was provided that in provinces entitled to four or more representatives, only three should be churchmen, army officers and lawyers. He felt that by this means a large number of non-professional, easily-controlled deputies would be chosen.

When the Congress was convoked on February 4, 1822, it was composed of 162 delegates (including representatives of Guatemala, which had voted to attach itself to Mexico), the number of educated men from army, church, and law being decidedly limited. There were in it three groups of political thought; the Bourbonists stood for insistence on obtaining a Bourbon prince to rule the country; the Iturbidists wanted to name the Liberator as emperor; while the republicans stood against all monarchical plans. They were able to work with the Bourbonists to delay awarding the royal crown to Iturbide, hoping first to finish the Constitution, into which they could readily inject suitable limitations upon the national hero if possible. The republican Constituents were not a little disgusted that Iturbide had been able, at the beginning of their session, to compel their acquiescence in the Plan and the Treaty by a show of force. When the Spanish Cortes repudiated O'Donojú and rejected the Treaty of Córdoba, as could have been foreseen, the Bourbonists were left without a possibility of choosing a Spanish prince, and they adhered to the republican party instead of to that of Iturbide, for personalist reasons.

It was not long before open conflict arose between the Constituent Congress and Iturbide. His lack of appreciation for the revolutionary republicans was crowned by his manifest intention to continue his membership in and his control of the Regency, using it to insure his own preëminence. It had been expected that he would resign from the Regency when the Congress met. Furthermore, the public treasury was bankrupt, and the Congress attempted to recoup finances by reducing all salaries, including those of the military, a measure which struck at Iturbide's supporters.

While financial matters, including means for paying the army, were causing dissensions, a royalist general at Vera Cruz, Dávila, tried to inaugurate a pro-Spanish counter-revolution which he asked Iturbide to join. The affair became known, and Iturbide asked to be allowed to appear before Congress to explain; when he did so, he accused several of the members of complicity in Dávila's design, but his proof consisted of letters which implicated himself rather than anyone else. The result was to add bitterness to a growing estrangement. The republican idea constantly gained adherents. The Congress began to pass measures limiting the power of the president of the Regency, Iturbide. It then went about removing his friends from the Regency, substituting liberal sympathizers; it voted that the army should be reduced from 36,000 to 20,000 men, and it proposed to pass a decree prohibiting any member of the Regency from holding military command.

This last measure meant that Iturbide was to be deprived of all connection with the army, his chief source of power. He therefore determined upon a bold stroke. Most of the army was still his, the church stood back of him; he was still, despite his quarrels with the Congress, a most popular public idol. By liberal use of money he prepared the way for a staged military and popular uprising. On the night of May 18, a sergeant named Pío Marcha, of the San Hipólito garrison, rushed wildly out of his barracks, summoned his companions in arms, and together they raised the cry: "Viva Agustín I." The populace came running at the commotion; they marched to Iturbide's home, continuing their shouted demands that he should be crowned emperor. Such a popular clamor could not be immediately acquiesced in, but it could be humbly listened to, and advice could be sought from firm adherents among the upper class who would urge acceptance. Finally with apparent reluctance the popular idol bowed to the will of the rabble.

Now legal confirmation had to be sought from an unfriendly Congress which wanted a republic. Many inimical members were prevented from attending a special meeting of that body, which was convoked at the unearthly hour, for Mexicans, of seven o'clock on the following morning. By only a part of the Congress, Iturbide was chosen emperor, in accord with the apparent will of the populace. The assemblage lacked some twenty-five members of having a legal quorum, and out of seventy-seven votes cast ten were against him even in the face of the popular clamor; but a trick of that mild variety was not an essential error. Besides, popular sentiment was turning from Congress, which had been sitting nine months without getting anything constructive done on the constitution. It was hoped that the monarchy, once established, would shortly provide an efficient government. There was still a strong monarchical party, and a large element of the population which believed in Iturbide.

He took the oath of his new office before the intimidated Congress, and on July 25 he was crowned in a stately ceremonial. Prior to the coronation he had taken care to provide for succession to the crown, and secure imperial titles for the members of his family.

Only among the radical republicans was the new Emperor unpopular at the beginning of his reign. There was even a brief period of harmony between the ruler and the Congress; the latter smothered for a time its resentment at having been coërced into electing him. But soon dissension began; it was fomented by Father Servando Mier, a sharp radical who bitterly attacked royal institutions and openly advocated republican principles. The Bourbonist faction desired the downfall of Iturbide, and there was no small group of influential Mexicans who lacked sympathy with his manifest attachment for the church.

In the month of August 1822, a group of radicals including Father Mier plotted to declare Iturbide's election as emperor unconstitutional and to proclaim a republic. Iturbide, learning of the plot, put fifteen suspected deputies into jail, and held them many months after failure to prove their complicity. This attack upon the legislative power alienated the Congress completely. It refused to accept Iturbide's plan to establish military courts; he proposed to reduce Congress to a membership of seventy. When Congress tried to mollify him by providing that he should appoint the supreme court, and that he should have the power of the veto, he countered with a demand that he be given the right to veto each article of the constitution then in process of formation. The exasperated Constituents could only reject such an absurdity, and they were thereupon, on October 31, immediately dissolved by irate royalty. In their place he set up an Instituent Committee which was expected to go on with framing a constitution which would conform to his views.

Agustín I had now committed his crowning fatal blunder. He might have succeeded, even for a time longer, with arbitrary measures, for he still had friends in the church. But he had been guilty of the capital political error of going against legality. He had dissolved a Congress chosen by a semblance of popular desire, at least acquiescence in it, and he had imposed a constitution-framing organization responsive to his will alone without any authorization from the politically conscient part of the people. As a result his further progress in governing the country had now to depend at every step upon force and not popular desire. The long-neglected republicans began to have their inning.

While Iturbide had been mismanaging the government in Mexico City a new political star was rising on the Vera Cruz horizon. There Antonio López de Santa Anna was perfecting plans for his own aggrandizement. He proposed an attempt to wrest San Juan de Ulloa from its Spanish garrison. Iturbide ordered his captain-general, Echávarri, to aid Santa Anna's plan. He did so, finding himself so near being taken prisoner when the attack failed, and

under such suspicious circumstances, that he wrote to the
Emperor his conviction that Santa Anna had planned to
sacrifice him for the sake of obtaining his command. Iturbide planned then to rid himself of the danger from such an
ambitious inferior by going to fetch Santa Anna in person
to Mexico City. Santa Anna dissembled acquiescence
until an opportune moment for escape while the two were
marching inland. Then he returned to Vera Cruz, and
pronounced in December against the Emperor. He was
joined in January, 1823, by a number of old republicans including Guadalupe Victoria, who on February 1 enunciated
their program under the Plan de Casa Mata. This pronunciamiento was issued by a group of adherents to the
Masonic order. Among them was Echávarri, leading
troops which he had been given in order to defeat Santa
Anna. It was an appeal to force, such as Yermo and Iturbide had made before-time in quest of power—the traditional method by which political renovation has been
sought in Mexico ever since—an appeal which Carlos
Pereyra justly calls a crime, with which the forward moving
portion of the Mexican people today are determined to do
away.

The Plan de Casa Mata enunciated a political program
which demanded the fall of the empire, the establishment
of a republic, the convocation of a Constituent Congress,
and the framing of a Constitution. Underneath all these
ideals was the invocation of personalism, which began with
Iturbide and still unfortunately dominates Mexican politics.

Endeavoring to stem the tide of opposition in a belated
appreciation of his position, the Emperor tried to reconvoke
the dissolved Constituent Congress and have it proceed
with framing a Constitution. Naturally this policy was
a failure. The members of the Congress had still fresh
memories of jail sentences and irrational opposition. Santa
Anna, disastrously defeated at Jalapa and about to flee
precipitately to the United States, was dissuaded from
such cowardice by Guadalupe Victoria. From Vera Cruz
other leaders like Guerrero and Bravo spread the movement

with astonishing rapidity. The imperialists were power-less to check it. Their army was largely officered by men who had sworn to uphold the Plan de Iguala, which Iturbide had swept into the discard when he became Emperor. Province after province fell away; in Vera Cruz Echávarri, recently made a Mason, remained inactive against Santa Anna. In the capital troops considered loyal went over to the republicans, marching out of the city in gala array.

Iturbide tried in vain to stem the tide by diplomacy, calling for an election of a new congress. When this measure failed, and when the old Congress, reassembled, listened coldly to his explanation of his conduct, he gave up the struggle, and abdicated the troublous throne on February 19, 1823, offering to go into voluntary banishment. The Army of Liberation, now called the Army of the Republic, marched into the capital on March 27. The Congress voted that the ex-emperor should be required to live in Italy, and granted him an annual pension of 25,000 pesos a year from its nearly bankrupt treasury. On May 11, after an unpleasant journey to Vera Cruz, during which his Masonic enemies sought to take his life, the disappointed pretender to imperial power departed with his family for Italy on an English armed merchantman.

Shortly after taking up his foreign residence, he became aware of plans by certain of the states of Europe to reconquer the young Spanish American republics, and began to plan, no doubt urged by ambition as well as patriotism, to come again to Mexico to save her from foreign enemies. Masonic foes, trailing him, reported his aspirations to Congress, which in April, 1824, passed a decree declaring him out-lawed if he should set foot in the country. Ignorant of this attitude, Iturbide landed at Soto la Marina July 15, where he was immediately arrested. The State Congress of Tamaulipas summarily passed sentence on him, and on the nineteenth he was most unjustly executed, following Hidalgo and Morelos in the path of glory.

The greatest moment in this man's life was that in which he had stripped the power of Spain from his country, and

he stood forth as the great Libertador. Of him then said
Bolívar, himself an aspirant for military glory: "Bonaparte in Europe, Iturbide in America; these are the two
most extraordinary men that modern history has to offer."
The Mexican Emperor wrote to Bolívar on May 29, 1822,
congratulating him on his successes and offering eternal
friendship, but Bolívar, seeing the monarchical trend of
Iturbide's ambition, refused to respond with the recognition of the empire which the overweening aspirant to fame
desired.

It is difficult to fathom the reasons for the idealism in
which Iturbide is enshrined in the hearts of a substantial
number of the better class Mexicans today. The removal,
in the summer of 1921, of his name from the wall of the
Chamber of Deputies by vote of the radical Congress then
in session, was reviled as an act of ingrates by conservative
people, though there was much popular sympathy with
the radical attitude. Iturbide was at best a vain, dissolute
young coxcomb, in whom honor was secondary to ambition.
He had only moderate military ability, and none as an
executive. He loved to trail his ermine robes through the
streets in theatrical grandeur. His elevation to an imperial
throne was too much for his creole confrères, who looked
askance on mestizo ascendance. The day of the mixed
race had not yet dawned for Mexico. Indeed, the salvation of the country at that moment lay in the choice of a
European prince and the development of a native royal
house, could such an evolution have followed the Treaty
of Córdoba.

But there was no help from that or from any other direction. With Iturbide's downfall, as Rodolfo Reyes has
well said, the Mexican chaos began, the struggle between
indisciplined liberalism and egoistic reaction. There was
to be a long and sanguinary struggle between written law
and living custom, between tradition and progress, centralism and federation, privilege and equality, between dictators and petty local tyrants, between military and clerical
tyranny, or against both in the name of individualism.

Anarchy one day to be replaced by tyranny the next. There were to be Spanish tradition, imitation of the United States, and French centralism, all in inextricable confusion. In his initiation of this period Iturbide by his foolishness measurably delayed the creation of a government which might have found harmony while the warmth of mutual renunciations was yet alive. As long as he stood for developing a personal union between Spain and Mexico through a Bourbon prince, he served a cause; when he listened to the voice of ambition he became a crass, vulgar self dupe. He cast Mexico into a witch's cauldron from which she has not yet escaped. And yet he was nothing more than a legitimate product of his milieu.

Francisco Bulnes, another able conservative, thought that Iturbide's Plan de Iguala benefited Mexico, because some plan of compromise was an absolute necessity; this one removed class warfare; it gave the Spaniards freedom from fear of extermination; it violated the creed of no real republican party, for there were few of such political faith as yet. A constitutional monarchy was an ideal of those times. Nor was there any demand for religious liberty. A Spanish monarchy would have stopped bloodshed; but Iturbide's first fault lay in the insincerity with which he proposed a Spanish occupant for a throne he intended to fill himself. It was worse than insincerity, it was a blunder concerning his own acceptability. He was only a mediocre person, who attempted by autocratic methods to ape the Napoleon whose grandeur dazzled the minds of many of his Spanish American contemporaries. He was crafty, unreliable, selfish, unscrupulous; he descended from his first ideal, a workable basis for society, to government by pure personalism. His one moment of grandeur was that in which he served as the agent by which Mexico's fetters to the Old World were dissolved. Then he stood as the symbol of a movement which unfettered an outgrown colonial system. Beyond that he was all ludicrous personal ambition. After him descended the deluge of anarchism.

CHAPTER XV

The Congress which Iturbide had summoned was in session when he proffered his abdication. After accepting it, with some show of punctilio for its injuries, this body deposited the Executive Power, so styled, in the hands of a military triumvirate composed of generals Nicolás Bravo, Guadalupe Victoria, and Pedro Celestino Negrete. This group was only intended to have temporary control, pending the completion of the Constitution and the proper organization of the country on a permanent basis. It was regrettable that the Executive Power should have been thought safe only in the hands of a committee instead of a single man, but the minds of those times were schooled to look for escape from autocracy by the use of numbers. It was worse that the men chosen for the task should all have been military; the choice is explicable in the long political experience of the Mexicans, in whose eyes the viceroy as captain-general was the symbol and impersonation of royalty and supreme executive authority.

The Executive Power soon organized a Cabinet, placing at its head one of the best known and ablest conservatives of the epoch. This was Lucas Alamán, who was made minister of foreign relations and of government. Other cabinet positions created were those of justice and church, treasury, and war and navy. With the exception of Alamán the cabinet offices were filled by unimportant men. The imperial council of state, created by Iturbide, was abolished, and the five captaincies-general which had superseded the twelve colonial intendancies were changed to command-ancies, indicating the military status which local adminis-tration was still to maintain although republican theories were to succeed autocracy.

The treasury was replenished by sale of tobacco and by a negotiation of a 16,000,000 peso loan from an English concern at a ruinous discount. The national colors, of green, white, and red bars, the green nearest the flagstaff, were adopted as symbolizing independence, the purity of the Roman Catholic religion, and the union of the Spanish and Indian bloods. The coat of arms, the legendary eagle sitting on a cactus and devouring a serpent on a rock which protrudes above a swamp, symbolical of the founding of Tenochtitlán, was also adopted.

The overthrow of Iturbide, first machinated by Santa Anna in order to further his own designs, had taken the form of a blow to establish a republic. The church and the army were both in confusion and divided in purpose. Unfortunately, the republicans were also torn with dissension, some of them favoring a centralist or unitarian form of government with the reins of power held by a group of officers in Mexico City. The others desired a federal form of government which should recognize the independent sovereignty of the provinces, yielding opportunity for wider freedom of prerogative by groups of politicians outside the capital. The centralists were supporters of French ideals of administration; the federalists based their theories upon the example evolved by the organization and government of the United States. The party still in control of the Congress was composed of former monarchists and Scottish Rite Masons. But the federalists and the former Iturbidists, aided by new provincial delegations, were able to force the Congress to declare itself in favor of the federal system, and to issue a call for a Constituent Congress which should take up de novo the framing of a national charter.

In the elections for this body the federalists seated most of their candidates, though there were some centralists who had been opposed to Iturbide. The Congress met on November 7, 1823. The leader for the federalists was that clergyman Miguel Ramos Arizpe, whose voice had been heard before in the Cortes of León which framed the

Constitution of 1812. Opposed to him as protagonist of centralist ideas was Father Mier, acrimonious hater of royalty. The plan of the federalists, to divide the country artificially into sovereign states, was decried by Mier as a debilitation of the country at a time when it most needed strength from union in order to oppose the threat of an alliance of European powers ready to help Spain to recover her lost American colonies. He sapiently called to attention the fact that federation meant to unite what had formerly been separated; as in the United States, for instance, old and independently created colonies had been federated to form a nation. But the provinces of Mexico had always been united; there was nothing to federate. Guatemala, which had joined the empire when Iturbide rose, had left it when he fell, with the exception of the provinces of Soconusco and Chiapas. To divide the provinces of New Spain, creating them sovereign states, was to deny the significance of her colonial history and court continuous division; already were they setting themselves up in a pretended and little understood sovereignty, forgetting the interests of the whole country.

The arguments of Ramos Arizpe (unfortunately for later developments) prevailed; he was backed by the fact that Santa Anna had proclaimed for a federal republic, though Father Mier's mordant characterization of him and his followers, that "they did not know what kind of an animal a federal republic was" needs no sustaining argument. The Mexicans, struggling for a liberal independence, had been tricked into a conservative one by Iturbide and the church. Now that they needed a strong central republic, they erred through accepting Ramos Arizpe's advice to imitate the organization of the United States, when their every experience should have taught them that in centralized power lay their security. Fear of centralist domination on the one hand, and regional sympathies and ambitions on the other determined the issue in favor of a decentralized form of government.

The Congress had indeed little time in which to hesitate.

Already whispers of proposed reaction were being passed about. The demand for something constructive was pressing. In three days' time Ramos Arizpe presented a draft of an organic law known as the Acta Constitutiva. This was little more than a translation—with establishment of a state church, certain local adaptations and other minor changes—of the Constitution of the United States. It was immediately promulgated to drown rising opposition, and remained in force until the completed Federal Constitution was made effective. The discussion of the resolution which involved the adoption of federalism had evoked a number of riots, fomented by sympathizers with Iturbide. These manifestations ceased when that unfortunate imperialist was executed.

After this, the interest of the Congress revolved about the question of whether the executive power should be held by one or by three persons. Fortunately, the decision was for but one chief magistrate; but most unfortunately, it was at the same time decided that the executive should be under restraint by the legislature. This theory, unfaithful to Mexican conditions, has only tended when enforced to tie the hands of the executive by the inane debatings of an ill-schooled legislature; on the other hand it has been the cause of numerous cuartelazos or military seizures of power. The Mexican system of government, to be successful, must be strongly centralized until political experience and judgment become more nearly universal than they are today.

The completed Constitution was published on October 4, 1824. The nineteen states were to be independent in internal affairs with the four territories centrally controlled. There were to be three branches of government, the executive, legislative, and judicial. The Roman Catholic religion was established. The federation was to have a president and vice-president. They were to be chosen by the state legislatures, each voting for two candidates, one of whom must not be a resident of the state in which he was voted for. This was to restrict campaigns for "favorite sons," and to bring forward national figures. The candidate receiving most votes was to be president, and the second choice vice-president. This weak system, adopted from the United States Constitution, brought opposite parties into control of the executive positions, and was responsible for several of the early violent transmissions of power during the next few years.

The Congress was to be comprised of a Senate to represent the States as sovereign entities, and of a House of Deputies to represent the people. The deputies were to be chosen every two years, one for each 80,000 inhabitants or major fraction thereof. The senators were to be chosen by the plural votes of the State legislatures, two from each State, one retiring every two years. The presidential form of government was secured by the provision that neither the president, vice-president, members of the Supreme Court, secretaries of state nor employees of their departments, might be elected deputies. Congress had the right of impeaching executive officers. The president must be a native Mexican, and might not be reëlected until the lapse of four years after retirement. The Supreme Court, and the Superior Courts of districts and departments, were to be manned by judges chosen in the same way as were the president and vice-president. The State Constitutions were to be framed on the same model, and their laws not conflict with those of the nation.

This federal imitation of the early Constitution of the United States was not blindly framed, as Emilio Rabasa says. The provinces had more confidence in themselves than they had in the center, and the long Revolution had taught them to seek all the liberties they could obtain. They also sought all the power of official position which would bring emoluments. They were, it is true, anxious to prevent usurpation of power by the capital, to such an extent that they passed by in silence obvious parts of the American Constitution, those which granted to the people a bill of rights guaranteeing liberty of conscience, or other individual guarantees, of which only a few are interspersed through the document. Traditionalist influence was jointly responsible for this with the fact that the charter was never, submitted to the people, nor was there existent a "people" which could discuss and amend the document or ratify it when it might be considered adapted to the needs of the nation. This was in strong contrast to the awakening of public opinion which accompanied the adoption of the Constitution of the United States.

The Constitution of 1824 was in many respects a commendable document. Though it established a unique religion it abolished the Inquisition. Torture, mutilation, and excessive penalties were prohibited, even though secrecy in trials continued and no attempt at a jury system was provided. A real effort was made to promote material interests, education, and intellectual progress. Its greatest defect was that it assumed to remove the Mexican people from royalism, in which they were immersed, without adequate popular education in democracy, either before or after its promulgation. Hardly had this promulgation taken place when the State legislatures began to propose amendments; they wanted to participate in all the independent functions of the national power, instead of endeavoring to accord to the new system all the prestige which loyalty and coöperation could give it. There were no great pamphleteers to issue a *Federalist* to make intelligible its essentials to the masses; and there were no masses with political sensibilities to arouse in its name.

The first national president elected under the Constitution was that Guadalupe Victoria who had distinguished himself by refusing a Spanish pardon during the dark days after Morelos and before Iturbide. As for the rest, this picturesque son of Sonora had little to recommend him for the high distinction he received on October 10, 1824, when, with General Nicolás Bravo as vice-president, he assumed the executive power. The nineteen States had been organized, the two Californias, Colima, and New Mexico, had been constituted territories, Tlascala had been left for future organization, and the Federal District had been created. The Congress and the courts had been instituted. The presidential term of office was to continue until April 1, 1829.

Victoria had been chosen by a clear majority in all the States, whereas Bravo had had to be designated by an appeal from the general electoral results to the decision of the Chamber of Deputies, as constitutionally provided in case of no majority. This government might well have been a happy and profitable one for Mexico; the country was normally prosperous, and public order was good. Victoria was enormously popular, and Bravo, who had been the main support of Morelos, was esteemed as a humanitarian who had once declined the opportunity to shoot down in retribution of his father's execution by the royalists three hundred defenseless prisoners whom he had taken in battle. But there were present many elements of weakness. There was, inevitably, a pronounced survival of militarism. Generals remained in each State capital as representatives of the Federal Executive. There was widespread disaffection toward radical ideals among the wealthy and educated part of the population, which included many of the old Spaniards. A campaign of expelling these was undertaken, and there were symptoms of unrest in the occasional pronouncement of a dissatisfied general, or in the disturbance caused by the return and unprincipled execution of Iturbide.

Victoria, with a passion for coöperation and a passive disposition, attempted to administer a government composed of officers drawn from all factions. The two important groups were members of the two branches of Masonry. The Escoceses, or Scottish Rite Masons, who had been organized in Mexico for some time, were royalists, conservatives, who favored the restoration of monarchy. Among them were such men as Negrete and Echávarri. The Yorkinos, or York Rite Masons, were the liberals, democrats, largely creoles and mestizos, generally less well educated than the Escoceses. The latter had been active during the Revolution. The Yorkinos had been encouraged by the American minister, Joel Poinsett, who thought he was helping democracy by organizing the liberals into such political clubs. He made the sad mistake of interfering in Mexican politics and getting himself so badly disliked that he was recalled.

The two political factions, stirred to white heat by fraternal jealousies, came to loggerheads over the foreign debt. The London bankers who were holding back a part of the 16,000,000 peso loan failed, there was insufficient revenue to meet budget expenses, and the cabinet, of Yorkino complexion, voted to suspend payment of interest on the public debt. This made them very unpopular, and Nicolás Bravo, the vice-president, rose against them in 1828 under the Plan de Montaño, demanding the prohibition of secret societies, the expulsion of Poinsett, and the removal of the cabinet, especially of the Secretary of War, Manuel Gómez Pedraza. The revolt failed; Bravo and his adherents were banished, causing loss of power and prestige by the Escoceses. Soon the Yorkinos also split, due to quarrels over the next presidency. The two factions were practically ended.

In the second presidential campaign, that of 1828, the liberal element championed the candidacy of General Vicente Guerrero. Though an ignorant man of the lower class, he was a popular war hero. He was Grand Master of the York lodges. His opponent, Gómez Pedraza, was also a York Mason, a faction of whom he led, combined with some Scottish Rite remnants. Thus an educated white man was pitted against one of plebeian extraction for the highest office in the land.

Gómez Pedraza received the electoral votes of ten out of nineteen State legislatures, having profited by the protection of the government. Guerrero had been supported by the American minister, Poinsett, and by numerous strong liberals. An appeal was made to the Congress by Guerrero's supporters to have it reverse the vote of the legislatures. The deputies did so, but the senators upheld Gómez Pedraza, whereupon the Guerrero party appealed to arms. They were soon successful in engaging the self-interest of Santa Anna, who, stationed at Vera Cruz, took it upon himself to declare Guerrero elected. President Victoria defeated Santa Anna, but the latter almost immediately obtained command of the troops that had bested him. The military uprising in the capital known as the Cuartelazo de La Acordada then ensued, and Gómez Pedraza, seeing his cause lost, resigned and fled the country. In January 1829, after Victoria's term had ended, the Congress, composed of Guerrero partisans, seated him as president and Anastasio Bustamante as vice-president. The "election" of Guerrero had violated the Constitution, just as that of Gómez Pedraza had violated the sense of justice of his opponents. The violence of Yermo against Iturrigaray, and of Santa Anna against Iturbide had become a traditional feature of political renovation. The characteristic fault of democracy, namely the attempt of the party in power to perpetuate its influence by controlling elections—a fault not unknown in more stable republics than Mexico, had now begun its yet unbroken sway over the country. Not appeals to arms, but unrighteous elections, are the bane of Mexican politics.

The choice of Anastasio Bustamante as vice-president was unfortunate. He was an opportunist of the first water. He had served long in Calleja's army, had been prompt to espouse the Plan de Iguala, was a firm supporter of Iturbide, and had been commandant of the Interior Provinces under him. When the empire fell, Bustamante joined the federals as a remonstrance against the monarchical party, whom he blamed for Iturbide's failure. He was soon ready for still another political adventure.

This came when in the summer of 1829 the Spaniards sent an expedition from Cuba to avenge the eviction of their nationals by the Mexicans during Victoria's term, and to take possession anew of Mexico if possible. The Congress gave President Guerrero full control that he might the more easily beat the Spaniards off, but when he had done this he was slow to relinquish his dictatorship. This was Bustamante's chance to stand for constitutionality and high principles. He was aided now in this by the ever ready Santa Anna, whose Plan de Jalapa set Bustamante's troops at that place in revolt against Guerrero. The latter took the field against his enemies, leaving General Bocanegra in possession of the office of president. Bocanegra "declared" for himself, and Guerrero was obliged to flee to the south. Bocanegra ruled five days, being ousted by General Quintanar, who placed Pedro Vélez, Chief Justice, in the presidential chair pending the installation of Bustamante. By February 1830 the latter was in the usurped position, the subservient but badly perplexed Congress having declared Guerrero intellectually incapacitated for the presidency. They would have declared Guerrero's election null, but that would have excluded Bustamante also.

Bustamante's revolt and seizure of power was a travesty on established government. It stood for no essential principle other than hankering for office. His government was a pure military despotism. Naturally, the holder of such power was fearful of a similar attempt against himself. The fear was justified when Guerrero's friends declared they would support him under arms. Bustamante hired assassins to do away with such a rival. When Guerrero established a sort of government at Valladolid early in 1830, Bustamante's troops drove him to Acapulco, where he was treacherously seized by an Italian sea-captain for a price, and subsequently executed by government order on February 14, 1831. He was one more martyr to the stormy struggle for Mexican political integrity; a man of no great parts, of some political trickery, but who had done much valuable service for his country and who had not merited death at the hands of so small a man as he that won momentary security by this political crime.

The outrage against Guerrero, with similar animus shown toward many of his partisans, soon called for spirited contest of Bustamante's tenure. It was again the watchful Santa Anna, always opposition candidate for preference, who grasped the opportunity. In January, 1832, he revolted under a demand for reorganization of the Cabinet and the proper observance of the Constitution, features of political necessity which had not occurred to him when he had helped seat Bustamante. Santa Anna was joined by many federalists, and Bustamante was ousted in September. He resigned his pretensions in favor of Gómez Pedraza, whom Santa Anna had thought of as a likely person to hold ad interim powers. Gómez Pedraza was shamelessly brought back from exile, and served the now remaining three months of the term for which a majority of the state legislatures had designated him, a term which he should have begun in 1829.

It was evident that Santa Anna himself expected to succeed Gómez Pedraza, and at the end of three months he did so, the vice-president chosen with him being Valentín Gómez Farías, a liberal who had already seen cabinet service. Thus the old misfortune was again repeated of employing a president and a vice-president of opposite political tendencies. The president-elect absented himself from the capital at the time when the transmissal of the executive power occurred, on April 1, 1833, perhaps with the purpose of allowing Gómez Farías to make himself and his party unpopular through advocacy of the radical program of reform which they had been espousing during the short incumbency of Gómez Pedraza.

The Congress which now met was dominated by liberals. While Santa Anna remained under various pretexts near Jalapa at his hacienda of Manga de Clavo (clove-spike), the aromatic designation of which lends a certain spicy flavor to this new Napoleon's political vagaries, Gómez Farías and his liberal coterie began to inaugurate a number of badly needed governmental reforms. Their first effort was toward reduction of the size of the army, which was unduly large and had become a ready instrument for revolt in the hands of ambitious generals. The cuartelazo as a means of renovating the government was seen to be an extra-Constitutional instrument sure to bring disaster in its wake.

More inveterate were the evils inherent in the condition of the Mexican clergy. The missionary zeal of the sixteenth century had long since failed in this great body; its members no longer sought the crown of martyrdom on Indian frontiers, but filled the convents in the cities, where they lived the lives of the privileged, contributing less than was their obligation to the spiritual needs of the country, and constituting a heavy economic drain upon its resources for their physical sustenance. In the secular arm, the tithes and obventions were monopolized to produce fat salaries for prelates and dignitaries, while in the lower ranks the priests of parishes lived in a penury which prevented their setting an example of higher standards of living for the common people.

Striking at the privileges of the clergy, the Congress voted first of all to remove its monopoly over the intellectuality of the nation by providing that education should be made free, lay, and obligatory. This move connoted the suppression of the church schools, which were doing the only valuable educational work in the Republic, and closing the University, which was now in an advanced stage of decrepitude. To carry out a program of national education a Direction of Instruction was to be provided. A still more vital blow was struck at the domination of the church when the Congress pretended to assume the old royal prerogative of the patronato. That is, it took upon itself, as repository of the exercise of sovereignty, the appointment of the officers of the church. Even more radically, it suppressed the legal collection of church tithes, and annulled the civil obligation of monastic oaths.

Nothing more courageous or more ill-timed could have been attempted by a party only recently come into power, with a hostile president and the wealthy and educated class clearly opposed. The greatest perturbation was visible among both army and clergy. Santa Anna reassumed the presidency May 16, 1833, in order to calm the storm. When armed resistance against the government broke out, the president relinquished the executive power to Gómez Farías and set out in June to suppress the disorder. In three days' time Santa Anna's troops revolted, "captured" him, and proclaimed him dictator, much to his satisfaction. But his sympathizers in Mexico City who tried to oust Gómez Farías were themselves defeated by the latter. The two executives alternated in control of the chief power several times, and there were projects formed to set aside the federal organization of the country for any other form of government, but Santa Anna, favoring federalism for the moment, was able to defeat rebels who sought the change. When he reassumed the presidency after his campaign, the liberal program which Gómez Farías and his party advocated was temporarily suspended.

The clerical party had raised the cry of "Religion and privileges" immediately upon the attempt of the reformers to invade the sacred prerogatives of the church. When Santa Anna resumed the executive authority on April 24, 1834, he soon dissolved the national Congress on May 31, as a part of his Plan de Cuernavaca, which denounced all liberalism, federalism, Masonic activities in general, and Gómez Farías in particular. He also disbanded the State legislatures, deposed governors and city councils, and filled the vacancies with adherents of his reactionary Plan. Indeed, he only retained one cabinet member as a secretary, and ruled in isolated grandeur as a dictator for a time, until new cabinet members were chosen during the summer. The conduct of the president-dictator now became so preposterously reactionary that remonstrances were continuous, yet he persisted in claiming that the federal constitution of 1824 was still the supreme law, and in resisting all attempts of its open enemies to replace it. After eight months of wrangling, during which officials were changed with senseless rapidity, the Congress which Santa Anna had called for December, 1834, met on January 4, 1835. The elections for it had been contested by a military-clerical coalition on one side and the supporters of Santa Anna and the Escoceses on the other. The military-clerical faction had won by large majorities.

When Santa Anna saw that he would have no control over such a Congress, he retired once more from the presidency to Manga de Clavo, leaving General Miguel Barragán in charge of his office on January 28, 1835. The Congress now listened to numerous pronouncements favoring a change to the centralist form of government, resolved its two houses into a joint assembly, and, under a decree of October 3, 1835, actually established centralism. Proceeding then with the duty which devolved upon them, its members set about drawing up a centralist constitution, which was promulgated on December 30, 1836. This new organic legislation was composed of seven separate but correlated laws, and was known as the "Siete Leyes."

This new Constitution of 1836 was the culmination of a nine-year struggle by the military-clerical reactionaries to do away with the federalist system established by the radical republicans in 1824. Thus since independence the country had swung through a complete cycle from the centralism of Iturbide to that of the same element restored to power during the political contortions of Santa Anna. The framing of the Seven Laws was the work of a constitutional assembly which had pleased itself in gathering in joint session at the houses of Congress for that purpose. No one had asked it to frame a constitution when it was elected. Its behavior may be characterized as a parliamentary coup d'état. Its constructive work has been characterized by its opponents, with a true Mexican love for a political bon mot, as "The Seven Plagues."

This Constitution had one virtue which no Mexican liberal charter framers have ever dared to include. It restricted the franchise. Only those possessed it who had at least 100 pesos income, either from property or wages. This restriction deprived the ignorant, indigent population of the vote, placing it definitely beyond the pale of temptation to political agitators. That was not the intention at the time, however, it being the effort merely to repose political power solely in the hands of the privileged class. If this provision had been included in the early and later constitutions, it would have been better for Mexico.

The legislative power was to be held by a bicameral congress. There were to be twenty-four senators, with property qualification of an income of twenty-five hundred pesos, chosen indirectly from lists submitted by the assemblies representing the twelve departments into which the previously organized states had been resolved. The Chamber of Deputies was to contain one member for each 150,000 inhabitants or fraction thereof over 80,000. Their income had to be at least fifteen hundred pesos annually. They were to be chosen by popular election, and might hold no office of civil, judicial, ecclesiastical, or military character.

The executive power was vested in a President chosen for a term of eight years with the privilege of reëlection. To secure a president, the Senate, the Supreme Court, and the Presidential Council were each to submit a list of three names to the Chamber of Deputies. This body was then to select three of the nine names, and the Departmental Assemblies were to make a final choice of one from among these three. No more cumbersome method, more definitely calculated to permit of machinations by a dominant despot like Santa Anna, could have been devised. It bore the external marks of a careful sifting process, however, and suited its framers. The President was to be assisted by a Council of thirteen members, two to be churchmen and two army officers. They were to be chosen by the Deputies from a list formed by the President from nominations made to him by the Senate. The President must have an annual income of 4000 pesos; he might choose freely his own ministers. The judiciary, composed of a Supreme Court, Superior Courts, auditing courts, and courts of first instance in the Departments, was to be chosen by indirect methods. But the most notable provision of this set of laws was that contained in the second of the seven, which created a hitherto unheard-of body, to be known as the Poder Conservador, or Conserving Power. This body was composed of five members, each forty years of age and having an annual income of 3,000 pesos. It was to be renovated by changing one member every two years. The function of this remarkable committee was to create and maintain an equilibrium between the executive, legislative, and judicial branches of the government. It was to secure the enforcement of the laws, and, upon especial occasions, hand down judgments interpreting the "will of the nation."

Such a carefully constructed machine for obstructing administration could hardly have pleased everyone. The radicals denounced its conservatism, the reactionaries its radicalism. Several states questioned its very doubtful validity. It displeased the church in a measure because it left open certain principles which paved the way for later attacks upon its privileged position. The army men were equally unhappy over it, while the radicals saw in it the end of all things governmental. The Constitution of 1836 was indeed a curious document. The Departments had no liberties, the legislative branch no initiative, the judiciary no independence; but the worst feature of all was that of subjecting the Chief Executive to the Poder Conservador, a body somehow superhuman, which might depose him, suspend Congress, annul laws, or reverse judicial sentences. It was responsible only to Deity, which it barely recognized. It demanded immediate submission to its commands on all hands, under penalty of charges of rebellion and the commission of the crime of "lese nation."

All these provisions for checks on the executive are traceable to suspicion of the character of Santa Anna, who it was expected would be the President under it, but whose sinister shadow, like that of the inglorious tribe of South American caudillos, was growing darker on the political horizon.

The cares of President Barragán, charged with inaugurating this new Constitution, were multifarious. Insurrection against its imposition broke out in numerous places, led by champions of the Constitution of 1824. These were to go on while a more serious problem confronted the country, that of the resistance of the American colonists in Texas to the exactions and limitations placed upon them by the centralist power; resistance which led to open revolt and the final secession of Texas from the Republic.

CHAPTER XVI

THE SECESSION OF TEXAS

TEXAS first came sharply to the attention of the white conquerors of North America through the explorations southward from Canada by the Chevalier de La Salle in 1682. His later attempt at colonization of the mouth of the Mississippi, which resulted in the planting of Fort St. Louis on Garza Creek, inland from Matagorda Bay, in 1685, drew the attention of the rulers of Spain and New Spain. Repeated efforts to discover and destroy the intruding French settlement revealed the fact that it had been a ghastly failure. Not much more successful were the early Texan establishments of the Spaniards. The mission system used by them there first in 1690, had a meager and transitory success, but in 1716 the effort of the church to hold the vast area of Texas by mission organization began to bear more tangible results. Efforts along the eastward shore of the Gulf of Mexico were less successful. The great area called Louisiana was seized and held by France, of which Spain was a mere appanage from about 1690 until the death of Louis XIV.

By the great continental struggle for mastery known as the French and Indian War, 1754–1763, the French lost forever their holdings on the mainland, and Louisiana became Spanish for the alleged purpose of compensating Spain for the loss of East and West Florida. In actuality the possession of Louisiana by Spain had the effect of bringing that power into frontier conflict successively with England and the United States.

In 1801 Louisiana was forced from Spanish control by Napoleon, who reassimilated it to France under the obligation never to alienate it, but in 1803 it became the possession of the United States "with the same extent it [had] in the hands of Spain, and that it had when France possessed it"—words taken from the Treaty of San Ildefonso, 1801, which left the problem of actual delimitation to later negotiations.

As a matter of fact, the boundary never had been actually determined by international agreement while the French and the Spanish had held Louisiana and Texas respectively. During the Spanish tenure of Louisiana the boundary line had been of negligible consequence. When Louisiana became American the problem of the southwestern boundary came into prominence, the division of the territory continuing to be a matter of dispute until 1819, when the United States gave up its "right" to all of Texas west of the Sabine River in the negotiations which resulted in the purchase of Florida.

Prior to this time the American advance into the southwest had been in process since the close of the Revolution under continuously increasing momentum. It began with the cross-boundary horse-trade of men like Philip Nolan, who is thought to have been in Texas as early as 1785, and was killed in Spanish territory in 1801. He was followed by a list of adventurers whom Spain was ever on the alert to circumvent, adventurers with no political purpose, like John Sibley, Banks, Davenport, and later the Patties. Then also there were the more dangerous visionaries, men like Aaron Burr, Magee or James Long, or the active agent of assimilation Zebulon Pike, whose projects had a political significance never gainsaid by American chroniclers, and the post-Napoleonic episodes of such French exiles as Lallemand, who treasured frayed vestiges of the French dream of colonial resuscitation in America.

Up to the time of the American cession there had been little need of boundaries other than the barriers imposed by distance and inhospitable wastes. A little arroyo had kept the two Latin nations from treading on each other's toes except on a few occasions. The insignificant Arroyo Hondo, accepted as the line about 1744, was all there was of practical division between the French Natchitoches and the Spanish

Adaes. As the westward movement of the Americans gained headway, the Spaniards looked upon each successive step with increased alarm. Fear was expressed that the Yankees would penetrate into Mexico's rich mineral district of the Interior Provinces. Burr's project of southwestern empire led to the establishment of a neutral strip between Arroyo Hondo and the Sabine River, which provided a harbor from 1806 until 1819 for all the outlawed denizens of the frontier who fattened there on crimes against citizens of both nations, neither of which would drive them out for fear of exciting the jealousy of the other. To this equivocal settlement were owing the subsequent troubles incident to the formation of the abortive Fredonian Republic which tried the patience of Mexico with her adopted colonists, and fanned the distrust which added to the impossibility of the Americans living in political inferiority to a Mexican régime.

The so-called Cachupin War, Magee's expedition into Texas, was another display of that ruthless contempt for unutilized sovereignty which increased the hostility of the Spaniards to things American.

Magee and Perry were both to pay with self-destruction for their dreams of Texan conquest, and Long gave his life to the assassin as a price of failure in 1819. Lafitte and his Galveston pirates might worry, but not effectually overcome the maritime commerce of the Gulf powers, particularly that of Spain. But the impotence of Spain gave the revolutionists of Mexico success at last, and the logical outcome was a spirit of gratitude on the part of the Mexicans which won for the Americans who had assisted in the revolt numerous valuable land cessions which were the immediate forerunners of the troubles which culminated in the Texan Revolution of 1836. This barest outline has given an inadequate idea of the succession of events which led to the inevitable clash of interests between the two races. It would be impossible to give a detailed account of the succession of conflicts within Mexico following the expulsion of the Spaniards from the country in 1821. It is only to be said that the colonization grant to the Austins by the Iturbide régime was confirmed ere that

fleeting empire's laws were entirely superseded. Then laws
for colonization were passed, and the way of the westerner
into Texas was legally opened.

In the year 1821 Missouri, the second state west of the
Mississippi, was admitted to the American Union; Louisiana
had been admitted in 1812. Thus the westward movement
brought organized American society to the border of Texas,
possession of which was disputed until the boundary treaty
of 1819. Moses Austin, engaged in mining and in land enterprises in Missouri and Arkansas, went to Mexico and obtained from Iturbide permission to plant in Texas a colony
of Roman Catholic citizens of Louisiana. Dying at the
inception of his enterprise, he bequeathed his ambitions to
his son, Stephen F. Austin, who alone of all the army of
empresarios, carried to anything like success the scheme of
colonization which the empresario system provided. Under
it the contractor was to bring into the province several
hundred settlers who were to be given liberal allotments of
land. They were to have these lands for the payment of a
nominal sum to the contractor or empresario, who got for
himself a liberal donation of land for bringing the settlers in.
The newness of the land and the lack of resources made it
seem reasonable that the colonists should be free for a period
from taxation and duties. Accordingly they were granted
immunity from these contributions for a period of seven
years, whereby were sown the dragon's teeth. The Mexicans
hoped to obtain from the settlers two benefits: trade between
them and Mexico and the building up of a strong aggressive
frontier colony which would be a barrier to the cupidity of
the United States. That such a curious misjudgment of the
Anglo-American temper could have occurred must be
charged to the lack of continuous government in Mexico by
men of practical affairs. Her leaders were visionaries imbued
with the theories of universal brotherhood which had up-
heaved the American nation, France, and then Spanish
America, a century too soon for the latter to profit by
democracy. With these ideals was combined the notion
that the plains of Texas were barren of real value, and the

gain they might get from sale was a return for nothing invested.

Whatever the policy, and whatever the self-deception, the movement proved a letting down of the bars to that mass of adventurous spirits which under some pretense, legalized or otherwise, must sooner or later have possessed itself of the land.

By 1827 there were about twelve thousand Americans across the Sabine. The greatest immigration occurred in 1825. Though the immigration orders issued in 1826 and 1827 tried to limit the influx of Americans, and demanded allegiance to the Roman Catholic faith as a prerequisite to colonization, the tide was not apparently diminished thereby. Only a spirit of jealousy was engendered between the two races. The contrast between American and Spanish attitudes toward the avowal of religious principles as a basis of the social order makes it possible for us to understand how little an obstacle such a requirement would be to the frontiersman, and how it became a subject of complaint by the Mexicans when it was so flagrantly disregarded. Probably nineteen-twentieths of the Americans pretended no allegiance to Catholicism.

The concessions or grants of lands to colonists soon led to troubles in Texas. Notorious among them were those of the grant to Edwards, made in 1825. Before a single year elapsed Edwards had quarreled with many of the earlier settlers, whose titles he would not recognize. These questions of title were followed by disputes over supposed usurpation of the powers of the state by the empresario and election quarrels, so that in 1826 the jefe político of the department, General Blanco, banished Edwards from the province. The reply of the dispossessed settlers was the organization of the ill-starred Fredonian Republic. This was led by Edwards, who drew the Cherokee Indians into his scheme by a proposal to divide Texas between the new State and the red men. It was also expected that the other Americans would come to the support of the venture. Instead, the Austin settlers joined the forces of the government to quell the insurrection, the Indians were detached from the enterprise, and the leaders were obliged to flee the land. Austin was instrumental in securing amnesty for those who would surrender. Nothing had been gained but a new cause for increased suspicion and distrust between the two peoples.

The Fredonian turbulence showed to what lengths many Americans outside the Austin grant would go to effect their ends. It was now plain to the leaders of Mexican politics that repression would have to be the policy if they were to remain dominant. Laws governing land grants had been but loosely enforced, and many immigrants had come and settled independently, "with no other title than that of the rifle." It was to stop this kind of immigration, and to check the incoming of new men to the established grants that the policy of the Mexican government now directed itself. This was made plain by two acts, the Emancipation Decree of 1829 urged by Tornel, and the Colonization Law of 1830 proposed by Alamán.

Tornel persuaded President Guerrero, after the refusal of the Senate to pass an emancipation bill sent up from the Deputies, to issue the decree. The aim was to limit the American farming population by forbidding immigrants to bring in slaves. The decree was, however, soon set aside as far as Texas was concerned owing to the firm representations of the local Mexican officials and many of the leading Texans. The industry of the Americans depended upon the labor of slaves, and those who were opposed to the institution of slavery on principle still believed that the colony would be ruined if the importation of slaves were to be stopped. When later slavery became again the target of Mexican opposition the Texans brought in the negroes under the fiction of indentured servants. Slavery never suffered any serious check at the hands of the Mexican owners of Texas. Neither was the move for the settlement of that region a preorganized plot of the slavocracy, as several American historians have averred. The question was at this time an incident in the internal history of Texas, the colonization of which was as inevitable as the centuries-long westward sweep of the Anglo-Saxon race had been.

Repeated proposals by the United States to purchase Texas had made it apparent to the Mexicans that there was more than danger in allowing admission of a strong colony of Americans. Hence the law of April 6, 1830, proposed by Lucas Alamán, Secretary of Foreign Relations. This law, couched in general terms, explicitly encouraged colonization by Mexicans in Texas, and was directed against the feared contingency by providing that no territory should be settled by inhabitants of another state immediately contiguous to the boundary of the lands upon which settlement was being made. Importation of slaves was forbidden, as a special discouragement. Independent settlers, not on regular grants, were to be ejected. Passports were to be required for admission. Unfulfilled contracts were to be suspended. This law was never adequately enforced. It did check immigration, and led to a vast amount of ill-feeling, but it was an impossible measure. General Terán was sent from the parent State to enforce it; he established twelve military posts in the hope of quieting the Americans, who were restless under the restrictions on immigration, land titles, and customs collection. The law was abrogated finally in 1833, after serving little purpose, and a policy of greater fairness to the American settlers was recommended to the state officers.

The original provision that the colonists should be exempt from customs duties on certain necessities for seven years had led to much abuse. Smuggling was popular, and when in 1831 the time of exemption expired there was widespread dissatisfaction at the enforcement of collections.

At the entry port of Anáhuac the Virginian adventurer Bradburn was particularly obnoxious to the Texans in his arbitrary methods of assisting George Fisher, the hard-spirited collector of customs. The colonists, after an affair in which the impetuous Travis and others espoused the cause of a woman outraged by one of Bradburn's soldiers, rose and drove the collector and the garrison away. Colonel

Mejía was sent to investigate the affair, but again Austin saved the situation, convincing the liberal minded Mejía that the Texans were not to blame, though Terán continued to hold Austin responsible for the disorders coincident with the collection of duties. Colonel Mejía succeeded in getting many of the soldiers in Texas to support the revolution in Mexico, and led them away, leaving old Colonel Piedras alone at Nacogdoches to surrender his command to the new movement for Santa Anna. The soil of Texas was without Mexican soldiers in August, 1832.

The union of Texas with Coahuila in 1830 as one State of the Union had been a continual aggravation to the Texans. Coahuila was controlled by a majority of Mexicans, while Texas was not largely enough American to avoid being dominated by the larger native population of the two provinces. The capital, Saltillo, was so far removed that the Texans were at great inconvenience in transacting legal business which required presence there. Another source of discontent was Santa Anna's decree reducing the militia, so as to deprive the Texans of their arms. The desire for statehood was brought conspicuously to the front when, after the expulsion of Piedras and the departure of the liberal army, a convention met at San Felipe on October 1, 1832, to consider the state of the country. The call for this convention stated that the reasons for the meeting were to check the current misrepresentations of the Texans as desiring independence, and the prevalent Indian raids. The acts of the convention in its six days' session were: to provide for the collection of the customs until the government could send new collectors; to pray for a reform of the tariff bill; to appoint land commissioners; to ask a grant of land for schools; and to petition for separate statehood. This convention being but lightly attended, another was called for the following spring, and in April, 1833, the desires of a larger group of the people were expressed in a more representative and more radical manner.

Austin in 1833 carried to Mexico the plea of the second convention, but found President Gómez Farías opposed to

Texan statehood. After waiting long in vain for a hearing, he wrote a letter advising the settlers to proceed with forming a state under the law of May 7, 1824, even though Mexico refuse assent. His letter was intercepted, and he was arrested at Saltillo and detained in Mexico City until the summer of 1835, by which time he had become convinced of the futility of hoping for stable conditions in Texas from the operations of the existing Mexican government.

During 1833–34 the state legislature of Coahuila-Texas was favorable to the American colonists, and passed a number of acts which benefited their cause. Among them were measures creating several new municipalities, political unity to the inhabitants being thereby secured. Texas was divided into three executive departments each under a jefe político, who was to be the direct representative of the governor within the department. Two of these new departments were American in population. The English language was made coördinate with Spanish for legal usage, and a judicial system was adopted which gave the Texans the right of jury trial.

In May 1834 Santa Anna was successful in dissolving the national Congress and many of the state legislatures, making himself dictator through a Council subservient to his bidding. In October of the same year this Council gave a hearing to the petition of the Texans, and the dictator, after the consultation, decided that Texas could not have separate statehood, but that the law of April 6, 1830, should be repealed if he found no good reason for continuing it in force. Most important of all, 4000 troops were to be sent to Bejar to "protect the coast and frontier."

Stephen Austin arrived from his vicissitudes in Mexico in September of 1835 to find a revolution gathering headway. He was given a welcoming banquet at Brazoria, at which he favored the General Consultation of the people of Texas which had been proposed by the municipality of Columbia for the fifteenth of October. On the twelfth of September a committee of vigilance and safety was organized. Austin was a member of this committee, and from the date of his beginning that work until the secession was far advanced he remained the leading spirit in the affairs of the incipient republic. His basis of action was Texas first, if possible under Mexico, but always Texas. In the present exigency that policy meant war as the only resource left, inasmuch as the national Mexican army of General Cos, fresh from despoiling Zacatecas, was already on its way to enforce obedience to the laws of the land which the resolute pioneers were setting aside with ruthless disregard for their governmental superiors.

The immediate outbreak of armed hostility was the attack on Anáhuac by Travis and the expulsion of the customs collector Tenorio against the advice of the still influential conservative element. But the nearer approach of Cos, and the consequent destruction of the hopes of the people that the rumors of his coming were false, filled the hearts of the populace with an excitement which reduced factional spirit. The advent of the fugitive liberal Zavala added to the enthusiasm of opposition. The capture of Thompson, captain of the *Correo*, sent to collect customs after the expulsion of Tenorio, assisted in bringing popular feeling to a white heat.

The policy of the Mexicans to disarm the Texans led to the demand of Colonel Ugartechea for the old La Salle cannon which the people of González had set up to keep off the Indians. The cannon was valiantly defended, the town was taken by the revolutionists, and soon skirmishes at Goliad and Bahía were added to the Saxon victories. In the middle of October Austin was before Bejar in command of a force of over 350, and Cos was lying inside with 500. Captain Fannin won a fight at Concepción at the end of October; during November Colonel Mejía made an unsuccessful attempt on Tampico with a shipload of American adventurers. The Mejía expedition had the sanction of a considerable number of the revolutionists in Texas, who believed that their cause would have better standing if it were made a part of the scheme to rid the nation of Santa Anna, and that transferring the fight to Mexican soil instead of Texan would give the conflict greater dignity.

On November 25 a Texan Commission went to the United

States for the purpose of negotiating a loan and securing volunteers for the war. Burleson was placed in command of the volunteers before Bejar, and on December 4 "Old Ben Milam" raised the war cry against the Mexican garrison; Cos was taken, paroled, and allowed to march out of the land beyond the Río Grande. His departure left the soil of Texas again without a Mexican soldier,—and soon without Texas troops as well—for the people could not be made to believe that the struggle had only begun, and the volunteers hastened home to Christmas dinners.

The people of Texas sent fifty-five representative men to Felipe de Austin on November 3 to constitute the General Consultation; there they issued a tentative declaration of independence, reciting the charges that militarism under Santa Anna had overthrown constitutional government, and that it was their duty and right to maintain government independent of the representatives of centralized military control. Loyalty was pledged to the republican principles of the Constitution of 1824, it being deemed likely that this attitude would secure the hearty coöperation of the revolutionary party of Mexico. The sympathies of the Americans were appealed to by proffers of land to those who would come to the standards of resistance.

The plans of civil and military government drawn up by this Consultation are described by Garrison as "triumphs of potential confusion and conflict of authority." The governor and his council had duties not clearly differentiated, with no method of overcoming deadlocks. The military plan created a volunteer and a regular army, with a major-general in command of all the forces of the state, though the troops before Bejar were later excepted.

Henry Smith, a radical, was made president, defeating the more conservative Austin. Sam Houston, of the same political group as Smith, was made commander of the regular army on November 12. Thus fully organized and officered as they were it ought to have been possible for the Texans to crown with signal victories the beginnings they had made at Anáhuac, Concepción, Goliad, and Bejar.

But first ridiculous then serious differences arose in clashes of authority between governor and council. The most significant result was the failure of a plan to carry the war into Mexico in the Matamoros expedition. Due to conflicting orders Fannin, Johnson, Grant and Houston, had each a turn at being considered the head of this expedition, and at one time two of them were in command. Finally a number of soldiers set out, but so small was the party that it hardly merited the name of expedition. The enterprise was a dismal failure, most of the troops under Grant and Johnson being cut to pieces; the frontier of Texas was left unprotected, and the reverses of the Álamo and Goliad were traceable to the dissensions between the branches of the new government. The Álamo, besieged by Santa Anna in 1836, was taken by assault on March 6; only one defender escaped.

Travis defending the Álamo with a handful against accumulating thousands is one of the most thrilling incidents in the history of this continent. The butchery of Fannin and nearly three hundred and fifty American volunteers while retreating from Goliad on March 27 is defended by Mexican national historians as summary justice to "pirates."

On the second day of March in the same year, whilst on the field all was loss, the reconvened Consultation at New Washington on the Brazos, now under control of more radical delegates than former gatherings of its like, passed a declaration of absolute independence. Even the peace-loving Austin had come to see the need for such a step since the Mexican liberals had not been attracted by the nationalistic tone of the previous declaration, and the Americans refused to extend financial aid without a hope that complete independence would make a loan more secure. Besides the declaration, the Consultation drew up a constitution, and reëstablished Houston in his command of the troops.

Meantime the invasion under Santa Anna had brought 2500 or 3000 men to San Antonio, where the heroic stand of Travis was made, whilst General Urrea was coming up from Matamoros with probably a thousand more troops against San Patricio and Goliad. Houston had ordered Fannin to add his four hundred volunteers to the main command, but Fannin delayed, and the fight at the Coleta and the subsequent massacre at Goliad had deprived the Texans of half their army. This catastrophe served to weaken further Houston's fighting force, as his undisciplinable men, fearful for the safety of their homes which lay in the path of the conqueror, left the standards of the Republic to hasten back to the defense of their homes or to move their families beyond the Sabine.

Hence the only possible movement for a month was a retreat; from Goliad northeast to Groce's, thence southeastward at slow rates of progress Houston's forces moved to the final scene on the San Jacinto River. The mutterings of the troops at the continued retreat from a position where the pursuing enemy might have been assailed with even chances of success were continuous. The real necessity was to keep out of reach of the Mexicans. It is sometimes suspected that Houston was trying to decoy Santa Anna over to the Sabine country, where the United States army might find an easy opportunity to interfere, and the mantle of protection might be thrown over the new "nation." Finally, however, General Rusk, sent to inaugurate a more vigorous policy, joined the army and succeeded in bringing on the fight which ended the war, without the aid of the American general Gaines who was watching against violations of neutrality and Indian raids with something of generous solicitude for the Texans.

On the nineteenth of April, Houston came upon his pursuer near Buffalo Bayou, or San Jacinto River. Here it seemed still doubtful whether the Texan would fight, but his officers were determined to bring on an immediate attack.

Accordingly an action was begun on the afternoon of April 21 which was a complete surprise to Santa Anna, though he knew that his opponents were near. But his own troops were worn with marching, and, confident that the patriots would not dare to attack in their weak condition, he and his men indulged in rest. The chief himself slept. His second spent the time shaving and dressing. Meanwhile the

Texans formed in the shelter of sparse trees, until, rushing forward, they gave the cry, "Remember the Álamo!" Then ensued a bad quarter of an hour for "The Napoleon of the West;" his advance guard of picked troops was borne back, his convict troops huddled around and impeded his veterans. General Urrea had disappointed him by not sending the five hundred best men of his command. Clubbed guns in the hands of the Texans, who took no time to reload after the first shots, and knives desperately wielded, were too much for the poorly led peón army. Six hundred out of about 1360 were killed; about three dozen escaped; the rest were gathered by Colonel Almonte and surrendered. Santa Anna was captured the next day, and all the munitions of the invaders fell to the conquerors.

Santa Anna feared for his life, not without cause, for the victory on the San Jacinto had hardly sated the Texan desire for vengeance on the author of the indignities the colonists had suffered, and it required all Houston's persuasion to keep him from falling into the hands of those who would destroy him. But Houston realized that the reputation of Texas in the eyes of the world depended upon the humanity with which its army could treat a conquered enemy, and Santa Anna was, after long delays, sent to Washington late in 1836 and thence back to his career of conquest in Mexico, where he continued to be a melodramatic and Machiavellian figure in the history of the unhappy country, but forgot his promises concerning Texan independence.

Seeing himself undone, he proposed entering into a treaty whereby he was to gain his liberty in return for efforts in Mexico to secure the independence of Texas. The Mexican troops were to cross the Río Grande, and war damages to private property were to be paid. This Treaty of Velasco was signed on May 14, 1836. Santa Anna's long detention and the hazards of his captivity freed his easy conscience from keeping the terms of the treaty imposed upon him; Mexico never acknowledged the independence of Texas, and indeed the new republic was never wholly free from prospects of repeated invasion. Tornel made heroic efforts to secure means for a return of the Mexican troops to Texas in 1836, but lack of funds was the unconquerable difficulty, and the expedition was abandoned. Generals were made and unmade over the issue, to no avail. Futile raids into Texas were of irritating frequency. Two expeditions did indeed reach San Antonio, the second as late as 1842, but served no efficient purpose. On the other hand an ill-starred expedition of the Texans in June, 1841, against Santa Fe resulted in defeat. Other aggressive acts by both sides kept up an impotent hatred for years. The probable effects upon the slavery struggle of the admission of Texas to the American Union delayed that act until 1845, when the ensuing events brought on the War with the United States.

CHAPTER XVII

ON the first day of March, 1836, just before the Texans won their complete but officially unacknowledged separation from the mother country, the Mexican president, General Barragán, died of a sudden fever. The Chamber of Deputies replaced him with another very pious but mediocre personage, José Justo Corro. His term was signalized by the recognition of Mexican independence, thus tardily, by Spain. The action was due to Spanish sympathy with the centralist and clerical régime imposed by the Constitution of 1836. In 1839 came the first Spanish minister, Ángel Calderón de la Barca, whose wife, Madame Calderón, a New England woman, most cleverly interpreted this period of Mexican history in her *Life in Mexico*. In 1837 the pope also recognized Mexican independence.

During Corro's term there was a well-intended movement started in Puebla to bring about harmony among the many jealous political factions, but the time was not ripe for concord. Santa Anna, still in obscurity because of his unsavory record in the Texas episode and in the crushing of federalists in Zacatecas, was nevertheless in the political offing, and peace internal was not to be had. Federalism and centralism were the specious shibboleths under which regionalism and individualism disrupted the country.

In this situation were affairs when Anastasio Bustamante returned from the exile in France which Gómez Farías had imposed upon him. Looked upon as fit centralist presidential material, Bustamante had little trouble in getting himself elected. He took office April 19, 1837, supposedly

291

for a term of eight years. He had promised great reforms, but speedily entered upon a reactionary policy which earned him severe federalist opposition. There was revival of the centrifugal spirit which had been shown just after independence among the northern states, in Jalisco and neighboring states in 1829, in 1833 in the nine states of the central north, and in 1836 in Texas and the whole northern frontier. San Luis Potosí and Sonora were ripe for secession during 1837, a plan being on foot to establish in the mountain states a new Republic of Sierra Madre. These plots were to continue for almost a decade longer in various federalist areas to the north and south.

At one time, in 1837, it seemed as though the federalists would succeed in reëstablishing themselves in Mexico City by putting Gómez Farías again in power. The condition of the country was desperate financially. All sorts of plans were tried to raise money, but without avail. There grew up a demand for mortgaging the property of the church, since that institution still had large resources, which the covetous eyes of politicians looked upon longingly. Thus was renewed the agitation for those assaults upon the privileged economic position of the great rival institution to the government, assaults which were to bring decades of political turmoil before Mexico was to be free of clerical domination.

The rather unusual powers of Bustamante as an administrator were prevented from developing legitimate scope by external troubles as well as internal ones. In 1838 occurred the aggression of France upon Mexico for the collection of damages to her nationals during various disorders dating back as far as 1828. One claimant was a French baker whose shop had been sacked by a mob, an incident which brought upon the French attempt to collect damages the name of "The Pastry War." The whole amount of the claims amounted to $600,000. A French fleet blockaded Vera Cruz for the purpose of enforcing collection and delivered an ultimatum which could not be heeded because of numerous federal attempts to embarrass

Bustamante's government. Santa Anna, endeavoring again to regain the prestige he had lost at San Jacinto, undertook to repel the French, who had landed. In the engagement with them he had the rare good fortune to have a leg shot away by a cannon ball. This sacrifice was used to cover up the lack of military acumen which had nearly led to his capture. The restored hero and his valuable leg were each given separate ovations in the capital; the French claim was adjusted through English intervention, in a treaty allowing the claims, and the episode closed.

In 1839 Bustamante had to take the field to repel another federalist attempt to seize the power for Gómez Farías. Successful temporarily, he had, two years afterward, to meet another insurrection against the Constitution of 1836 led by General Paredes and Santa Anna. The most of the fighting occurred in Mexico City, where comparatively little damage of material nature was done.

There was justification for the very general discontent elicited by the system of government provided by the Constitution of 1836. The most remarkable feature of that system was the absurd super-committee called the Poder Conservador. This group of men, who were supposed to possess that political omniscience which would enable them to interpret and compel obedience to the will of the nation, actually exercised its privileged position to thwart the very interests it was supposed to promote. There was a quick and general revulsion of sentiment against it all over the country. The press began to demand the restoration of the Constitution of 1824. After two and a half years of trial, the Congress attempted to amend the Constitution so as to make it more responsive to the popular will, but the Poder Conservador refused to accede to the proposed changes. Thereupon the radicals attempted to vote the Poder out of existence, but were defeated. After a great deal of disorder, numerous fruitless conferences between party leaders, and indecisive battles between contesting military aspirants for power, President Bustamante was seized in his own apartments by the federalist general Urrea on July 15, 1840. A struggle between the opposing factions left the government for the time intact, but in August, 1841, General Paredes in Jalisco declared for a new Constitution and the renovation of the executive power by conferring it upon "some citizen worthy of confidence," by which he meant Santa Anna, with whom he had a secret understanding. About the same time General Valencia "proclaimed" in Mexico, and Santa Anna himself in Vera Cruz. Now began a series of military plots and counterplots headed by Santa Anna, Paredes, and Valencia. A Plan was agreed upon at Tacubaya, a suburb of Mexico City, by nearly two hundred followers of these three military chiefs. It was really nothing but a military coalition manipulated in the personal interests of Santa Anna, utilizing the general discontent as an excuse for advancing his ambition.

The Plan de Tacubaya, promulgated on September 28, 1841, declared that the Poder Comservador had, by the "will of the nation," ceased to exist. General amnesty was announced for political offenders of all descriptions, and a Congress to frame a new Constitution was demanded. First, a Junta of Notables, chosen by Santa Anna, named that worthy as Provisional President. He, in accordance with the Plan, began by abolishing all the existing arms of government except the judiciary. President Bustamante attempted to retain his power by declaring for federalism, but failing to win support by this means he gave up the contest and sailed away to Europe. On October 7, 1841, Santa Anna entered the capital as Provisional President; thus, after defeat and disgrace in Texas and capture by his enemies had been added to his many opportunist political antics, he was in possession of the supreme power of the country once again.

On June 10, 1842, the assembled Congress of patriotic citizens who had been elected to produce a new constitution proved to be in the hands of proponents of federalism. What Santa Anna wanted was a centralist form of government with himself as the center. This he unequivocally declared to the constituent body when he addressed it at its opening, though he intimated that he would graciously acquiesce in its decision. When, however, two attempts had unsuccessfully been made to produce a framework of government which would suit both himself and the Congress, he retired from political control, as was his wont when crossed. In his place he left Nicolás Bravo and Valentín Canalizo with orders to alternate in exercise of the executive power. Bravo, being of centralist tendencies, quickly dissolved the federalist Congress and reassembled the Junta of Notables which had been convoked by the Plan de Tacubaya. This new body, which in fact represented no one but Santa Anna, soon produced a third fundamental charter on June 13, 1843, which it called the Bases Orgánicas de la República Mexicana.

These Bases Orgánicas were a most cynical attack on popular rights under an assumption of the form of democracy. It would be hard to tell which of the two constitutions, that of 1836 or that of 1843, was more highly centralized or worse for the country as political matters stood. The men, there were eighty of them, who drew up the document of 1843, desired nothing less than a federal system, and yet they feared on the one hand to make the central power too strong because of their apprehension of Santa Anna as a prospective dictator, and on the other that if they did not meet his demands for practically unlimited power through the Bases he would declare for that very federalism they so much despised. Hence their document proved to be a governmental absurdity, for it created a "constitutional" despotism. There was to be a popular representative government, but every voter must have an annual income of two hundred pesos. This provision deprived nearly all common laborers of the franchise. The system of selective elections filtered the desired candidates through all the stages at the will of the central power. The territory of the country was divided into departments. The sovereignty was declared to reside in the nation and not in the people. The Congress was made a nullity through the large veto power given the president. The judiciary depended on him, and his cabinet had no independent prerogatives. In the Departments, the assemblies were subservient to the governors, whom the president appointed. Perhaps the worst feature of the whole organization was the provision that the president might, by his so-called exceptional powers, initiate special local laws for the various departments, whenever and however he wished. He was also empowered to impose fines not exceeding five hundred pesos on whoever should disobey him or show disrespect for the laws. He might declare war as he saw fit; he might expel dangerous foreigners at his own pleasure. These are some of the outstanding features of the charter under which Santa Anna enthroned himself in power with the backing of the church and the army. There was in fact no other aristocracy created by Mexican conditions. Here was the apogee of personalistic centralism.

Under a benevolent despot, the system evolved by Santa Anna might have worked. But his purpose had been entirely selfish. Thoroughly ensconced in the power by election in 1844, he began to rule with the most barefaced corruptness. He and his entourage were guilty of the most open immorality. Graft lost all vestiges of refinement. Huge sums expended in pleasures led to demands upon the people for still greater sums to be expended, it was alleged, upon preparations for resistance to the United States, France, and England, whose interests in the outcome of the Texan situation were matters of grave concern to the presidential power. In his personal dress and bearing the dictator displayed a presumptuous elegance which was irritating, and in his demands for money he aroused more than suspicion of his intention to do nothing for the country. Sensing the bitterness of the opposition, he again left the presidency, this time in charge of Canalizo, retiring to Manga de Clavo but placing a large body of troops between himself and the capital in case he should need them.

But in his lust for power he had forgotten the political virtue of gratitude to General Paredes, who had manipulated

the first steps of his rise to power when he overthrew Bustamante. Paredes had been placed in charge of the military
department of Jalisco, but his ambition was not sated by
this preferment, nor was he pleased by the effort made to
belittle his prestige by Santa Anna, who knew him to be the
only other general powerful enough to aspire to the presidency. In the congressional group Santa Anna was roundly
censured by such liberals as Gómez Pedraza, Llaca, Olaguíbel, de la Rosa, and others, while there were many throughout the country who resented the failure of the President to
limit his activities to the broad powers conceded by the
Bases, and who groaned under the new burdens of taxation
which the personal centralism imposed.

Paredes denounced the ad interim President, Canalizo,
and called an assembly in his department to demand that
the government should obey the spirit of the Plan de Tacubaya; he also demanded cessation of forced loans and increased automony in the Departments. Five northern Departments adhered to him. There were as many which
adhered to Santa Anna, who took the field and led troops
against Paredes. But Congress, which constitutionally had
the power to prevent the President from leading armed
forces, opposed his policies as well as his activities, for
which it was indefinitely dissolved by Canalizo, the entire
functions of government being assumed by him in the name
of Santa Anna. The popular anger against this act was so
great that the Department of Puebla and the garrison and
people of the capital rose and swept Canalizo out of power,
caused the Congress to reassemble, and advanced the President of the Council of State, José Joaquín Herrera, to the
chief executive power, on December 5, 1844. Thus the
country was broken up into three loyalties. Paredes in the
north, the Congress in the center, and Santa Anna supported by the Departments of Puebla and Vera Cruz, all
sought preëminent political control. But the Senate and
the Deputies both protested against Santa Anna's attitude,
calling upon the army to submit to the legislature's control.
Santa Anna marched upon the capital, and Paredes marched

upon Santa Anna. After ineffectual battles before Mexico City and later before Puebla, the would-be dictator was captured, was shortly tried, and banished from the country "forever." There was a party which demanded his execution for palpable dishonesty, even high treason in subverting the Constitution; but a spirit of somewhat greater political tolerance was growing up in the country among the liberals led by such men as Gómez Farías and Herrera, the moderate president, and, after all the turmoil was over, a general amnesty was declared for all but Santa Anna and a few of his closest associates. None of the political criminals was executed, varying terms of banishment being substituted.

About a year and a half later, Santa Anna's "perpetual" exile ended, and he returned to his native country with the encouragement of the United States forces, which hoped to utilize him in effecting peace in the war then being waged between that country and Mexico. When he returned, it was as a declared federalist, and it was evidently not his intention to hasten terms of peace. By a pronouncement called the Plan de la Ciudadela, in August, 1846, still another constituent congress was convoked, while a provisional decree reëstablished temporarily the old Constitution of 1824. In 1847 Santa Anna proclaimed a new Acta Constitutiva and an Acta de Reformas, which reëstablished the federal principle of government. The work of this constituent congress was led by a moderate in politics, Mariano Otero. The federalism which he introduced was destined to survive the war with the United States, and to continue in a struggle gigantic which was to terminate in the Revolution of Ayutla and the War of the Reform. But in the meantime the fortunes of Mexico were gravely altered by the occurrences of the inevitable War with the United States which had grown out of the border conflict over the colonization, secession, and annexation to the latter country of the old province of Texas.

CHAPTER XVIII

WAR WITH THE UNITED STATES

THE war with the United States which began in 1845 had both remote and proximate causes. Among the former were natural racial antipathies which had been formed during the colonial epoch of both Spain and England. These antipathies had had their origins in nationalistic and religious rivalries which antedated the buccaneering period of the Elizabethan seamen. They had not grown less when the English colonists confronted the Spanish along the Louisiana frontier after the Seven Years' War drove France from the continent, nor had they been abated when the ships of the Americans began to visit the Pacific ports of New Spain before the end of the eighteenth century, nor when, shortly after the nineteenth century began, Louisiana was bought by the United States and the westward movement of the Americans took on new vigor. In all these situations the aggressiveness of the virile Anglo-Saxon people was met by an obstructionist policy on the part of the Spaniards and Mexicans, a policy born of dislike, but prompted more acutely by fear of loss of territory.

The proximate causes were bound up with the problems arising out of the American colonization of Texas, its subsequent secession, and its annexation by the United States. Texas, we have seen, obtained a treaty from Santa Anna acknowledging her independence in 1836. This treaty had not been ratified by the Mexican government, that is, the independence of Texas had never been formally recognized. It had not, on the other hand, ever been effectively disputed. The people of Texas had maintained their independence for nine years, and their government had been recognized by several foreign nations, including the United States. The

299

latter power acknowledged Texan independence in the spring of 1837. By many persons in Mexico and the United States this was considered only a preliminary to annexation. Mexico broke relations with the United States after Texas was recognized, and served notice in 1843 that annexation would be held an act of war.

The steps toward disagreement between the two governments had been continuous since the unfortunate career of Joel R. Poinsett, first minister of the United States to Mexico, in 1825. Though Poinsett had a hard position to fill, he rendered his own success impossible by interfering in Mexican politics. He attempted to teach lessons of democracy through organization of York Rite Masonic lodges to oppose the Scottish Rite lodges, which held the political power. This move was practically forced upon him, as his mission depended on a republican Mexico. He ended by failure to press to completion any treaty of commerce or boundaries, or effect any purchase of territory, and wound up by becoming an issue in an armed uprising, which demanded his expulsion. He had made himself the victim of factional discords, for all united to execrate him; thus he dealt a severe blow to the idealism in which Mexicans had held the American people as friends of democracy and republicanism. It is a matter of the keenest regret that there could not have been found for this position a minister who understood diplomacy, or who might at least have had the acumen to attend more strictly to the mission on which he entered Mexico. His influence was largely minimized, it is true, by the fact that he was instructed to urge the unacceptable purchase of Texan territory. This made the Mexican government suspicious and its course was not irreproachable in delaying ratification of the treaties and in discriminatory action in completing negotiations of the same character with England. But the Americans were in a position to be feared as aggressors, while the English were not, as they had, through Mexico's first foreign loan, effected a virtual protectorate over the newborn Republic.

The prospect of purchasing part of Texas was made

even more remote by the undiplomatic character of Poinsett's successor, Anthony Butler. He was "a national disgrace," says Justin H. Smith, "a cantankerous, incompetent rascal." Like Poinsett, whom Smith defends, Butler also proved unsatisfactory to Mexico, and his recall was asked for in 1835, a full year after Jackson had characterized him as a "scamp."

The colonization of Texas by Americans, encouraged by Mexico at first in the fatuous hope that the settlers could be restricted to Catholics, and that these would create a buffer state against the westward sweep of the American nation and its anticipated aggression on Mexican territory, was recognized as a mistake by the Mexican government as early as 1825. It would have been better for Mexico to have yielded gracefully to natural developments, effecting an advantageous sale of Texan territory when Poinsett suggested it, but such a step was impossible given the Mexican frame of mind toward territorial integrity and national sovereignty. No government could have maintained its power after such a transaction. The psychology of the weaker nation was against any change that would disclose feebleness. Hence when the Texans seceded it was only natural for Mexicans to suspect that the United States government had had an interested share in promoting the movement. Though this was probably untrue, the fact that a part of the American people also had a like suspicion tended to bolster the Mexican attitude. And when Americans as individuals or in organizations lent aid to the Texans the Mexicans could hardly be blamed for failing to distinguish between popular sympathies and governmental action.

Another unsatisfactory situation arose in 1829 over the question as to whether the Sabine or the Neches river was the true boundary between the United States and Texas. The United States seemed to have its eye on the region west of the Sabine, and General Gaines was sent to occupy the area between the two rivers for the declared purpose of holding the predatory Indians of the frontier in check.

The Mexican government believed this to be an invasion of national territory, and sanctioned the departure from Washington of a special minister whom it had sent to settle the boundary issue. Popular feeling in Mexico was hot against the United States for this encroachment, and when American recognition of Texan independence followed, the fact was considered proof of a long-cherished design to obtain the seceded territory.

This sentiment was re-enlivened in 1842 by Santa Anna, who doubtless desired to arouse anti-American feeling in order to stifle complaints against his internal policy. He encouraged raids into Texas, and planned an armed expedition to reconquer it. His foreign minister took the American government to task for alleged aid to the enemies of Mexico, but dropped discussion upon Secretary Webster's tart reassertion of American neutrality. In both countries there was deeply hostile feeling over the Texas question. This was heightened when Commodore T. A. C. Jones of the American Pacific squadron, believing war inevitable, and probably even then existent, in October, 1842, seized Monterey, California, without authorization and had immediately to withdraw in some humiliation at his hastiness in anticipating an obviously coming event. In 1842 and 1843 the American government further irritated the Mexican government by urging discontinuance of raids into Texas for recovery of the lost territory as senseless and futile.

Anyone who has the slightest understanding of the Hispanic American spirit must recognize that each of these incidents was inflammatory to the Mexicans. But the Americans had also had many grievances. There was the execution by Santa Anna's order without trial of twenty-two Americans and their leader caught in 1835 at Tampico under the liberal revolutionist Mejía. Americans could not look upon these men as deserving such a fate, as the Mexicans did. Then there began in 1837 a renewal of the policy of keeping Americans from settling in Mexican frontier states. In 1840 a number of Americans in California were arrested, and sent to Mexico, and their property confiscated. Their legal offence was that of being in Mexican territory. When in 1841 Texas attempted to seize New Mexico, some American citizens joined the expedition. Upon its failure, they were sent to Mexico and treated inhumanely while prisoners, the American government protesting. In 1843 American trade with New Mexico, which had slowly developed, was forbidden by Santa Anna. Other trade restrictions followed, designed to stop commercial intercourse. Again, in 1843, the Mexican government ordered the expulsion of all Americans from its territory. And finally, there were large unsatisfied claims of many American citizens for forced loans and loss of property and life in disorders in many Mexican "revolutions." A convention which imposed payment of $2,000,000 in claims to Americans was effected in 1843, but never completely fulfilled.

In that same year the international tension began to grow more acute. Not only was Mexico still intransigent on the question of Texas, but it began to be feared that the Lone Star Republic was hoping to add the west and northwest, including Oregon, to its domain. There was visible discontent among the inhabitants of the Mexican northwest over their habitual misgovernment, and there were those in the slave area of the United States who could see economic advantage in a union with such an enlarged and independent Texas. Such a political aggroupment would have been as disastrous as secession of the American South would have been had it succeeded when attempted a few years later. The nations of the Old World would have viewed such aggrandizement with alarm. It would have involved North America in the complications of European politics, and Mexico in annihilation.

Naturally Mexico was also apprehensive over American interest in such an expanded Texas, and its announcement, on August 23, 1843, that it would consider American annexation of Texas as tantamount to a declaration of war, was not unnatural under the circumstances. In November the Mexican minister at Washington, J. N. Almonte, asseverated that war would be declared upon announcement that the annexation had been consummated. The Americans felt that they had free right to act on Texas as though the latter were, as she was, actually independent; however, to avoid complications, she offered negotiations looking toward financial compensation, but the overture was rejected. The proffer was even used by Santa Anna as an added cause for war. The American people have never been quite able to understand the spirit of a Mexico which has repeatedly manifested its willingness to embark upon a warlike course even though the prospect of winning has been materially nothing.

When, therefore, President Tyler signed the joint resolution of annexation, the Mexican minister asserted that his nation would maintain her claim to Texas by every means available, called for his passports and went home. The American minister in Mexico was speedily dismissed on receipt there of news of this action.

Mexico immediately prepared for war without formally declaring it. Troops were moved northward preparatory to crossing the Río Grande into Texas, which was yet national territory in Mexican opinion. Even yet the American president tried to conciliate Mexico by offer of a liberal settlement of the annexation difficulty through concessions to be made in a boundary treaty. The administration of President Herrera was disposed to conciliation. His tenure was not strong, he had only recently superseded the Santa Anna régime, he knew what costly losses defeat would entail, and he felt that Texas was already lost to Mexico and out of her power. He consented to receive an American minister, and John Slidell was sent to Mexico, where he arrived on November 30, a decidedly unwelcome visitor. By that time Herrera's government was about to fall, he was afraid of the popular effect of a peaceable settlement, and timorously refused to open negotiations. At this juncture General Paredes, at the head of a coali-

tion of church, army, and monarchical groups, which were
desirous of supplanting the federal party, revolted under
the allegation that Herrera was planning to compromise
the dignity of the Republic by entering into negotiations
concerning Texas. Paredes was under orders to move
his army to the frontier to aid General Arista in the imminent clash with the United States forces. Instead of obey-
ing, he marched in January 1846 upon Mexico City and
seized the political power, Herrera having given up without
a blow on December 29. Paredes at once assumed a
hostile attitude toward the United States. Slidell, who
had remained to see what success he could attain from the
new administration, was rebuffed with short shrift early
in March.

The Americans had already planned to defend Texas
as soon as annexation had become a fact. The Texans
claimed that their territory extended to the Río Grande.
This had been the American view when the Louisiana
Territory was purchased, the United States considering
Texas a part of Louisiana until the purchase of Florida in
1819, when the area west of the Sabine River was ceded
to Spain. Since that time no boundary between Texas
and Coahuila had been definitely established; the secession of Texas from Mexico had left the question open, the
citizens of the new republic claiming jurisdiction to the
Río Grande. The United States accepted that line at
annexation, and now prepared to defend it. American
troops under General Zachary Taylor, stationed at Fort
Jesup on the western line of Louisiana, were sent to Texas
in July, 1845, and stationed at Corpus Christi, south of the
Nueces at its outlet. By October the forces there assembled
numbered about 3,900 men. In March, after news of the
failure of Slidell, Taylor moved upon Matamoros, at the
mouth of the Río Grande. Here General Arista arrived on
April 24, with orders to attack the Americans. Arista
ordered General Torrejón to cross the river on April 25
with 1,600 cavalry. There Torrejón encountered Captain
Thornton commanding some sixty American dragoons;

several of them were killed trying to cut their way through the Mexican cavalry, and the remainder surrendered. The war which Mexico had considered as existing ever since Texas was annexed was by that action formally opened. President Polk had sincerely tried to avoid it; Herrera had been anxious to do so. Both had been prevented by popular clamor in each country. Mexico had been drawn into it by the ambition of Paredes and his clerical party; the United States by land hunger and ideals of "Manifest Destiny."

The Mexican forces at Matamoros under Arista numbered nearly 6,000 men, cavalry, infantry, and artillery, of both volunteer and regular organization. The men were good fighters, but the officers were of quality indifferent or worse. Arista's plan of campaign was to cut the American communications with the Gulf, north of Matamoros. The Mexican leader took suitable positions for this purpose before Taylor realized it or began to protect his lines by falling back upon the Gulf coast. On May 8 the Mexicans were met at Palo Alto, and after a long engagement, driven from the field. They were overtaken by the pursuing Americans at the Resaca de la Palma, an old course of the Río Grande, and there driven across the river into Matamoros the next day. On May 17 they evacuated the town, falling back on Linares. By the first week in July the Americans were ready to proceed with the invasion of Mexico. Troops were sent by boat to Camargo, the head of navigation of the Río Grande, four hundred miles inland, whence the march overland to Monterrey, in Nuevo León, was undertaken.

The Mexicans had been nonplussed at the defeat of Arista at Matamoros. They knew of the inefficiency of Taylor's operations, and realized better than the Americans did what would be the cost of a northern invasion such as was proposed. In June General Paredes was elected president, and his Congress voted to repel the invasion, the church contributing a million pesos for the cause. But the president's power soon waned. He feared to take the field lest an uprising in Mexico unseat him. He was a monarchist, and had been planning to aid in setting up a monarchical system, but his plans went awry, and the army began to call for its old chieftain and hero, Santa Anna, still in exile. In August, 1845, the garrison at Vera Cruz "pronounced" for him, and for a return to federalism, with active prosecution of the war. Santa Anna landed at Vera Cruz in the same month, and proclaimed his enmity to monarchical plans and ecclesiastical power in politics. Though not as enthusiastically received as he had expected to be, he succeeded in having the federal Constitution of 1824 re-proclaimed and a government organized in which he characteristically declined an active part. On September 17 he was given command of the army. Thenceforward he bent his plans to meet Taylor in the north, in order to defeat the invader and reëstablish himself in supreme power. His "Liberating Army" was concentrated at San Luis Potosí.

General Mejía, who had superseded Arista after Matamoros, planned to harass the Americans by guerrilla warfare, and make a determined stand only at Monterrey. That city was as well fortified as the meager resources and the unhappy political condition of the country would permit. The Americans arrived before it on September 19. In heroic fighting against manfully defended works, they won a costly triumph after three days, and on September 26 the Mexican forces marched out without being paroled, and retired south of a line across which neither army was to pass during eight weeks unless under orders from its central government.

When the armistice so arranged was repudiated by the American government, General Taylor promptly decided to occupy Saltillo. in Coahuila, because of its strategic value, though the American secretary of war advised against any advance beyond Monterrey because of the hostility which was being encountered among the Mexican people. Saltillo was occupied without resistance on November 17.

Meantime another campaign in the character of a diversion was being conducted in the state of Chihuahua. It was believed that conquest of that area would hasten the desire of Mexico for peace. This movement was led by General Wool from San Antonio, Texas; it began in September, 1846, and advanced by way of Monclova, which was occupied October 29 without resistance just before Taylor's armistice stopped troop movements. As there was great hazard in maintaining communications in Chihuahua, though the regular Mexican troops in that State had moved back into Durango, Wool moved his command from Monclova to Parras in Coahuila, with the purpose of joining Taylor. He effected a union with Worth's command at Agua Nueva, south of Saltillo, on December 21, having made a successful march of nine hundred miles through Mexican territory without meeting any armed resistance whatsoever.

Tampico, on the Gulf coast of Tamaulipas, was taken by a maritime expedition in October, the Mexican defenders having withdrawn because of their ineffective condition prior to the advent of the Americans. Thus practically all of northeastern Mexico was then controlled by the invading forces. General Taylor desired to hold that area defensively for a war indemnity and for American claims. This meant controlling a line eight hundred miles long in hostile country with less than 15,000 men against an enemy numbered at some 50,000 under Santa Anna, an obvious impossibility.

New Mexico, northernmost and most neglected of Mexican inland territory, so neglected that it had even proposed in 1837 to secede as Texas and California had done, well known to the Americans because of the Santa Fe caravan trade, was another region which lay in the path of conquest. An expedition, which it was hoped might be bloodless, was sent under Colonel S. W. Kearny to effect the occupation of the region. His troops began leaving Fort Leavenworth in June, 1846, for the Santa Fe road. Kearny announced at Las Vegas, which he reached on August 15, that the Americans had come to assimilate and benefit the New Mexican people, and not as conquerors. But the governor, Armijo, had assured the inhabitants that the invaders would brutalize them, and had organized a formidable resistance to the travel-weakened Americans. But the ferocity of the officers and of the people alike soon waned, the resistance gave way, and the occupation of Santa Fe was effected on August 18. Fortifying the place, Kearny soon added the remainder of the province to his conquest, and then set out at the end of September for California.

From Santa Fe it was thought wise again to send troops into Chihuahua, the number of them at Santa Fe being superfluous. In December therefore Colonel Doniphan set out from Valverde, New Mexico, to effect a union with General Wool, whom he expected to meet at the city of Chihuahua. Moving to Paso del Norte, now Ciudad Juárez, he defeated a Mexican force which offered but feeble-hearted opposition, and set out for his objective over the Chihuahua desert-plain, a march of two hundred and twenty-five miles. Beating resistance again at Sacramento, near Chihuahua, he entered that city, soon continuing to Saltillo, which he reached on May 22. From Saltillo the force returned to the Río Grande, reaching New Orleans in June, where it was mustered out. A long march of 3,000 miles had been made with no strategic gain for a force of over 900 men who might have been employed to better purpose. They had, however, assisted in delivering a caravan of American merchandise in Chihuahua, and had demonstrated the practical defenselessness of the Mexican northlands.

The Californian coast had excited an increasing amount of interest in the United States since 1822, when the New England hide trade with that region began. By 1845 there were probably eight hundred Americans, and numerous other foreigners, in the westernmost Mexican province. The ill-governed natives had rebelled against the Republic in 1836, had been reduced by Santa Anna's troops in 1843, and had again driven out the representatives of the central power in 1845. In May of 1846 it seemed likely that the province would be sold to some foreign power. There was no ability in Mexico to control or improve the area. The Californians were ready for any change that would bring prosperity and good government. The Americans were the most ready to accept the trust, though the French and the British in the territory also entertained similar expectant attitudes.

The value of California became better appreciated, and demand for its acquisition by the United States became vociferously popular in 1845. Newspapers and even members of Congress in 1846 urged forestalling the loss of the territory to England by obtaining it in payment of the Mexican bonded debt. The value of the port of San Francisco to the rich American whale fisheries of the Pacific was an added inducement.

The first armed forces of the United States reached California in December, 1845. They were not soldiers, but armed explorers under Captain John C. Frémont seeking a road to the Pacific. Though his purpose was avowedly peaceful, he was thought by the military governor, Castro, to be aiming at exciting rebellion. Desiring to avoid a clash, Frémont moved his forces from Monterey toward Oregon, but, overtaken by Gillespie, who bore a verbal message from the American secretary of state, Buchanan, he returned to the Sacramento and shortly after indulged his personal ambition in the Bear Flag uprising at Sonoma. The complications which might have arisen from this American declaration of Californian independence were averted by the seizure of Monterey on July 7 by Commodore Sloat, commander of the American Pacific squadron.

Though the action was accompanied by declaration of its benevolent purpose, the Mexican officers Alvarado and Pico, withdrawing to the south near Los Angeles, seemed preparing to offer resistance. Soon Sloat turned over his squadron to Robert F. Stockton. Frémont and his men were taken into the service of the navy, and were moved to Los Angeles, to conquer the south. The Mexican troops did not attack him. At Los Angeles Stockton on August 17 proclaimed the authority of the United States and appointed Gillespie commandant, with a meager force of fifty men. Soon revolt broke out. The Americans were obliged to surrender, and Gillespie sailed from San Pedro for the north early in October. Stockton sent them back with reinforcements, but they were repulsed.

While this indecisive condition prevailed Kearny was approaching from New Mexico. As his small party of one hundred dragoons gained the vicinity of San Diego a force of Californians of about the same number under Andrés Pico met them at San Pascual on Warner's Ranch and defeated them, but was unable to follow up the advantage. Kearny reached San Diego on December 12. Stockton then moved against Los Angeles with about four hundred men from the north, and occupied it after trifling resistance by Flores on January 10, 1847. Meantime Frémont, coming tardily from the north, reached the Cahuenga Pass north of Los Angeles, where, after having taken no active part in the recent operations, he accepted a surrender from the Californians which gave them all the immunities they asked. Stockton reluctantly confirmed the so-called treaty, by which California was definitely divorced from Mexico.

But the conquest of all these northern areas did not have the expected result of bringing Mexico to terms. A change of policy on the part of the United States became imperative. It was seen that an advance of Taylor's forces farther south would necessitate too long a line of communications, but it was seen that a blow must be struck at the heart of Mexico to make her yield by taking the capital by way of Vera Cruz. This was almost equally hazardous, for it involved maintaining several hundred miles of communications after a forced landing at a most unhealthful port. General Winfield Scott was chosen to head the expedition. General Taylor, now being superseded in the chief command by Scott, was ordered to maintain his forces on the defensive at Monterrey.

Taylor's political ambitions, for he was an avowed candidate for nomination for the presidency of the United States, led him to disregard orders which he deemed intended to relegate him to obscurity. At the end of January, 1847, he advanced his available forces from Monterrey to Saltillo so as to seem to be upon the aggressive. South of the latter city he established his camp on the Hacienda of Buena Vista. Santa Anna, staking his military and political fortunes on hopes of a victory, had gathered a force at San Luis Potosí, from which point he began a dramatic northward march toward Saltillo on January 28, 1847. On the cruel march of two hundred miles he lost several thousand of his troops through desertion or diseases caused by privations, arriving near the American positions with some 15,000 men. Skirmishes between outposts began on February 21, and on the twenty-second and twenty-third the Mexicans attacked in the battle of Buena Vista. Near to triumph at one moment, Santa Anna was at the end completely routed though his men had fought with a courage equalling that of the Americans. He was obliged to retreat southward, leaving Taylor master of the north in Monterrey.

There was abundant work for Santa Anna in the south. Scott's army of over 12,000 men disembarked just south of Vera Cruz on March 7, and began bombarding the city on the twenty-second. It surrendered on the twenty-ninth. No outside aid had been rendered it. Scott's bombardment of a city full of civilians was justified by the haste necessary if his troops were to avoid the terrible diseases of Vera Cruz. Santa Anna, having returned to Mexico to put down a revolt of students called polkos, assumed the presidency with no opposition, and set about opposing the Americans. He established fortifications at the pass of Cerro Gordo on the road inland, toward Jalapa, and considered his position impregnable. But the Americans turned the position in a flank attack on April 17 and 18. Santa Anna fled to Orizaba. The invaders pressed on to Puebla, occupying it on May 15, in spite of attempts at resistance by Santa Anna. The city was glad to welcome the Americans. By August he was before Mexico City ready to invest it.

After these victories, the Americans hoped that peace could be obtained. President Polk sent Nicholas B. Trist to Scott's headquarters to negotiate with the Mexicans. The Americans demanded the cession of New Mexico and California for a cash consideration, while Santa Anna's commis-

sioners, after accepting $10,000 cash and a promise of
$1,000,000 when peace should come, entered a claim for the
return of both banks of the Río Grande and of California
with war indemnities for damages caused in the invasion.
The Americans could then do nothing else but press forward
to the capture of the capital. Santa Anna's plans for its
defense had been elaborate. There were over 20,000 defenders, with fortifications all about the city. He was
waiting attack while planning to fall on the flank and rear of
the invaders. Battles were fought in the suburbs of the city
at Contreras, Churubusco, Molino del Rey, and Chapultepec, in which the defenders were successively driven inward
upon the capital. On September 13 the city itself fell, and
the victorious Americans marched into the Plaza de la
Constitución.

The negotiations for peace had been carried on by Trist
and by four Mexican commissioners. The American demands, sent from Washington, were for all territory beyond
the line of the Río Grande to New Mexico and thence along
the Gila and Colorado Rivers to the Gulf of California and
down the middle of that body of water. Other demands
concerning free transit of Tehuantepec, money compensation
for territory taken, and for adjustment of private claims,
were also presented. The Mexicans, torn with dissensions
over the peace issue as they had been during the whole conduct of the war, were unable to guide their commissioners.
They resisted cession of territory as best they could, prolonging the peace debates at Querétaro, while Santa Anna
prepared new defenses and advised resumption of hostilities.
When these had brought about the Mexican defeats at
Churubusco, Molino del Rey, and Chapultepec, Santa Anna
vainly attempted to break the American line of communications at Puebla. After this there was a cessation of armed
resistance.

Santa Anna had been followed in the presidency by
General Anaya in April, 1847, and by Manuel de la Peña y
Peña on September 26, after the capital fell. Peña urgently
wanted peace. Trist had lost his position as commissioner

for the United States by order of October 4, because of Polk's mistaken lack of confidence in him, and was only deterred from leaving Mexico because it was too difficult to provide him with an escort. The Mexican peace party under Peña was most anxious to effect a treaty, and at the same time fearful that harder terms would be exacted than under previous proposals. Trist therefore seized the opportunity to treat with the Mexicans although he was no longer the accredited representative of the United States. The representatives of Mexico clung tenaciously to hopes of modifying the terms, which were substantially those of the armistice. Finally, when General Scott offered to protect the peace government against the intransigent opposition if a treaty should be signed, the last difficulty was removed. On February 2, 1848, at Guadalupe Hidalgo just outside the capital, a treaty was signed whereby the war was ended.

By this treaty Texas was definitely relinquished, and the American conquest of New Mexico and California was acknowledged. All the territory south of the Río Grande which had been conquered was restored to Mexico. All claims against Mexico dating earlier than the treaty were relinquished, and the small sum of fifteen million dollars was paid for the territory transferred. Though there was an active propaganda in the United States for absorption of the whole of Mexico—a move which was favored by a respectably large element of Mexican opinion and desire—and in spite of the irregular standing of Trist, the demands of the war party, and the vacillations of Polk, the treaty was ratified on March 10, with slight modifications. These modifications were accepted in a prompt ratification by the Mexican Congress. In July the American forces departed from Mexican soil.

The effect of the war upon Mexico was to reduce its size by considerably more than one-half if Texas be included in the reckoning. A great area remote from the political and economic life of the Republic was taken out of its hands, and the problem of American infiltration was, for the time being, removed. An appreciable sum of money was turned into the public treasury, which might have undertaken with it the much needed rehabilitation of the country. Mexico was not yet free, however, from ambitious and troublesome political aspirants, and she received scant spiritual rejuvenation through her trials. Santa Anna, it is true, modestly or opportunely removed himself again into voluntary exile, but that was only a temporary blessing. He was yet again to return and intrude his personal ambitions upon a struggle for social and economic readjustment which had been already in process when the Texas conflict became acute. The rise of the mestizo element in opposition to clerical domination was yet to come in the Revolution of Ayutla.

The effect of this war upon the United States was even more serious than it was upon Mexico. It accentuated the hostile feelings of the North and the South over the slavery issue, for the acquisition of such a vast area rendered the spirit of competition for control of the Senate particularly keen and this vast westward sweep of the ill-appreciated upstart democracy of America had its repercussion in Europe, where royalty feared the spread of the successes of republics. That mental attitude assisted in preparing England, France, and Spain for the steps which resulted in the majestic attempt of Napoleon III to throw his influence athwart American aggrandizement in a struggle which delayed Mexican reorganization after the War of the Reform for many weary years.

Much that is heated, or subtle, or forced, has been written as to the justification of the United States in entering and prosecuting this war. It was desired by militarists in Mexico, and they have a heavy responsibility for it. They deserved worse punishment than they received. But their course, once the fatal step of colonizing Texas with Americans had been taken, was obviously the inevitable course which a proud, sensitive, weak, and politically ignorant people would follow. The cruelties of her military men and the suspiciousness of her rulers are not to be condoned. The ambition, the restlessness, the aggressiveness, of the American westward sweep, is not to be defended, praised, or condemned as an attitude toward Mexicans. The American side of the war had no element in it that calls for characterization as just or unjust. The whole process is to be observed as a biological phenomenon, in which the historical facts are largely accidentals of that process. The forces in conflict were larger than the settlement effected. Two races met and clashed on a coveted frontier, and the battle went to the strong. It was inevitable.

CHAPTER XIX

THE REVOLUTION OF AYUTLA

WHEN the issues of the War with the United States had been settled, Mexico was again free to return to the endless conflict between her own racial and economic groups. The period now to come was one of a continuation of former troubles. There was the strife for power on the part of the rising mestizo group, which aimed at the emancipation of the country from ecclesiastical domination, and at the release of the government from control by military adventurers who dominated through identity of interest with the church. That organization fought with all its power to retain its political and economic ascendancy. The contest took the old form of centralism versus federalism, the church and the army with their chief influence in the capital favoring central control, while the provinces, with interests dominated by the new social group of the mestizos and their creole sympathizers, were federalistic by reason of the factors of geographical location and economic determinism. Weaving in and out among these general elements of factional discord was the personal ambition of Santa Anna, who sought by any and all means to seize and control absolute power. His own activities were for a time delayed because of his voluntary exile at the close of the war with the United States, but it will not be long before we shall see him again return to his country to embroil it in the struggle which was to end in his permanent elimination as a political factor and in the Revolution of Ayutla which all but won for Mexico her opportunity to shake off the clerical-military control and become in fact a modern state.

The National Congress which met at Querétaro during the occupation of the capital by the Americans chose General

Anaya for acting president of the Republic in November, 1847. His term was to end in the following January. The former Chief Justice, Manuel de la Peña y Peña, leader of the peace party which had negotiated the treaty with the United States, served as head of the nation from January 1848, to the end of May. On June 3, General José Joaquín Herrera, who had been president in 1845 when the war began, was returned to the executive chair by virtue of an election. De la Peña returned to his position as Chief Justice of the Supreme Court. The government was supported by the liberal party, but it had as opponents the old monarchist group, of whom General Paredes was the leader and hope, and the Santanistas, whose name sufficiently describes their aims and ambitions. These hostile elements rendered doubly difficult the task before Herrera, that of reorganizing the government offices, establishing the national credit, and uniting the country on a peace basis so that prosperity might return.

He was honestly and honorably engaged in these constructive policies when disorders broke out in many parts of the country. In Aguascalientes General Paredes revolted, alleging discontent with the treaty with the United States. He was defeated and fled the country. General Leonardo Márquez, who was fighting rebel Indians in the Sierra Gorda, attempted a revolt in favor of Santa Anna, but General Bustamante reduced the revolt to nothing. Indians in Mizteca and troops in San Luis Potosí proved temporarily troublesome; there was a revolt in Zacatecas, and Yucatan was torn with interracial strife. Throughout Herrera's mild-mannered but honest government the alignment of Indians against whites in many places served to prevent the coming of internal peace. The period saw also a flurry of excitement over a proposed Tehuantepec canal treaty with the United States, which was rejected because it conceded internal police powers to American military forces. In 1850 one of Herrera's cabinet officers, General Mariano Arista, a liberal of pronounced views and great personal energy, was elected president over a number of candidates, among whom was the ever ambitious though still absent Santa Anna. Arista was inaugurated in January, 1851.

This man was as much of an opportunist and egoist as Santa Anna, without the skill in political intrigue of the latter. He had been a royalist but had joined the revolution when it was about to win. His career in early command of the Mexican troops against Taylor had not been devoid of the earmarks of incompetency and even of treachery. He was nothing but a pocket edition of the caudillo or guerrilla leader type, possessing no constructive policies of his own and no outstanding virtues to balance his personal ambitions. His administration bent its efforts toward replenishing the national treasury and reducing expenses. In the pursuit of the last named object the expedient of cutting down the pay-roll was attempted, combined with large reductions in the size of the army. Arista had not the acumen to see what Porfirio Díaz realized twenty-five years later, namely, that the non-industrial mestizo type would have to be made contented at the public expense before the real beginnings of national peace could be realized. Retrenchment was necessary if government was to be operated within income and if foreign creditors clamorous for their dues were to be satisfied. But the cabinet changed with kaleidoscopic rapidity, just as Herrera's had done, members resigning rather than face popular protests. Public safety suffered because the government had no control; discontent spread rapidly. In July of 1852, a revolt under the "Plan del Hospicio", originating in Guadalajara, spread over most of the country under the encouragement of the conservative element. It was but a condensation of opposition which had previously showed numerous localized manifestations. Three-fourths of the country was hostile to Arista; his cabinet resigned in a body; without friends finally among clergy, army, or in the states, the president himself resigned on January 5, 1853, rather than immerse the country in the horrors of a civil war then visibly prospective. For a single month his place was filled by Juan Bautista Ceballos, Chief Justice of the Supreme Court.

Ceballos was expected by the politicians to follow a moderate course. He accordingly released a number of political prisoners, declared amnesty for others, and called upon the governors of the states to aid him. But the Guadalajara revolt which had unseated Arista kept on growing, and Ceballos proposed to stem the movement by declaring for it and becoming its head. He proposed a federal constitution and a new choice of president. The Congress raised a great outcry against this suggestion, whereupon Ceballos dissolved it. The two houses then met privately and attempted to choose a new president, but a declaration of military officers gave to General Manuel Lombardini the control of the country in a movement for bringing Santa Anna back from Nueva Granada and making him chief executive. That wily politician had long been in correspondence with clerical and centralist friends in Mexico in order to bring about his return. He arrived on April first, 1853, and on the fifteenth, after a triumphal progress from the coast to the capital, was installed in the presidency, to which he had been elected before his return.

The return of Santa Anna meant power to the army, power to the church, the end of prospects of social and economic reform. The conservatives supported him on a program of cessation of political activity against the church and security for the proprietors of huge landed estates against the progressive ideas of the times. His accession to power was marked by amnesty to the opposition, but this was of scant importance in view of the prompt dissolution of the Congress and the abolition of the State Assemblies. Santa Anna made himself absolute dictator. He absorbed the militia, which had been created by state influence to foster federalism, by taking it under his own control; he increased the regular army so as to gain adherents through military appointments, reëstablished the Order of Guadalupe, and gave himself the title of Most Serene Highness. To save his country from the ruin which would ensue if his control should be lost to it, he acceded to the desires of his flatterers and proclaimed himself, on December 16, 1853, Perpetual Dictator.

At the end of this same month the sale to the United States of the Mesilla Valley was effected by Santa Anna on his own autocratic responsibility. The funds received for this area, otherwise known as the Gadsden Purchase, furnished the means whereby the dictator could pursue his despotic career with greater freedom. This alienation of national territory has been more bitterly execrated by Mexicans than most of Santa Anna's other arrogations of authority. This was several months after the death of Lucas Alamán, who had favored Santa Anna's recall and had accepted a cabinet position while hoping for the establishment of a throne in Mexico with a foreign prince upon it. Alamán believed that a foreign royal house, with a genuine courtly life, would awe the Mexicans into respect for law as the old viceroys had done. After Alamán's death several Mexicans continued to try to interest Europe in such a proposal; hope was entertained that Spain would assume a protectorate, but the idea did not grow as rapidly as did Mexican fear of the overambitious dictator.

In the midst of all his vain pretensions, Santa Anna had been unable to give the country peace. In Guerrero there was critical opposition to him by old Juan Álvarez, who had once been his supporter and coöperator in the war with the United States, and now southern regional chieftain. When it seemed that Álvarez was to be menaced by government troops he raised the standard of revolt on February 20, 1854. On the first of the following month a pronouncement at Ayutla in Guerrero was issued by radical leaders. It was on the eleventh modified to gain adhesion of certain moderates, among whom was Ignacio Comonfort, commander at Acapulco.

The Plan de Ayutla demanded the removal of Santa Anna and a call for a constituent congress to frame a federal constitution. It was hailed at once as the beginning of a great popular movement. Although Santa Anna went in person to besiege Acapulco, he was defeated there and returned to the capital. Revolution spread rapidly, discontent being fomented by the sale of the Mesilla.

The dictator now tried to trim his sails to the gale. He planned changes in his cabinet; he instructed his governors to be more moderate. He called an election for the coming December which was to be a popular expression as to whether he should continue in office and if not who should succeed him. The election was of course unanimous for him, but the country was bitterly against him. Pardons, amnesty, imprisonments, campaigns, all were tried in vain. Finally, feigning a journey to Vera Cruz only, he went to that place on August 9, 1855, resigned his powers to a triumvirate, and went into exile in Cartagena. That was the end of his political importance, though he afterward returned to Mexico and lived there until his death in 1876.

Under the Plan de Ayutla, now triumphant in the capital as elsewhere throughout the country, a temporary president in the person of Álvarez was chosen by the junta which the revolution had provided for that purpose. Álvarez presided over the nation from October 4 to December 12. During this brief period new alignments of political interests occurred. The extreme liberals, who were dubbed "Puros," stood for the measures which Gómez Farías had advocated in 1833, while the reactionaries stood for clerical and military privilege and the ascendancy of the great landholders. The civil war of economic, racial, and social interests was now about to enter its most bitter stages.

Álvarez, a full-blooded Indian, entered Mexico in November accompanied by a body guard of his own race, a circumstance which recalled the campaigns of Hidalgo and filled the educated and privileged class with alarm. The movement did indeed have a racial significance. Álvarez placed in his cabinet Ignacio Comonfort, a creole, as minister of war, and Benito Juárez, a Zapotec Indian, as minister of justice. Melchor Ocampo was made minister of foreign relations, Guillermo Prieto of the treasury, and Miguel Lerdo de Tejada of Fomento. All were strong liberals save Comonfort. Juárez had been exiled by Santa Anna, but had participated in the revolution. The choice of these men served notice on the country that a reform program loos-

ening the clutches of special privileges was to be inau,
rated. This was a hard blow to the conservative elem
which had made a counter move from San Luis Potosí to o
throw Santa Anna even while the Revolution of Ayutla w /in
progress, and which had also, in another movement, held the
capital for a brief period before the triumph of the Plan.

The liberal party which had placed Álvarez in power soon
became sharply divided. Juárez began his ministerial program by issuing a law on November 23, 1855, which came to
be called by his name. The Ley Juárez struck boldly at
ecclesiastical privilege by suppressing all special courts, the
military and church establishments being denied cognizance
of any civil suits whatsoever. It was a courageous but inopportune enactment. It raised a furor. The clergy claimed
that religion had been attacked, though nothing of the kind
had happened. It raised the battle cry of "religión y fueros,"
—religion and privilege— and egged the army men on to
rebellion and deeds of violence. The liberals who opposed
Álvarez, and the moderates who feared the church, asked
him to give up his presidency to Comonfort, who had shown
a less intransigent attitude. This he did on December 12,
1855. Comonfort's elevation to the presidency was a loss to
liberalism.

The opinion of the time was that Comonfort had had
notice from General Manuel Doblado that he was going to
be asked to assume the presidency; it was also thought that
he had even promoted the movement in belief that a more
moderate spirit in public affairs was the first necessity. The
move by Álvarez was a more or less equivocal one, as he left
the presidency in Comonfort's hands under the pretense
that he was merely doing so temporarily. It was a time of
unusual stress, for the monarchical clericals were rampant
in their opposition to the reform program initiated by the
Ley Juárez. The liberals should not have announced such a
program nor attempted to enforce such a law without being
sure that they would not have to swap horses while crossing
the stream. So far as the loss of Álvarez was concerned, it
could hardly be deemed irreparable.

Comonfort began his administration on December 11, 1855, as a decided moderate.   With the government organized, discussions began concerning the form and character to be given to the prospective constitution which the liberals had been for years demanding.   The movement was dominated by the advanced opinions held by such men as Arriaga, Mata, and Guzmán, all of whom were more liberal in their tendencies than President Comonfort.   On the whole, the opinion of the country at large was not very hopeful of the promised benefits from a new federal constitution.   The people had seen too many constitutions come and go without materially affecting the character of the government or improving the condition of affairs.   Many citizens had grave doubts of the efficacy of an anti-clerical propaganda.   The liberals themselves were not as clear cut as they should have been in their determination to break with the old forces of clericalism, for in spite of the growing sentiment for widened participation in la causa pública by the newly developing mestizo class, the fear of the church and the privileged aristocracy was deeply instilled in their hearts, and they faltered when they should have been strong.

The government circle meantime proceeded with its program to end clerical domination.   It started with a decree for suppressing the Company of Jesus, following this by the notable Ley Lerdo, initiated by Lerdo de Tejada and passed by the Congress on June 25, 1856, by a vote of 71 to 13.   This law struck at the basis of ecclesiastical domination by prohibiting civil and religious corporations from holding real estate not used for worship and allowing tenants of such properties to purchase them on very liberal terms.   It should be noted particularly that the Ley Lerdo did not deprive the church of its wealth.   It did not confiscate property.   It did decree the necessity of alienating the agricultural property of the church.   This property was to be sold, and much of it was sold, at public auction, the proceeds being turned over to the church.   That is, it was a law intended to disamortize the lands so long held in mortmain by the church.   It was expected that the sale of church property would bring it

into the hands of the people in small tracts; but t
the church was so great that those of small means
reluctant to purchase, and the huge estates wer
up intact by newly enriched families of creoles wno had
hitherto been landless. So far as its purpose of creating
small properties was concerned, it was a failure. It was of
value in creating a new landed aristocracy. But it gave to
the church large sums of money which it had to reïnvest in
some new way. The economic advantage of the church was
in no whit diminished, though its pride was seriously im-
paired, and it threw itself with vigor into the policy of over-
throwing the liberal government which had assailed it.

Still another blow was struck at the church by the passage
of the law named after José M. Iglesias, its initiator. The
Ley Iglesias aimed to exclude the clergy from influence in the
exercise of civil rights by citizens. It was an amplification
of the spirit of the Constitution of 1857. The cemeteries,
until then under church control, were placed under a newly
created Department of Public Hygiene. This move had two
purposes; to deprive the church of burial fees and to create
hygienic conditions for interments. Another bill limited
fees for baptism, marriage, and so forth, the aim being to
reduce in every way possible the subsidiary influence of the
clergy in matters not purely of the faith.

These laws were beneficent in their purpose, and their
complete and rapid fulfillment ought to have had the warm
coöperation of the Mexican church. Its opportunity to
minister to the spiritual and moral needs of the people, a
service in which it has often been negligent when it was not
hostile, would have been measurably increased. It chose,
however, to consider that the normal aspiration of the
liberal party to win self expression in governmental processes,
that is, the attack upon the church as a political and economic organization, was an attack upon its proper spiritual
functions. It resisted with envenomed fierceness, bringing
on the movement which really did assault its spiritual
dominion and lose it the support of the very large proportion
of Mexican men. The church must answer for a large

measure of responsibility for the havoc which its mistaken policy has wrought in Mexico.

During 1856 the Constituent Congress had been framing the new federal Constitution which was promulgated on February 5, 1857. This document provided for the re-establishment of representative, republican, and popular government, in form at least. It was distinguished from the previous federal Constitution of 1824 by the liberal character of its provisions. In its so-called Bill of Rights, it set forth the rights of man, proclaiming freedom from forced labor, slavery, religious vows, or any other infringement of personal liberty. Freedom of speech, press, petition, and assembly were guaranteed. Titles of nobility, hereditary privileges and prerogatives were swept away. There might be no retroactive laws, no special courts. The domicile was declared inviolate. Imprisonment for debt was abolished, as were actual judicial costs, though justice never became "free" in Mexico, as was theoretically intended. Private property might not be taken in time of peace without the owner's consent, unless for public use; nor even in time of war without previous payment. The attack on church ten-ure of real estate, provided in the Ley Lerdo, was incorpo-rated in this Constitution, and monopolies, except those of public utilities operated by the government, were abolished.

The provisions of the Constitution, prescribing the form of government, the powers of functionaries, the separation and description of the powers of the states and of the federal union, were in the main not unlike the same features of the Constitution of the United States. It was specified that the Constitution might be amended by a two-thirds quorum of Congress, subject to the later sanction of the State legisla-tures. No state religion was established; indeed the docu-ment was entirely silent upon the question of religion. This was a real advance in intellectual freedom, as the silence confessed movement rather away from clerical influence than toward it. A final provision concerning the perdurability of the Constitution, contained in Article 128, is eloquent witness to the perturbed course of Mexican political life,

and proof of the uncertainty with which its framers viewed
their own work. The statement reads:

"This Constitution shall not lose force . . . even if its
observance be interrupted by rebellion. In case through
public disorder a government contrary to its provisions is
established, as soon as the people recover their liberty its
observance shall be reëstablished, and those who have
figured in the rebel government or who have coöperated with
such government, shall be judged by this Constitution and by
the laws issued in conformity with it."

Such was the Constitution which the liberal group led by
Benito Juárez and his confrères sought to impose upon their
country for the purpose of freeing it from clerical and military domination. Under its ægis the bitter War of the
Reform was to be fought, and out of that war was to come
the European Intervention and the attempt to establish a
foreign empire. Under this Constitution Maximilian was
to lose his life, vainly hoping that his blood might be the last
to be shed for Mexican liberties. Under it Porfirio Díaz was
to govern the country for the span of thirty-seven years
with a sway as despotic and more efficient than the rule of
the most autocratic of the old Spanish viceroys. To enforce this Magna Charta Francisco Madero was to fight, to
lose, and achieve martyrdom. In the name of it Venustiano
Carranza set about effecting reforms which ended in framing
a new document which though based largely on the old, is
still changed enough to bring its originators under the
penalties of the Article quoted above if ever the defenders of
the old Constitution of 1857 should gain the upper hand.
The government set up under the auspices of Álvaro Obregón, which maintained the Constitution of 1917 intact,
became the object of attack by the conservative elements,
foreign and domestic, which held vast economic stakes in the
country.

The Constitution of 1857 was promulgated on February 5,
and it was to become effective on September 16, the anniversary of Hidalgo's Grito de Dolores. During the year 1856,
while the Constituents were sitting, and during the period

following the promulgation of the Constitution, the country was full of armed revolts against the Ley Lerdo, which, as we have seen, deprived the church of the privilege of holding lands. The new body of law was not inordinately popular even with the members of the Constituent Congress. Very often the proceedings of that body were interrupted by lack of a quorum. Several of its members never attended it at all. Many of them were anxious as to the course which events might take after the promulgation should occur; fear of the church, and lack of political stamina prevented the law-makers from becoming heroic figures.

One of the provisions accompanying the adoption of this Constitution was of course the regulation that all public officers serving under it must take public oath of allegiance to it. This was the acid test. The church early voiced vehement disapproval of the Constitution. The archbishop of Mexico, Lázaro de la Garza, sent out a circular to all the bishops, declaring that Articles 3, 5, 6, 7, 13, 27 and 123 (which curtailed the power and economic influence of the church), were of such character that no faithful Catholic could swear allegiance to it. He ordered that if any persons who had taken the oath should present themselves thereafter for administration of the sacraments, they must first be obliged to make a retraction of their oaths to support the national Constitution. This they must do publicly or else send notice of their retraction to the government. Hence many public servants were cast into deep consternation, for they knew that on the other hand they would be dismissed from their positions if they rejected the oath. Papal confirmation of the attitude of the Mexican church made their quandary even worse.

On the crest of this wave of trouble, Ignacio Comonfort took office on December 1, 1857, as elected president. His first address before the Congress tended to confirm previous suspicions that he was something less than a moderate. He wobbled in his statement that it was obvious that certain amendments to the Constitution were necessary. The church had begun to expect something from him, and his speech was taken as a covert announcement of his expected coup d'état in its favor. In reality, Comonfort's genuine objection to the Constitution was that it gave the ascendancy to the legislative over the executive branch of the government. His advisers suggested that he should ask for amendments remedying this defect. If the Deputies should refuse them, he should carry out his own ideas relying upon military force, meanwhile asking to be granted extraordinary faculties as executive. Still others advised him to ignore the Constitution through a coup d'état or cuartelazo.

Two weeks after Comonfort's inauguration the head of the army and tool of the clerical group, General Félix Zuloaga, issued a pronunciamiento against the liberal Congress. Under his "Plan de Tacubaya" of December 17, the new Constitution was declared set aside as not in conformity with Mexican usages; the supreme power was to be vested in Comonfort as president by pronouncement instead of under the Constitution. The Congress was dissolved, and Comonfort was to call a new one within three months to frame a new organic law which should be submitted to the *people* for approbation. If it should not be approved, it should be resubmitted to the Congress for reshaping to suit the popular demands. In reply to this "Plan" the Congress decreed that Comonfort was no longer to be considered as president. That gentleman had by his desire for moderation succeeded merely in making himself a man without a party. He was perturbed when he found himself deserted by his liberal friends, dismayed when the clericals insisted that he should betray his party. Once the Zuloaga "Plan" was pronounced he repented of his previous connection with it, and actually fought for two days in his palace and in the defenses of the city against the proponents of conservatism. But the reaction was too strong. There were daily defections among his troops. When he began fighting one morning he commanded 5,000 soldiers, all but 500 of whom had deserted before nightfall. Seeing himself defeated not by arms but by public opinion, he resigned his presidency and took safety in flight to the United States on January 21, 1858. Such were the events which culminated in the Three Years' War or War of the Reform, which lasted from 1858 to the beginning of 1861.

It was the paltering policy of Comonfort, who acted under the impulse of traditional fear of the church, believing that the state could not enforce its decrees against its intrenched privileges, which brought about the protraction of the strife for administrative and civil liberty, and in the end plunged Mexico into a sea of blood through foreign intervention. It was not the time for moderate policies.

CHAPTER XX

THE WAR OF THE REFORM

FOR a number of years after the fiasco of Comonfort's attempt to establish a moderate régime there were to be two continuously rival claimants to the political power. The party which was ultimately triumphant was led throughout by Benito Juárez, the Zapotec Indian student, lawyer, statesman, governor of Oaxaca, chief justice of the Supreme Court, and finally President. The reactionary party was led by an ever shifting array of generals who are now called the anti-presidents, among whom Zuloaga and Miramón were the most conspicuous, until the foreign intervention came.

When Comonfort fled in January, 1858, the reactionary party in power in Mexico City placed General Zuloaga in the presidency. He immediately restored the special privileges of the army and clergy, and annulled the reform legislation enacted under the liberal leaders; but he had the widespread liberal movement to cope with, a prospective war for damages with Spain to forefend, and dangerous rivalries in his own camp. The states of the northern interior and the west coast, under the leadership of the state of Jalisco, entered into an agreement to support the Constitution of 1857 and to dislodge the reactionary party from the capital. This coalition supported Juárez in his claim to the presidency.

Upon the seizure of the power by Zuloaga, Juárez had left Mexico City secretly, being unable to establish his authority in the capital. He was able to do that in Guanajuato, however, traveling thither concealed in a closed carriage for which the explanation was given that it contained a sick family. The Mexican love for a political quip quickly fixed on the Juárez cabinet group the nickname "the sick family," a phrase of utility for describing the vicissitudes of the liberals, who were often in serious straits and frequently had to seek safety in flight. From Guanajuato they were presently driven to Guadalajara. In the latter town a body of their own troops mutinied and were on the point of executing Juárez and his cabinet in the governor's palace, but were dissuaded at the critical moment by Guillermo Prieto. The attempt by the liberals to hold the northern and western states in a coalition was prevented by defeats of the liberal army at Salamanca. The Juárez government was obliged to leave Guadalajara and betake itself to Colima on the Pacific coast. Thence it made its way via Panamá, Havana, and New Orleans to Vera Cruz, obtaining transportation on an American steamer. The governor of the state of Vera Cruz offered it a friendly welcome and refuge. In the state capital the liberals believed they could set up and maintain their government, since they would have there the advantages of a friendly local administration, control of the chief maritime customhouse, and closer proximity to any possible outside friendly assistance. Accordingly the liberal government was installed in Vera Cruz on May 6, 1858. The struggle in the west had been intrusted to the Juárez minister of war, Don Santos Degollado, who had been given ample powers to raise funds and prosecute a campaign against the reactionaries. These had now spread their forces over San Luis Potosí, Zacatecas, and Guadalajara, but their organization was not strong enough nor their numbers great enough, to attempt to hold more area. Their chief leader in the field was the very young but audacious and cruel General Leonardo Márquez.

During 1858 the liberal military leaders Santos Degollado in the west, and Santiago Vidaurri in Nuevo León and Coahuila, though widely separated, prevented the conservatives from penetrating northward beyond San Luis Potosí or southward beyond Guadalajara; if they had been united they might have defeated their common enemy. But instead of joining Degollado in besieging Guadalajara in September, Vidaurri himself suffered defeat at the hands of

the conservative leader Miramón at Ahualulco. Then
Miramón wrested Guadalajara from Degollado, who had
occupied it, and drove him southwestward to Colima in
complete defeat. Miramón was clever enough to strike at
both his enemies while they were divided. In this he was
aided by the brilliant Vidaurri's personal ambitions. That
frontier hero cherished a desire of reducing the entire north
to his own leadership as a possible stepping-stone to the
presidency. He was fighting for his own interests and not
for the Juárez government.

General Zuloaga was not making a flowery success as
president in Mexico City. When he tried to restore church
lands alienated under the Ley Lerdo he came into conflict
with foreign nations whose citizens had bought these lands.
He angered the Mexicans by reducing the States of the
Republic to mere military departments. He could not take
Vera Cruz from Juárez. He could not assemble a Constitutional Congress because of the widespread civil war. When
he could get no more money from the church, he resorted to
a tax levy which secured nothing but trouble. His party
split. It controlled only the towns where it had large garrisons. The United States minister demanded his passports
because he could secure no redress for forced loans from
Americans. Finally the failure to secure a Congress brought
about his ruin. In reality he was only tolerated by his own
adherents, the sparkling Miramón being the real leader.
Two pronouncements against Zuloaga occurred in December,
and he very soon resigned, seeking refuge in the British
legation. England had recognized the conservative government. Miramón returned to Mexico City and reinstated
Zuloaga with a rather sardonic toleration, but within a week
made himself president through action of a junta of friends,
assuming the office on December thirtieth.

In February of 1859 Miramón seriously undertook the
capture of Vera Cruz. He set out with a force which proved
too small, and soon found it necessary to give up the attack
and return to the capital. Meantime Santos Degollado
attacked Mexico City to draw Miramón back. He was near

to success when he suffered defeat at the hands of the conservative leader Márquez at Tacubaya, one of the suburbs of the capital, on April eleventh. Here Márquez brutally executed a number of native and foreign physicians who had been captured after serving the liberal forces in the battle. For this butchery he was called "The Tiger of Tacubaya." Miramón returned from Vera Cruz just after this victory for his faction, and Degollado was obliged to give up the effort to secure the capital.

Now the liberal party at Vera Cruz sought to strengthen its position in the country by making war measures of the reform legislation which had been the cause of its overthrow. If the civil war was ever to be ended, it could only be through depriving the church of its revenues by taking its lands for the nation. This would provide the revenues necessary for victory; it would yield much more money than the church could possibly contribute to the conservatives, and it would at the same time dry up the sources of their revenues. The only trouble was that the best lands, which the liberals sought to nationalize, lay in territory still controlled by the conservatives. But the decrees could be, and were, issued in anticipation of victory, while an order for the extinction of the monastic bodies accompanied it. The law of nationalization, drawn by the same Miguel Lerdo de Tejada who had written the Ley Lerdo in the time of Comonfort, was an advance upon the policy of the latter law, in that it contemplated not purchase but actual confiscation of the estates of the church.

Other reformative measures then issued at Vera Cruz as a challenge to the enemy and an appeal to the moderates and liberals included the establishment of marriage by civil contract, making it independent of the church sacrament. Another law, like the previous Ley Iglesias, secularized the cemeteries and prescribed burial outside the limits of cities. Still another separated church and state; another introduced the jury system; another provided for liberty of the press; another made all church obventions optional only; still another abolished the hated alcabala and capitation taxes.

There were also measures for improving the schools, dividing huge estates to create a middle farming class, creating a railroad building program, establishing a national register of statistics, and in general attempting to equip Mexico with a public administration free from priestcraft and military chicanery and make it in every sense of the word a modern Christian nation. Such was the program, announced during dark days, which the liberals were attempting to establish for Mexico at the very moment when the European powers England, France, and Spain, abetted and misguided by a handful of Mexican monarchical schemers, were plotting the forceful occupation of Mexican territory to compel payment of debts; while Napoleon III was building up the fanciful fabric of Maximilian's empire, and the United States was preparing to enter its death struggle against disruption in the slavery controversy.

The great protagonists of liberty who seconded Benito Juárez in this reform program were Santos Degollado, Melchor Ocampo, Miguel Lerdo de Tejada, Juan Antonio de la Fuente, and Ignacio Ramírez. It was not long before the ambitious Vidaurri turned traitor to them. Though he was defeated and driven out, the liberal leader Manuel Doblado suffered defeat at Las Vacas, and Miramón with guile suborned a liberal leader at Guadalajara and won another victory there.

While these actions were occurring Juárez was attempting to provide a way to escape the threat of foreign intervention for collection of claims by an arrangement with the United States for a loan. The negotiations finally took form in the McLane-Ocampo Treaty. This provided for granting the United States perpetual unlimited transit across the Isthmus of Tehuantepec and across the north Mexican states to the Pacific under conditions which meant practical derogation of Mexican sovereignty in those areas. Intervention in force by the United States was provided for in case of disorders. There was also a declaration that Americans in Mexico should be exempt from all levies and loans, forced or otherwise, such as had caused so much trouble previously. The amount of money which the liberal government was to receive for these stipulations was insignificant. The United States was to pay four million dollars, but half was to be used to pay American private claims. This treaty was an unfortunate attempt on the part of the United States to "save Mexico." It was sharply opposed in Juárez' own cabinet by Juan Antonio de la Fuente and other liberals. In England, it was held that the treaty would soon leave Mexico a mere appanage of the United States. The Mexican conservative government violently protested against it. Newspapers in the United States expressed wonderment at the small recompense proposed, since an offer twelve years before of fifteen millions for the Tehuantepec transit had been refused, and an offer to buy Lower California in 1857 for ten millions had met the same rejection. Objections were made against the measure as providing possible extension of the slave area. It was also thought that intervention of this character to help the Juárez government would anger France, Spain, and Rome. Moreover, it was feared that the Catholics in the United States would resent aid to such an anti-clerical party as was that of Juárez, and would cause ruin of any political party which might ratify the treaty. Fortunately, in view of these considerations, the American Senate refused ratification May 31, 1860, thus saving the liberals in Mexico from further dissensions over the issue. The negotiation of the treaty by consent of Juárez has been bitterly attacked by Francisco Bulnes, the modern Mexican conservative publicist, who deems it one of the serious manifestations of personal weakness on the part of the great liberal patriot.

After the victory at Guadalajara just mentioned above, General Miramón undertook a second time to capture Vera Cruz from the liberals. For this purpose he ordered a consignment of arms and ammunition from the friendly Spaniards in Havana, sending a small vessel to bring them. Juárez declared this craft piratical, but having no vessel with which to capture it, he arranged with Captain Jarvis of the American navy, who had orders to prevent the attempted coöperation with Miramón, to act for the liberals. The

Saratoga and two small Mexican vessels attacked the conservative vessels in the harbor of Antón Lizardi and captured them. This solicitation and acceptance of American naval intervention by Juárez has brought strong condemnation upon his head by his Mexican critics who stickle for a foolish isolation. If he believed in his own cause he would have been more culpable had he allowed the munitions to land, as such an act might have spelled ruin to the cause he believed essential.

At any event, without them Miramón was again unsuccessful. He was obliged to raise the siege of Vera Cruz on March 16, 1860, and return to the capital again. It seemed for a time as though neither side could gain any advantage over the other. But now events began to move toward a solution. The reactionary general Díaz de la Vega was defeated near San Luis Potosí, and Miramón, taking the western field again, was routed at Silao by the united forces of Generals Zaragoza and González Ortega on August 10. Then came a bloody attack on Guadalajara, from which the murderer Márquez had to flee before the strategy and courage of General Zaragoza. On December 22 again his eight thousand followers suffered final defeat at San Miguel Calpulalpam. This was the only sizable force left to the reactionaries; its defeat meant the termination of the Three Years' War.

It had been a bitter conflict. On the liberal side it was a struggle for freedom of thought and speech, for the extinction of clerical participation in affairs of state, for the nationalization of great areas of land held by the church, for the normal participation of laymen in government, for complete equality of all citizens before the law, for intellectual progress and modernity. On the conservative side the ideal was church and army control, with a foreign constitutional monarchy in the background. All the old Spanish abuses based on the colonial conception of political society were to be perpetuated: special privileges, absence of liberty of conscience, class domination. The reaction was a death struggle for the regular army and the clergy, opposed by the militia and leaders of the states. Geographically it was a war of the outside against the center. The clergy made it a holy war. Their coffers were open to it early and long. Their soldiers marched to battle wearing crosses and scapularies, bearing pictures of saints and other symbols of religion. The liberals were the Philistines, and they were the Chosen People. The population went into the war with religious fervor on each side. Non-combatants wore the chosen distintivos or badges of the cause of their predilection. Brutal reprisals characterized the action of both sides in the later months of the struggle. Prisoners had short shrift. The spirit of extermination animated everyone. During the last year and a half of the war, no less than seventy battles were fought, most of them until the final stage being won by the reactionaries.

The triumphant liberal army entered Mexico City on December 27, 1860. They had many sympathizers there, and their army now numbered some 25,000. The great military "hero of defeats," as he was styled, was Santos Degollado. But the march of triumph was led by González Ortega. Happily, the latter accorded to Degollado full measure of recognition before the multitudes for his successful organization of the now victorious army, so that no foolish envy was aroused. Happily too, there was free rein given to the civil government under Juárez. Miramón was exiled. Zuloaga fled to the mountains, claiming the presidency, where he was supported by Márquez, Mejía, and a few other irreconcilables.

Juárez and his government occupied the capital on January 11, 1861. His first measure was to expel the Spanish minister, who had done all he could to assist the reactionaries. He also ordered expulsion of the archbishop of Mexico, the bishop of Michoacán, and other notable clergymen who had opposed the liberal cause. Several of his cabinet members disapproved of these measures as usurpations of power by the executive during a time when the legitimate rule of the country had been reëstablished. They believed that such action should have been left to the judiciary. So strong was the opposition that De la Fuente, Ocampo, and Llave resigned their cabinet offices in protest.

The decree of expropriation issued concerning church properties was promptly put into effect. A large amount of land in the Federal District and the State of Mexico then changed hands under the execution of this decree, and many valuable paintings were taken from the monasteries and placed in the San Carlos Academy of Fine Arts. At the same time the Augustinian church and convent were taken over for a national library, and thousands of books were transported thither from the libraries of the holy orders. Hundreds of them are duplicates of antiquated religious treatises of scant value, but the collection, as a whole, housed in the fine old church, is one of the finest attractions of a city wherein marks of culture are by no means scarce.

While these and other active policies of the Reform were being carried into effect, the opponents of the government continued active in guerrilla warfare outside the capital. Though General Escobedo was sent in February, 1861, with troops to check the depredations of Márquez and Mejía, he was captured after defeat at Río Verde, and the Tiger Márquez ordered him shot, but he managed to escape after Mejía had interceded for him. After Ocampo left the cabinet he went to live on his country estate near Maravatío, where he engaged in a simple country life which was soon rudely ended through his capture by guerrillas acting under Márquez, who vindictively had him shot. The wantonness of this vengeance aroused the people and the government to intense indignation. Rewards were offered for the heads of the assassins. Santos Degollado was released from a court process in which he was a defendant to lead forces to attack them, but he fell into an ambush on the Monte de las Cruces, and was in his turn summarily executed by the conservatives. The same fate befell General Leandro Valle in June. Finally Márquez was defeated in August by González Ortega, but not before he had become powerful or audacious enough to threaten the very outskirts of the capital.

Meantime, Juárez had, even yet while in Vera Cruz, appealed to the country for vindication of his policies by election to the presidency on the platform of the decrees issued there embodying the program of the Reform. He felt that he needed a vote of confidence from his followers if he were to enter boldly upon the reconstructive work which he conceived of as essential. It was a bold, but a logical and necessary measure. His strongest opponent in the election was his immediate associate, Miguel Lerdo de Tejada, who was of course of the same political faith. As Lerdo died in March, before the election, Juárez was opposed by González Ortega only, hence these two men were voted for by their party for the offices of president and chief justice respectively. They were installed as legally elected officers on June 1. This "election" was merely a personal vindication. The opponents of the liberals were rebels in the field or unarmed citizens not voting. It would have been inconceivable that any other than a liberal could have won, though even within the ranks of the liberals the Reform program was not always supported with enthusiasm. While the anti-clerical agrarian expropriations were at their height, the opponents of the President in the Chamber of Deputies, to the number of fifty-one, addressed a memorial to him requesting him to resign his office. Happily, a petition asking him not to resign, signed by fifty-two of his supporters among the Deputies, could be considered a "vote of confidence."

It was indeed a precarious triumph which the liberals had won. Though there was manifest a better appreciation of law and order by the liberals, and though foreign opinion, notably the American and British, expressed confidence in Juárez, his Indian birth made him the object of great aristocratic derision, and his determination to carry out dispossessal of the church from its properties earned him the bitter reproaches of the clericals. Even so, success might have been won but for lack of funds. The chaotic finances of the country proved the rock on which the Reform movement broke. In July, 1861, the Congress approved an earlier decree of Juárez suspending for two years payment of interest on the external national debts. This measure was for the purpose of securing a breathing spell for the country while the customs receipts could be applied to quelling the guerrilla fighting at the edge of the capital. There were no other resources available for this life-and-death demand, but the customs receipts had been pledged in nearly their entirety to the payment of the external debts.

The suspension of interest payments for two years would have been a serious move in a time of normal foreign relations, but in the peculiar situation of Mexico at that time it was a most hazardous thing to do. At a later day, beginning in 1913, Mexico was able to discontinue fulfillment of her international financial obligations for more than eight years without bringing on armed intervention to force collections, largely because foreign creditor nations were temporarily unable to make demands. But the spirit of the middle nineteenth century was aggressive on collection of claims to a degree not manifest in the present decade. The European creditors of Mexico had waited long for settlement of just claims, while their nationals had gone on adding many doubtful ones. Loans had been made to all the successive revolutionary governments, each of which was unable to meet even its own debts. Readjustments had been made, had lapsed, and been questioned, until it seemed as though there was no way out of the tangle.

The French claims against Mexico, for robberies, murders, and ransoms of French citizens, had been dealt with in conventions of 1851 and 1853 whereby several millions of dollars were recognized as just obligations. Then there was the notorious J. B. Jecker claim. Jecker, a Swiss who had been in Mexico, arranged in 1859 to lend her $15,000,000, on an issue of bonds in such a way that Mexico was liable for $16,800,000. After the bonds were issued Jecker paid $1,470,000 but went bankrupt before paying any more. Through his friend the duc de Morny, a relative of Napoleon III, he then became a French citizen, and with this advantage pressed his claim for the full amount of the loan. Juárez would recognize obligations only to the extent of the amount actually received. Because of these conditions France broke diplomatic relations with Mexico in July, 1851. The Juárez government recognized total French claims to the amount of $2,860,762.

England's grievances were because of outrages against British subjects, including officials. There had also been much destruction of property, and several seizures of British funds. England had recognized the conservative government as soon as the liberals deserted the capital. In September, 1860, the liberals seized from 80,000 to 100,000 pounds sterling of British funds, other amounts also being taken at the same time from the French and Spanish. In November, Miramón seized $660,000 belonging to the British, in Mexico City, although he gave a receipt for it. The British government then offered to recognize Juárez if he could establish himself in Mexico City and would assume responsibility for these seizures. On those terms he was so recognized on February 22, 1861. There were also loans, amounting to 19,208,-250 pesos, claims of over 4,000,000 pesos, and other liabilities, which were to be met by sixteen percent of Mexican customs duties. Juárez recognized as valid British claims to the extent of $69,994,542.

The Spanish claims against Mexico were for over 10,000,-000 pesos for outrages, unkept conventions, and the expulsion of Spaniards, including the ambassador. Then there was the problem of the liability of the Juárez government for obligations assumed by the Miramón party, whose pseudo-government had celebrated the Mon-Almonte Treaty. This agreement obligated Mexico to assume responsibility for claims by Spanish subjects because of outrages and forced loans which had occurred under Santa Anna's government. In return for their acknowledgment of these liabilities, the reactionaries were to receive Spanish aid in establishing a foreign protectorate. With the terms of this treaty in mind the determination of Juárez to expel the Spanish ambassador, Mon, who had negotiated it with Almonte, can only be characterized as legitimate and necessary. The claims by Spain against Mexico were recognized as valid by Juárez to the extent of $9,460,986.

Instead of decreeing suspension of interest payments on

the debts for a period of two years, as he did, Juárez might
have sought other safer expedients.   It would have been
wiser to have sought a shorter moratorium, or to have tried
for a suitable refunding, or to have eliminated one or other
creditor nation from the list of exigent creditors by conciliatory measures. But the simple, straightforward mind of
Juárez moved toward the consummation of his ideals with a
courageous directness in spite of overpowering difficulties.
The American nation which had already befriended him was
involved in difficulties which rendered it incapable of giving
assistance against the European plot which aimed at checking
democratic government in America, and at reducing the
growing power and prestige of the United States.   The
creditor nations were bent upon collection of their claims,
for which their nationals clamored. But the ulterior motives
behind the determination to intervention would have made
the happy settlement of the foreign debts a matter of disappointment to the French and the Spanish, if not to the
English. For the two Latin powers had ambitions for
continental holdings in North America which the actual
contingency seemed to bring within the realm of possibility.

Indeed, Europe as a whole had not, in 1860, forgiven
the United States for her independence and her hated innova-
tion of a successful democracy. She was an upstart nation
which had not pleased England in the acquisition of Texas,
California, and Oregon. She was viewed with alarm in
Europe because of her rapid expansion. England in particular, having aided the Spanish American colonies to obtain
their independence as a suitable retribution for the assistance which Spain had given the United States in their Revolution, had obtained a large share of Spanish American trade
and was anxious to secure more of it. Moreover, her heavy
loans to Mexico constituted a large measure of her means of
commercial infiltration. The French had hoped intermittently ever since 1762 for an opportunity to reëstablish a
North American empire. Like England, France desired to
restrict the area and the trade prosperity of the United
States. The French interest in establishing buffer states in

Sonora and Baja California had been eloquent testimonials of this attitude. Napoleon's dream was to destroy Anglo-Saxon preponderance and revive Latin glory. Spain cherished the hope of some renewed relationship of her ruling house with her once-best province. When therefore the United States became involved in the Civil War the moment was ripe for an intervention which had so many apparent justifications and so much animus in the ulterior motives of England, France and Spain.

CHAPTER XXI

FOREIGN INTERVENTION—THE SECOND EMPIRE

WHEN the European creditors of Mexico were apprised of the suspension of payment of interest on the national debt, there were already two Mexicans in Europe who were seeking to bring about intervention. They were José María Gutiérrez de Estrada and José Manuel Hidalgo. Monarchism had always had strong adherents in Mexico. The clerical party considered that a monarchy would prove a bulwark to the church, united as these two institutions were in interests. Statesmen like Lucas Alamán believed that a foreign prince would overawe and quiet the disturbing factions which prevented internal peace. Sordid place seekers like Santa Anna even toyed with the idea now and then, encouraging it in the hope of intercepting and absorbing the movement before it should actually bring a foreign ruler to Mexican soil, as Iturbide had managed to do. Many projects had been formed from time to time, but they had proved illusory until now. With Gutiérrez and Hidalgo was General Juan N. Almonte, who gave great impetus to the cause of monarchy by gaining the ear of Napoleon III, while his associates made a favorable impression on the French Empress. Napoleon conceived the idea of aiding the Mexican refugees by finding them a monarch. He would make the Mexican empire an ally or even a protectorate of his own, for the benefit of French trade and political supremacy.

The desires of the Mexican monarchists marched with the current of proposals which were passing between the courts of the nations which held Mexican debts. It was in November of 1858 that the idea of a united intervention in Mexico was proposed by Mon, the Spanish ambassador at Paris, to France, for the purpose of establishing a firm government in

Mexico. During 1859 the Spanish prime minister and Mon kept up some correspondence on the matter, agreeing that it was a necessary move but would require some "moral suasion" and diplomacy. In April, 1860, Spain, after repeatedly sounding out both England and France, found them ready to effect a combination for establishing a firm united government which all members of the distracted nation should recognize and obey. The Spaniards thought that the mere announcement of the formation of such a government would cause all the Mexican conservatives to rally around it and coöperate in the plan. In May of the year mentioned, a conservative constitution to be imposed upon Mexico was drawn up in Spain and sent to England for criticism and approval. Fortunately for the study of constitutional plans for Mexico, this philanthropic document appears to be no longer extant.

The Spanish scheme, which was one of only thinly disguised reconquest, met with a cool reception in England. The English attitude was that no force should be used in imposing an outside government upon the Mexicans, who must accept the proffered regeneration gladly and willingly. Furthermore, the Protestant form of worship must be guaranteed, a provision which proved unacceptable to Spain. Although the French court to all appearances agreed to the Spanish suggestion and to the English limitation prescribing friendly intervention only, the project languished after June of 1860. Spain then took up the matter alone, attempting to enter Mexican waters with a fleet. In this movement she met with hostility from the United States, which then had a naval force off Vera Cruz. On September 2, 1860, Secretary of State Cass notified the Spanish minister that: "The United States will regret any unjust claim against Mexico, and will not permit any hostility against the legitimate government of the Republic of Mexico." By August, 1861, it was evident that the United States was so implicated in the internal problems of secession that she could no longer maintain this intransigent attitude. In that month Mon wrote from Paris to Madrid that he considered the occasion propitious for placing a Bourbon prince or a near relative of the Bourbons on the throne of Mexico. To this the Spanish government replied that it was then preparing an expedition against Mexico, and that orders to that effect had already been sent to the captain-general in Cuba. This move was to avenge the expulsion of Spain's ambassador to Mexico. In September Carl Schurz was told that Spain was about to make war upon Mexico to secure redress for damages and insults. Secretary of State Seward expressed the attitude of the United States government when he declared that it would not intervene in such a war if conducted according to the laws of nations, did not infringe upon the rights of the United States, and had not the object of acquiring territory or of subverting the republican form of the government of Mexico.

With these limitations, the expression of which gave evidence of the reservation with which the United States viewed the project, and the bases upon which future intervention might possibly be premised, Spain moved to interest Napoleon III in the enterprise, and the latter obtained a reluctant consent from England to participate in a joint intervention.

With this end in view, a treaty was signed at London on October 31, 1861, by England, France, and Spain. Austria and Belgium were not signatories, but they approved the convention, and the pope gave its purpose his blessing. Under this document it was agreed by the signatories to send a joint expedition composed of land and sea forces to seize and hold the Mexican coast. No attempt was to be made to establish or impose any kind of government upon the Mexicans, but the duties collected at the customhouses were to be used to meet the overdue claims, in accordance with plans to be drawn by representatives of the three powers. An invitation to the United States to participate in the intervention was extended, though the movement was undertaken before a reply could be had from that power.

The Spanish contingent of six thousand men, first to

arrive at Vera Cruz, on December 14, 1861, found that there were no representatives of the new liberal government there to receive it. While there was no open hostility, there was no enthusiasm, nothing but apathy. It was at once apparent that no debts could be collected without a march into the interior. This was no part of the joint plan. On January 7, 1862, the French arrived with three thousand troops, the English contingent being composed of some seven hundred marines in four large battleships and several smaller vessels.

The Commissioners of the three intervening powers met in Vera Cruz to determine upon a course of procedure. The attitude of the French presented grave difficulties. As a matter of fact Napoleon had deceived England with regard to his intentions, for as early as January, 1861, he had decided to place upon a throne in Mexico the Austrian archduke Maximilian. His pretense that he did not seek to establish any form of government was therefore simply lying. In pursuit of Napoleon's policy the French commander at Vera Cruz had granted admission into Mexico of the monarchists Gutiérrez de Estrada, Hidalgo, and Almonte, and with them had come the recently expelled archbishop of Mexico, Labástida. These conspirators against the independence of their country were now engaged in opposing the Juárez government and preparing the people for the imposition of a foreign prince.

It was plain that the French sought to impose impossible conditions upon the Mexican liberal government, for they demanded twelve million pesos for damages and claims, with no accounting and no proof of their validity required. The Jecker bonds were to be recognized completely, and Vera Cruz and Tampico were to be administered by France until the claims were satisfied by duty collections. The claims of the Spanish and English were more moderate; the English position, as chief creditor of the national debt, made it possible for England to demand settlement for a total of some $40,000,000; while the Spanish claims were for less than $8,000,000. The chief Spanish item was due to the failure of the Mon-Almonte Treaty, as a logical sequel to the defeat of the conservative party.

While busily preparing for national defense by calling upon all Mexicans to come to the support of their government, Juárez attempted to ward off hostilities by conferring with the foreign representatives. A preliminary conference at La Soledad, near Vera Cruz, outlined a program for discussion to be held at Orizaba in April, 1862. At Soledad it was agreed that the European troops should be moved inland to healthy towns away from the tropical diseases of Vera Cruz, that the Mexican liberal government should be recognized, and that if satisfactory settlement of the debts and claims could not be made at Orizaba, the troops would be marched back to the coast again before they should be employed in any aggression upon the Mexican government.

When the Orizaba conference convened, General Almonte had been admitted to the country by the French. He had at once set about the destruction of the Juárez government which the French representative, the count de Saligny, had joined in recognizing. Secretary Doblado remonstrated against this violation of the Soledad agreement, asking that Almonte and his associates be at once sent out of the country. When the conference met at Orizaba, Saligny maintained that the Juárez government had now added so many new grievances against his country that he could no longer treat with it. He declared that France could now be appeased only by a march against Mexico City. The Spanish leader, General Prim, was quick to realize that the claims of France, exorbitant and arbitrary, were intentionally provocative, and that whether they should be acceded to by the Mexicans or not, there was no further hope of Spanish domination of the intervention or the imposition of any Spaniard, himself or another, upon a Mexican throne. He therefore decided to abandon the enterprise, and sailed away to Havana. The French forces had been reïnforced meantime, in order that they might equal in number those of Spain. Prim had left without securing any agreement in regard to the Spanish demands against Mexico. The English were more deliberate, attempting to effect a settlement before they departed; the agreement they entered into was, however, later repudiated by their government.

There had been no concerted action among the allies since April 9, and the French troops which came under General Laurencez were intended to permit of independent action in case of need. When the Spanish and British withdrew from the intervention France was thus left free to act, and her authorities believed that their forces in Mexico were adequate for her needs and purposes. They immediately decided to march to the interior. On April 20 they occupied Orizaba, ignoring their obligation to return to the coast before commencing hostilities. At the same moment the Spaniards were leaving the place for the coast. General Almonte then issued a proclamation to the Mexican people urging their adhesion to the French cause, and Orizaba, under clerical influence, declared for him as supreme chief, while Mexico City voiced its adhesion to Juárez. On the whole, the masses of the people maintained an indifferent attitude in the face of an unwarranted aggression which they could not prevent. The French declaration in April, 1862, naming Almonte as supreme chief of the nation, was followed immediately by the advance of the French forces toward the capital. It was joined by the forces of the infamous General Márquez. The first objective was Puebla, which General Laurencez expected to take with ease. Indeed, the city was ill defended, but its commander was the Coahuiltecan, General Zaragoza, who had given a good account of himself in the War of the Reform. The French commander, obsessed with the idea that victory was to be easily acquired, foolishly struck at the fortified heights of the place in such a way that his seven thousand choice troops were repulsed with astonishing carnage. The battle was fought on May 5, a date ever since glorious in Mexican history. It brought fame to Zaragoza, and to young Porfirio Díaz;

the latter probably won the last phase of the encounter by repelling an attack on General Zaragoza's right wing. The fact that unskilled Mexican soldiers could decisively defeat such a splendid army as Laurencez led was most heartening to Juárez and his associates. The French were nonplussed at their reverse, but though there were scathing speeches in the Corps Législatif, that body voted money for the purpose of sending to Mexico sufficient troops to redeem French military honor, as did the Senate. The defeated Laurencez withdrew to Orizaba, where he was superseded late in September by General Forey, who had brought thirty thousand troops to compel the Mexicans to accept Napoleon's program. Forey was ordered to proclaim himself military dictator over Mexico. In doing so he asserted that while the Almonte party would be kindly treated, the French would abstain from participation in the Mexican quarrel, awaiting a decision. He would defer to the faith of the people in the matter of religion, but expected Mexican troops to do the chief fighting for the establishment of stable conservative government. Forey's orders also directed him to endeavor to induce Almonte to call a convention for the purpose of declaring whether a monarchy was wanted or not, and, in case it was, he was to suggest Maximilian of Austria for the crown. With his large army he was able to begin a second advance toward Mexico City. Puebla, again besieged, managed to hold off the enemy from March 23 to May 17, 1863, but though the garrison held out to the point of exhaustion, it was finally obliged to surrender. The officers were captured and refused to give parole. Some of them were taken to France and others were sent into Mexico City. While they were being taken to Vera Cruz for deportation Porfirio Díaz and a few others managed to make their escape, most fortunately for the cause of Mexican political independence.

The fall of Puebla left the capital open to the advance of the victorious French. It was useless, with his force of only six thousand troops, for Juárez to offer direct resistance, so he retired once again northward on May 31, and set up his government in San Luis Potosí in June, continuing there until nearly the close of the year. While he was entering San Luis, the French were about to enter the capital. There Forey, after a staged welcome for these would-be liberators scant in show of enthusiasm, selected a supreme council of thirty-five monarchists, who in turn named a regency of five men, led by Almonte. This regency or junta called a convention of two hundred and fifteen notables which on July 8 speedily pronounced itself in favor of establishing a monarchy, with an hereditary, moderate, Catholic prince, to be styled "Emperor of Mexico." So thoroughly was the convention prepared for this program that it offered the newly created crown without discussion to Maximilian, providing that if that prince should decline the honor, Napoleon should name an alternate.

The monarchical ideal in Mexico had contemplated a Spanish prince in the first place, and Spanish intervention had been premised on such an arrangement. It had been hoped that Don Juan, the Spanish Pretender, would accept nomination, but that gentleman had declined to become interested in a program which would be likely to remove him from his aspiration to the throne of Spain. It was a simple matter for Napoleon to turn then to Maximilian, but not so easy to prevail upon that idealist to accept. When in 1861 Gutiérrez de Estrada urged Napoleon to seize the opportunity presented by the internal struggle beginning in the United States, he found the French ruler in a peculiarly receptive frame of mind. This man has been characterized as the greatest visionary that ever wore an imperial crown. He desired, as Musser says, to emulate his glorious uncle. He desired to give France a strong foreign policy so as to divert the attention of his subjects from affairs at home. Like other monarchs of Europe, he feared the growing power of the great republic of the western hemisphere, the expansion of which seemed likely to exclude France from the Gulf of Mexico and from all commercial and political influence in the New World. This danger could be averted, and the course of empire changed, if a strong Latin power could be established in Mexico. It was really the recrudescence of the old French dreams of rehabilitation on the North American continent which had survived ever since the tragic losses of the Seven Years' War.

Napoleon believed that the Confederacy would win the Civil War, and he did all he could to bring about such an event, planning to establish Maximilian in Mexico whilst the American struggle would be protracted by Confederate battleships which he allowed to be built in French ports. Several vessels were being prepared when the results of Gettysburg and Vicksburg taught Napoleon that his hopes were unlikely to be realized. He then attempted to intervene in the Civil War, and to detach Texas from the Confederacy, in the hope that he might in some way check the Northern success which began to seem inevitable. No doubt he was moved also by the desires of his empress, Eugenie, who was deeply solicitous for the welfare of the "persecuted" Catholics in Mexico, and it may even be that the scheme to give Maximilian a throne was intended to repay Austria for the annexation of Lombardy and Piedmont by the Treaty of Villafranca, in 1859, when it seemed that a united Italy might prove a menace to French ascendancy.

Whatever may have been his motives, the event proved that in his machinations he committed two costly mistakes. He overestimated the strength of the Catholic party, and he underestimated the power of Juárez and the Mexican determination to defeat intervention. He was in no position to realize that in all her disorder Mexico was forging out a national consciousness premised on liberal doctrines. Second, he failed to judge accurately the cohesive power of the American union. In short, himself a monarchical anachronism, he had no conception of the vigor of nationalism and republicanism which animated the Western Hemisphere. He paid for his sanguine hopes by being shouldered with an enormous debt for the Intervention; his troops in Mexico prevented him from helping Austria when that country went to war with Germany, and the death of Maximilian kept Austria from helping him in the Franco-Prussian War.

Maximilian himself, before giving up his chances as heir of his brother Francis Joseph of Austria when approached with the offer of the Mexican throne, demanded guarantees of success. He specifically requested the effective assistance of England and France, and a clearly decisive expression of choice by the Mexican people, as the necessary antecedents to his assumption of the imperial crown. This attitude he reïterated on October 27, 1861, three days before the Convention of London asserted the purpose of the signatory powers to impose no form of government upon Mexico. Two years later, on October 3, 1863, Maximilian received a statement of the vote of the Assembly of Notables. While accepting the designation, he then again reïterated his demand for a popular election, which even Napoleon himself thought desirable for the effect it would have in conducting foreseen diplomatic correspondence with the United States. The fact that an election would be, and was when taken, merely a farcical procedure, did not seem to have occurred to these two royal visionaries. Elsewhere, in Spain and England, the ephemeral character of the Napoleonic enterprise was by that time thoroughly appreciated. The conditional acceptance of Maximilian brought the French to make an attempt to meet his requirements. A new campaign was begun in Mexico to get an expression from the interior towns. Forey and Saligny, whose dual control of the expedition had proven slow and unsatisfactory, were recalled, and Bazaine was placed in complete control of the enterprise.

The situation now became momentarily favorable to the Intervention. Morelia, Querétaro, San Luis Potosí, and Guadalajara were captured by the French and clerical combination, the Juárez government being driven northward into Durango. Even so, the ground held by the Intervention was only a small wedge in the center of the country, including most of the populous cities. This seemed to satisfy Maximilian, now become eager for his adventure. Leaving Austria with his young and ambitious wife Carlota, he went

The Coach of Maximilian and Carlota
Museo Nacional

to Paris in March, 1864, and on to London, in the hope of moving the reluctant English to espouse his cause. Though unsuccessful in this, the young and romantic couple returned to their home at Miramar, where on April 10, 1864, they formally accepted the Mexican throne, in the fond belief that the vast majority of the Mexicans wanted them.

In the Convention of Miramar, signed that day, it was agreed that the French forces in Mexico should be reduced to the number of 25,000 in 1866, to 20,000 in 1867, and that they should all be replaced by Maximilian's Mexican forces in time, save the foreign legion of 8,000, which was to remain six years. The maintenance of the French expedition was to be at the charge of the new imperial exchequer, under new bonds added to the old debt, adjustment of which was to be speedily forthcoming. A treasury was created for the new government by a loan of 221,600,000 francs, sixty-three percent only of which was forthcoming, with six percent interest. The loan, though unpopular, supplied sufficient funds from sale of bonds to begin with. On April 14, 1864, Maximilian and Carlota embarked for their voyage to Mexico, passing by way of Rome, Gibraltar, the Madeiras, and Jamaica, and arriving at Vera Cruz on May 28. Dampened somewhat by their cool reception there, they proceeded by easy stages in their elegantly silvered coach to the capital. Characteristic receptions met them on the way. At Córdoba the Indians met them with garlands and bouquets, saying: "Thou comest like the rainbow, to dissipate the clouds of discord; sent by the Almighty, may He give thee strength to save us." The fancy of the return of the bearded Quetzalcoatl from the East, to govern Mexico with the clemency and justice of his old mythical reign, was read into this advent of the handsome young monarch for which the reactionaries had been so long machinating. Many were the marks of attention which seemed to augur a propitious opening of the reign of the new savior of the country.

Arriving at his capital on June 12, and assuming the government of his war-torn empire, Maximilian did not delay long in disappointing the expectations of his sponsors, the clericals. Received with enthusiasm by the monarchists of Mexico City, the Emperor began to display a desire for harmonizing the opposing factions, a sense of need of cooperation among the divergent groups among his new subjects, which served only to demonstrate how ill-prepared he was to understand the trend of Mexican history and its effects upon the passions of the contending parties. Removing the Regency, which Almonte had headed, it being no longer useful, he chose his council of ministers largely from among those who had supported monarchical aspirations. But in order to effect his purpose he labored hard, with ultimate success, to induce the conspicuous liberal leader José Fernando Ramírez, to accept the portfolio of minister of state. Still other liberals were added in the vain hope of reconciling the more hostile republicans to his empire. But the flat refusal of Mariano Riva Palacio to enter the cabinet showed that republican opinion could not be so readily purchased. This was a shocking surprise to the Emperor, who, while a member of the conservative group of society, was at heart a liberal in politics and intended to govern by liberal methods.   His determination to do so effectively was thwarted by his own acts, since his conservative supporters were offended and made jealous by his use of liberals as helpers in organizing his government.

The general policy of regeneration which Maximilian hoped for met its first serious difficulty when he refused the demand of the clericals, expressed by the archbishop, that the church lands which had been seized by Juárez should be restored. To have done this would have been unjust to the purchasers of those lands from the Juárez government, an idea which made scant appeal to the clericals. Naturally their enthusiasm for the Emperor was measurably dampened by his refusal to accede to their desires, as he practically endorsed the reform policy for which the republican patriots had fought so long and were still in the field to maintain. The Emperor suffered also in his executive character from an irresolute disposition which permitted him to be influenced by each successive adviser. He was thus often inconsistent and inconsequential where he should have been resolute and tenacious. Cruel and satirical in his comments concerning absent supporters, often ungrateful toward his warmest friends, he lacked the essentials of personality needful to build up a solidarity among his entourage which might have aided him in the hour of fate. The Empress on the contrary was an energetic ambitious woman of solid character who might have saved his life had she continued at his side until the success of the liberals.

In August, 1865, Maximilian made an expedition into the cities of Querétaro and Guanajuato, during which the staged enthusiasms of the populace and the fawning flattery of his official family convinced him, as he wished to be convinced, that he was genuinely popular with the people. At the same time he was falsely informed that Juárez had abandoned Mexican soil. He at once concluded that the liberal cause was crushed and that the remaining forces in the field were mere irreconcilables who would never be moved by defeat but required extermination before peace could come. He therefore issued on October 3, 1865, his famous decree ordering that members of "Juarist bands" taken under arms should be shot on sight without trial. The decree horrified even Mexico; it raised a furor of condemnation in the United States Congress, where vehement speeches were made against the Intervention and the Empire. Many barbarous acts under this decree alienated the sympathies of numerous friends who had seen in Maximilian a hope of establishing a real and permanent government in Mexico.

The year 1864 had drawn to a close with the republicans in the south led by Díaz, generally successful, but in the north their successes were less decisive. Juárez was forced northward to Chihuahua, where he continued until August, 1865, at which time he was again driven northward, finally establishing his government at Paso del Norte, now Ciudad Juárez. During 1865 the Empire was at its strongest. An imperial constitution was promulgated; an effort was made to encourage immigration, refugees from the decaying Confederacy being among them. Senator Gwinn of California planned an abortive colony in Sonora for some of these; a great outcry from the Mexicans, who saw in the movement a possible repetition of the Texas episode, was accompanied by the opposition of the United States to the project. One of the most hopeless features of the imperial position was the impossibility of reaching a solution of the financial question. The obligations assumed toward France were enough to embarrass a peaceful country, but the addition of war expenses, coupled with the old debts, kept the interventionists' organization in continuous straits.

When the Confederate surrender at Appomatox relieved the long tension in the United States, it became possible for Secretary Seward to take a more decisive attitude toward the Napoleonic dream. Though there was popular demand that the Union armies be turned at once on the French interlopers, it was thought that the best effect could be obtained at the smallest expense by giving secret aid to Juárez in the shape of men, money, and munitions. General Bazaine, in spite of his victories in the north, was unwilling to pursue the liberals to Paso del Norte, fearing complications if armed clashes should occur along the border, where volunteer American bands were aiding the republicans. With the North triumphant, Napoleon saw that there was no longer hope of decisive victory. On February 12, 1866, Secretary Seward demanded the withdrawal of the French forces. The demand was complied with, at a date earlier than had been specified in the Miramar Convention. The first troops were to go in November, 1866, the second in March, 1867, and the last in November, 1867. Since it had been all too well manifested that his tenure rested exclusively on the French arms, Maximilian in this exigency deemed it wise that he should abdicate; but with characteristic irresolution he hesitated; Carlota set forth on her ill-fated voyage to Europe to endeavor to retain the backing of Napoleon and of the pope. The perplexed and irresolute Emperor was induced, by new promises of aid from the Mexican Church, and by the self-seeking counsels of Miramón and Márquez, to remain in his quaking Empire. Even his mother wrote to him, urging him to stay rather than compromise his honor. Between hopes and fears, ignorance and selfish counsels, he hesitated and was lost.

The French troops were finally withdrawn, Bazaine leaving Mexico City on February 5, 1867, and the last of his forces embarking from Vera Cruz on March 12. The republican troops eagerly occupied the route in his rear as he neared the coast. Maximilian was led to believe that Márquez and Miramón could still save his throne without French aid. He returned in January, 1867, to Mexico City from Orizaba, whither he had gone while under the impulse to abdicate, now determined to consult the will of the nation as to whether he should continue his attempt or not. If he could not receive the vote of confidence of the Mexicans, he hoped to be able to treat with Juárez for terms whereby he might turn over the government to the liberals and leave the country with credit if not with glory. Strange hallucination of a deserted and harassed soul!

In Mexico City the quondam liberal Vidaurri, whose instinct of self interest gave him some intelligence amid the general fear which clutched Maximilian's advisers, proffered the sage counsel that the Emperor should show his good faith by abdicating in anticipation of the convocation of the congress which he desired should voice the will of the nation regarding him. But Maximilian declined this opportunity, and listened to those who desired that he alone should receive the entire blame for the Empire. They knew that upon his departure they would pay dearly for adhesion to the lost cause.

The republican successes had reduced the Empire to the capital and a few State capitals when Miramón with his old audacity suddenly seized the republican capital, Zacatecas, Juárez and his ministers escaping capture only by rapid flight in a well executed ruse which led their pursuers off their trail. Maximilian, deceived into thinking this was a presage of complete victory, wrote to Miramón ordering that the republican leaders if caught should be tried by court martial. But Miramón was defeated on February 6 at San Jacinto, and fled without receiving this letter. When Maximilian learned of his defeat he became dismayed to the point of incoherency of ideas. First he adopted the recourse of appealing to Porfirio Díaz, whom the French themselves had earlier thought of utilizing when it had become evident that the foreign throne was tottering. Díaz was at the time moving from Oaxaca upon Puebla. To the proffer of Maximilian that he should assume charge of affairs, Díaz shrewdly replied that he was subordinate, being in a military capacity, to the republican government, and hence could not enter into political relations with the enemy.

It was now evident even to Maximilian that there was no hope of assembling the congress upon which he had built his faith for a solution of his problem. While the French army was embarking for Europe his generals one by one suffered defeat or abandoned his cause. The territory he controlled was a mere fraction of what it had been. In this situation he took council with his minister Lares, who gave him a quixotic piece of advice. This was that he place himself at the head of the army; ostensibly because he no longer had confidence in his mutually jealous generals, also that he might be removed from too close supervision of the ministry, which was making exhaustive efforts to provide resources wherewith to keep the monarchy alive. It was still Maximilian's hope that he might be able to present to Juárez an imposing front which would impel the liberal leader to arrange terms under which the foreign prince might relinquish his unsuccessful political tenure and leave the country. Lares also advised that any pact which Maximilian might offer to enter into with Juárez should above all include an agreement that the clergy should be restored to the position of power and privilege which it had enjoyed prior to the War of the Reform. That is, a liberal reform Emperor was to enter an agreement with a liberal reform President to bring about the restoration of the one thing they were agreed upon in opposing! On such a mission Maximilian left the capital with sixteen hundred men to join his army, then largely concentrated at

Querétaro. Lares remained in charge of the imperial government in the capital, defended by five thousand troops. Puebla with twenty-five hundred, Vera Cruz with a small force, and Yucatan with another, constituted the only points now held by the Empire outside of the general concentration from more northern points at Querétaro. The latter was a strongly clerical town, most loyal to the Empire, but entirely unsuited for a stronghold, since it is almost surrounded and entirely dominated by low hills which the imperial forces were too scant to occupy.

Maximilian reached Querétaro on February 19, 1867. He had there about nine thousand soldiers. He realized that he was opposed, not by a demoralized band bent on pillage, but by a "homogeneous army whose stimulus is the courage and perseverance of a chief moved by a great idea— that of defending the national independence. . . ." So he had written to one of his ministers shortly before setting out for the north. Now, surrounded by the last of the imperial generals, his fate was in the hands of such indifferent strategists as Miramón, Márquez, Méndez, Mejía, who constituted with Maximilian the "five tragic M's." There the imperial forces spent the time, instead of marching out to meet enemy troops in detail before they could unite, in waiting until the republicans could gather sufficient forces to invest the place. They began to gather early in March, soon proving numerous enough nearly to surround the city. From March till mid-May General Escobedo, the liberal military commander, with from fifteen to twenty thousand men kept Querétaro in a state of constant siege. General Márquez made unwearying efforts to increase his strength after being outvoted in a council of war in which he had urged retiring upon Mexico City. On March 22 he slipped away unobserved by the enemy to the capital to obtain help. Two days later the liberals were beaten in an attack, losing 2,000 men killed and several hundred prisoners. They now determined to starve the imperialists out. The besieged were reduced to great straits while waiting vainly for the return of Márquez with reënforcements. But that aspiring genius, finding Puebla hard pressed by Díaz, went to its relief, justifying the suspicion of his associates at Querétaro that he sought a government there for himself when the Empire should completely drop to pieces. The weeks passed, news being brought at last that Márquez had been annihilated and that Puebla had fallen. On April 27 Miramón made a fierce assault on the southern side of the iron ring which hemmed him in, preparatory to cutting a way out. Unexpected success left him dazed, and before he could affirm his victory Escobedo had him more tightly encompassed than before, with hundreds lost in killed, wounded, and prisoners. Now dejection seized the imperial forces; desertions became more frequent. There were only about five thousand defenders left. The troops and the city were approaching starvation. The citizens bore their trials patiently; Maximilian was a model of good nature, comradeship, and reckless bravery.

Finally, as a last desperate effort, it was determined that the defenders should cut their way through the republican ring and make their way to the Sierra Gorda to the northwest, where they could still hold out by guerrilla warfare. It was no longer thought feasible to try to get back to Mexico City. On the night of May 14 all was ready, rations distributed, horses saddled and waiting. But Maximilian still hoped for a chance to surrender, and on the eve of departure sent General Miguel López to interview Escobedo. López revealed the unhappy situation of the besieged, but was denied the capitulation which Maximilian desired. On the contrary the republican forces made their way into the city and took the convent of La Cruz. Maximilian, told of this by López, thereupon repaired to the Cerro de las Campanas, one of the low hills near the city, and there gave up his sword at dawn on the fifteenth.

He was promptly tried by court-martial in the Iturbide Theatre, together with Miramón and Mejía. Méndez, when taken, had been summarily shot. The royal prisoner had the sympathy of the entire world during his month of trial. His efforts to obtain permission to leave the country were all rejected. Friends made every effort to obtain clemency. The court-martial convicted him of filibustering, treason, and of ordering inhumane executions under the infamous decree of October 3, 1865. He never had a chance before his judges, though he was ably defended by Mariano Riva Palacio and several other able republican lawyers. A protest from the United States, which country had contributed effectively toward Juárez' success, failed to arrive in time to save the prince. It was believed that he might, if released, be again persuaded by adherents to renew his pretensions, or prove the center of renewed foreign complications. Juárez and Lerdo de Tejada felt that events had placed executive clemency beyond their power. The northern republican army men generally demanded that justice be done. Abortive eleventh hour plans for escape proved futile, and were exposed.

On the morning of June 19, after an early mass, the three prisoners were carried to the Cerro de las Campanas, where Maximilian had surrendered. A square of four thousand soldiers enclosed the field. Embracing his condemned companions in a last salute, and pressing his hand to his heart, the brave unfortunate, with the prayer that his blood might be the last to be shed for Mexico, received the fatal volley. Men in Mexico have always known how to die with composure, though in vain, from Quauhtémoc to Carranza, but the prayer that blood may cease to flow still awaits answer.

Two days later Mexico City fell before Díaz. Márquez made good his flight. The war and the Empire were ended. On July 15, 1867, Juárez and his ministers again reëntered the capital and set up anew the sorely tried Republic. Several hundred imperialists were imprisoned and tried, but only two, O'Horan and Vidaurri, were executed. The war had caused the loss of probably 40,000 lives, in over a thousand encounters. There was less retributive vengeance by the victorious liberals than the reactionaries had practiced, though there was some confiscation of property and marked display of bitterness by liberal politicians.

What had been gained by the War of the Reform and the

foreign intervention? The conservative attempt to affirm the identity of church and state had failed. The belief that bad debts can be collected by costly and unjust exercise of force had been proven a ghastly error. Thousands of lives had been lost, millions of treasure expended; finance, commerce, industry, agriculture, education—all the comforts and amenities of modern life—had been sacrificed. Yet there had been a gain in national consciousness. During the struggle the people of Mexico had come to identify the liberal Constitution and the Laws of Reform with the existence of the nation and the preservation of liberty. Thus, as Rabasa says, the concepts of the foreign ruler, the invading French army, and the conservative party all were fused in the popular mind in one idea of treason to the country. Whatever there must have been of confusion in this identification of ideas where there should have been merely association of them, the effect was to create a simple mental image around which to rally the sentiment of patriotism and loyalty. Thus the church, the invasion, the reactionary party, all became the fused object of hatred. The prestige of the clerical influence had weakened enough to permit popular sanction of the Laws of Reform which had served as the ægis of those who had fought to prevent the country from betrayal to foreign control and identity of church and state. The liberals, a mere handful unable to make headway with their ideas in 1833 and still a minority in 1858, had now become a majority through the superiority of their cause and through the adhesion of those who always join a successful movement. Even so, a few more years of readjustment were to pass before these laws, incorporated into the Constitution as basic, received the approval of the Congress and of the State legislatures—not only because they were necessary and just, but because they interpreted the will of the people of the Republic.

CHAPTER XXII

THE RECONSTRUCTION PERIOD

WHEN the liberals found themselves in control of the country once more there was some natural demand that retribution should be visited upon the defeated party, although Juárez from the first manifested a conciliatory spirit toward the lost cause. Under a law of August 16, 1863, a large number of estates belonging to reactionaries were confiscated. Many of the old families were thus reduced to penury. The President soon saw the futility of this course, and fines were imposed instead of confiscation, lessening the severity of punishment for those reactionaries who were not adjudged guilty of actual treason. Some of the liberal newspapers soon began to agitate for the usual law of amnesty. Juárez and his immediate cabinet members saw the advantage of a general political pardon; the administration did, indeed, execute punishment as mildly as possible without incurring the risk of dissension among its more vindictive partisan adherents, who were already beginning to sniff the spoils of victory. Owing to their attitude the actual amnesty proclamation had to be delayed for some time.

Gradually the government resumed its functions under new organization. The secretariat of fomento, or improvement of natural resources, was reëstablished. Changes in the personnel of the cabinet were effected. The State governments which had moved to seaports for security during hostilities were ordered back to their legal capitals. With his usual disregard for consequences when moving toward a desired end, Juárez reduced the army to 16,000 men. This measure left two-thirds of the soldiers who had fought the French and Maximilian to shift for themselves, and created discontent among a number of army officers who later made trouble by leading revolts. The judiciary was reorganized, with Sebastián Lerdo de Tejada ad interim chief justice, and the legal status of civil acts consummated under the Empire was established by decree. Liberal newspapers which had been suppressed by Maximilian's government were restored. Efforts scant in success but none the less sincere were made to establish just practices in elections, to raise municipal government to a respectable status, to create a bicameral national legislature, and to evoke a permanent American continental congress. Measures were undertaken for creating a number of badly needed technical schools, and the railroad problem received much attention.

But the country feared the discretionary powers which Juárez still exercised, and there was impatience at the continuance of martial law, even for the protection of free elections. When, in August, 1867, general elections were called to choose a president, a new constitutional congress, and officers of the supreme court, popular unrest began to appear. The trouble centered about a proposal to allow the ordinary Congress to amend the Constitution. Many liberals opposed this as an abrogation of states' rights. A party of them which stood for adherence to existing constitutional procedure wished to elect Porfirio Díaz president. Another group favored Sebastián Lerdo de Tejada. Juárez himself sought reëlection as a vindication of the course he had taken when, in 1865, he had continued as president after expiration of his term, although the strict constitutional method demanded that General Ortega, chief justice, should have succeeded him at that time. Ortega was undesirable to the liberals because he had been long absent from the country, and had pro-French leanings. In the elections, held in October, 1867, Juárez was elected by 7,522 votes in 10,380. When the Congress met, the President surrendered his wartime discretionary powers. On December 25 he assumed office as constitutional President for a term to expire November 30, 1871. His earliest act, in addressing the newly opened Congress, was to acknowledge gratefully the moral support which had been given him by the United States throughout the intervention. American claims were adjusted, and amicable relations between the two republics were cemented in 1869 through a visit to Mexico by William H. Seward, ex-secretary of state of the American Union. Friendly relations with the most important European countries were gradually resumed, Mexico undertaking adjustment of the debts of those who presented claims.

But the process of reconstruction was hindered all through this presidential period by military revolts in eight or nine states. Generally, these entities refused to coöperate with the Juárez government, the governors maintaining themselves as independent regional chiefs. This was the logical aftermath of foreign intervention, during which no central government enforced its orders in many of the states. The desire of Juárez to continue his old cabinet officers also roused frequent jealousies and crises. Harmony among the liberals was once again impossible after the danger of foreign aggression was removed. Partly this was due to the dissatisfaction of minorities defeated in the national elections by the government party, which had no doubt procured its retention of power by questionable means. As Rabasa says, this was the fault of the untimely grant of manhood suffrage by the Constitution of 1857. The incapacity of the ignorant lower class to understand the franchise made it the prey of political aspirants. It was imperative for Juárez to control votes in order to establish the results of the long struggle through which the country had passed. His long tenure, especially when in January, 1868, he began to ask plenary powers of Congress for dealing with conspirators, made his enemies suspect him of seeking to perpetuate a personal dictatorship. As a result of all these contributing causes the year was marked by great public insecurity. Everywhere life and property were unsafe until at the end of the year the government succeeded in restoring a semblance of order. The next year saw a repetition of numerous revolts animated by desire to overthrow Juárez. The most conspicuous success of the administration during the presidential term was the enactment of a general amnesty law in October, 1870. This measure relieved many imperialists and later conspirators of the consequences of their political acts, but did not succeed in restoring peace.

The presidential campaign of 1871 only added to the emotional perturbation. The best friends of Juárez urged him not to stand as candidate again. It must be admitted that he shone, not as an administrator, but as the exponent of a principle. He was intransigent, an idealist; charged by conscience with the national preservation under great odds, he rose to spiritual grandeur. But the president of Mexico must be intensely practical. Now he believed that he was still needed to continue the enforcement of the Constitution until it should become engrafted in the national political subconsciousness. He stood once more for the presidency, again opposed by Díaz and Lerdo. His tenacity armed the opposition. Díaz was a popular military hero, with a claim to distinction because of his unquestioned services during the war. Lerdo was popular because of the great name of his brother Miguel, who had written the Laws of Disamortization and Nationalization of clerical estates. He had won some official following by feathering his own nest while making political appointments as the friend of Juárez. The meagerly participated in election gave no one a majority; Congress, deciding the issue, in October declared Juárez once more elected.

This was too much for the friends of Díaz, who alleged corruption in the popular election—no doubt correctly; but they neglected their own wish to have committed the same sin, and flew to arms in protest. Díaz was urged to join them, and did so by a pronouncement from his hacienda of La Noria on November 8. The battle cry was for free and honest elections, a thing then and yet unknown in Mexico. The Plan de la Noria claimed to want them, but its process and program were their direct negation. The essence of the movement was the ambition and egotism of Díaz, as the cause had been those of Juárez and the mistaken constitutional provision that the lower class people of Mexico should possess the manhood franchise.

The Plan de la Noria advocated reconstruction of the government by a popularly elected convention which should choose a provisional president and frame a new organic law. There was to be no opportunity left for any president to succeed himself. Congress was to be limited to powers largely economic and to confirmation of appointees to secretariats. Municipal autonomy was advocated, and a number of unpopular taxes were to be done away with. Under this program the revolt spread in spite of the fact that many liberals criticized it as an assault upon the Constitution. There was fighting in Oaxaca, Zacatecas, Durango, and Yucatan. Díaz even made a rapid move with a detachment of cavalry upon Mexico City, in the illusory hope that his friends there would rise as he drew near. Undeceived, he rode on to Jalisco, a little later making his way into Tepic (now Nayarit), in the mountain fastnesses of which region he sought safety with the bandit chieftain Manuel Lozada. The Díaz insurrection, though no longer imposing in actual force, still maintained scattered bands afield in nearly all parts of the country. The government had been fairly successful in the fighting, but the decision had not yet come in mid-July, 1872, when a new power entered the political arena.

It was the hand of death. Juárez, first taken seriously ill in 1870, had felt for some time that his days were shortening. His passion for the establishment of pacific conditions supported him through numberless trials and disappointments, until victory seemed almost at hand. He was not to see it. On July 18, 1872, he left his office somewhat earlier than was his wont, retiring to his home, where he was seized with an affection of the heart from which he died late in the night, amid family and friends. The nation paused from civil strife for a moment to honor the distinguished Indian who had not failed to give his best at every moment of his life that Mexico might endure. The hero's body was laid to rest among the country's distinguished dead in the pantheon of San Fernando. There his effigy lies on a marble monument, beside which, in later days, Porfirio Díaz was wont during the anniversary memorial service for Juárez, to place laurels on the tomb of his great predecessor, to the bitterness of whose last days he had added in no small measure.

Sebastián Lerdo de Tejada, chief justice of the supreme court, constitutionally indicated for the succession, qualified as president on the day after the death of Juárez. His problems were difficult. Neither of the three militant "political" parties—Juarists, Porfirists, and Lerdists, was in a majority nor was any of them in safe military control, though the old Juarists held the momentary ascendancy. Lerdo, staunch friend of Juárez during the Intervention, had yearned for the presidency at the prior election. He had the valuable qualities of persistence and purpose, but was vain, domineering, and suspicious. Pertinaciously retaining the old Juárez cabinet, he thus antagonized both his own personal followers and those of Díaz. The latter hero he hoped to eliminate as a dangerous rival by having him proscribed when Díaz attempted to make conditions under which he would accept Lerdo's amnesty proclaimed in July. Many former rebels availed themselves of this clemency, and returned to political positions as governors of states or other preferments. But Díaz held out for a postponement of the general election which Lerdo had called until the country should be quite pacified. This was in the hope of making more certain his own political chances. He also objected with the characteristic modesty of an insurgent to being deprived of his general's salary for the period during which he had been fighting the recognized government of Juárez.

The President disliked receiving orders from a rebel, and would not modify his amnesty terms. The federal troops busy at pacification moved from success to success. One by one the supporters of the Plan de la Noria gave in their allegiance to Lerdo. Díaz had finally to abandon hope of effecting an arrangement whereby his chances at the polls would be strengthened, and was constrained to accept amnesty unconditionally on October 26, the day upon which the secondary elections for president were being held. Lerdo won them decisively, receiving nearly 10,000 votes, Díaz 600, and others 136. Obviously the status of the franchise was wretched for a nation numbering many millions. Congress on November 16 declared Lerdo president-elect by one hundred and fifty votes against three. The election, if procured, was at least acquiesced in by the nation. But the President, installed on December 1, was silent on the questions of free suffrage and no reëlection which had agitated the La Noria insurgents. Díaz he proposed for a European embassage. The Lerdists and Porfirists hoped for a coalition cabinet, as both parties had supported the successful candidate. But Lerdo owned no obligations save to constitutionality, and took his own council.

At that time the bandit of Tepic, Manuel Lozada, schooled as he had been by many revolutionary leaders who had sought refuge with him as Díaz had done, declared himself independent of the central government. Marching eastward from Tepic with a horde of bloodthirsty Indians numbering thousands, he threatened Guadalajara, but was defeated and returned to Tepic. In July he was caught in the mountains and executed. After the pacification of the region, Lerdo continued to govern it as a federal military district in opposition to the will of the State of Jalisco and that of several Deputies. This invasion of the integrity of statehood weakened Lerdo's support in Congress.

That body performed one momentous act before it adjourned. It approved, on May 29, 1874, of the incorporation into the Constitution of the Laws of Reform. These historic laws, which had cost at least eight years of civil war, completely disestablished the church, eliminated it from participation in politics, and attempted to break its economic domination. Freedom of religious worship was declared. Marriage by civil contract became the only legal basis of conjugal relations. The religious oath to speak truth in lawsuits was legally superseded by simple affirmation. All men were declared free to labor, worship, and be educated as they might choose. Monastic vows were made no longer civilly binding. These laws were affirmed by the State legislatures, and became a regular part of the national Constitution on November 12, 1874. The liberals were now able to reckon on the support of public opinion as they had not been in 1833 and 1857, and 1861. Through years of bloodshed the Reform was won at last.

Though the full effect of the Laws of the Reform has never been felt, they have not been without influence on the nation. At their inception they met some opposition in Indian uprisings instigated by clericals, as in Michoacán in 1874. Such disturbances were by no means comparable with the bloody civil strife which had gone on since 1855, however. As a matter of fact, the Revolution of Ayutla, the War of the Reform and the Intervention had liberalized Mexico. Henceforth there was no open attempt by the church to dominate politics. Church and state were definitively separated; only with the tacit consent of Díaz did it continue its economic dominance, providing fuel for the flames of revolt which broke out in 1910.

During the two following years there was a gradual return to almost peaceful conditions. Rebellions in Yucatan, Coahuila, and elsewhere, were of local significance and not against Lerdo. But he steadily acquired enemies by neglect of his old partisans and by continuous antagonism toward the Díaz party. The press assailed him; prominent men challenged his acts. His party began to lay plans for perfecting control of the coming elections. Díaz saw that there would be armed strife if his ambitions were to be realized, and departed to Brownsville, Texas, to prepare a revolt. This was soon forthcoming under the lead of one of his partisans, General Fidencio Hernández, who "pronounced" the Plan de Tuxtepec on January 15, 1876, at Tuxtepec, Oaxaca. He soon seized the State and proclaimed Díaz head of a new "revolution," which spread like wildfire. When it was strong enough, Díaz entered Mexico from the north, and on March 31 published at Palo Blanco, just below

Matamoros, an amended form of the Tuxtépec pronouncement which he styled the Plan de Palo Blanco.

These Plans declared that Lerdo's government was sub-
versive of the laws of the land; that elections were controlled
by the President; that the States had been deprived of their
independence; that the courts were subservient to the executive; that municipal autonomy was dead; and that most of
Lerdo's administrative acts had sacrificed the country to
foreign investors. His dictatorial rule must end, and force
alone could effect this. However true the accusations, the
Plans read more like a Díaz program, in the light of later
events, than a promise of reform. Stripped of their verbiage
they meant that the ambition of Díaz could no longer be
delayed.

With all this warning, Lerdo stubbornly continued to
perfect plans to succeed himself in the summer elections, or
rather to procure a favorable composition of Congress so
that that body might declare him elected. This was done in
October. The chief justice, Iglesias, determined also to
attempt to forestall Lerdo's illegal election, by pronouncing
himself constitutionally the proper occupant of the office.
Iglesias set up a counter government in Guanajuato at the
end of October.

While this second revolution was going on, Díaz, who had
come down from the north on a steamer in disguise, had
organized forces in his own state, Oaxaca, and now was advancing upon Mexico. At Tecoac his forces met those of
Lerdo on November 16 in a severe engagement which lasted
several hours. Díaz was nearly defeated when he was re-
inforced by General González, companion of his plots in
Brownsville. The new troops saved the day. The Lerdists
lost three thousand men and all their impedimenta. That
single battle was enough to drive Lerdo out of Mexico City in
panic. He went to New York, where he died in 1889.

Iglesias tried to effect an agreement with Díaz whereby
the former might assume the presidency constitutionally.
Díaz consented, providing Iglesias would subscribe to the
Plan de Palo Blanco, and effect a coalition government, but

before negotiations were completed he entered Mexico and assumed the provisional presidency. Iglesias left the country for the United States. There were now three claimants to the executive power, two in flight seeking means of restoration, and one in actual possession of the power, laying plans to consummate legitimacy in his tenure.

CHAPTER XXIII

THE RISE OF PORFIRIO DÍAZ

THERE was little of especial brilliancy or power in the military career of Porfirio Díaz to justify his aspirations to the presidency of the Republic. The elections of his competitors, Juárez in 1871, and Lerdo de Tejada in 1875, were as free from suspicion of being representative of the popular will as any of his own ever were to be, but save for his own revolts they were as generally acquiesced in. They were simply procured elections, as was inherently necessary under party government with manhood suffrage in a nation having no political education. It is true that these men were elected through subversion of the franchise; their administrations were marked by frequent outbreaks, insurrection, unsafety of life and property, fiscal chaos, and administrative ineptitude. But these were traditional evils which the ambitions of Díaz, in his two "revolutions" of La Noria and Tuxtépec, only augmented for the sake of personal vanity. True, his military successes merited reward; he had done yeoman work in Oaxaca, at Puebla and Mexico, against the French and Maximilian. But Doblado and Degollado had given equally valiant service in the Juárez cause, and had been content with the voluntary rewards conceded by their fellow-citizens.

Moreover, although Juárez and Lerdo had to fight insurrections, the country was making notable political progress under them. During their combined periods there occurred three presidential and four legislative elections in which proper form at least had been observed. Congress was functioning legally, though with asperity and passion in debates. Each president held to his office during his entire constitutional period. This was vastly better than had been

375

the case before the fall of Maximilian. The reason lay in the respect for law which had developed under the Constitution of 1857, in the improved condition of the national army, and in the destruction of the conservative party, which meant elimination of church intervention in public affairs. The Plan de la Noria protested against the indefinite reelection of Juárez, the subservience of Congress, and the impotence of the Supreme Court. The warfare introduced by this pronouncement was a negation of whatever civil advance the country had made. It was a pretorian appeal for the expulsion of the president-elect, Juárez, and a demand for the exaltation of the militaristic principle once more. In the name of personal ambition Díaz put himself politically in a class with Bustamante, Santa Anna, Paredes.

The death of Juárez put an end to the unseemly contest. This was a great tribute to the departed hero. But it was only an armistice. Lerdo de Tejada had as a civilian rendered as conspicuous service to the country as had Díaz as a military leader. His tenacity of the presidency, his stubborn self-will, and his hostility toward the defeated Díaz party led ultimately to the Plan de Tuxtépec, which was simply another pretorian demand, but attempt to justify it included denunciation of Lerdo's Stamp Law and a pronouncement against reëlection of the president and governors of states. It demanded the removal of the proud and inflexible Lerdo. Díaz, as has been said, after adventurous hazards, overcame the government in a single battle, soon entered the capital with a large army, and, shortly getting rid of José María Iglesias, assumed the executive power. Iglesias was soon bested in a small fight in the state of Guanajuato, and fled to the United States, leaving the way clear for Díaz to realize the ambition he had treasured for so many years.

A well chosen cabinet was speedily formed, containing men whose political aptitudes and status tended to strengthen the new ruler. Then elections were called in obedience to tradition, in order to allow a chosen portion of the people to legalize by form of democracy the seizure of power by

military force. On the following day, May 2, Díaz was by
the newly elected Congress declared constitutional President
for a term to expire November 30, 1880. At first there were
armed uprisings to quell, notably that led from Texas into
Coahuila in June, 1877, by General Escobedo (who had
commanded the federal army at the fall of Querétaro and
had been war minister under Lerdo de Tejada) in favor of
the presidential pretensions of the latter refugee. In 1878
Escobedo made a second entry from the American frontier,
but was captured. A similar move by Amador was defeated.
On April 9, 1878, the United States recognized Díaz as
head of the de jure government. Recognition had been
delayed because of unquiet border conditions.   Here General Ord for the Americans, and General Treviño for the
Mexicans, worked harmoniously for the control and dis-
persion of bandits who molested the inhabitants of both
nations by forays across the international boundary.

In June, 1879, a more serious insurrection fomented by
old followers of Lerdo in Vera Cruz proved the turning point
of the Díaz period in internal disorders. Governor Mier y
Terán was ordered to suppress the uprising energetically.
There were two Mexican gunboats in the Gulf charged with
the duty of admitting vessels to the port of Alvarado. The
crew of one of them without warning left its commander on
shore and put to sea in mutinous support of the Lerdists.
Their act convinced Mier that the conspiracy, of which he
had been apprised from Mexico, was really in existence.
Acting upon orders from Díaz, sent in the famous telegram:
"Aprehendidos infraganti, mátalos en caliente"—When they
are caught in the overt act, kill them in cold blood—he
seized nine alleged conspirators and promptly had them
shot. Some of those executed were innocent. The execution
caused a profound sensation in the entire country. The
force of the "iron hand" was recognized as supreme. Its
effect was to cement a peace which endured with only minor
interruptions throughout the entire Díaz régime. At the
first sign of a revolt, swift and ruthless punishment descended. Bandits were exterminated or set against each

other, in an organization which built up out of these doubtful elements the "rurales" who protected life in the provinces as the old Acordada had done in colonial days. In 1879 the national elections recurred. Díaz could not be reëlected in the face of his promises made in the Plan de Tuxtépec. The logical successor, Justo Benítez, who had been a staunch supporter and adviser of Díaz, could not be trusted to return the presidency to the latter at the end of four years, so General Manuel González was supported for the candidacy. It was certain that he would acquiesce in such a rotation of the executive office. The governors of the states, who really held the power of deciding the elections, abandoned Benítez for González, and the latter was overwhelmingly elected, though three candidates appeared against him. His term of four years was relatively placid politically because he was free from machinations to succeed himself and Díaz was recognized by all as the logical man for the next president.

González was an intelligent person. Under him, the country progressed notably. That was the epoch of the initial steps in railroad building toward the northern frontier. There was a general atmosphere of speculation; many roads were rapidly though poorly built. Concessions for survey and colonization of the public lands were begun. There were visible in many directions the beginnings of the general prosperity which characterized the era of the absolute Porfirian power which was to follow. The presidency of González would have left for itself a grateful memory in the hearts of most Mexicans, had it not been for the avarice of his associates, which toward the end of his term brought upon him a most thorough-going unpopularity. These people attempted to monopolize all the business which the government controlled for their own private gain. But in spite of this weakness the extraordinary administrative capacity of González brought Mexico into a condition of economic well-being through the solution of the many budgetary troubles inherited from the earlier period of disorder. González was able to conclude his term in peace because there was no conspicuous effort to have him reëlected. During his tenure he maintained consistent loyalty toward his old military chief. At first he made him Minister of Fomento, but Díaz gave up that office in May, 1881. In 1882 he was chosen a member of the Supreme Court and Senator at the same time. Holding the second of these positions for a short interval, he soon resigned in order to accept the governorship of the State of Oaxaca. Early in 1883 he made a visit to the United States, where he was received in triumph.

The political influence of the revolution of Tuxtépec ended with the retirement of González on November 30, 1884. On the following day Díaz began the long rule which was to end only with his exile in May, 1911. The Plan de Tuxtépec had become only a memory to be blotted out as soon as possible. It had been enunciated and fought for primarily to abolish reëlections of presidents and governors, but now that ambition was realized, those very policies of Juárez and Lerdo which Díaz had sought to upset became the imperious necessities of the new dictator. The country looked on with apparent apathy at his usurpation. War weary after two generations of political turmoil, they asked nothing but peace. That, Díaz was eminently qualified to provide. The event proved the justification for his unconscionable egotism. Success came because foreign infiltration of capital brought increased tax receipts and prosperity to the federal government, and because there were no ultra-radicals to emasculate his government such as have menaced the success of the early rulers of the twentieth century.

The political problem of Díaz after 1884 was how to consolidate and perpetuate his power. He had learned much since he ceased to be merely a successful revolutionist. His choice of a real coalition cabinet composed of strong men from the various political factions demonstrated at one and the same time his political fairmindedness and his acumen. He was now an able politician dominated by two complementary springs to action, personal ambition and desire for the material prosperity of the nation. Ambition was gratified, but the fabric built to establish national prosperity failed to endure because of the essential weakness of the one-man system and of the faulty administration of justice; the glory of Mexico proved evanescent for the added reason that Díaz adhered to the mistaken idea that the lower classes could not be educated with profit to the nation.

It was the business of General Carlos Pacheco, the only old revolutionary still in the cabinet in 1884, to initiate an amendment of the Constitution which would permit re-election of the president in spite of the Plans of La Noria and Tuxtépec. This action on Pacheco's part was conclusive evidence that the popular spirit which had initiated those revolts against Juárez and Lerdo had now completely died out; it was also an indication that any attempt to revolt against Díaz over prospective reëlections would be summarily dealt with. The labors of Pacheco were consummated through the inspired actions of Congress and the State legislatures.

Another feature of settled policy which the President early developed in order to stifle opposition was that of playing his supporters off against one another before they could develop sufficient strength to oppose him. Each of his ambitious followers thus found in turn that the only way he could prevent a disagreeable rival from rising to the supreme power was to work for the continued retention of the President. Those who openly opposed him were either purchased or eliminated. Those who listened to reason were rewarded by large grants of land and assistance in exploiting them. But they were at the same time deprived of political influence by the bestowal of official prestige upon their local rivals. This was the same method, practiced in the States, that had succeeded in nullifying the ambitions of the chief officers of the cabinet. Of course every material beneficiary of this system was interested in the prolongation of peace, hence in maintaining Díaz indefinitely in the presidency.

Immediately upon the beginning of his second term, Díaz succeeded in bringing his cabinet officers, Romero Rubio, Manuel Dublán, and Carlos Pacheco, into open conflict with each other regarding the succession. He also managed to eliminate his old friend and tool Manuel González by having him brought to book for alleged financial irregularities during his presidency. Upon pretext of disloyalty, the governors of the states of Coahuila, Nuevo León, and Mexico were removed, and their González supporters were supplanted by Díaz adherents. This quiet warfare against unfavorable governors made it possible for the President to secure an amendment to the Constitution which permitted a single reëlection for the period 1888–92. It was yet too early to provide legally for continuous reëlection. That was to come later.

In 1891 the two most serious aspirants for presidential honors, Manuel Dublán and Carlos Pacheco, died. Their deaths ought to have cleared the political situation for Romero Rubio, but now Díaz began to play against him Joaquín Baranda, Minister of Justice, and Teodoro Dehesa, administrator of the port of Vera Cruz. Romero Rubio was clever enough to lay aside his political ambitions; he was father-in-law of the President, and did not wish to break with him. He set about the difficult task then of developing a governing group among the younger men of the country.

The Constitution of 1857 had been amended on May 5, 1878, to prohibit the immediate reëlection of the president. On October 21, 1887, the law was published which permitted a single reëlection. On December 20, 1890, occurred the final amendment which permitted indefinite reëlection. It was in evidence of conscientious respect for the Mexican fetish of absolute legality in the matter of form that Díaz caused these amendments to be passed. On the other hand it was an ironical historical dénûment that the champion of the revolutions of 1871 and 1876, which were fought to establish the principle of no reëlection, should be the man who checked the political development of the country by building up legal perpetuity in the presidency in his own behalf. Those who magnify the virtues of Díaz in contrast with those of other Mexican presidents who have observed the same egotistical policy with less success have sought to justify his actions by that success, seeking to read into the motives of the great Dictator a prescience which he could not possibly have possessed.

Had Díaz felt himself as strong as his admirers considered him, he might have given up his old policy of playing dangerous rivals against each other once these had disappeared. But this system had worked successfully; besides, political habit had now been formed, and caution was a potent motivating power. There was still one old adherent, Bernardo Reyes, who might at any time, and who did finally, become a menace at an inopportune moment. Reyes was placed on the frontier in charge of the Third Military Zone, which included the states of Nuevo León, Coahuila, and Tamaulipas. He also had some authority, tacitly exercised, in Durango and Zacatecas. By his activities on the frontier against a number of military officers who were attached to Manuel González, and by his repressive punishment of a number of incipient revolts, he won the reward of being made constitutional governor of Nuevo León. Here he came into conflict with Governor Garza Galán of Coahuila, to the benefit of Díaz, who allowed their rivalry to serve his own purposes.

While these personalisms were perplexing the face of internal affairs the great financial problems which menaced the external phases of government were acute. The ministry of Hacienda was bestowed, after the death of Manuel Dublán, upon Benito Gómez Farías. There was still pending at that time the problem of the English debt, which had originated in part just after the formation of the republic. Negotiations for the recognition of an indebtedness of £17,200,000 were begun during the closing days of the term of Manuel González, with attendant rioting and bloodshed in the capital because it was believed that the President planned to steal the conversion fund. When Díaz desired to effect a national loan in order to be able to reorganize his finances, the necessary preliminary was the conclusion of these negotiations. This was effected, though with some renewed rioting

and strenuous official opposition. This strong step toward
financial soundness was shortly followed by the appointment
of Matías Romero as minister of finance, Benito Gómez
Farías having in less than a year demonstrated his ineptitude
for the portfolio. Romero's service to the treasury for
a number of years marked him as one of the most distinguished public servants of Mexico's modern era. With him
as subsecretary was a young man whose fame as a financier
was one day to outshine that of his patron. This was the
French creole, José Ives Limantour, son of that Limantour
who made a fraudulent land claim to a large part of the San
Francisco peninsula in the early years of the American occupation. In May of 1893 Limantour himself became secretary of the treasury.

The stability of the Díaz régime was in large measure due
to this astute promoter-financier. To him Mexico owed
many economic reforms. Among them was the abolition of
the hated alcabala which had been inherited from Spanish
times and had been a source of confusion and strife throughout the entire independence period until 1906. Thus was
belatedly fulfilled one of the promises of the Revolution of
Ayutla, a project which had baffled every timorous treasury
head until Limantour braved the danger of a political and
economic crisis, proving by the change that it was a beneficial one for the country.

Another great service performed by Limantour was the
establishment of the monetary system on the gold basis.
This measure was taken to correct depressions which occurred in the silver market, Mexico having been, until 1905,
on a silver basis alone. The rise in silver prices which followed shortly afterward assisted business and banking to a
decided degree, though the change had only a year or so in
which to operate freely. By 1907 Mexico's financial status
reflected the economic crisis through which the United States
and other countries were passing. In that year a French
loan of twenty-five million francs had to be negotiated
in order to cover shrinkage in government revenues. Financial recovery was not complete when the crop failures of

1909 caused further depression which found its dénûment in the Madero revolution. This chain of casualties not even the genius of Limantour was able to conjure. Indeed, it is fairly evident that his bold financial management was in some degree responsible for the tragic end of the Díaz power. The full success of his plans required that he should have continued another lustrum at the helm in finance. The revolutionary financiers who have succeeded him have not yet been able, with vastly increased amounts from taxes at their command, to begin to put the country on the credit basis in which Limantour left it.

The third great contribution of Limantour to the strength of Mexico was the consolidation into a national system of a large part of the railways which had sprung into existence during his generation. This consummation, effected by buying up quietly in the open market large blocks of the stocks of the various American-built railways which extended in several main arteries toward the United States, was brought about in opposition to the railway mergers being effected by E. H. Harriman. The Mexican government feared that financial control in one hand of all the great railways would impair too greatly the economic independence of the country. The nation began under Limantour's policy to operate the railroads acquired, with gradual lessening of efficiency and decrease of service until the chaotic conditions of the recent revolution reduced the lines to almost complete impotence, from which the recovery has been slow and uncertain. It is difficult to see, however, that the plan of nationalization of the roads had very profound influence in adding to the general disintegration during the revolutionary epoch.

Other financial operations carried into effect by Limantour included various refundings of the national debt. These reductions in the rate of interest on Mexican government bonds, thinks Ramón Prida, were not due so much to the skill of Limantour as to the logic of events, they being purely automatic reactions to the widespread belief that Mexico had reached a stability which rendered her safe from further revolutionary disorders. It was, as the same writer says, the iron hand of Díaz which had brought about these conditions and this faith in Mexican credit.

Not even such an astute coadjutor as Limantour was to be immune from the political jealousies the fostering of which had become a fixed mental habit with the distinguished Dictator. Though it could mean nothing but power lost through friction, Limantour found himself obliged to struggle for his ministerial program against the political ambitions of Joaquín Baranda, Minister of Justice, and Governor Teodoro A. Dehesa of the state of Vera Cruz. Díaz used their services but played them one against the other with all his aboriginal cunning, until finally Baranda was able to defeat Limantour's proposed assumption of the executive power while the President should absent himself on a triumphal tour of Europe for a year in order to permit a peaceable transmission of the administration to new hands. A third hand in the political game was that played on the northern border by General Bernardo Reyes, whose patent ambitions led him to aid first one group and then the other, as the chances of success seemed to lie.

The reëlection of Díaz in 1888 was another travesty on the elective process. A few State governors, urged by cabinet officers, asked the President to consent to stand, and he did so, merely sending out his orders concerning procedure to the several authorities of the country. In 1892 he felt that the form of an election ought to be observed, possibly for its effect on foreign opinion. Señor Rosendo Pineda, Minister of Gobernación, advised the imitation of the convention system of nomination which prevails in the United States. For this purpose a number of prominent men were invited to organize a so-called political party. It took the name of Liberal Union; its subordinate clubs were organized throughout the country, and a convention was called to nominate Díaz as candidate of the Liberal Party. The municipal presidents, summoned to Mexico City for the celebration of the Grito de Dolores in September, 1891, went back to their towns as warm propagandists of the Liberal candidature.

Reyes in Nuevo León, not knowing that this party had the President's sanction, opposed it, and organized a small one of his own which he later tried to affiliate with it. Though unsuccessful in so doing, Reyes avoided a break with Díaz by causing his adherents to vote for him. Reyes lost his cordial standing with the clique in the capital later called "Científicos," however, and this rift in the political groups of the friends of the Dictator served to keep the latter in power for a time longer.

Of course the convention nominated Díaz. He accepted, but refrained from comment on the soi-disant "platform" which accompanied the oft-accepted kingly crown. It was in this convention of 1892 that Justo Sierra, famous jurisconsult and educator, uttered the oft-quoted phrase: "This people is hungering and thirsting for justice"—for a justice never realized in Spanish times, nor even yet attained, though seas of blood have flowed in its name. The election was once more "nearly unanimous." There was insignificant opposition by a small metropolitan paper, La República, the editors of which were driven out of the country for their temerity.

The Liberal Union had given rise to the idea of the organization of a great political party which should start Mexico on the road to democracy under the authority and prestige of Díaz. The nucleus of the group, which wanted to effect a methodical reformation in political procedure, began to be called "Científicos." The Mexicans love a political joke, and because of the lean and flaccid faces of some of the organizers of this group, the phrasemakers dubbed it the "Cien tísicos," that is, the "Hundred Ptisicky Ones." Their purpose was, however, a serious and laudable one. Their program included a plan to make the judiciary respectable and independent by making the judges irremovable. They advocated wider educational facilities, reforms in taxation, and abolition of internal customhouses. It was also proposed to give a measure of liberty to the press, which had been maintained in servile subjection to the executive. A new law for the presidential succession was also called for.

Essentially, of course, the "practical program" was to prevent Reyes from establishing a new military dictatorship. The liberal press of the days of Juárez and Lerdo had been destroyed under President González, when a special type of jury authorized by the Constitution to try "newspaper crimes" was abolished. This supposed exemption under a special jury had indeed proved useless; what was needed was an uninfluenced judiciary. There grew up, in the effort to restrict liberty of the press, the use of a practice which Prida, himself a jurist, dubbed "judicial psychology." This was, in brief, the sentiment that "newspaper crimes" should be tried, not in accordance with the letter of the law and the demonstrable facts of the case, but in accordance with whatever interpretation the judge might care to put upon the writings under investigation. Such a policy made it impossible for the newspapers under Díaz to criticize the government, because he created and removed judges at will. A law to make them irremovable passed the Chamber of Deputies in December, 1892, but it never was brought up in the Senate, either during the régime of Díaz nor yet in that of Madero the apostle, though it was then again urged. Thus the newspapers failed to lead or follow public opinion.

When the election of 1896 approached, it was deemed wise to provide a law of succession in order to remove the chief executive office from the hazards incident to the advancement of the chief justice to the presidency in case of the incapacity of the incumbent. This was done by providing that the minister of foreign relations, and after him the minister of gobernación, should succeed in emergencies until the Congress could convene to choose an ad interim president.

The election, which was to be "popular," was managed by the organization of the Círculo Nacional Porfirista. This group failed in its purpose of outwitting the Científicos, whom Díaz mistrusted, because nobody would join a "Porfirio Circle" if he pretended to be an independent politician. Nevertheless, the Círculo carried the election without disorders in spite of the fact that the repeated reëlections brought popular discontent and uneasiness. The government sought a victim to condemn, and fixed the blame for the unrest upon the Científicos, because they had criticized the President's procedure. Now everyone who wanted to injure his enemy denounced him as a Científico, and a general hue and cry was raised against the whole group. Its original members remained indifferent to criticism however, and soon came to be surrounded by friends and acquaintances to whom the name was extended. Many of them were favored by Díaz in handling public enterprises in which they grew immensely rich, for which they are still paying a full measure of public odium or political exile.

These original Científicos had little real influence over Díaz. Indeed, he made no secret of refusing to accept their advice, or that of anyone else, through a personal vanity which led him to fear that to do so would be to yield to undue influence.

The real Científico group had the weaknesses of its strength. It had no great political power with the Dictator; in the administration its one great man was Limantour. Its essential mistake was in its sense of security and self-sufficiency. Its program was to prevent the succession of another military dictatorship, but to seek its opportunity when Díaz should die, as it was felt he soon must. The Científicos believed that all things come to him who waits, but during the waiting they failed to take decisive steps to oppose Díaz, largely through conservative respect for his ancient prestige, or fear of American intervention. Limantour was a ruthless administrator who irritated opponents instead of attracting them. His fiscal manipulations were popularly credited to the group which was associated with him. Hatreds were heaped upon hatreds, while the Científicos injured themselves in public opinion by success in their professions, by unmeasured pride of wealth and position, an inconceivable disdain for their enemies, and especially an imperturbable calm in the face of attacks upon them in the public press. They were too haughty to seek to attract followers or bid for popularity through personal liberality or approachability.

Were they responsible for the ills which have befallen them and their country? They represented the brain power, the intellectual and economic aristocracy of the Republic. But they also personified the disdain of the upper caste for the common people and their aspirations. Had they been good politicians, they might have succeeded in winning a popular support which could have forced Díaz to develop a more genuine spirit in government. In this they would have run the danger of elimination one by one as they rose to conspicuous influence. They should have perfected a close and efficient organization ready to establish a definite plan of liberal government six years before the last election of Díaz. Had they anticipated Madero by that length of time, Madero would never have happened. But given the political atmosphere in which they lived, and the prostitution of justice which characterized their courts and their administrative offices, such prescience was impossible. Even prescience, had it existed, and it was present in the minds of a few, would have failed to bring concerted action; the iron hand had taught its lessons too well. Mexico moved inexorably toward the fate which ambition had stored up for it.

When the time came to discuss the election of 1900, General Díaz brought forward again the project which he had often mentioned previously of placing José Limantour in the presidency, but also of placing Bernardo Reyes in the war ministry in order that the civilian presidency might have strong military support. Limantour and Reyes agreed, but very shortly Joaquín Baranda, Secretary of Justice, and Governor Dehesa of Vera Cruz discovered that Limantour was disqualified under the Constitution, for, while he had been born in Mexico, his parents were foreigners at the time. The argument was finely drawn, but enough doubt was created to make Díaz feel that it would be dubious policy to give Limantour control in face of the legal doubt. Hence he determined to accept reëlection once more pending further study of the case or suitable constitutional amendment eliminating Limantour's hypothetical disability. Accordingly a convention was assembled, the National Porfirist Circle performed its accustomed duties, and Díaz was again reëlected on July 17, with no opposition worth mentioning.

Limantour was obliged to content himself with getting Baranda out of the cabinet and the old promise, again repeated, that he should be made president next time. This was merely to mollify him, however, for Díaz had no real intention of giving up his power.

After the reëlection of 1896 he had consented to a meager provision for the succession by allowing the constitutional establishment of the vice-presidency in the French form. But the concession merely provided that in case of the death of the incumbent the two houses of Congress should designate his successor. This made it plain to everyone that Díaz intended to hold office until death. If the constitutional provision had been put into actual use inevitable revolution would have resulted, for it would have imposed an unknown personality in the presidency.

Upon the occasion of his sixth reëlection at the age of seventy-four in 1904 a constitutional amendment established a genuine vice-presidency of the American type. At the same time the presidential term was extended to six years, against Científico opposition, which tried but failed to impose an anti-reëlection clause. Just before the election Díaz nominated Ramón Corral, Minister of Gobernación, for vice-president, and the two were "elected" by a stupified and disgusted people, for Díaz was no longer desired, and Corral had been absolutely unthought of for the position. The vice-president reaped all the unpopularity which should have fallen to Díaz. His failure as chief executive, should occasion arise, was a foregone conclusion. Díaz should have imposed Limantour in 1900 and then stepped down, supporting his successor with his own prestige. His own great work was done, and upon it he should have been content to rest his fame.

Not even his worst enemies deny the contribution which the great Dictator made to his country's prosperity.

The most signal success was attained with the national treasury. Where previously all had been confusion and debt, the revenues rose gradually, especially under Limantour; in 1900 the revenues reached 74,000,000 pesos and 110,000,000 pesos in 1910. Reserves were created and parts of them applied to harbor works, schools, and public works. It became possible to effect a national loan with no unusual security, so good was the national credit. Old debts were refunded. A favorable loan in 1904 made possible the railroad control already mentioned, and their consolidation into a national system.

The building of these railways had itself been a triumph of a few short years. In 1876 there had been only 691 kilometers built; by 1890 there were 8,948 kilometers, while in 1900 and 1911 there were 14,573 and 24,717 kilometers respectively. Half the main lines were at the latter date under government control in actuality, and the remainder of the system was under the strategic influence of the nationally owned portion. All but six of the State capitals were connected by rail with Mexico City, as were five of the principal seaports. Railway construction was carried out in Mexico on an average subsidy per kilometer of $8,935, about half the average subsidy given in Chile, and something over one-third of that given in the Argentine Republic.

The Porfirian prosperity was due to uninterrupted peace, railway expansion, and the suppression of the alcabala. It was due to these reforms that capital flowed in, increasing the national production, developing commerce and industries, and raising wages; each of these in turn produced augmentation of material prosperity. Finally, the change of the money standard from silver to gold had wide-reaching effect. It stabilized the value of Mexican silver money while the white metal was subject to serious fluctuations elsewhere.

The benefits to commerce were palpable. In 1873 the sum of exports and imports was 51,760,000 pesos; in 1893 it was yet only 154,085,000 pesos; whereas in 1910 the total was 499,588,000 pesos. In 1910 exports exceeded imports by 87,916,000 pesos. There are no known figures for the corresponding increase in internal trade. Mining grew rapidly. In 1880 the production of gold and silver totaled 31,000,000 pesos. By 1910 it totaled 124,000,000 pesos. The 1910 copper yield gave Mexico second place in the world's production with a value of 26,000,000 pesos. Petroleum development grew from 10,345 barrels in 1901 to 1,005,000 in 1907 and nearly 13,000,000 in 1911, though these figures are small compared to the annual production since that time. It now runs into the hundreds of millions.

Into these enterprises went mostly foreign capital; figures are all unreliable on this subject, but the Mexican government in 1910 estimated investments since 1886 at nearly three billion pesos, of which 664,000,000 pesos were native, the preponderant part of the foreign investment being American. There was also important investment of English, German, and French capital.

During the Porfirian epoch factories grew by thousands, including sugar mills, smelters, cotton and woollen mills, chemical works, breweries. In 1910 the textile factories numbered 135, employing 33,000 hands. The smelters and mines employed many thousands more, at wages hitherto unheard of. The growth of factories was accompanied by development of hydraulic power. Puebla, using the Río Atoyac, developed into a manufacturing center with many thousand horsepower. Guadalajara utilized the falls of Juanacatlán in the Río Lerma. In Hidalgo the Cascada de Regla, in Mexico City the Río Tlalnepantla, and, more important than all, the great Necaxa reservoir producing 127,560 horsepower for the capital, were among the important developments of this order.

The thorough organization of the banking system, the construction of harbors at Vera Cruz, Puerto México, and Salina Cruz, the completion of the drainage for Mexico City, the erection of scores of modern artistic public buildings as beautiful and useful as any in the world, situated in many provincial cities as well as in the capital, all attest the material wealth which one short generation could produce on the wreck of fifty years of anarchy. With all the movement, development practically paid for itself as it went. There was only an insignificant national debt of $438,000,000, and the reserve which had been accumulated for emergencies amounted to $70,000,000.

Even more surprising was the security of life and limb throughout the land. For four centuries robbery, banditry, and violence had characterized the land, affecting its travel, its business, even its architecture. Under Díaz Mexico became the safest country in the world, without exception. It was policed by some three thousand rurales, a small number of municipal gendarmes, and an army of insignificant proportions in reserve. This peace was, as Rabasa says, not a forced one, but spontaneous and natural, after the first years of the dictatorship. Order, work, peace, well-being, had transfigured the nation. It stood in 1910 as the fairest and brightest example of Hispanic American solidity.

The miracle appears the greater in view of the methods whereby Díaz perpetuated his rule. In a so-called republic, which had shaken off the forms of despotism, a man who fought through two revolts to establish freedom of elections ruled the land over a third of a century with a power never once derived from a legitimately conducted election but always nevertheless resting on the known consent of the governed. It was the apotheosis of benevolent caciquismo, as the rule of Santa Anna was that of malevolent caciquismo. Díaz had no precedent in Mexican history; few of the benevolent despots of eighteenth century Europe equalled his majestic performance. He won the hearts of his people, who long loved him while they feared him, who admired him when they wished his government ended, and who respected him in exile and mourned him in death.

CHAPTER XXIV

FRANCISCO I. MADERO

GENERAL BERNARDO REYES hoped to be the successor of Díaz. It was his program to organize support in the frontier states under his control by forming Masonic lodges in which his friends might labor covertly in his behalf. Such lodges were organized in Chihuahua, Zacatecas, Jalisco, and San Luis Potosí. In this manner he would be able, in the event of the expected demise of the President, to thwart the pretensions of Limantour, who also hoped to secure the coveted ascendancy, and that by the aid of Don Bernardo's military coöperation.

In 1901 Reyes was summoned to Mexico and made Minister of War, in which office he continued for a part of 1902. At that time his political organization was widely spread over the country. In the capital he began to organize a pseudo Second Reserve for the army which was nothing more than an agency through which he might disseminate his propaganda the more efficaciously. His partisans were augmented, curiously enough, by the adhesion of many men who were blind to the prospect that his régime, should it dawn, would become a military autocracy with all the malevolent features which characterized the rule of Díaz, but with little of its genuine strength or greatness. When Reyes timorously suffered himself to be eliminated by the foreign mission which Díaz cannily imposed upon him in 1910, it was his Masonic lodges and Reyes Clubs which served Madero as the nuclei through which was inaugurated the revolution which began in the autumn of that year.

Reyes was a person of only ordinary abilities. His military career demonstrated no great mental or administrative gifts. He was a sergeant in the patriot forces which ended

Maximilian's empire in 1867. He supported Lerdo de Tejada and Iglesias during their troubled epochs with only moderate enthusiasm. When the Plan de Tuxtépec triumphed he was a colonel, soon becoming a brigadier as a reward for a minor victory. Energetic and astute in his military command of Nuevo León, he was an intelligent administrator of the reconstructionist plans of Díaz. But his partisans admired him in all his vicissitudes, and he was ably supported in his ambitions by his son Rodolfo, an attorney of some ability and prestige. Reyes counted on his personal friendship with Díaz to protect him from executive wrath against his aspirations, and upon his supporters to bring him success. He was the outstanding military personage, and naturally counted the military tradition as a personal asset.

His political activities were largely responsible for the easy launching of Madero's revolution, which broke soon after Reyes had for the time being given up his political aspirations. The Madero propaganda fell welcome upon the ears of the followers of Reyes, their major desire being at all hazards to prevent the reëlection of Díaz. Socialist agitators, the brothers Ricardo and Enrique Flores Magón, and the brothers Vázquez Gómez, with their anti-Porfirism, also contributed to the preparation of the minds of the people for the wave of remonstrance against the atrophied government which began to sweep over the land during the year of the Centennial. The marked service which Madero performed in this epoch was that of accepting the leadership of the revulsion when there was no one else who had the courage to do so. Reyes might have had the honor, but his indecision at the critical moment cost him his predominance. He might have come out openly as a candidate for the vice-presidency, and would probably have won in the elections of 1910. But this would have been tantamount to a disavowal of Díaz. Again later, when he feared Díaz and fled from Monterrey to Galeana, he might have launched a cuartelazo and been successful. But his judgment as to the propitious occasion was at fault. When he finally did take up arms, in 1911, it was against a Madero untried and unproven, at the beginning of his tenure, when yet he had the halo of a redeeming apostle, and no one was ready to follow Reyes in a counter-revolution. The world had been astonished in 1908 when Díaz gave his famous Creelman interview, published in *Pearson's Magazine* for March. In that interview the old President had declared that Mexico was now ready for democracy; that he would welcome the formation of a political party which should put forward an opposition candidate; that he would surrender the power to such a candidate if legally elected. This was an electrifying statement. It amazed all America, including Mexico. It started a whirl of political agitation. Demagogues began fierce attacks upon the Científicos, especially upon Limantour. Díaz with his old time self-interest permitted these attacks, even covertly encouraged them. Madero turned the situation cleverly to his own advantage. He published his famous book, *The Presidential Succession in 1910*, in the fall of 1908. It was a mildly expressed protest against the Díaz régime, though like all public utterances of the epoch, it abounded in adulation of the declining executive. It was, on the heels of the Creelman interview, a clarion call to rebellion.

Like Creelman's article, it circulated widely throughout the Republic, being twice reprinted before 1910. Its effect upon a restive people was extremely disquieting. The anti-reëlectionists, whom Emilio Vázquez Gómez was leading against Ramón Corral's enforced candidacy for the vice-presidency, soon came out openly against the reëlection of Díaz as well. Many men of affairs joined in the expression of discontent against the administration or its chief officers. In January, 1909, appeared the Democratic Party, apparently also a party of protest against reëlection, numbering among its members several prominent men outside the administration group. The first director of the party was Don Manuel Calero, a friend of Díaz.

The Anti-Reëlectionist Party, organized about the same time, met in convention in Mexico City and, moving more rapidly than the Democrats, nominated Madero for president and Dr. Francisco Vázquez Gómez for vice-president. Madero had already interviewed Díaz, confiding to him his project of organizing a political party. Díaz apparently failed to fathom the seriousness of Madero's program, for he took no measures to curb it until it was too late. Meantime the Reëlectionists began to campaign in opposition to Madero and to the Democrats. Public disorders attended their propaganda in Guanajuato and Guadalajara. In the latter city the anti-Díaz manifestation was in favor of Bernardo Reyes. There were no demonstrations against the Madero campaign or that of the Democrats. The latter were practically all Reyists, but their propaganda for Reyes was covert.

Díaz evidently still believed that he ought to retain the power, in spite of his advanced age, the storm which followed the Creelman interview, and the growing opposition. The Reëlectionist Club had been organized in response to this personal conviction. The friends of Díaz were forced into this body for fear that if they did not organize it he would support Reyes or his nephew Félix Díaz. With either choice they would have to resort to revolution against a military dictatorship, in the wake of which loomed the spectre of American intervention. The Reëlectionists were the Científicos, the Catholics, the rich, conservative class in general. They were warmly supported by the sympathies of many self-interested foreigners. The Reyists supported the reelection of Díaz, but opposed that of Corral. Reyes himself gave out an interview with this purport. But Díaz by that time doubted his sincerity and placed General Gerónimo Treviño, enemy of Reyes, in command of the northern military zone where the principal Reyes support lay. Then it was that Reyes fled to the Sierra de Galeana, ostensibly for his health. Treviño soon made his plans untenable, and he returned suddenly to Monterrey, where he was shortly advised by Manuel Calero, emissary of Díaz, to accept a European mission. He accepted and went to France, arriving there in the summer of 1910. Madero's campaign instead of that of Díaz was thus materially benefited.

During this political campaign the police were ordered to watch all meetings and report all the speeches. When it became evident that Madero, on his famous "swing around the circle" seeking support for his candidacy all over the Republic, was indulging in personal attacks upon him, Díaz ordered his opponent arrested for statements he had made at the railway station in San Luis Potosí. This was astutely done upon the declaration of a friend of Corral, upon whom the president was willing to have the odium for the arrest fall. Madero was seized in Monterrey; inspection of his correspondence proved that he was preparing an armed revolt. Yet he was allowed to have the liberty of the city of San Luis Potosí, where he was first imprisoned early in June. From that place he made his flight four months later in disguise into the United States. He had been let out of prison on July 20, just after the "reëlection" of Díaz and Corral had taken place. The declaration of the stereotyped result was announced by the Chamber of Deputies in October.

When Madero was safely out of reach he issued from San Antonio, Texas, on October 5 his call for revolution, under the title of the Plan de San Luis Potosí. It was a sweeping denunciation of the reëlection of Díaz and Corral, and an announcement that he, having been deprived of an opportunity to receive the vote of the people, assumed the leadership of armed revolt to nullify the election. In November he entered his own country and began to recruit followers. The call was espoused by Pascual Orozco and Abraham González in Chihuahua, where armed movements were already in progress against Governor Terrazas. Over a dozen other small rebel leaders, including Francisco Villa, very shortly adhered to Madero's cause. Díaz refused to consider the revolt serious, or to send troops to suppress it. His disdain for the Utopian ideas of Madero made him incapable of realizing the danger.

The plan of the revolution was that there should occur simultaneous outbreaks on November 20 in many places. This became known when Madero's correspondence was seized. A revolt plotted in Puebla by Aquíles Serdán thus became known. Serdán was shot on November 18 after defending his home in an attempt to arouse the city in his support. Other disorders occurred in the south, while the northern revolt spread. Finally the government was compelled to send troops to restore order in Chihuahua. Efforts to treat with the rebels failed, as did the first military actions. Ciudad Guerrero and Parral were lost in November, though the federal troops gained a number of small advantages, including the preservation of Chihuahua.

Madero had crossed the border from San Antonio into Coahuila, but not encountering sufficient support, went back to San Antonio in December. There confronted with prospective arrest for violation of the neutrality laws, he was obliged to enter Chihuahua. Again in the north attempts were made to consolidate all the rebel forces, and to take some positions of minor importance, but without conspicuous successes. At Casas Grandes on March 5 the rebels were routed; by a little decision on the part of the federal troops they might have been annihilated. Meanwhile Pascual Orozco had isolated Ciudad Juárez, opposite El Paso, and began to move against it for the sake of establishing communications with El Paso, where there was prospect of obtaining arms and ammunition. The operations of the government troops were mismanaged by Porfirio Díaz, Jr., who served as director of campaign because of the illness of the President. Ciudad Juárez fell to the rebels on May 9 in a sharp action in which Villa won distinction. Few troops were involved. Madero was not present. But the prestige of the government was gone. The revolution begun in November had triumphed in seven months with only one real fight. Public opinion, not military success, had won it.

In the meantime efforts of political character had been made to save the situation. Limantour, who had gone to Europe before the Centennial Celebration, was induced to return in March, 1911, upon the oft-repeated asseveration by Díaz that he should have the executive power reposed in his hands. Dissociating himself now from the Científicos, with whom he had long been identified, Limantour called for the resignation of the cabinet in a body, and at the President's behest formed a new one. It was composed of a coalition group of younger men who were to initiate the clamored-for but belated political reforms demanded by the opposition. The transitory character of the new cabinet was immediately recognized. Francisco Bulnes, old war horse of the Científico group and political writer of force, at once dubbed it the "High C Cabinet," a *bon mot* which everyone accepted with a chuckle, for it was foreseen that it would survive only as long as a singer could maintain a very high vocal note.

This change of cabinet was a palliative intended to gratify the popular demand for a renovation of the personnel of the administration. Cabinet officers it should be remembered play a stronger rôle in Mexican politics than in American. The ministry formed on March 28 had as secretary of Foreign Relations Francisco L. de la Barra, just returned from the post of ambassador in Washington. He was a polished gentleman, a Catholic in politics, acceptable to the conservative element, Limantour's choice. The secretariat of Gobernación (Interior Affairs) remained vacant. The secretary of Justice was Demetrio Sodi, son of an old friend of Díaz and justice of the Supreme Court. Public Instruction was intrusted to Jorge Vera Estañol, law-partner of Manuel Calero, who had suggested him. This gentleman served a few months later as secretary of Gobernación when it came to arranging peace terms with Madero. Manuel Marroquín y Rivera in Fomento, as friend of Limantour, Norberto Domínguez as Postmaster General, were also new. General González Cosío, innocuous with the portfolio of War, and Limantour at the helm in Hacienda, completed the list. These officers were not formally approved until April 25, a trifle more than two weeks before the fall of Ciudad Juárez.

Essentially, the change in personnel meant no material change in program. Real policy remained the same. Limantour moved cautiously, endeavoring to calm the rebels and steer clear of American intervention, always the Díaz and

Científico bogey. But in his negotiations with them his fear of trouble caused him to be easily outwitted by Dr. Francisco Vázquez Gómez, whose demands that the government agents present credentials, acceded to, really meant recognition of the rebels as belligerents. The chief effect of this was merely to give the revolution added favor in the minds of the American public. The sole administrative program which was developed during Limantour's short rule was the passage of an anti-reëlection law, and a land-division law. Neither of them had any efficacy because they were measures forced upon the government and because the Revolution moved too rapidly.

When Limantour called for an armistice and sent Francisco Carbajal to treat with the revolutionists, Dr. Francisco Vázquez Gómez, who seemed to be chief spokesman for the latter, demanded the resignation of Díaz, that of all Científicos in the Chamber of Deputies, the appointment of eighteen revolutionary state governors, and payment of a large indemnity to the revolutionary army. The government refused the indemnity and the resignation, yielding the other points, but insisting that no rebel military ranks should be recognized. To these terms Madero assented, but the Vázquez Gómez brothers remained intransigent and prevailed. Negotiations were broken, and the armistice ended. It was then that Ciudad Juárez was captured and occupied on May 9. This action had not been ordered by Madero. That national savior soon suffered another contretemps when two days after the capture of the frontier town, Pascual Orozco arrested him in the municipal palace in chagrin because Venustiano Carranza and not himself had been named minister of war in the revolutionary cabinet. Madero succeeded in reïmposing his authority, but he continuously demonstrated, even at this early period, his scant capacity for administrative authority. Jorge Vera Estañol and Rafael L. Hernández continued the negotiations with the successful rebels until May 21, when a treaty was signed.

Under it Díaz and Corral were to resign before the end

of the month; Francisco de la Barra was to assume the ad interim presidency and call general elections. Indemnity was to be left to the new government to settle, hostilities were to cease immediately, the revolutionary army was to be reduced gradually, and destroyed communications were to be restored.

When these terms became known, every doubtful revolutionist joined the exultant side for the sake of booty. Díaz could not bring himself to resign. Disorder prevailed in the capital, where the populace clamored for the bitter renunciation. Under pressure of mob violence, ill, tormented by Limantour, who now obtained consolation for many executive snubs, the old ruler resigned on May 25, 1911. Corral's resignation, cabled from Paris, was received and accepted by the Deputies simultaneously with that of Díaz. With Mexico a howling mob egged on by former beneficiaries of the government, Díaz set out for Vera Cruz on May 26 under an escort led by General Victoriano Huerta. The port city had never been his friend since the famous telegram, "Mátelos en caliente" of 1879, but now the tragedy of the loss of the great leader smote the citizens, who gave him a ringing ovation as he sailed away on a German steamer to end his days in Paris.

De la Barra assumed control on May 26. He at once accepted a cabinet imposed upon him by the revolutionists. It was in reality a coalition cabinet, with the Madero family dominant. The Vázquez Gómez brothers conducted their secretariats without consulting President de la Barra. Emilio Vázquez Gómez, in charge of Gobernación, began to draw on the treasury lavishly for everything revolutionary. Madero partisans were turbulent everywhere. The great apostle entered the capital in triumph on June 7 amid hozannas and strewn flowers. The legal president was at once a nobody. Madero held Mexico in his hand, and his business offices conducted revolutionary affairs under the nose of the ad interim government. So also in the new political circles there went on a struggle for the vice-presidency-to-be. De la Barra and Gustavo Madero, for unlike reasons, succeeded in wresting this candidacy from Dr. Francisco Vázquez Gómez, secretary of Public Instruction, and in eliminating Don Emilio from the government. The latter had until that moment been popularly styled "The Black President," while De la Barra was dubbed "The White President."

When the fight for the vice-presidential candidacy was over, José María Pino Suárez had won, and the Vázquez Gómez faction had become disaffected. The primary elections took place on October 1, and the secondary elections on October 15, 1911. They were a foregone conclusion so far as Madero was concerned. The Constitutionalist or Madero party dominated the situation, though Bernardo Reyes had interposed his own candidacy for the presidency. Reyes, who had met and become reconciled with Limantour in Paris, had been called home by the latter to support the tottering Díaz power with his sword. He moved too slowly for this; reaching Havana, he was prevented from entering Mexican territory by the revolutionists, who stipulated that he remain in foreign parts as an item of their convention with Díaz. But through the agency of his son Rodolfo he effected his entry, reaching Vera Cruz on June 4, and agreeing to support Madero and accept the portfolio of war in his prospective cabinet. Madero had hoped thus to prevent Reyes from attaching himself to a possible reaction, but when he saw that the Reyes faction was smaller than he had been led to believe, that the promise to Reyes was unpopular, and that as minister of war the General would have too much power, he sought release from the agreement. Reyes also desired to end it, and this was done early in August. The candidacy which Reyes launched never was popular, however. He had outlived his opportunity. The revolutionaries all mistrusted him, radical and conservative wings of the group alike.

He made no showing in the elections. Madero's choice was almost unanimous, naturally, though his early popularity had waned, due to the conflict with the Vázquez Gómez group. Pino Suárez received a smaller majority, for much the same reason, yet it was a clear majority. The winners were inaugurated on November 6, 1911, for a term to expire on November 30, 1916.

After the result of the election was known, De la Barra obtained permission to read an apologia for his administration before the Deputies on November 4. His fine phrases did not conceal the fact that he had been actually a failure, for reasons largely beyond his control. He had allowed the treasury accumulated by Díaz to be dissipated, he had permitted cabinet officers who had been forced upon him to absorb the presidential functions. And he had of necessity submitted to being snubbed by the revolutionaries who actually managed affairs outside of official positions. He had no control over the cabinet, the governors, nor the congress. He was in reality only a technically constitutional stop-gap, and should have been superseded immediately after the expatriation of Porfirio Díaz, for the good of the country. His entire ad interim tenure was vitiated by the activities of the Reyists, the Vázquists, and the "Porra," or rabid anti-Reyes faction which staged street disorders for political effect. One intelligent thing De la Barra did; he refused to try to retain the presidency as some of his friends urged. But at the same time he foolishly became a candidate for vice-president, and so lost influence with everyone. After the elections he joined the Reyes and Vázquez parties in denouncing them as having been procured by the Maderists, thus swelling the chorus of discontent which produced a spirit of rebellion against Madero even before he was inaugurated.

The Madero-Pino Suárez government retained from the De la Barra régime Manuel Calero, Manuel Bonilla, Ernesto Madero, Rafael Hernández and General González Salas in the cabinet. These were relatives of Madero or conservatives or both. New members were Abraham González, Manuel Vázquez Tagle, and Miguel Díaz Lombardo. The first was an ignorant revolutionist, the latter two were conservatives. The new government was well received and had an auspicious beginning. But it was almost immediately beset by a revolt begun in November, led by Bernardo

Reyes in the name of Félix Díaz. This reaction was manifest in Yucatan, in the Laguna region, in Ramos Arizpe, and in Michoacán; Reyes was arrested in the United States on November 19, 1911, was released under bonds, and entered Mexico under arms on December 16, but found no support and was taken to Mexico, where he was imprisoned until the Tragic Ten Days of February, 1913.

One of the most serious problems of the presidents of Mexico is that of dominating the state governors. Due to the social and political tradition of centralism the life of every régime depends on this. It is usually done by direct or indirect intervention in the state elections. Madero followed the historical form, but characteristically hesitated between candidates in Vera Cruz, Aguascalientes, Tlascala, Michoacán, and Oaxaca. In the latter state Emilio Vázquez Gómez was implicated in dissident schemes. There were also gubernatorial troubles in Guanajuato, Puebla, San Luis Potosí, Guerrero, Sinaloa, Tamaulipas. In all of these local troubles a firm and ready judgment by the President and the Minister of Gobernación might have effected prompt solutions, but González Salas had no will to do, and Madero could brook no advice. He lost his apostolic affability, and in his conferences became stubborn and impertinent. The executive authority for which he was temperamentally unadapted was destroying his nerves.

The Vázquez Gómez brothers were inimical to Madero ever after Don Emilio left the cabinet on August 2, 1911. Their enmity was chiefly for Gustavo Madero, who had succeeded in imposing Pino Suárez in the vice-presidency. Francisco Vázquez Gómez, "the brain of the revolution," had aspired to rule the country from the vice-presidential position. The two brothers prepared the way for disorder by intriguing with Reyes and Díaz; the money which Don Emilio had disbursed while in the cabinet serving to attach adherents to their projects.

The worst of Madero's troubles were the revolt in Chihuahua under Pascual Orozco and the Zapata movement.

Orozco, who thought himself the winner of the revolution, was snubbed by Madero in the matter of appointments, and took up armed revolt on March 3, 1912. He shortly controlled all Chihuahua, and believed that the government's peace proposals meant fear of him. His military successes were not great, but operations against him were crude, uncertain, and expensive. Operations against Zapata were futile because of jealousies among the government's generals and the real sympathy which the radicals felt for the movement in Morelos.

Madero sent Manuel Calero to serve as ambassador at Washington, on April 9, 1912. In his place in the cabinet was named Pedro Lascurain, who had had no political activities before this, and who was to cut so sorry a figure at the time of Huerta's usurpation in 1913. Díaz Lombardo was forced out of the ministry to make room for the Vicepresident, whom Gustavo Madero desired to make more active in the administration by giving him a portfolio. Rafael Hernández, Minister of Fomento, attempted to control the Congress for Madero, and in order to enlist the sympathies of members promised them government aid in the coming elections. When these promises were not fulfilled there was added a new element of opposition. When the congressional elections occurred, Gustavo Madero had one list of candidates and the President another. The Catholic party also put up candidates everywhere. The state governors could not decide which candidates they were expected to support. Great disorders attended the voting; when it was over, the Constitutional Progressive Party, that is, Gustavo Madero, had a small majority, the opposition being scattering and disorganized. The session which followed was an orgy of fierce passions. Nothing of moment was done, but the government continued it in extraordinary session, in which it remained until Madero's fall. The opposition was more clever in its program, led by the "Quadrilateral," than were the government members.

The northern and southern rebellions, linked by the

activities of the Vázquez Gómez brothers, continued to harass the administration. When Pascual Orozco, the son, began to menace Torreón, Madero sent General Victoriano Huerta against him in April, 1912. Battles were won near Conejos and at Rellano by the government forces, which also frustrated Orozco's efforts to cut their communications. On July 3 at Bachimba Orozco was decisively beaten, his disorganized forces maintaining only guerrilla warfare thereafter until the Tragic Ten Days. Huerta returned to Mexico and was superseded by several officers, the command being broken up to meet the changed conditions of the conflict. Huerta, disgruntled, began to grumble. He and other military men who had not been promoted by Madero began to conspire against him.

The election for governor in the state of Vera Cruz proved another stumbling block for Madero, whose uncertain attitudes produced a serious situation. There were five active candidates; Madero at first favored Hilario Rodríguez Malpica, his chief of staff, but finding him unpopular, began to vacillate between his old newspaper friend, Manuel Alegre, Tomás Braniff, and Antonio Pérez Alegre. Becoming involved in incertitudes, he broke promises he had made to Braniff. Madero descended to accusing Braniff of using money in the election, and Braniff retaliated by declaring that the President spoke untruthfully. Madero intervened when a money pact was made between one of the candidates and the state governor to deliver the election, removing the governor and sending orders to the legislature to elect his ad interim candidate, whose business it was to be to prevent the election of Guillermo Pous, a popular but conservative candidate. Pous received a majority of the votes, but he was counted out by the legislature, which was amenable to presidential control. Porfirio Díaz would have managed it more cleverly, but he had had no popular elections to contend with.

In Tlascala the retiring governor refused to surrender the government to his successor. When the latter seized the palace, he was besieged, and called for federal help.

The revolutionary troops which were sent aided the wrong side, and the governor-elect did not obtain his office until forces of the regular army put him in possession of it. These were not the only disorders of local character in which the President intervened with an uncertain hand.

The atmosphere was full of criticism of Madero. The newspapers called for rebellion, the putative chief of which would be the much talked of but little esteemed Félix Díaz. He procured his release from the army and installed himself at Vera Cruz, and on December 16 his followers rose against the government. But the federal army remained in general faithful to Madero, though the commanders of the little naval vessels in the port tried to go over to Díaz. The possession of Vera Cruz gave the latter enough war materials to arm 8,000 men and equip them with artillery and machine guns. There were also large resources in customs and cash to be had for the seizing. The Madero government realized the danger, especially in case the cuartelazos should spread, and sent General Joaquín Beltrán to recover the lost city.

Díaz endeavored to induce Beltrán to join his cause. Beltrán refused, but so courteously that Díaz believed that he intended to give his adherence in the act of battle. Subordinate officers when approached either refused without indignation or declared they would be guided by their superiors. Díaz therefore persisted in believing that the government forces would come over to him up until the moment of his arrest on October 22, after the formal engagement, which entailed few casualties, had closed. Shortly he and a few of his companions were sentenced to death by a court-martial, and confined in San Juan de Ulloa. The friends of Díaz succeeded in having execution of the sentence delayed while legal methods were undertaken to have it set aside. Public sympathy for Díaz was aroused when the government rebuked the cadets of the Military College at Chapultepec for opposing "La Porra," which demanded immediate execution. While the government dallied with legal forms the whole official body in the capital began to conspire against it. Those enemies of Madero who had hoped that the blow struck at Vera Cruz would succeed now looked about for a new military leader. Bernardo Reyes was still in prison in the capital and his friends decided to prepare for his release and renewed rebellion. Díaz was transferred to Mexico City through the influence of plotters within the official entourage of the President, and imprisoned in the military prison of Santiago, while Reyes was detained at the Ciudadela. General Manuel Mondragón, co-conspirator with Díaz, secured the allegiance of many artillery officers, while General Gregorio Ruíz prepared the minds of cavalry officers. Reyes and Díaz were in constant communication through and with mutual friends. There were attempts to draw into the general conspiracy the disaffected groups headed by Alberto García Granados, the Vázquez Gómez brothers, Zapata, and others, but these groups were radicals, whereas the Reyes-Díaz uprising was essentially reactionary.

Madero went along blissfully unconscious of the impending storm, thinking himself still a popular idol and believing there was strength in the masses. He finally came to hold the opinion that his brother Gustavo, hated as he was for having manipulated the congressional elections, was the greatest drag on his administration, and prepared to sacrifice him by sending him on a protracted mission to Japan. This was the signal for vicious attacks on Don Gustavo. He was thought to have been planning to succeed his brother; the political groups were all tired of the whole family, looking upon it as the source of all their misfortunes. Don Gustavo was about to set forth to his disguised exile when the blow fell which destroyed first himself and then the government of which he was, though without official position in it, the clearest minded and strongest member.

On February 8, 1913, the preliminaries for the second cuartelazo were all arranged. The artillery officers who were compromised bade their families unusually impressive farewells. Everyone, even Rafael Hernández and Madero, were cognizant of the proximity of the storm, but Madero still believed the people were with him, and neither he nor his cabinet took alarm.   Only Gustavo Madero realized the situation, but he was unable to secure action, largely because so many officers were involved in the rising.   On the morning of February 9, General Mondragón and Colonel Aguillón induced regiments at the Cuartel San Diego in Tacubaya to rise and procure the fall of the Madero government. Many other garrisons joined them, and marched upon Santiago prison to release General Reyes; this was effected without a blow.   Reyes then led a column, with the cadets of the Military College of Tlalpam as vanguard, to the Penitenciaría to release Félix Díaz.   Here also the prisoner walked out of the building at dawn with none to resist or question him.

Meantime, General Lauro Villar, head of the federal army and loyal to Madero, had taken position with a handful of only one hundred and twenty men in the National Palace to defend the government.   The revolters prepared to attack the Palace, General Reyes riding exposed to Villar's fire at the head of three thousand rebels.   In front of the Palace, at the first shots, Reyes fell, dead by a pistol bullet.   The rebels fell back at this show of resistance.   There had been some three hundred men killed and wounded in the brief affray. General Villar, exemplary guardian of Mexico's military honor and official good faith, had been seriously wounded, suffering a fractured clavicle.   The President, arriving at the Palace some two hours later, found him still on duty, and, ordering him relieved for medical attention, placed the military fortunes of the government under the general who had accompanied him from Chapultepec to the Palace, Victoriano Huerta.   Thus began the Tragic Ten Days.

CHAPTER XXV

VICTORIANO HUERTA

THE President made his way across the city from Chapultepec on the morning of Sunday, February 9, to the National Palace as soon as he heard of the fighting there, under a strong military escort of cadets and still loyal soldiers. There was some skirmishing along the principal business streets, but no action of consequence, although Mondragón and Díaz were in force in the vicinity, and knew that Reyes had been killed. General Huerta had been named Commandant of the Plaza as soon as word of the wounding of General Villar was received. The designation of Huerta was made by García Peña, minister of War, rather against the wish of Madero, who had no great confidence in the man.

Having reached the Palace with the President, Huerta set about its defense. The forces available were small, and Madero shortly set out for Cuernavaca, returning next day at nightfall with troops under General Felipe Ángeles, who was fighting Zapata in the south. The rebels meanwhile seized the Ciudadela, the commander of which, General Villareal, had been killed defending it. He had been treacherously shot by his aide while organizing the defense of the arsenal. If Mondragón and Díaz had been capable of decisive action that day, they might have won their aim. But they hesitated until Madero had men and ammunition, and thus plunged the heart of the capital into the midst of a battle which lasted from the ninth to the eighteenth of February—The Tragic Ten Days.

The rebels seized supplies from the city stores. They seized the Y. M. C. A. Building and the Belem Prison; the walls of the latter were opened by shells, some two hundred of the prisoners being forced into military service in the Ciudadela.

411

On the morning of February 10 cannon fire from the Ciudadela began to be directed upon the National Palace over the tops of the buildings in the principal business district. That night the government forces cut the lighting wires which served the region of the Ciudadela. On the morning of the eleventh, Díaz and Huerta held a secret conference in which the downfall of Madero was agreed upon, Huerta reserving decision as to the moment when the President's arrest should occur until he could ascertain what portion of his forces he might count upon in such a treacherous course. Immediately thereafter preparations began for investing the Ciudadela by government forces. Action began by the command of Huerta, who sent a regiment of loyal rurales against the Ciudadela at a round trot, as if they were on exhibition. They had been giving distinguished service to Madero. As they advanced they were cut to pieces by machine gun fire. Their sacrifice was intended to make the proposed task of treachery easier. There were no further attempts at attack on the fortress. It suffered little, as did the combatants on either side. The populace, however, was seriously affected; houses were injured and many lives were lost between the two ineffective fires. This disregard of non-combatants by both Huerta and Díaz, whose agreement prevented any real military operations but only sought the elimination of Madero, is a serious indictment of both the leaders.

In view of the state of siege in which the city was, the American ambassador, Henry Lane Wilson, urged Pedro Lascurain, Minister of Foreign Affairs, to convoke the Senate to discuss means for ending the situation. Twenty-seven senators convened on Saturday, February 15. These gentlemen, urged by inclination and the fear of American intervention, appointed a committee which should interview the President and recommend that he resign in order to end an impossible condition of affairs. Madero refused to see them, and flatly declined their suggestion. The senators continued their endeavors to obtain both the President's resignation and the renunciation of Díaz, without success.

On the morning of February 18 they were summoned by Huerta and shortly afterward met the President in an interview in which they again asked him to resign. Again, though after a heated argument, were they unsuccessful. Madero would not listen to advice.

That afternoon the plot of Huerta was carried through. He had called the senators in the hope that they would order him to take the decisive step he desired, that is, pronounce with their sanction, but they declined to assist him. He therefore resolved to arrest the President and Vice-president as they were, under his protection in the National Palace. His long-cherished dream of power, which probably dated from his first military successes against Pascual Orozco, was about to come true. Gustavo Madero was induced to leave the Palace under pretext of an invitation to dine at a restaurant in the city, where he was shortly arrested, confined in the Ciudadela, and brutally murdered.

Lieutenant Colonel Jiménez Riverol then went to the Chamber in the Palace in which Madero and Pino Suárez were, together with some friends and cabinet officers, and attempted to seize the executives. A mêlée ensued, in which Jiménez Riverol was killed. Madero was then arrested by General Blanquete, together with his cabinet officers and Pino Suárez. On the same evening they were joined by Felipe Ángeles, who was imprisoned for faithful adhesion and loyal service to his chief. The cabinet members were shortly released and sent home.

On the next day Huerta sent for Pedro Lascurain. He abandoned the idea of obtaining the support of the Senate for his usurpation, but impressed upon Lascurain the imperative need that Madero should present his resignation in order to give his usurpation the aspect of legality before the Felicista party might begin to do away with the prisoners as they had already done with Gustavo Madero. Huerta promised that the President and Vice-president, as soon as they had resigned, should be sent to Vera Cruz and embarked freely for any foreign port which they might choose. Lascurain transmitted this information to Madero, who had already heard it from the lips of General Juvencio Robles. Madero, angered at the intimation, at first refused vehemently, but finally consented, demanding as a condition guarantees for the lives of Pino Suárez, Ángeles, and himself. Gustavo Madero had met his end in the following manner: While Félix Díaz was absent from the Ciudadela on a call at the American Embassy, a number of his associates began to celebrate their victory with wine and song. In their enthusiasm they set forth and burned the building used by *La Nueva Era,* a newspaper created by Gustavo Madero and published in the interest of the fallen régime. When Díaz returned from making his celebrated pact with Huerta, the carousal in the Ciudadela was at its height. The revelers began to demand the immediate execution of Madero and Pino Suárez. But Huerta when appealed to, refused; there had yet been no resignations. But Don Gustavo had nothing to resign, and during the early hours of morning, while it was yet dark, he was given over to the Felicistas. He was surrendered to General Mondragón and taken into a small plaza, where he was brutally maimed while expostulating with his prospective executioners, who maimed him to silence him. Then he was riddled with bullets. He was murdered, not executed. Shortly afterward Adolfo Basso, thought to have fired the shot that killed Bernardo Reyes on February 9, fell before a firing squad on the spot where Don Gustavo had perished. He also had been turned over to the assassins by Huerta. Later in the day still another, Manuel Oviedo, jefe político of Tacubaya, was likewise executed in the same little plaza, on which the statue of the martyred Morelos looked down. Since the days of the execution of the patriot of Chilpancingo there had never been a more dastardly public crime in Mexico.

The civil strife into which the country had been plunged had been a matter of profound concern to the Diplomatic Corps. The dean of the body, Henry Lane Wilson, held the opinion after the events of February 9 that the government of Madero no longer existed, and asked the Diplomatic Corps to join in withdrawing recognition from it. The Hispanic American countries, with the exception of Guatemala, declined to do so. The Belgian minister agreed with Wilson. The latter then suggested that the Corps request Madero to resign as the only means of reëstablishing order. This proposal was opposed by the representatives of Chile and Cuba, and was not presented to the Corps openly. The Spanish minister, Señor Cólogan, at the suggestion of some of his colleagues, intimated to Madero the advisability of resigning. Madero declined, but asked Cólogan to endeavor to arrange an armistice.

Henry Lane Wilson was inimical to Madero throughout the Tragic Ten Days. The Embassy was the center of anti-government activity. Huerta and Díaz visited him there on the night of February 18, and talked with him concerning their pact for the division of the governmental powers they had seized. There the names of the prospective ministers were discussed and agreed upon. Wilson then submitted them to the foreign ministers, who were waiting in an adjoining room, and asked their comments, in case any of the appointments seemed inappropriate. The ministers merely took note of them, but made no comment. They then listened while Rodolfo Reyes read to them what is popularly known as the "Pact of the Ciudadela." Huerta and Díaz shortly thereafter left, singly. The members of the Corps, on taking their farewells, expressed solicitude for the lives of the imprisoned executives. Mr. Wilson seemed not deeply moved. His associates noted that he had felt free to lend his influence to the destruction of a legitimate government and to listen to plans for the organization of the usurping faction, but when it came to proposals to save the lives of the prisoners, he had no plans, nor even suggestions to offer.

On the afternoon of February nineteenth Wilson called the Diplomatic Corps together again and, reading Huerta's report that Madero had been made prisoner, asked them to recognize the new power. Wilson then bent his efforts to securing the President's resignation. When the relatives of the latter urged him to intervene to save his life, he declined to assume any interest, or to submit the request to the Diplomatic Corps. Finally, after warm discussion among its members, they agreed to ask Huerta to save Madero's life. The ministers of Spain and Cuba went to see Huerta, who was not available, but General Blanquete assured them that Madero's life was not in danger, and that when he had resigned he would be permitted to leave the country at once. Details of the proposed departure were discussed and agreed upon, but Huerta could not be found to ratify the agreement.

The Señores Cólogan and Márquez Sterling then went to Madero's prison, where he agreed to place his resignation in the hands of the minister of Chile, who should deliver it when the prisoners had got safely aboard the Cuban cruiser *Cuba*. The resignations were written and signed, and given to Lascurain to show to Huerta. Madero asked that General Ángeles, imprisoned with them, should lead the escort to Vera Cruz, and would not be dissuaded when it was pointed out how remarkable this request would be considered. The effect was to rouse the suspicion of Huerta that a rescue would be attempted; this sealed the fate of the prisoners.

It was planned, but without consulting Huerta, that they should set out that night for Vera Cruz at ten thirty. But when Huerta was found by Madero's friends, he insisted that the resignations should be submitted to Congress at once. He urged that he was without legal power to protect the prisoners until their resignations should be accepted, and he intimated that danger might occur to them unless they were prompt. Once in the presidency, he would fulfill all the responsibility of his power.

Lascurain weakly vacillated, consulted the Madero family, acquiesced, surrendered the resignations. Passing at once to the Chamber of Deputies as acting president, he nominated Huerta Minister of Gobernación, to whom the oath was administered. Lascurain then promptly resigned. The Deputies ratified the procedure with but eight dissenting votes. Lascurain had been President of the Republic approximately half an hour. Huerta himself remained in the Chamber while the business was transacted, and assumed the ad interim presidency constitutionally under the law of succession by virtue of possession of the portfolio of Gobernación.

It was evident that the lives of the prisoners were in extreme danger, notwithstanding the assurances of the usurper. Everyone but Madero realized this. As the night came on, the expected preparations for the journey to Vera Cruz did not materialize. The prisoners were left alone all night, only Márquez Sterling remaining with them. Huerta had omitted to issue orders for their departure, and none of Madero's friends was able to see the new President for three days. In that interval the assassin's plot was matured.

On February 22 the new cabinet discussed appropriate methods of disposing of Madero and Pino Suárez. It would have been a difficult problem even had there been no personal or political passions to consider. What the details of the discussion were, or the conclusion reached, have never been so definitely proven that responsibility for the deeds of the night of February 22 could be fixed beyond peradventure. The narrative of Prida covering this period places the blame directly upon Huerta and his cabinet.

Late on that night the prisoners were taken from the National Palace, being told that they were to be conveyed to the Penitenciaría. Quickly they were put into two automobiles, with a few rurales for guards. Many versions circulate as to what transpired thereafter. One statement is that the automobiles were conducted to a side of the Penitenciaría on which there were no doors. There forced to alight, they were assassinated in the act. The crime was charged to Major Francisco Cárdenas. He disappeared shortly from Mexico, and in 1920, when his extradition from Guatemala was demanded by the Obregón government, was reported to have committed suicide after being taken prisoner. From the moment he learned that the murders had occurred, Huerta denied complicity, and the report was given out that the prisoners had perished in an attempted rescue. In spite of all his protestations, it is recognized that the moral responsibility for the occurrence rested upon him. It formed the basis of the determination of the Democratic administration of the United States not to recognize him, and was the beginning of his downfall.

Huerta now bent his efforts toward consolidating his power. In the Chamber his program was intrusted to the deputies José María Lozano, Nemesio García Naranjo, Francisco M. de Olaguíbel, and Querido Moheno, who became known as the "Parliamentary Quadrilateral." The cabinet, which Félix Díaz had imposed in his pact with Huerta, was soon reorganized by its aid. To this end elections for president and vice-president were set for October 23, 1913. The Díaz supporters began to work for the election of Don Félix. But Huerta began to remove the friends of Díaz from their offices by various astute measures. Cabinet positions were given to Dr. Aureliano Urrutia in Gobernación, Garza Aldape in Public Instruction, and General Blanquete in War. There were incessant changes in the various cabinet positions, nearly all of them registering diminution of the Díaz influence as time went on. Esquivel Obregón and Rodolfo Reyes were among the first to be eliminated. Robles Gil soon followed. Federico Gamboa had become minister of Foreign Relations when De la Barra resigned that office early in the Huerta régime.

While these and other numerous changes kept occurring in the cabinet, the non-conforming Chamber of Deputies, containing many old Madero men, was opposing Huerta's cabinet nominations and his fiscal policy. It seemed necessary to eliminate the Deputies. The occasion was given by an event which occurred in the Senate. On September 23, Senator Belisario Domínguez of Chiapas asked the upper house to depose Huerta, and a few days later his accusation against the government became public property. In it Domínguez said in substance:

"Huerta is an old soldier, without the political and social experience needed for his assumed office, who makes himself appear strong by commission of acts universally disapproved. He practices terrorism because he believes it the only policy, and because his brain is unbalanced and his spirit disoriented through the method by which he has risen to power. The spectre of Madero haunts him, and for relief he issues orders to kill. He fears everyone, lest someone betray him. Yet he thinks he is the only man capable of governing Mexico. In this course he is dragging us toward intervention by the United States. Mexicans must prevent this; the Senate must prevent it. If you will commission me, I will face Huerta with your petition signed here by you all. He will probably kill me, and then, when he reads my speech, he will kill himself. . . .

" Huerta's presidential message is full of falsehoods. The truth is that during the government of Huerta nothing has been done toward pacification. The situation is worse. The revolution has extended to nearly all the states. Many friendly nations refuse to recognize this government as legal. Our money has depreciated, our credit is gone. Our press concedes the truth. Our fields are abandoned; many towns are destroyed. Hunger and misery threaten our entire country. . . . "

The rabid speech ended with repeated accusations that Huerta had risen by treachery and was implicated in the assassination of Madero and Pino Suárez. On October 7 the Senator disappeared. His fanatical tirade had brought the ruin he anticipated. The Chamber of Deputies ordered an investigation; this was an open invasion of the functions of the judiciary, and on October 10 the government ordered the arrest of over one hundred members of the body. Huerta issued a proclamation on the next day, declaring that the legislative and judicial functions, added to the executive, were now reposed in himself. This arbitrary usurpation was only an accompaniment of numerous acts of terrorism by which Huerta and his ministers sought to impose their sway. The terrorist program was for a time under direction of Dr. Aureliano Urrutia, who held the portfolio of minister of Gobernación during the summer of 1913, when political assassination reached its greatest activity. The policy of vindictive punishment of suspected enemies within was dictated by fear of the insurrection in the north and of the hostile attitude of the American government.

In the state of Coahuila, Venustiano Carranza was the leading political power when the usurpation of the presidential office by Huerta occurred. Carranza had been one of the conforming senators under Díaz; he represented Coahuila from 1900 to 1902 as substitute, and from 1904 nearly continuously until 1911 as proprietary senator. He was candidate for the governorship of the state in 1910, with the sanction of President Díaz and Reyes, but when the latter was sent to Europe Díaz repudiated Carranza's candidacy. It was not long thereafter that Carranza joined Madero's revolution, receiving first a military command, and later, in 1911, becoming Madero's provisional minister of War. After the fall of Díaz he returned to Coahuila to complete the term of the governorship to which he had been elected. He was so serving when Huerta sent out his telegrams of February 18, 1913, bidding for the adhesion of the state governors and the revolutionary leaders immediately after his seizure of Madero.

Carranza, backed by the Coahuila legislature, refused to recognize the usurpation, thus saving the self-respect of the people of Mexico, Huerta being independently rejected by only one other man, General J. Refugio Velasco, commandant of Vera Cruz. Carranza announced the dissidence of Coahuila on February 19 and called on all state governors within reach to join him. When the murders became known, he refused to listen to the later overtures of Huerta's emissaries, and made his way with troops toward Monterrey and Cuatro Cienagas. Soon joined by a number of adherents, he and they drew up their platform on March 26 under the name of the Plan de Guadalupe, which was merely a rejection of Huerta, and launched their armed protest. Many residents, both foreign and native, advised submission to the usurpation. Huerta's invitation had been accepted by Pascual Orozco, Emilio Vázquez Gómez and others, but in general the northern country pronouncedly rejected it when Carranza's attitude became known. Sec-

onding the Coahuila movement were Governor Maytorena
of Sonora, and Generals Álvaro Obregón, Benjamín Hill,
and Salvador Alvarado in Sonora. In Chihuahua Francisco
Villa, guided by the military genius of General Felipe
Ángeles, became a strong factor in the war against Huerta,
the federal army, and the clerical and foreign groups.
The Constitutionalist revolution had its greatest strength
in Coahuila and Sonora; soon its leaders were able to control
Durango and Zacatecas as well, while the mountainous
regions of Hidalgo, Vera Cruz, San Luis Potosí, and Querétaro quickly joined the "First Chief." The greatest early
successes fell to Villa, and he was tacitly recognized as
military leader. His victories at Casas Grandes and San
Andrés enabled him to attack Torreón in the rich cotton
belt, of which he became master on October 10. Pressing
to the frontier, he possessed himself of Ciudad Juárez on
November 16. Success at Tierra Blanca made it possible
for him to defeat Orozco at Ojinaga, and drive the federal
forces to intern in United States territory at Fort Bliss.
Villa then returned to Chihuahua, set up the revolutionary
government, and invested Torreón, which had meantime
been evacuated. Torreón fell to him on April 2, 1914, and
another victory at San Pedro de las Colonias nearly annihilated the federal forces.

While endeavoring to defeat his enemies in the field,
Huerta had sought to affirm his usurpation by the traditional appeal to the form of legality in a so-called national
election. While preparations for this were going on, he
continued his campaign for obtaining recognition from the
United States. The intimacy with that government for
which he had been led to hope by the patronage of Henry
Lane Wilson was rendered impossible when in July President Woodrow Wilson recalled the ambassador and demanded his resignation. The attitude of the Democratic
administration was indicative of a determination to preserve the remnant of what had been conceived of as Madero's
"social revolution," and to prevent Huerta from consolidating his treacherously acquired power. To this end Presi-

dent Wilson, steadfastly refusing recognition, in August 1913 sent John Lind as his personal representative to Mexico to hold conversations with the Huerta government. His object was to secure the latter's acquiescence in Wilson's demand that an armistice be declared and that Mexicans of all political adhesions should join therein, but that Huerta himself should not offer his candidacy. The remarkable thing was not that Huerta should refuse, as he did, of course. The startling inconsequence of ideas was that President Wilson could have conceived that Huerta could have been humanly capable, after his recent activities, of accepting such a proposal. Acquiescence, though essentially it was what he had once agreed to with Félix Díaz, would have been tantamount, not only to complete personal abnegation, of which he might conceivably have been capable, but to desertion of his supporters who, with himself, would have been promptly subjected to a retributive violence at the hands of their enemies which would have done Mexico little good in the final analysis. Lind's mission failed for this chief reason, as well as because he himself was not temperamentally qualified to cope with an intricate Hispanic American political condition. His argument should not have been based on Mexican constitutionality, but upon international morality. And such an argument would have had little weight with Huerta. Further inacceptability was added to his proposals by reason of his suggestion that acquiescence in them would smooth the way for obtaining the financial help of which Mexico was so much in need. This was considered a publicly offered bribe. The "elections" therefore occurred on October 26, 1913, attended by more than the habitual interference on the part of the administration. The foregone conclusion of the vote was rejected by the reassembled Congress, which, however, in default of any more satisfactory solution, requested Huerta to continue at the head of affairs until a "genuine" election could take place.

The rejection of the Wilson-Lind suggestion was followed by a warning from the United States government to Americans in Mexico to leave the country. This was a move similar to that made by President Taft some time earlier during the troubled days of 1912. On December 2, 1913, President Wilson addressed the American Congress, announcing his continued adherence to the policy of non-recognition, and proclaiming that of "Watchful Waiting" which was maintained from that time with few exceptions. and those during Wilson's term, until the spring of 1923.

The American government aided the revolutionary faction in February, 1914, by removing the restriction upon shipment of arms across the border. The financial boycott was another method used to destroy Huerta. While Secretary of State Bryan demanded punishment of crimes of violence against Americans in Mexico, the United States Congress was bitter in its denunciation of the American administrative policy, and demands for intervention were loud and insistent. While popular feeling was excited over the general conditions, the unhappy Tampico incident of April 10 occurred. A party of American marines from the gunboat *Dolphin*, of the fleet which had lain in Mexican waters since the beginning of general disorders, landed at a wharf in Tampico within prohibited area to obtain gasoline. They were arrested by the Mexican military officer in immediate command, though presently released with the regrets of his superior. Admiral Mayo, in command of the American vessels, demanded an apology and a salute to the flag in satisfaction of the affront. Wilson sustained the demand. Huerta declined to comply except under proviso that the salute should be returned gun for gun. President Wilson then obtained from Congress authorization to use force to procure redress, and on April 21 Vera Cruz was occupied by an American force.

The immediate duty of the American occupation was to prevent delivery to Huerta forces of a cargo of munitions being brought in on the German steamer *Ypiranga*. The munitions were later delivered at another port. There was sharp street fighting in Vera Cruz, in which several American and many Mexican lives were lost; Huerta ended diplomatic contacts on April 22. War loomed imminent. In principle it actually existed.

Spread of hostile activities was averted by the prompt offer of mediation by the A B C powers of South America. At their instance a conference met at Niagara Falls, to which the revolutionists, the Huerta party, and nine Hispanic American countries were invited. The Carranza group accepted only "in principle," and its representatives, arriving in June, played the part of observers rather than of participants. The effort to avert war took the form of an attempt to find a provisional president who would prove acceptable to all parties concerned. In this the Conference was unsuccessful, as the Carranza forces declined to participate officially in the deliberations, their chief's attitude being one of resentment against the constructive intervention in Mexican internal affairs. Huerta's representatives had few instructions, little influence, and less authority. His appeal to Carranza for aid to repel the Americans had been properly rejected by that governor and self-styled chieftain, for Huerta had, since his dissolution of his Congress, no legal authority, let alone moral, upon which to base his claim to the administrative power. The net result of the Conference was to affirm the oft-repeated dictum of President Wilson, "Huerta must go."

Very shortly, the continued successes of the revolutionists, aided as they were by the intransigent attitude of the United States, brought Huerta to a realization, not of the heinous rôle he had played in Mexican history, but of his immediate physical danger. The forces from the north had been steadily drawing nearer while the last phases of his discomfiture were being enacted. Early in July he had made a futile effort to carry out "elections" again, but these resulted more ineffective than the early effort of the preceding autumn. It was evident that there was no help through intervention by Hispanic American nations, no recognition from the United States, no loan from any source, no funds of any kind, no hope of escaping ultimate defeat at the hands of his enemies. On July 15 Victoriano Huerta dictated a bombastic resignation acknowledging in effect that he had been forced out of office by President Wilson—a final admission of impotence which seals his obliquy in history for Mexicans. The remnant of power which he left behind was confided to the hands of his Chief Justice, Francisco S. Carbajal, now made Minister of Foreign Relations, whose sole governmental function was to be the surrender of the executive power to the Constitutionalist Army within a month. Huerta fled, a German steamer taking him away under the protection of Emperor Wilhelm's flag. Some two years later he made his way back into the United States from Europe, to foment armed activity in Texas against the power of Carranza. In this violation of the neutrality laws of the United States he brought about his arrest by agents of the American government. Being taken ill, and evidently with little time to live, he was released from confinement, and presently died in the same year. At no time in his career since his seizure of Madero had he given a solitary indication of moral force, sensitiveness to the genuine welfare of Mexico, or ability to conduct an organized government, even of dictatorial type. The agencies, whatever they were, which encouraged his ambition to seize the administrative power, made a most serious mistake. It was unwise to attempt to impose the "iron hand" of one who had not grown into the minds of the people as born to command, as Díaz had. The determination to keep Reyes from seizing the power after Díaz, and the unrest caused by Madero's preachments of a new social and economic order had created a situation which no egoistic autocracy could manage. Another step in consciousness of nationality had been taken.

CHAPTER XXVI

CARRANZA'S PROGRAM OF REFORM

VENUSTIANO CARRANZA emerged from the sepulchral solitude of one of the later Díaz senates, to become, first of all governor of Coahuila, then a partisan and cabinet member under Madero, and finally, as governor again, the bearer of the standard which fell from the hand of Madero when the latter was betrayed and assassinated. Why did Carranza repudiate an old and decadent dictatorship to defend a Utopian régime professedly democratic but minus in all essentials the elements of either autocracy or democracy? And why, when the success he nearly achieved lay within grasp, did he resort to that dictatorial form of control he had so loudly denounced and so bitterly fought?

His enemies have always said that his rejection of Huerta was based on opportunism rather than principle; that he was preparing for revolt against Madero at the time of the Tragic Ten Days, and that his early appearance in the field against the usurper was due to his self-interested forehandedness in possessing troops (of which there were in truth but few) rather than to efficiency and precision after the event. Félix Díaz and Huerta, did they forestall him in this attitude, and give him the opportunity to appear as the champion of legitimacy and democracy, whereas if he had not been anticipated he would have become the chief antagonist of the falling Apostle?

Had Carranza been heartily sincere in his attitude of desire to preserve constitutional forms, he would have refused to recognize the resignations of Madero's cabinet, upon whom successively the law imposed the right and duty to ascend to the presidential power. They had resigned under coercion, as had Madero and Pino Suárez. None of

426

them, however, so far as is now known, made any effort to preserve constitutionality. They must have been afraid of Huerta and Díaz, either unwilling or unable to take the field for a cause which had been considered dear to the hearts of the liberal Mexicans. But Carranza had been close to Madero, minister in his provisional cabinet, and charged as governor of an important state with preservation of the revolution-born government. Possessed of strategic position and armed forces, it was not beyond reason that he should have arrogated to himself the distinction of leading the revindication of Madero. Constitutionally of course, his action in imposing himself was as much of a nullity as was Huerta's, but he had the adhesion of Governor Maytorena of Sonora, and that of a number of regional celebrities who were regarded as military men in a country where military pretension is not unusual.

The movement led by Carranza immediately took the name of Constitutionalist. It was to defend the constitution which Huerta had violated in spirit at the first stroke, and habitually and constructively ever afterward in all essentials. For the sake of logic—logic which forgot the law of succession, as has been said—Carranza denied himself any claim to the presidency, but styled himself First Chief of the Constitutionalist Army encharged with the Executive Power. Operating under that abnegating but cumbersome appelation, he declared that he was governing without the aid of the National Charter, in a "preconstitutional period" which lasted until the promulgation of the new Constitution in 1917. Such a period in Mexico could only mean one free from legal restraints, subject to the will of him who held the largest army at his back.

This attitude was exemplified by his resuscitation of the old decree against traitors promulgated by Benito Juárez in 1862 to provide a mode of procedure against Mexicans who espoused the French Intervention. But Carranza himself had no constitutional status, as has been pointed out, hence his orders to shoot Huertistas on sight contained a legal inconsequence which mocked the claim of respect for constitutionality which he asserted so vehemently. Like Huerta, like Díaz, he sought to justify his ambitions and his attitude under a cloak of legality, whereas it was not the logic of law but that of events, the unrolling of the political screen, which justified his action. Carranza, like Madero before him, found the opportunity for mastery thrown at his feet. Whatever may have been the complex of his motives, it would have been, taking all the factors into consideration, other than human for him to have acted in any other way than he did at the beginning of his movements.

Nor could his cause succeed without the secular accompaniment of an attempt to establish a classical Spanish American dictatorship. Those who upbraided him for doing so failed to appreciate the traditional spirit of Mexican history. They forgot that from the time of old Spain's conquest to that moment there had never been a successful government in Mexico which had not been a dictatorship. The crowning achievement of Díaz was his success in making that institution work better than any of his predecessors, Spanish or Mexican, had been able to do. And all his critics agree that his ultimate failure was due to the inherent weakness of the dictatorial system, its incapacity to perpetuate itself by transmitting the power, clothed with a prestige which is personal and not institutional, to a new personality which can preserve the filiation of authority intact. It was the failure of Díaz to find the apt successor he sought, either in Limantour, Reyes, or Corral, which gave Madero his opportunity as an agitator.

But Madero successful as agitator was a dismal failure as ruler. He breathed upon the apathetic masses of Mexican society the fire of discontent, and they believed his promises of a new social order, in which opportunity should come to the dispossessed and the indigent, with the removal of the privileged, the enterprising and the successful element from power. His movement was an explosion of pent-up hatreds of the lowly against the better bred. It was not a movement for a better government in essence, but a movement for the reversal of the relative positions of the social classes in the political and economic scheme of things. It was not a plan to get rid of dictators, but to put the dictatorship into the hands of a new element.

It was such an aroused proletariat that Madero had sought to control, and it was his attempt to control it by utilizing the remnants of the traditional social structure that gave his rule its illogical character and assured his failure. This failure gave Carranza his opportunity to find emergence from semi-obscurity to power provided he could dominate the new situation. He had some military power behind him by virtue of his governorship; his cause grew in force through the adhesion of northerners who, as provincials, had found scant opportunity for self-assertion in the Madero movement and were not included in or who were suspicious of the Huerta power, which was essentially metropolitan. But Carranza lacked the traditional element of political success— he had no military training or prestige; he was civilian in heart and belief, and his plan for the perpetuation of his movement contemplated establishing the civil power in supremacy by the aid of a newly formed military caste in a land where all pomp, prestige, and power had for centuries been identified with the regalia and authority of either the church or the army. The church as a political power had been swept away by the Reform, to return by tacit consent under Díaz, but the instinct for military predominance had survived, fostered by the tradition of Díaz and developed into a more potent influence during the social exacerbations of the Madero period and the exigencies of Carranza himself.

As has been said, Huerta fled on July 15, 1914, turning the executive office over to Francisco S. Carbajal. The rule of the latter was brought to its foredestined close by Secretary Bryan's urgent suggestion that he relinquish the power to Carranza. Obregón, as leader of the Carranza forces, entered Mexico City within a month after Huerta's flight, but when Governor Maytorena of Sonora rose against the Constitutionalists Obregón and Villa were sent north to combat him. There they quarreled, Villa, after failing in an attempt to execute Obregón, declaring himself dictator of the north and renouncing the Carranza movement. Obregón escaped to the capital, where he supported Carranza in a projected convention for nominating a civilian president, Carranza himself of course being the candidate. General Pablo González also supported Carranza, but he was opposed by a powerful group of northern revolutionary celebrities including Villa, Felipe Ángeles, Blanco, and former governor Maytorena of Sonora. Carranza called the convention in Mexico for the purpose of obtaining the nomination, but the rival faction manipulated its removal to Aguascalientes, within territory under the control of Villa. There the anti-Carranza faction naturally secured the ascendancy, and under the designation of Conventionalists a Villa-Zapata contingent occupied Mexico City and imposed Eulalio Gutiérrez as their provisional president. Carranza was forced to fall back upon Vera Cruz, which became his capital until he could recuperate strength. Emiliano Zapata had driven him out of Mexico City on November 21 and he entered Vera Cruz as the Americans, delayed in their evacuation, moved out on November 23. Some ten days after the arrival of Zapata, Villa entered and held the capital for about two months. Zapata sallied to fight Carranza forces early in December, but was beaten. Villa was obliged to evacuate on January 19, Obregón reëntering for Carranza on the twenty-eighth. But again the agrarian hordes from Morelos under Zapata swarmed in and reigned supreme in a very orgy of plebeian domination from March 11 until July 10, 1915, when Carranza was able to return.

During a part of 1914 Villa had been much in the limelight. In his "government" in Chihuahua and other parts of northern Mexico he seemed for a time to be the leader of the substantial element in the Republic which might restore constitutional order and resume the normal organization of society. Emissaries were sent to him by President Wilson with a view to determining his fitness for such a task, but he was judged not to possess the qualities to warrant American support. His genuine military successes were due to the skill of General Ángeles. His star never rose higher. He was hard pressed by General Álvaro Obregón, who defeated him in April at Celaya, then near León, and finally forced him far to the north and out of military significance. In the interval the condition of the country was disastrous. Not only Mexicans, but foreigners, especially Spaniards, suffered severely. Many of the latter, including their minister, were expelled from the country. There was no constitution, no capital, no law, no authority. In March President Wilson secured permission from the various leaders to remove foreigners from Mexico City under American protection. His notes of remonstrance to Carranza over treatment of foreigners were answered by ungracious acceptance of responsibility for their safety. But the First Chief's power was really not equal to the task. Zapata was still dominant in the south, chiefly in Morelos; Villa was a veritable scourge to enemies and had many supporters in most of the wide north; Manuel Peláez controlled the Tampico oil fields, defied Carranza and levied monthly tribute from the oil producers. There he continued as a complicating factor until 1920. In all parts of the country banditry and destruction of railroads, life and private property were rampant.

After the decisive defeats of Villa, President Wilson urged the Mexican leaders to drop their differences or the United States would "use means to help Mexico save herself and help her people." In August, 1915, the A B C powers, joined by Bolivia, Guatemala, and Uruguay, urged the Mexicans to erect a provisional government and call general elections. Carranza protested against this "new policy of interference." The American State Department issued, jointly with the six powers above named, an appeal for a conference and offered assistance to bring about peace. Carranza again rejected the proffer as intrusive, he being then successful against Villa, who by the same token accepted. In September the conference of the American powers agreed to extend recognition after an interval of three weeks to the faction which should then have demonstrated greatest success in maintaining order.

This interposition of outside influence led to the recognition on October 19 by nine American powers of Carranza as de facto president. It was a victory which the Constitutionalists had not won by clear-cut military domination of a measurably significant portion of the country. The step was in reality one of emergency, and justifiable if at all, because of the desperate need for peace and in the hope that it would prove efficacious in bringing it. Recognition elicited from Carranza renewed acceptance of responsibility for safety of foreign lives and property. Formal diplomatic relations with the United States were resumed in December, 1915, by the appointment of Henry P. Fletcher as ambassador to Mexico and the reception of Eliseo Arredondo as representative of the new Mexican government in Washington. Fletcher did not go to Mexico at once, and his residence there was short and intermittent; the attitude of Carranza on numerous international perplexities was in part at least responsible for this.

The recognition of Carranza came, as has been intimated, after a course of procedure which had held out to Villa a hope that his might have been the favored faction. Revenge for this slight animated Villa, whose attitude toward Americans had been rendered hostile by added considerations. On January 10, 1916, eighteen Americans were shot down by Villistas at Santa Ysabel while on their way into Mexico at Carranza's invitation to reopen mines. The American Congress passed resolutions in both houses demanding armed intervention in retribution. Carranza promised to punish the perpetrators of the wanton atrocity, and some time later two Villa leaders, one of them said to have been responsible for the Santa Ysabel massacre, were executed by the Carranza government.

Another outstanding consequence of the snub to Villa was his raid upon Columbus, New Mexico, which occurred in the following March. In that surprise assault, seventeen Americans and a much larger number of Mexicans were killed. The American border troops, sent in pursuit of Villa across the border on a "hot trail" began a movement which soon resolved itself into a punitive expedition under General

Pershing. By a peculiar quixotism, the American president
ordered the United States forces to refrain from using Mexican railways, out of deference to Mexican sovereign rights.
Hence the movement was forced to utilize motor-trucks
across the Chihuahua desert, with the result that delay and
transportation exigencies allowed the vicious outlaw to
keep beyond reach. He was among loyal supporters who
aided him in every way possible. American forces were
commanded to keep out of Mexican centers of population to
avoid complications with the inhabitants. With these
handicaps, the expedition failed of its prime object, the
capture of Villa dead or alive, though advanced cavalry was
more than once upon point of success. The expedition took
on political aspects in the United States, for its withdrawal
during the progress of the presidential campaign became a
strategic impossibility.

In Mexico the effort aroused keen resentment among
Americans and Mexicans alike, but for diametrically opposite
reasons. The Americans thought that the armed intervention should have progressed to the point of establishing
general peace, while the Mexicans joined in resenting it as
a violation of their sovereignty. Carranza had given reluctant and qualified consent to the expedition, but soon
began to object to it, inquiring how far the American troops
would penetrate and how long they would remain. There
were 12,000 American troops below the border and 18,000
along it, the latter group being largely increased as the
expedition progressed. General Obregón, Minister of War,
conferred with Generals Scott and Funston at El Paso,
urging withdrawal of the invading army. The Mexican
forces, which ought to have been more anxious than the
Americans to capture Villa, failed to extend any aid; their
attitude became continually a growing menace to the expedition. On May 10 the American State Department
again urged remaining nationals to leave the country. On
the twenty-second Carranza protested sharply against the
"invasion and violation of sovereignty." The false rumor was
circulated that Villa was dead; he had been wounded and

was in hiding, protected by sympathizers. The attempt to take him was given up, American troops remaining, as Carranza was notified, only as security against disorders. Their presence soon precipitated a sharp crisis. On June 21 a troop of American negro soldiers, moving, in opposition to the declared Mexican desires, "in a direction other than northward," was attacked by Mexican forces at Carrizal. A number of them were killed; nearly a score who surrendered were promptly released in compliance with a sharp demand from the American government.

In July the expedition was being withdrawn, and Carranza suggested mediation by Hispanic American powers to formulate methods whereby the border phases of disagreements might be solved. The offer was accepted, but the commission which sat until January 15, 1917, failed to find a satisfactory remedy because Carranza would not agree to allow American troops to be sent in pursuit of raiders. They were however, repeatedly so sent during the remainder of his tenure, with only pro forma protest. The expedition was entirely out of Mexico on February 5, 1917, having been in the country eleven months, at a cost of a total of over $130,000,000. The result had not clarified the situation. It made Francisco Villa a countryside hero, but while it failed to unite the Mexicans for national defense it left a deep feeling of outraged sovereignty and a permanent fear of armed intervention. It seemed to Carranza to justify the international rôle which he assumed as protagonist of the Hispanic American nations against the aggressive attitude of the "Colossus of the North."

The event of greatest significance to the internal administration of Mexico during the presidency of Carranza was the adoption and promulgation of the Constitution of 1917. Although the Constitution of 1857 was an extremely liberal document, reflecting in its oft-amended forms the ideals of segregation of church and state and the mechanism of genuine democracy, those features were almost entirely in abeyance during the long reign of Díaz. Under Madero and Huerta the observance of the Constitution waned appreciably. Huerta had no conception of the forms of government at all. The Constitutionalists went to battle to restore the desecrated document, but the first three years of Carranza's power were designated by him as a Pre-constitutional Period in order that he might with legal logic issue decrees conceived to embody the principles of the social revolution. That was the characterization the Carrancistas gave it, rather than that of political or agrarian revolution. Social revolution contained the three elements; there were, in spite of its critics, Mexican and American alike, and there still are, in the revolution, traits of desire for genuine social and economic reform which if engrafted will yield some measure of compensation for the bitter trials Mexico has endured and has caused the world. But they are yet far from realization, obfuscated by treachery, personal ambitions, peculations, false theories and foul murders within, and by selfish interests and ignorance and lack of realization from without. Carranza was one of the chief contributors to the delay.

The program of the social revolution began to be unfolded by Carranza in his decree of December 12, 1914, at Vera Cruz. There he invoked the spirit of Benito Juárez who, in a like extremity, launched his campaign against the landed power of the church. But Carranza's reforms contemplated a more complete upturning of society, an extirpation of all the vices Mexico was heir to, the complete substitution for a régime of oppression of one of liberty.

The reforms which Carranza sought to impose by his own dictum were: the establishment of a divorce law in order to place family life on a more rational and humane basis; the invigorization of the liberty of the municipalities as an imperative prerequisite for the inauguration of free government; the immediate restitution of their lands to towns which had been dispossessed of them through the rapacity of recent military dictators; and the dotation of lands to towns which lacked the areas needed to provide even the prime necessities of life. Municipal officers were elected by the inhabitants of all the cities on September 3, 1916; the office of vice-president was abolished, and the presidential term was reduced from six to four years. These measures were directed against the return of such a despotism as Díaz had wielded. On each of these contemplated reforms much might be said against their efficacy to overthrow age-old vices in any country; much has been written to show that they were not the expression of any general desire by the Mexicans, and that none of them have yet been realized. Other reform features included genuine ending of the economic and political power of the church, and breaking up the great haciendas. At any event, they constituted the nucleus of Carranza's political theory.

To put them into proper effect, giving them the sanction of basic legislation, it was necessary to incorporate them in the Constitution. Hence a convention was called to sit at Querétaro in November 1916. Only delegates who had supported Carranza were allowed to attend it. This arbitrary exclusion of political opponents was at least logical. Instead of amending the old Constitution, however, the convention promptly produced a document largely new but retaining many sections of the old one. The new Constitution, promulgated on February 5, 1917, served one valuable purpose. It reduced the Congress to a four months' session each year, extra sessions being at pleasure of the executive. In this and other ways it made the legislative branch inferior to the executive, reversing the rule of the prior document. It put the paper system of government more completely in accord with the dictatorial genius of the country. Reforms in judicial procedure and in administration were of advanced democratic character.

Whatever the benefits of the new Constitution, these were not the features which have given it its great notoriety. The salient points of interest in it are its new application of the principle of eminent domain and its care, meticulously expressed, for the welfare of the laboring classes. With these also marches the determination to destroy the evils of authoritative control of the people by the church either through education or religion. It is dedicated to the rule of reason and of the proletariat. Not only is the Constitution antireligious, or more correctly speaking anti-clerical; it is also anti-foreign and anti-monopolistic, and it embodies the theory of social reorganization in the exhaustive way in which it attempts to protect the laboring class and forestall all its difficulties. It is in fact an attempt to institute a régime of state socialism.

The paternalistic attitude toward labor is demonstrated by the provisions of Article 123. These are dangerous because they lack discrimination in details and because they are theoretical rather than practical. They attempt to create conditions instead of controlling existing ones. Some of them, ideal for a highly industrialized society, are applied to domestic laborers, with evil results. But some of them are admirable. Special favor is extended to woman and child labor. Nursing mothers are to have rest periods, there is a minimum wage provision and an eight hour day. Accident compensation, legalization of certain strikes, arbitration of disputes, and other provisions have social value, but the general tendency is to make laborers the privileged class. This element, especially the part found in the ranks of skilled and semi-skilled labor, has become excessively class-conscious during the revolution. The sympathy felt for it among certain of the government officers has tended to make it self-assertive and in many cases actively anarchistic. One of its constitutional privileges, that of having three months' notice or three months' pay in case of discharge, would work a serious disadvantage to industry should it be generally enforced.

While the labor condition offered problems of moment, the most serious situation under Carranza's régime arose from the attempt to enforce the provisions of the famous Article 27. This article unfolds the theory that the subsoil products (minerals and oils) were never legally alienated by the Díaz government, and asserts that the proposed resumption of direct dominion over such subsoil products by the nation is to be undertaken for the good of society.

The full import of Article 27 was not at first well understood. But it soon became evident that the government intended to apply it in full vigor and to give it retroactive force as affecting properties acquired before promulgation of the Constitution, notwithstanding that Article 14 of that document prohibits retroactive laws. As a matter of fact, if the article is not retroactive or to be so applied, it needs amending in that sense. Purchasers of national and private lands under Díaz had been given fee simple rights in perpetuity, with right to all subsoil products. Prior laws had been repealed and new ones framed to make this possible. But Carranza, by decree of February 19, 1918, indicated that his government proposed to resume proprietary rights in subsoil products by imposing royalties on petroleum, and superficie taxes and graduated ground rents intended to penalize holding undeveloped oil areas. On July 31 he attempted to obtain obedience to this decree, which most oil producers had refused on the ground that acquiescence would impair their titles, by another decree declaring their holdings open to denouncement if their declarations were not made in a specified time. Decrees of August 8 and 12 were of the same purport but extended the time granted for compliance. The revolutionary theory was that the nation had never had legal authority to alienate subsoil products. It based this opinion on certain of the precepts of old Spanish law, and claimed that Díaz had violated Article 72 of the Constitution of 1857 by legislating in favor of alienation of subsoil products. Foreign oil producers began remonstrance through diplomatic channels on April 2, being sustained by their national state departments. The petroleum condition was acute during the remainder of Carranza's tenure. Foreign interests demanded that Article 27 should be amended so as to protect their acquired rights. They were unwilling to accept mere legislation, had it been forthcoming, because successive congresses might reverse the law. By the same token they were unable to accept court decisions which might declare the article non-retroactive. They did, however, interpose suits before the Mexican Supreme Court, claiming that the oil decrees were unconstitutional because the extraordinary legislative powers of the president did not extend to the case in point. These suits were some of them decided in favor of the companies, but not until Obregón had been over a year in power, in 1921 and 1922.

In January, 1920, Carranza was forced to yield to the oil men to the extent of allowing them to resume the drilling which he had attempted to stop. The concession was made without prejudice to either side in the pending legal controversy, and before this reached its conclusion Carranza had been driven from power.

During his entire rule Carranza was warmly opposed by nearly all the important foreign and the remaining native financial interests of the country. Many foreigners were sent out of the country by executive order under Article 33, which amplified the powers originally used by Santa Anna under the Constitution of 1843. His chief supporters were those who were unmolested by his revolutionary program. Among these were the numerous foreign Protestant missionaries, whose work for the lower strata of society was recognized as in consonance with the governmental program for the amelioration of their condition. They, like other students of the situation, believed that a president of Mexico who ruled by consent of an appreciable number of Mexicans could do less harm than an intervention for the sake of special interests, an intervention which might work to the serious complication of the affairs of the United States. This was especially true during the period in which the latter country was involved in the war in Europe, and it was due very largely to that conflict that the Mexican situation dragged, with no remedial action from without. The Wilsonian theory of "self-determination" was also a contributory factor.

The attitude of Mexico during the World War presented another serious cause for dissatisfaction with Carranza. Mexico observed officially a "rigorous neutrality" as he called it in his message of April 15, 1915, to Congress; this neutrality was, however, only a thin concealment of sympathy for Germany, as shown by Carranza's suggestion of an embargo by American nations on supplies and war materials for the belligerents. At that time such a policy could have helped no one but Germany. The French, Italian, and American residents did all they could to counteract Mexican official hostility, with some good effect. In March, 1917, the world was amused and angered at the disclosure of the infamous Zimmermann note, in which the German minister proposed to align Japan and Mexico against the United States. As a reward for such hostility, Mexico was to be given the old Spanish southwest lost in the war with the United States in 1848. Both Japan and Mexico denied knowledge of the note. There were other disclosures about the same time which indicated that there had been a "Plan of San Diego" by which Carranza had hoped to invade some parts of the southwest and reconquer it. These were never authoritatively proven. Other acts of hostility to Americans developed in the denial of opportunity to the American Red Cross to help succor starving persons in Mexico, and in the abduction of William Jenkins, consular agent at Puebla, who escaped from bandits who had taken him from his own home, only to be charged with complicity in rebel activities and with having procured his own capture to stir up international trouble; he was later released without any final decision by the Mexican courts.

CHAPTER XXVII

THE CARRANZA DÉBÂCLE

THE initial steps in the movement which resulted in the flight and death of President Carranza began to be chronicled in the daily press dispatches of the United States as early as the end of March, 1920. Weeks before that time some of the details of the proposed revolution were passed about by word of mouth, the contest in Sonora being freely predicted along the lines which it actually followed. It is thus evident that the waning power of the government had been accurately gauged during the winter, while Obregón was making a political tour of the Republic. During the year 1919 the power of the Carranza régime was apparently at its highest, though that power was never complete nor supported by a large or economically significant part of the population. It will be remembered that Carranza had been recognized as de facto head of the Republic of Mexico in October, 1915, after he had refused to abide by promises he had made not to assume the presidency, and had quarreled with Francisco Villa and others of his companions in arms against Huerta. Recognition was bestowed, not in full confidence, but in the belief that Carranza led the party which had made the most effective campaign against the prevailing disorders and which was most likely to succeed in the pacification of the country.

Adequate justification for that recognition would have developed had there come speedy elimination of banditry, had the power been consolidated on a civil instead of a military basis, and had a reasonable if not a grateful attitude toward the United States been shown. But pacification was unduly retarded by the policy of the military arm, which persisted in treating banditry and rebellion as opportunities

441

for self-enrichment not to be too suddenly ended. Thus the military arm, largely revolution-created to serve as the bulwark of the government, which had but a precarious tenure in the public esteem, became the weakness that worked the downfall of the chief under whose sign manual it pillaged the country and outraged its citizens.

This military situation was abundant cause for nonfulfilment of many of the promises under which the Carranza revolution was waged. There were many contributing causes in internal affairs. It is true that the program of the revolution was more amply laid down in the Constitution of 1917, but the Constitution was never really in force and acceptance within the controlled area. It was and is too idealistic for practical use. Its Utopian provisions for bettering labor conditions were not enacted into law or generally observed under decrees. Its emancipation of the peón class was nullified by the condition of semi-warfare which pervaded most areas outside the large cities. The financial condition of the Republic left much to be desired, although commerce was growing, although tax receipts were higher by one-half than they had been in the heyday of the Díaz régime, and although business was conducted almost entirely on a basis of metallic currency. The educational system had been left in the hands of the states and municipalities as a part of the revolutionary doctrine, even in the Federal District, and only in a few places—notably not in the capital, did it receive adequate attention. Promised improvements in the operation of the courts still left the people "hungering and thirsting for justice;" the unsanitary jails were continuously crowded with untried prisoners. The legislative branch broke with the executive in so far as it could. It refused to pass the oil legislation recommended, and withdrew the extraordinary war powers under which Carranza had been exercising dictatorial control. The City of Mexico, given rein as a "free municipality," one of the shibboleths of the revolution, was lax in police regulations, sanitation, education, administration of justice, and direction of public morals. Personal safety, even in the Capital, was without guarantees. The President had disregarded electoral formalities, imposing his own candidates as governors in numerous states, and had used these gentlemen to further his design to seat his own candidate as his successor, had arrested the partisans of Obregón, and imprisoned, upon flimsy charges, the members of Congress who opposed his political program.

In external affairs the non-payment of the interest on the public debt, and the observance of a neutrality in the Great War which veiled only too thinly a wish for German success fathered by the thought that a European friend might rise up to check the hegemony of the United States upon the American continent, combined to complicate a difficult situation. Coupled with this inane foreign policy were the effects of the attempt at "revindication" of the rights of the nation to the subsoil deposits of petroleum. The conflict grew tense when revindication attempted to affect retroactively lands held by foreigners in full titular ownership under the laws of the Díaz régime, which permitted private ownership of subsoil mineral oil. Possibly the new legislation would have left owners in possession and permitted profitable operation of oil properties; but suspicion that the opposite course might be taken, backed by American ideas of the sanctity of contracts, threw the oil producers into an opposition which was extremely embarrassing to the government.

Thus in both internal and external affairs Carranza, instead of addressing himself to righting conditions which menaced the life of the body politic, undertook to revolutionize the government upon a socialistic theory while a corrupt military oligarchy and a none too honest set of civilian officers vitiated whatever was good in the new plan by the most cynical grafting.

It is a mistake to think, however, that these attitudes and conditions were entirely new, or entirely chargeable to Carranza. Many of them are inveterate evils which will not disappear suddenly under any government. There had been a perceptible improvement in some of them during Carranza's incumbency, and those who hoped for and believed in the ultimate development of ability by the Mexican people to govern themselves felt that the first great step in improvement would come from the demonstration of stability through peaceable transmission of the presidential office. That was the one great hope of the Carranza régime. But in the mind of the President the essential thing was to transmit the power to a man who would continue his own program. He made the fatal mistake of. quarreling with Obregón, the most popular man of his own party, who was ambitious to succeed him, and who had a stronger influence over the military than did the President. If nothing succeeds like success nothing fails like failure to recognize the possibilities, or rather the probabilities, of a situation. Upon Carranza's power to transmit the presidency to a successor who could command the confidence of the faction in control depended the justification of his program. The débâcle, then, was caused by the personal attitude of the President rather than by the many contributory influences which made his tenure so precarious.

The political campaigns of would-be successors were waged for a year and a half; their acerbity contributed not a little to the unrest and disorder of the country. Early in January of 1920 the well-known fact of Obregón's lead in the race was recognized. He was a popular revolutionary idol. He was the only man who had ever defeated Villa. He had fathered several startling attempts to amend the new Constitution, thereby earning the enmity of Carranza. He had practically admitted that he would start a revolution if there were not a fair election. It was generally felt that if he did so he would surely win, as the majority of the military were for him.

About the same time it began to be announced that Ambassador Ignacio Bonillas would presently return from the United States to Mexico to quicken his candidacy, which had the backing of the President, and which had been talked of for six months at least. Almost simultaneously General Pablo González surrendered his military command in the

south to begin his formal campaign, which haa oeen thought
to have Carranza's support before Bonillas was brought forward as a civilian candidate who would free Mexico from
her "plague of military men."

Late in January a force of picked military police were sent
to Mazatlán and Hermosillo in Sonora to fight Yaqui supporters of Obregón, who controlled that state politically.
These traditional enemies of whatever central government
may exist had been on the warpath several months. Obregón was at the time in Guanajuato, and his interests were
being advanced in the United States by General Salvador
Alvarado of Yucatan fame, who had been recently arrested
for fomenting social revolution, but who had escaped. On
February 11 an assembly of governors in the capital, called
by Carranza, issued a declaration that the coming elections
would be held peaceably and honestly, they themselves
vouching maintenance of law and order. Pablo González
issued a manifesto advocating friendly relations with foreign
powers, abolition of the military caste, and liberal amnesty
laws. Carranza again reïterated his declaration that he
would not hold the presidency after expiration of his term,
and that if no executive were elected Congress would name
one. The Bonillas candidacy began to develop active character under the vociferative propaganda with which the
government urged it upon the people.

While all these discordant appeals were being made to the
small political element, the country continued in serious disorder, evinced by the murders of several Americans and
others. In the midst of such conditions it was announced
that the American State and War Departments were keenly
interested in a report of the arrival at Agua Prieta, in Sonora,
of a large force of federal troops presumably sent to prevent
the armed forces of that state from supporting Obregón.
These State forces were under Adolfo de la Huerta, the
governor, a young man of radical tendencies, a follower of
Obregón, the prospective Substitute President of the Republic, and minister of Hacienda under Obregón.

At this juncture, De la Huerta announced that a strike

was threatened by the employees of the Southern Pacific of Mexico. This had been predicted a full month before. While Bonillas was being given an apparently enthusiastic welcome in Mexico City on March 22, Obregón and González began to try to harmonize their bitter antagonisms in order to oppose him. Obregón had need of the alliance. By the end of the month General Diéguez stood ready to invade Sonora for Carranza to seat a new civil governor, C. G. Soriano. The Obregón soldiery was preparing to repel the invasion, as the Sonora group had no will to see their government taken from them in the way Carranza had taken possession of the states of San Luis Potosí, Guanajuato, Querétaro, Campeche, Nuevo León, Tamaulipas, Jalisco, and Vera Cruz.

On April 3 the railway strike began. Carranza threatened to operate the road with soldiers. This was the signal for the officials of Sonora to begin revolution. On the ninth day they anticipated Carranza, under the pronouncement of the Plan de Agua Prieta, by seizing the railway and operating it with strikers, whose terms were conceded. The State officers next seized the customhouse and post office at Agua Prieta and garrisoned the town. The legislature in an all-night session voted to secede and to constitute the "Republic of Sonora" an independent entity until assured that the rights of the State would not be invaded.

At the moment of the uprising Obregón was under technical arrest in Mexico City charged with complicity in revolutionary plans fomented by one Roberto Cejudo. The military operations of the new Republic were placed in charge of General Plutarco Elias Calles, who had recently resigned from the national cabinet to enter the campaign for Obregón. His immediate task was to repel invasion by Diéguez, who was expected to advance from Chihuahua by way of Pulpito Pass. But the Chihuahua forces, after having been denied railway transportation through United States territory from El Paso to Douglas, refused to advance. The attempt of Carranza to deal with the revolution from the eastern side was thus rendered futile.

In the meantime Governor Iturbe to the south in Sinaloa announced that he was "still loyal"—he should have been, for he had become a multimillionaire by virtue of his governorship—but neutral between Mexico and Sonora. He was looking for an opportunity of escape. The troops of Sonora now began to advance upon the Sinaloa border in order to bring that State into open revolt and control the coast. They took Culiacán on April 17 and pressed on to Mazatlán and Tepic. By April 15 Obregón had escaped from the capital in disguise, with General Benjamín Hill, and had made his way to the southwest. He was said to have established wireless communication whereby to direct the revolution. On April 18 the State of Nayarit (formerly Tepic province) indorsed the Sonora movement; all the interior towns of Sonora adhered to the cuartelazo of Agua Prieta, and practically all the Yaqui and the Mayo Indians of the region did so as well. Michoacán to the south soon joined in defection; in Chihuahua numerous army officers cast their contemplated lot with the rapidly growing movement to change the national leader. On April 21 Benjamín Hill, the "original Obregonista," was said to have advanced to Contreras, on the outskirts of the capital, with troops from Guerrero. Zacatecas was confessedly in rebel hands. Tuxpam in the oil regions was threatened, troops at Linares revolted, and Mexico City was cut off from communication.

The Liberal Constitutionalist Party thereupon made a demand that Carranza should relinquish his office, and, under declarations contained in the Plan de Agua Prieta, set up Adolfo de la Huerta as supreme commander until such time as the states joining Sonora should make a choice. A provisional president was to be named as soon as the Plan should be adopted by the Liberal Constitutionalist Army. The Plan announced a policy of protection to all citizens and foreigners and the enforcement of all their legal rights. Especially was emphasized a determination to develop industries, commerce, and business in general. Finally, the antiphonal strophe habitual in the Mexican system of government by cuartelazo was added: "Effectual suffrage, no reëlection." The legal government continued to camouflage the situation by absurd claims of strength, but its position was serious. The effort to send troops into the north failed, and Governor Iturbe of Sinaloa threatened to evacuate that State and Nayarit unless he could be reïnforced. Obregón was nearly ready to advance from Guerrero to the capital; more than 50,000 troops had joined the prospering cause.

On the last day of the month Washington received dispatches saying that Carranza was planning to leave the capital, but at the same time it was known that Pablo González had cut rail communication with Vera Cruz. He had recently been obliged by Carranza to withdraw his candidacy in order to compel Obregón to follow suit, it was claimed. This may have influenced González to assist the cuartelazo. He had left Mexico City on a feigned errand; and, once safely outside, had revolted with numerous subordinates on May 3. A rumor spread that Carranza's remaining generals, summoned to advise him, had recommended that he resign not later than May 15. The enemy now numbered twice the total of the government forces.

On May 5 President Carranza issued his last manifesto. He declared that he would fight to the finish, that he would not resign, nor turn the power over to anyone not his duly elected successor; he said:

"I must declare that I consider it one of the highest duties which devolve upon me to set down affirmed and established the principle that in future the public power shall not be the prize of military chiefs whose revolutionary merits, however great, may serve to excuse future acts of ambition. I consider that it is essential for the independence and sovereignty of Mexico that the transmission of power shall always be effected peacefully and by democratic procedure, that the cuartelazo as a means of ascent to power shall forever be abolished entirely from our political practices. And I consider, finally, that the principle must be kept inviolate which was adopted by the Constitution of 1917, that no man shall rule over the destinies of the nation who has tried to climb to power by means of insubordination, the cuartelazo, or treason."

While this declaration was being penned, and was being given to the press by the Secretary of Hacienda Luis Cabrera, the man who above all others was responsible for the unpopularity and the mistaken attitude of Carranza, the exodus had been planned, and was immediately put into execution.

It was an exodus, not a flight. Professor J. H. Smith has said of the departure of President Herrera from Mexico during the stormy days of the Mexican War, that he "left the palace with the entire body of his loyal officers and officials, his mild face and his respectable side-whiskers—in one hired cab." Had Carranza limited his contingent to those who were genuinely loyal a cab might have sufficed. Self-interest held a large number still in his political family. The proposal was to transfer the government to Vera Cruz, whence so many hard-pressed forlorn hopes have been able to "come back." Twenty-one trains, collected and equipped at great effort, were to carry away 20,000 troops, carloads of records, and millions of treasure. The dispatches said 27,000,000 pesos were taken, but, after the disaster, Pastor Rouaix, ex-secretary of Agriculture, upon returning to Mexico on May 18 with the booty, said that it was worth 100,000,000 pesos. In addition to the troops, there was a carload of employees of state, the Cabinet, the Supreme Court, and the Permanent Commission of Congress.

Misfortune attended every step. There was delay and confusion in getting off. Attacks on the convoy began almost at once. Before they passed La Villa the last four trains were cut off. Tools for tearing up the track in the rear had been left behind during the first attack, and a wild engine, driven against the fugitives' last train, wrecked artillery and aviation equipment, and killed or wounded railway employees. After delay at Apizaco on May 8 and 9, the loyal forces went on to San Marcos. Beyond that place they engaged revolutionary troops, taking four hundred prisoners. On May 12 they reached Rinconada, where they learned that General Guadalupe Sánchez had gone over to Obregón, deserting General Cándido Aguilar, the President's son-in-law, and that there was no longer hope of a stand at Orizaba, where Aguilar was to hold the ways, for he, deserted, had fled.

Finally, after his trains were cut to pieces and unusable, and his troops had been defeated at Aljibes, Carranza, maintaining imperturbable sangfroid, gave up hope of escape by rail and set out for the Puebla mountains, trusting perhaps in the aid of the Cabrera family, which was strong in the region.

While making his way northeastward, presumably toward some small gulf port, he was betrayed by one Herrero, a "general de dedo" (that is, a general so dubbed on the field of battle by merely being pointed at with the finger, and told orally: "You are a general") of sufficient obscurity to suggest that he might have been someone's agent. The President was done to death on the night of May 18, while he slept with his dwindled retinue in a mountain shack at Tlaxcalantongo, in the State of Puebla.

Thus far bloodshed had been insignificant. Obregón, who had entered the City of Mexico unresisted on May 8, had sent flying columns to capture Carranza, issuing repeated orders that he was not to be injured, and endeavoring to induce him to surrender upon reïterated assurances of personal guarantees. All overtures had been spurned. It was evidently intended to save his life. The considerations of humanity, of old associations, even of recognition itself demanded this. The pig-headed country gentleman, who was unsuccessful at managing the mature men of his organization, knew how to play his last card so as to diminish his opponents' profit to the minimum. Obregón's tart reply to the telegram sent by some thirty followers of Carranza announcing the final disaster, was evidently addressed as much to the public of Mexico and of the United States as to the remnant of the lost cause. The revolutionary party immediately took energetic means to demonstrate its non-complicity in the deed.

Most of the official family which remained with the fleeing President to the end were imprisoned for a time in Mexico City, but nearly all were shortly released. General Juan Barragán, the youngster under thirty who was the military genius of the last régime, escaped, and fled across the border, there to intrigue against the Obregón government with other ex-Carrancistas.

The body of Carranza was brought back to Mexico City on May 24 after an investigation, partly financed by Obregón personally, which disproved the claim of Herrero that the President had committed suicide. He was buried in the cemetery of Dolores, according to his known desire. Mexico gave itself up to uniform manifestations of regret and respect. It was anticipated for a time that the revulsion of feeling would develop into armed opposition to the revolution; there were some armed clashes in the north, and a rebel named Osuna was for some time in the field, but his forces were small and he met prompt defeats. None of the rebel activity had a purpose of vindicating Carranza.

On May 25 Adolfo de la Huerta was chosen Substitute President by the reorganized Congress. He served the un-expired term of Carranza, that is, until the end of November, 1920. One of the young men of the north, he had been an active revolutionist for years. He has interested himself in labor legislation, and reaffirmed his interest in the proletariat ever after his rise to the presidency. His ideas were moder-ately tempered by the acquisition of power, and he renounced in a measure his inveterate animosity toward capital. Obregón took private offices in the capital during De la Huerta's ad interim period, where he was announced to be "obey-ing" the new régime. The Cabinet was formed from the rad-ical group. The Minister of War, General Plutarco Elias Calles, was for a time in Carranza's cabinet as Secretary of Commerce and Industry; the latter position was given to Alberto Pani. The treasury was intermittently in charge of General Salvador Alvarado, whose career in Yucatan as an independent Socialist governor, and later as an opponent of Carranza and supporter of Obregón, made him well known.

His connection with the Obregón government was only transitory. His land program, at best a highly provocative one, was given great acerbity by numerous acts of wanton abuse of power. The ministry of Communications and Public Works was intrusted to General Ortiz Rubio, that of Agriculture and Fomento to General Enrique Estrada, while the name of General Jacinto B. Treviño was connected with various cabinet positions, as were those of Antonio Villareal, Morales Hesse, Santiago Martínez Alomía, and others. Foreign relations were at first committed to Miguel Covarrubias, who had had a diplomatic career of some forty years. Representation of the new government at Washington was in the hands of Fernando Iglesias Calderón. Félix F. Palavicini, old war horse of the early revolution, editor of *El Universal*, a strong pro-ally during the Great War and capable publicist, was given a mission before numerous courts of the Old World in which he had very meager success. The legation at Madrid was raised to the rank of an embassy, a courtesy reciprocated by the Spanish government, and ministers were exchanged. The new rector of the University of Mexico, Lic. José Vasconcelos, well-known educator and littérateur, at once began a program of popularizing education and extending the influence of the educational work by advocating a federal secretariat of Public Instruction.

Public opinion in Mexico received the new order with optimism. Among Americans it was recognized as a reorganization of the power within the group which Carranza himself led, but the sentiment was frequently voiced that the change could not be for the worse. It was developed rather in personal attitudes than in declared principles of government. The men who led the new movement were known by word and deed as pronounced radicals. The swing of the pendulum has been steadily toward more radical idealism ever since Independence. It has been noticeable, however, that in all cases of actual acquisition of power, radicalism has been left in the stage of theory, and pronounced materialistic conservatism, for the benefit of those who govern, has usually eventuated.

In the United States the Obregón movement was received with favorable comment in circles in which Mexican business interests are important. The leading article in the May number of *The Americas*, published by the National City Bank of New York, said in part:

" Now that events in Mexico are moving towards final settlement, there is every reason to believe that the plans repeatedly made and postponed may be put into execution, and trade relations established between the business men of this country and the merchants of Mexico that will be permanent and profitable to both groups. . . . In spite of troubles that may come during the next few months and outward appearances that make it appear that Mexico is merely keeping up its favorite pastime of revolution and civil war, there is sound reason for believing that constructive influences are at work and that a happier and more prosperous epoch is nearly at hand."

It was futile to expect that mere change of leadership from one coterie to another within a small fraction of the politically significant element of the population would work an immediate miracle. The congressional elections were set for the first Sunday in August, and the presidential election for September. Most of the governors were changed and the municipalities reorganized, with Obregonistas in place, hence the machinery was well arranged for peaceable elections. Obregón was given a clear field by the definite renunciation of González. The old conservative element put forward a candidate, but the action was merely nominal, the Catholic Party as a political influence being weak. The problem of Villa and his old defenders of the Constitution of 1857 continued to perplex the new government until a convention was arranged whereby that redoubtable bandit became a peaceful hacendado in Durango.

The new Congress was potent in capacity to promote discord, as was the old. The official class as a whole was new and untried. When such difficult problems as the oil controversy came before Congress there was great divergence of opinion and no legislation was obtained though it was demanded by both internal and external conditions. The oil men asked to have the Carranza decrees annulled and the program of legislation definitely settled. Among the Mexicans there was no unanimity concerning annulment of the decrees or solution of numerous problems raised by Article 27 of the Constitution. President De la Huerta's favorable decrees were of course only temporary in their effect.

The Mexicans expressed confidence that the United States would announce recognition at an early date, but the Republican administration refused to grant this in the absence of treaty stipulations guaranteeing American lives and property.

The one conspicuous aspiration of the Mexican nation since the advent of Obregón has been to secure recognition by the United States without yielding to the demand that American lives and property rights be guaranteed by treaty as a previous condition repeatedly enunciated by the Secretary of State, Charles E. Hughes. Such a treaty Obregón has held it beyond his competency to sign, alleging that it would give greater security to foreigners than to Mexicans. Many alternatives have been attempted, including favorable Supreme Court decisions in oil suits pending since the time of Carranza, and proposals to amend Article 27 so as to make it unmistakable that confiscatory measures will not be employed against American property owners. The more recent attitude of the American administration, seeking a reasonable solution of outstanding problems without insistence on any specified form of agreement, has met with sympathetic response in both Mexico and the United States. At the moment when this book is undergoing final revision, press announcements are made that an adjustment is again to be attempted under more auspicious circumstances than have hitherto existed.

The government under President Obregón has demonstrated a clever facility in self-preservation in spite of the obvious weakness inherent in its virtual position as a de facto government only. A well safeguarded recognition will

make for stability, and the problem of stabilizing social
conditions in Mexico is one of almost as much direct moment
to Americans as to Mexicans. The United States cannot be
wholly at ease while Mexico harbors manifestations of social
unrest. Proletarian disorders, as accompaniment of revolutionary legislation favoring laborers and landless peons,
commingled with political incertitude and personal and
regional bitternesses, all indicate that the day of the en-
thronement of social and political sanity, consent in majority rule, and sensitiveness to the demands of justice
whether internal or external, has not yet fully dawned in
Mexico. But its coming is desired by thousands of loyal
conservative and liberal Mexicans who cherish the hope that
their growth in national consciousness shall be directly encouraged by the United States.

BIBLIOGRAPHY

SOURCES, AUTHORITIES, AND ADDITIONAL READINGS

This bibliography is intended to be comprehensive but not exhaustive. The attempt is made to present a reasonable proportion of the sources and authorities without burdensome inclusion of the less significant items. A general topical survey is given of the chief works of importance, after which appear special lists of Additional Readings for each chapter of the text. These lists offer amplification of the subject treated in the chapters, and certain of the most significant sources and authorities. Effort has been made to place each item nearest the topic for which it is most useful; in order to avoid undue repetition of titles many works are noticed but once, although they bear on the contents of several chapters. Even so, it is obvious that many meritorious works have necessarily been omitted.

BIBLIOGRAPHIES.—It would be a work of supererogation to attempt a survey of the numerous bibliographies of Spanish American historical literature of the colonial epoch which contain items referring to Mexico. The interested student will find them in F. Weber, *Beiträge zur Charakteristik der älteren Geschichtsschreiber über Spanisch-Amerika* . . . (Leipzig, 1911), and in José Toribio Medina, *Biblioteca hispano-anericana (1493–1810)* (Santiago, 1898-1907, 7 v.) Tomo VI, *Prólogo*, Sección III, pp. CXI–CXX. Mr. C. K. Jones of the Library of Congress has translated Señor Medina's "Advertencia sobre las obras de bibliografía hispano-americana" as "Critical Notes on Sources" and published these in form supplementary to his *Hispanic American Bibliographies* (now in press) first printed in *The Hispanic American Historical Review*, Vol. IV, No. 4 (November, 1921) 783-799. Mr. Jones has also published in *The Hispanic American Historical Review*, Volume IV, No. 2, (May, 1921) the section of his *Bibliographies* referring especially to "Mexico, Nueva España," in which 232 numbers (753 to 985) cover the essential bibliographical aids to the study of Mexico to the present time.

There is no continuous bibliography of Mexican literature. A complete survey of the colonial period (that is 1539 to 1800) may be obtained by using García Icazbalceta, *Bibliografía mexicana del siglo xvi* . . . *de 1539 a 1600* (Mexico, 1886), Vicente de Paula Andrade, *Ensayo bibliográfico mexicano del siglo xvii* (Mexico, 2d ed. 1889), and N. León, *Bibliografía mexicana del siglo xviii* (Mexico, 1902–08, 5 v.). For the nineteenth century some materials are given in the latter author's *La bibliografía en México en el siglo xix (Boletín del Instituto Bibliográfico Mexicano*, Num. 3, Mexico, 1902). Manuel de Olaguíbel, *Memoria para una bibliografía científica de México en el siglo xix* (Mexico, 1889) is a partial aid to one class of Mexicana for the past century.

More available to American students are the partial lists which follow: *Index to Publications, Articles, and Maps relating to Mexico in the War Department Library* (Its *Subject Catalogue* No. 3, Washington, 1896); the *List of Materials on Mexico in the New York Public Library* (Its *Bulletin*, October-

December 1909) gives an excellently classified arrangement of official documents, general and special works. Exceedingly useful also are the bibliographical lists published in the preliminary pages of the first volumes of the following parts of H. H. Bancroft, *Works* (San Francisco 1882–90): *History of Central America* (1882–1887, 3 v.); *History of Mexico* (1883–1888, 6 v.); *History of California* (1884–1890), 7 v.); *North Mexican States and Texas* (1884–1889, 2 v.); *History of Arizona and New Mexico* (1889). The lists published by Bancroft constitute a printed guide to the nucleus of the present Bancroft Library at the University of California.

The National Library at Mexico City has published José M. Vigil, *Catálogos de la Biblioteca Nacional* (Vols. 1–9, 1889; Primeros suplementos de las divisiones 3a, 5a, 6a, y 8a, 1895, 1897; 9a, 1893); Luis González Obregón, *The National Library of Mexico 1833–1910* (Mexico, 1910), and its special list of Mexicana, *Catálogo especial de las obras mexicanas o sobre México en la Biblioteca Nacional de México* (Mexico, 1911). This work lists also the manuscripts in the collection.

The monumental work of José Toribio Medina, *La imprenta en México, 1539–1821* (Santiago, 1907-12, 8 v.) is supplemented by his smaller lists, *La imprenta en Guadalajara* (1904) . . . *Oaxaca* (1904) . . . *Vera Cruz* (1904) . . . *Mérida* (1904) . . . *Puebla* (1908).

Valuable Mexicana are listed in the *Catalogue of Books relating to North and South America in the Library of the late John Carter Brown*, Pt. I, 1482–1601 (Providence, 1875); Pt. II, 1600–1700 (Providence, 1882). Justin Winsor, *Narrative and Critical History of America* (New York, 1888–1889, 8 v.), lists items, especially in Volume 8, down to 1886, referring to Spanish America. J. N. Larned, *Literature of American History, a Bibliographical Guide* . . . (Boston, 1902) contains valuable materials, these being supplemented by E. C. Richardson and A. E. Morse, *Writings on American History, 1902* (Princeton, 1904) and A. C. McLaughlin, *Writings on American History, 1903* (Washington, 1905). In the annual lists edited since 1906 by Grace G. Griffin, *Writings on American History* (1906–1918) appear sections indicating partially the vast current output on the history of America south of the United States. Channing, Hart, and Turner, *Guide to the Study and Reading of American History* (Boston, rev. and augm. ed., 1912), list items topically. H. Keniston, *List of Works for the Study of Hispanic-American History* (New York, 1920) gives a practical list of the general bibliographies (pp. 1–10), collections and individual works (11–31), and New Spain and Mexico (385–448). Fairly satisfactory acquaintance with current publication in the general field of Spanish American history and geography can be derived from *Petermann's Mitteilungen aus Justus Perthes' Geographischer Anstalt*, (Gotha, 1855–192-) and in H. Wagner's *Geographisches Jahrbuch*, (Gotha, 1866–192-). Reviews also appear in *Revista de archivos, bibliotecas, y museos*, (Madrid, 1871–192-), *Revue d'histoire moderne et contemporaine* (Paris, 1899–191-), *Revue de l'histoire des colonies françaises* (Paris, 1813–192-), *Boletín de la Real Academia de la Historia* (Madrid, 1877–192-), *Revue de l'Amérique latin*, (Paris 1922-), *The English Historical Review* (1886–192-), and *The American Historical Review* (New York, 1895–192-). A wealth of current lists, in reviews and bibliographical notes, has been presented in *The Hispanic American Historical Review* (Baltimore, 1918–192-). In Mexico City, *El libro y el pueblo* (1922-) issued by the Secretariat of Education, and *Biblos* (1918–192-) published by the Biblioteca Nacional, contain notices of interest.

Special Periods.—Among the aids devoted to special periods of Mexican history may be mentioned: Henry E. Haferkorn, *The War with Mexico, 1846-1848, a select Bibliography* . . . (Washington, 1914), William T. Lawson, *Essay on the Literature of the Mexican War* (1882), Justin H. Smith, "Sources for a History of the Mexican War, 1846-1848" (*Military Historian and Economist*, January, 1916). Exhaustive on this period is the latter author's " Appendix—The Sources" in his *The War with Mexico* (New York, 1919, 2 v.). The bibliographical appendices in the works of Genaro García constitute the available printed working lists of the nucleus of the García Library at the University of Texas; they are found in his *Juárez; refutación a Don Francisco Bulnes* (Mexico, 1904), *Don Juan de Palafox y Mendoza* (Mexico, 1918), and *Carácter de la conquista española en América y en México* (Mexico, 1901). The current revolution is represented by H. I. Priestley, "Mexican Literature on the Recent Revolution" in *The Hispanic American Historical Review*, Vol. II, No. 2, (May, 1919) pp. 286-311; C. K. Jones, "Bibliography of the Mexican Revolution," *Idem*, 311-314, and the latter author in "Recent Acquisitions of the Library of Congress mainly treating of Mexico in Revolution" in the same *Review* for November, 1918, Vol. 1, No. 4, pp. 480-481. More complete on this phase are J. B. del Castillo, *Bibliografía de la revolución mexicana de 1910-1916*, in *Concurso de bibliografía y biblioteconomía convocado por la Biblioteca Nacional* . . . (Mexico, 1918).

Sources in Print.—Among general collections of printed sources should be mentioned the *Colección de los viajes y descubrimientos* . . . (Madrid, 1825-1837, 5 v.) edited by M. F. Navarrete; the *Colección de documentos inéditos para la historia de España* (Madrid, 1842-1895, 112 v.), has the first 110 volumes indexed by G. P. Winship in the Boston Public Library *Bulletin*, XIII, October, 1894. The set usually attributed to Pacheco and Cardenas, *Colección de documentos inéditos relativos al descubrimiento conquista y colonización de las posesiones españolas en América y Oceanía* . . . (Madrid, 1864-1884, 42 v.) has a chronological table of contents in Volume XXXIII. The entire set has a *Chronological Digest* by B. M. Read (Albuquerque, 1914). The documents are poorly edited, but the material is of supreme importance. The continuation, *Colección de documentos inéditos de Ultramar; segunda serie* (Madrid, 1885-1898, 11 v.) has the contents topically arranged. The *Colección de libros y documentos referentes a la historia de América* (Madrid, 1904-1918, 19 v.), the *Nueva colección de documentos inéditos para la historia de España y sus Indias* (Madrid, 1892-96, 6 v.) the *Colección de libros raros y curiosos que tratan de América* (Madrid, 1891-1912, 21 v.) and F. J. Hernáez, *Colección de bulas, breves, y otros documentos relativos a la iglesia de América y Filipinas* (Brussels, 1879, 2 v.) contain many items of importance to Mexico. H. Ternaux-Compans, *Voyages, relations et mémoires originaux pour servir à l'histoire de la découverte de l'Amérique* . . . (Paris, 1837-41, 20 v.), as well as the collections of voyages edited by A. Churchill, W. Dampier, R. Kerr, Pinkerton, and Prévost, contain valuable source material on Mexico.

The outstanding sets of documents relating especially to Mexico include: Fortino H. Vera, *Colección de documentos eclesiásticos de México, ó sea antigua y moderna legislación de la iglesia mexicana* . . . (Amecameca, 1887, 3 v.); *Colección eclesiástica mejicana* (Mexico, 1834, 4 v.); Luis G. Pimentel, *Documentos históricos de Méjico: Tomo I, Descripción del arzobispado de México* (1887), Tomo II, *Relación de los obispados de Tlaxcala, Michoacán, Oaxaca, y otros lugares en el siglo XVI* . . . (1904); and the *Archivo mexicano: Documentos para la historia de México* . . . (Mexico, 1852–1853, 2 v.). The *Documentos para la historia de México* (Mexico, 1853–1857, 19 v. in 17) are of prime importance for the history of the Mexican northwest. They are indexed in Genaro García, *Índice alfabético de los "Documentos para la historia de México" publicados en cuatro series por D. Manuel Orozco y Berra (Anales del Museo Nacional de México*, 2a época, tom. 3, Mexico, 1906, p. 523–540). The *Documentos inéditos ó muy raros para la historia de México* . . . published under the editorship of Genaro García and Carlos Pereyra (Mexico, 1905–19, 35 v.) deal with episodes of the colonial epoch, the independence, and the French Intervention. J. García Icazbalceta's, *Colección de documentos para la historia de México* (Mexico, 1858–66, 2 v.) like his *Nueva colección de documentos* . . . (Mexico, 1886–92, 5 v.) deals largely with primitive Mexico, Indian society, the labors of Father Mendieta and other early Franciscans. J. E. Hernández Dávalos, *Colección de documentos para la historia de la guerra de independencia de México, de 1808 a 1821* (Mexico, 1877–82, 6 v.), indexed by Genaro García in *Anales del Museo Nacional de México*, 2a época, tom. 4 (Mexico, 1907) 225–305, is complemented by the latter's *Documentos históricos mexicanos, obra conmemorativa del primer centenario de la independencia de México* . . . (Mexico, 1910, 6 v.). Antonio Peñafiel, *Colección de documentos para la historia mexicana* (Mexico, 1897–1903, 6 v.) is entirely concerned with Mexican antiquities.

MANUSCRIPT SOURCES.—The unpublished documentation for the history of Mexico is as yet only partially listed. A comprehensive survey of the manuscripts in the various Mexican archives is H. E. Bolton, *Guide to Materials for the History of the United States in the Principal Archives of Mexico* (Washington, 1913). C. E. Chapman, *Catalogue of Materials in the Archivo General de Indias for the History of the Pacific Coast and the American Southwest* (Berkeley, 1919) is a more intensive list of documents concerning a smaller field within the larger. R. R. Hill, *Descriptive Catalogue of the Documents relating to the History of the United States in the Papeles Procedentes de Cuba deposited in the Archivo General de Indias at Seville* (Washington, 1916), and W. R. Shepherd, *Guide to the Materials for the History of the United States in Spanish Archives (Simancas, the Archivo Histórico Nacional and Seville)* (Washington, 1907) combine with J. A. Robertson, *List of Documents in Spanish Archives relating to the History of the United States, which have been Printed or of which Transcripts are Preserved in American Libraries* (Washington, 1910) to present valuable guides to materials primarily appertaining to the history of Mexico. Since 1910, however, the transcripts added to American libraries number into the hundreds of thousands, while many documents have since then been printed. In Spain the work of Pedro Torres Lanzas, *Independencia de América; fuentes para su estudio; catálogo de documentos conservados en el Archivo General de Indias de Sevilla*, 1a serie (Madrid, 1912, 6 v.) is supplemented periodically by the lists of *legajo* contents published by the *Boletín del Centro de Estudios Americanistas* (Seville, 1913–192–). The works by Bolton, Hill, Shepherd, Robertson, listed above, are issued under the general editorship of Dr. J. Franklin Jameson, Director of the Department of Historical Research of the Carnegie Institution.

LEGISLATIVE DOCUMENTS.—The published laws offer bountiful opportunity for study of the political institutions of Mexico. Aside from the general legislation contained in the *Recopilación de leyes de los reinos de las Indias*, which appeared first at Madrid in 1681 and went through numerous editions until

1841, there are many works directly Mexican. Among these are Vasco de Puga, *Provisiones, cédulas, instrucciones de su Magestad . . . para la administración y gobernación de esta Nueva España . . . desde el año 1525 hasta . . . 1563* (Mexico, 1563, reprinted Mexico 1878, 2 v.); J. F. Montemayor y Córdova de Cuenca, *Sumarios de las cédulas, órdenes, y provisiones reales, que se han despachado por su Magestad, para la Nueva España* (Mexico, 1678) is complemented by Eusebio Beleña, *Recopilación sumaria de todos los autos acordados de la real audiencia y sala del crimen de esta Nueva España, y providencias de su superior govierno* (Mexico, 1787). Among the epochal legislative documents of the colonial period stand the *Real ordenanza para el establecimiento e instrucción de intendentes de ejército y provincia en el reino de la Nueva España* (Madrid, 1786), the *Reales ordenanzas para la dirección, régimen y gobierno del importante Cuerpo de Minería de Nueva-España, y de su real tribunal general* (Madrid, 1783) and the *Reglamento y aranceles reales para el comercio libre de España e Indias . . .* (Madrid, 1778). Fabián Fonseca and Carlos de Urrutia, *Historia general de real hacienda, escrita por . . . orden del virrey, Conde de Revillagigedo* (Mexico, 1845–1853, 6 v.) contains much documentary legal material on economic subjects of the colonial epoch. It was epitomized by Joaquín Maniau y Torquemada as *Compendio de la historia de la real hacienda de Nueva España, escrita en el año de 1794*, and published in J. N. Rodríguez de San Miguel, *Pandectas hispano-megicanas*, II, 168–190; reprinted as separate, Mexico, 1914, with notes and commentaries by Alberto M. Carreño. The survivals of old Spanish laws in force in Mexico after independence give point to J. N. Rodríguez de San Miguel, *Pandectas hispano-megicanas, o sea código general comprensivo de las leyes generales, útiles y vivas de las Siete Partidas, Recopilación Novísima, la de Indias, autos y providencias conocidas por de Montemayor y Beleña, y cédulas posteriores hasta el año de 1820* (Mexico, 1852, 3 v.). B. J. Arrillaga, *Recopilación de leyes, decretos, bandos, reglamentos, circulares y providencias de los supremos poderes y otras autoridades de la República Mexicana* (Mexico, 1834–1866) contains much of the important colonial as well as the early republican legislation. J. M. Zamora y Coronado, *Biblioteca de legislación ultramarina* (Madrid, 1844–49, 6v.) and A. X. Pérez y López, *Teatro de la legislación universal de España e Indias . . .* (Madrid, 1791–98, 28 v.) serve as alphabetical guides to the important legislation. The *Recopilación de las leyes del gobierno español que rigen en la República, respectivos a los años de 1788 y siguientes . . .* (Mexico, 1851) contains some of the same material. The monumental work called *Legislación Mexicana*, begun in 1876 by M. Dublán and J. M. Lozano and continued until the current revolution, comprises over one hundred volumes, and contains all the significant legislation of the epoch covered. The *Colección de las leyes fundamentales que han regido en la República Mexicana, y de los planes que han tenido el mismo carácter, desde el año de 1821 hasta el de 1857* (Mexico, 1857) is of value in tracing constitutional development. Special periods are represented by the *Código de la Reforma* (the laws of 1856–61; Mexico, 1861) and the *Código de leyes, decretos y circulares expedidas . . . desde 1863 hasta . . . 1867* (Mexico, 1867) which present the body of legislation promulgated during the struggle maintained by Benito Juárez to preserve the national integrity. The Maximilian period is represented by the *Boletín de las leyes del Imperio Mexicano* (Mexico, 1863–1865) and the *Colección de leyes, decretos y reglamentos que interinamente forman el sistema político, administrativo y judicial del Imperio . . .* (Mexico, 1865, 8 v.). For the Díaz period the important legislation is contained in the various editions of the Constitution, noted below. For the Carranza period the Constitution of 1917, the *Codificación de los decretos* . . . (Mexico, 1915) and the *Recopilación de las circulares* . . . (Mexico, 1916) form the best legislative historical materials.

The *Memorias* of the Cabinet officers, and the *Boletines* of their secretariats are replete with useful legislative documents, but are too numerous for inclusion here.

CONSTITUTIONS.—Among the bodies of law which have affected the life of the country since the beginning of the wars of independence the following are the most important: *Constitución política de la monarquía española*, Cadiz, 1812; *Decreto constitucional para la libertad de la América Mexicana sancionada en Apatzingán a 22 de octubre de 1814.* (1814) 1815; *Acta constitutiva de la Federación Mexicana* n.p., n.d. [1824] 1882; *Constitución federal de los Estados Unidos Mexicanos, sancionada por el congreso general constituyente, el 4 de octubre de 1824.* (1824) Mexico, 1882; *Bases y leyes constitucionales de la República Mexicana decretadas por el congreso general de la nación en el año de 1836.* Mexico, 1837; *Bases orgánicas de la República Mexicana acordadas por la honorable junta legislativa establecida conforme á los decretos de 19 y 23 de diciembre de 1842 y sancionadas por el supremo gobierno provisional con arreglo a los mismos decretos el día 12 de junio del año de 1843.* Mexico, 1843; *Código fundamental de los Estados Unidos Mexicanos.* Mexico, 1847; *Estatuto orgánico provisional de la República Mexicana decretado en 15 de mayo de 1856.* Mexico, 1856; *Constitución federal de los Estados Unidos Mexicanos, sancionada y jurada por el congreso general constituyente, el día 5 de febrero de 1857.* Mexico, 1857 (Translation in McHugh, *Modern Mexico.* Reprinted with successive amendments, Mexico, 1868, 1882, 1884, 1891, 1905, 1913); *Constitución política de los Estados Unidos Mexicanos. Ed. oficial.* Mexico, 1917; there are many reprints and translations of this latest constitution. The most useful is that by H. N. Branch, published in parallel columns with the Constitution of 1857, in a Supplement to the *Annals* of the American Academy of Political and Social Sciences, Philadelphia, May, 1917.

The various *Planes* which supplemented these basic laws down to 1857 are in the *Colección de las leyes fundamentales* listed above. For those of La Noria, Tuxtépec, and Palo Blanco, see Bancroft, *History of Mexico*, VI, 379, 419–423, and citations. Madero's Plan de San Luis Potosí is translated in Carlo de Fornaro, *Carranza and Mexico*, 219–230; Carranza's Plan de Guadalupe appears in A. Breceda, *México revolucionario*, 395–399; and Obregón's Plan de Agua Prieta in *La Caída de Carranza* (Mexico, 1920) 195–202.

The history of constitution making may be studied in I. A. Montiel y Duarte, *Derecho público mexicano. Compilación que contiene importantes documentos relativos a [todas las constituciones desde el Plan de Iguala hasta la Constitución de 1857]* . . . (Mexico, 1871–1882, 4 v.); F. Buenrostro, *Historia del primer congreso constituyente que funcionó en el año de 1857* . . . (Mexico, 1874–83, 10 v.); F. Zarco, *Historia del congreso extraordinario constituyente de 1856 y 1857*, (Mexico, 1857, 2 v.); J. M. Gamboa, *Leyes constitucionales de México durante el siglo XIX. Discurso* . . . *con apéndice que contiene íntegras todas las constituciones* . . . (Mexico, 1901); F. F. Palavicini, *Un nuevo congreso constituyente; artículos publicados en la prensa de Vera Cruz* . . . (Vera Cruz, 1915); Emilio Rabasa, *La constitución y la dictadura* . . . (Mexico, 1912); reprinted with prologue by Rodolfo Reyes as *La organización política de México* (Madrid, 1917). See also Rabasa, *El juicio constitucional*, (Mexico,

1919.) For recent American studies of the present constitution, see Additional Readings for Chapter 27.

Important translations into English of the essential laws governing activities of foreigners in Mexico are: L. Hamilton, *Hamilton's Mexican Law; a Compilation of Mexican Legislation . . . and Mexican Mining Law . . .* (San Francisco, 1882); J. Kerr, *A Handbook of Mexican Law, being an Abridgement of the Principal Mexican Codes* (Chicago, 1909); F. Hall, *The Laws of Mexico; a Compilation and Treatise relating to Real Property, Mines, Water Rights, Personal Rights, Contracts and Inheritances* (San Francisco, 1885); J. Wheless, *Compendium of the Laws of Mexico officially authorized by the Mexican Government, containing the Federal Constitution with all Amendments, and a thorough Abridgement of all the Codes and Special Laws of Importance to Foreigners concerned with Business in the Republic . . .* (St. Louis, 1910); H. W. Halleck, *A Collection of Mining Laws of Spain and Mexico* (San Francisco, 1859); M. G. Reynolds, *Spanish and Mexican Land Laws . . .* (St. Louis, 1895); J. M. White, *A New Collection of Laws, Charters, and local Ordinances of the Governments of Great Britain, France, and Spain, relating to the Concessions of Land in their respective Colonies . . .* (Philadelphia, 1839. 2 v.). F. X. Gamboa, *Commentaries on the Mining Ordinances of Spain . . .* (London, 1830, 2 v.) may be studied in connection with *Documentos relacionados con la legislación petrolera mexicana* (Mexico, 1919), and C. Díaz Dufoo, *La cuestión del petróleo* (Mexico, 1921). The recent revolutionary laws are translated in *The Mexican Year Book* (Los Angeles, 1921).

GENERAL HISTORIES.—Among pertinent general histories of Spanish America are: A. de Herrera, *Historia general de los hechos de los castellanos . . .* (Madrid, 1601-15, 8 v. [in 4]); B. de Las Casas, *Historia de las Indias . . .* (Madrid, 1875–76, 5 v.); G. F. de Oviedo y Valdés, *Historia general y natural de las Indias* (Madrid, 1851- 55, 3 pts. in 4 v.); J. de Torquemada, *Primera [segunda, tercera] parte de los vientiún libros rituales y monarquía indiana . . .* (Seville, 1615, Madrid, 1723). The *Sociedad de Geografía y Estadística*, and the *Sociedad Científica "Antonio Alzate,"* have published several series of valuable *Anales.*

Among the more important general histories of Mexico outstanding items are: I. Álvarez, *Estudios sobre la historia general de México . . .* (Zacatecas, 1869–77, 6 v.); L. Alamán, *Disertaciones sobre la historia de la República Megicana hasta la independencia . . .* (Mexico, 1844–49, 3 v.); ——, *Historia de la conquista de Méjico . . .* (Mexico, 1844, 2 v., a translation of Prescott); ——, *Historia de Méjico desde los primeros movimientos que prepararon su independencia . . .* (Mexico, 1849–52, 5 v.); A. Cavo, *Los tres siglos de México* (Mexico, 1836–38, 2 v.); F. Cervantes de Salazar, *Crónica de la Nueva España . . .* (Madrid, 1914); J. Sierra, ed., *Mexico, its Social Evolution* (Barcelona, 1900–1904, 2 v. in 3); V. Riva Palacio, ed., *México á través de los siglos . . .* (Barcelona, 1888–89, 5 v.); M. Rivera Cambas, *Los gobernantes de México . . .* (Mexico, [1872]–73, 2 v.); ——, *Historia antigua y moderna de Jalapa . . .* (Mexico, 1869–71, 5 v.); N. de Zamacois, *Historia de Méjico desde sus tiemvos más remotos . . .* (Mexico, 1877–82, 18 v.). Aside from these there are many short compendiums, among them N. León, *Compendio de la historia Mexicana* (Mexico, 1902, 1919); L. Pérez Verdía, *Compendio de la historia Mexicana* (Mexico 1883, 1892, 1906, 1911); and C. Pereyra, *Historia del pueblo Mexicano* (Mexico, 1909, 2 v.). Partial lists of special works are contained in the following sections referring to the chapters of this book.

ADDITIONAL READINGS

Among the many works consulted by the present author, those which appear under the following names in the lists below are especially deserving of grateful acknowledgment for the use made of their scholarship and authority: Keane, Bancroft, Bandelier, Alexander, Joyce, Radin, Spinden, Waterman, Hackett, MacNutt, Moses, Bolton, Garrison, Haring, Barker, Holway, von Humboldt, Rives, Noll, J. H. Smith, W. S. Robertson, Burges, Bourne, Dunn, Ward. For interpretations of Mexican history by Mexicans, or by other writers in the Spanish language, full use has been made of the scholarly writings of Alamán, Sierra, Riva Palacio, Zamacois, León, Pérez Verdía, Herrera y Ogazón, G. Estrada, González Obregón, Navarro y Lamarca, G. García, Artíñano y Galdácano, Fonseca and Urrutia, Solórzano, J. Enciso, A. F. Villa, Romero de Terreros, Rivera, Torres Quintero, Bulnes, Rabasa, Rivera Cambas, Iglesias Calderón, Esquivel Obregón, Rodríguez del Castillo, Fernández del Castillo, Trejo Lerdo de Tejada, R. H. Valle, Calero, Gamio, and Ramón Prida.

Joint research with graduate students in Mexican history has yielded such pleasurable profit that recognition is due to those student collaborators who have contributed to the author's opportunity to prepare this volume. Among these are Sister Mary Austin, *Hipólito Villarroel and the Reforms of Charles III*, a résumé of the field covered by four students, in studies and translations of Villarroel's *Enfermedades Políticas:* Loretta Wilson, Helen Lamson, Josephine Cuneo, Josephine Kravchyk; Grace H. Arlett, *The Movement for Constitutional Government in Mexico before 1857;* Sibyl Blakeley, *American Investments in Mexican Railroads, Mines, and Petroleum;* Dorothy Bitner, *The American Navy in the War with Mexico;* Lois Dyer, *History of the Cabildo of Mexico City, 1524–1534;* Edna Fisher, *Medical Knowledge and Practice in New Spain during the Sixteenth Century;* Lillian E. Fisher, *The Spanish American Viceroyalty of the Sixteenth Century;* Audrey Hollenbeck, *Diplomacy of the Carranza Régime;* Constance Hughes, *Trade Gilds of New Spain;* Elizabeth Kravchyk, *A General Survey of the Mexican Land Problem;* Sister Margaret Mary, *The Viceregal Administration of Luis de Velasco II;* Sister Mary Redempta, *The Viceregal Administration of Álvaro Manrique de Zúñiga;* Marguerite C. Sinclair, *French Commercial Relations with the Spanish-American Colonies;* Bessie Roach, *The Revolutionary Land Program;* Vera Stump, *The Successors of Columbus to 1535, with Bibliographical Guide;* Jane E. Swanson, *Life and Work of Benito Juárez;* Rolland A. Vandegrift, *The Defense of the Spanish-American Colonies, 1513–1542;* Margaret S. Woodruff, *The Diplomatic Relations of the United States and Mexico, 1896–1911.*

CHAPTER I. THE LAND OF NEW SPAIN.—H. H. Bancroft, *History of Central Amercia*, II; ——, *Resources and Development of Mexico;* A. T. Bird, *The Land of Nayarit;* Bureau of American Republics, *Mexico, a General Sketch* (1911); M. Chevalier, *Mexico Ancient and Modern;* C. C. Colby, *Source Book for the Economic Geography of North America,* Chaps. XIII, XVI. *Encyclopædia Britannica,* 1910 ed., at the word "Mexico," and 1921 revision, same; T. J. Farnham, *Mexico, its Geography, its People, its Institutions;* A. Fortier and J. R. Ficklen, *Central America and Mexico;* A. von Humboldt, *Political Essay on the Kingdom of New Spain,* I; A. H. Keane, *Central and South America,* II; *The Mexican Yearbook* (New York, 1908–1914) issued by the Mexican Government, and for 1920-21, and after, edited by R. G. Cleland, Los Angeles;

H. I. Priestley, *José de Gálvez, Visitor-General of New Spain, 1761–1765;* T. A. Rickard, *Journeys of Observation;* M. Romero, *Mexico and the United States* (numerous other contributions by the same author); T. P. Terry, *Terry's Mexico; Handbook for Travelers* (Boston, 1909). V. L. Baril, *Le Mexique, résumé géographique . . . industriel, historique, et social;* F. Cervantes de Salazar, *Crónica de la Nueva España;* M. Chevalier, *Le Mexique ancien et modern,* I, Pt. 3; E. Domenech, *Histoire du Mexique,* I; M. Orozco y Berra, *Apuntes para la historia de la geografía en México;* E. Pierron, *Datos para la geografía del Imperio Mexicano;* M. Rivera Cambas, *Historia . . . de Jalapa,* I.

CHAPTER II. THE ANCIENT MEXICANS.—H. B. Alexander, [The Mythology of] *Latin America,* Vol. XI of *The Mythology of all Races,* L. H. Gray, ed. (Bibliography); H. H. Bancroft, *The Native Races of the Pacific States,* II; ——, *History of Mexico,* I; A. Bandelier, "Social Organization and Mode of Government of the Ancient Mexicans" (Peabody Museum, Twelfth *Annual Report,* II, No. 3); L. Biart, *The Aztecs, their History, Manners, and Customs;* Bureau of American Ethnology, *Bulletin No.* 28, *Mexican and Central American Antiquities, Calendar Systems, and History;* J. W. Butler, *Sketches of Mexico in Prehistoric, Primitive, and Colonial Times* (Bib.); F. X. Clavigero, *The History of Mexico* (C. Cullen, ed.); B. Díaz del Castillo, *The True History of the Conquest of New Spain;* T. F. Gordon, *The History of Ancient Mexico* (chiefly from Clavigero); A. V. D. Honeyman, *The Aztecs (Indian Races);* T. A. Joyce, *Mexican Archœology;* E. K. Kingsborough, *Antiquities of Mexico;* W. Lehmann, *A History of Mexican Art;* ——, *Methods and Results in Mexican Research;* Z. Nuttall, *The Fundamental Principles of Old and New World Civilizations;* E. J. Payne, *History of the New World called America,* I, Bk. II, II, Bk. II; P. Radin, *The Sources and Authenticity of the History of the Ancient Mexicans;* L. Spence, *The Civilization of Ancient Mexico;* ——, *The Myths of Mexico and Peru;* H. J. Spinden, *Ancient Civilizations of Mexico and Central America;* ——, *A Handbook of Maya Art;* F. Starr, *In Indian Mexico;* C. Thomas and J. R. Swanton, *Indian Languages of Mexico and Central America;* T. T. Waterman, *The Delineation of the Day-Signs in the Aztec Manuscripts;* ——, *Bandelier's Contribution to the Study of Ancient Mexican Social Organization;* J. Winsor, "The Progress of Opinion respecting the Origin and Antiquity of Man in America" (*Narrative and Critical History of America* II, 369–411).

J. de Acosta, *Historia natural y moral de las Indias* (also English translation, C. Markham); L. B. Boturini, *Idea de una nueva historia general de la América Septentrional;* E. C. Brasseur de Bourbourg, *Histoire des nations civilisées du Mexique et de l'Amérique-Centrale;* D. Durán, *Historia de las Indias de Nueva España;* W. Lehmann, "Ergebnisse und Aufgaben der mexikanistischen Forschung" (*Archiv für Anthropologie,* neue Folge, vi, 1907); M. Orozco y Berra, *Historia antigua de la conquista de México;* J. de Tobar, *Relación del origen de los Indios que habitan esta Nueva España* (In Códice Ramírez).

CHAPTER III. THE INVASION OF THE MAINLAND.—J. S. C. Abbott, *History of Hernando Cortez; The Anonymous Conqueror, Narrative of some things of New Spain . . .,* published by the Cortez Society, (*Documents and Narratives concerning the Discovery and Conquest of Latin America*); translation in García Icazbalceta, *Colección de documentos,* I, and in Ternaux-Compans, *Voyages,* Tome X.; Bancroft, *History of Mexico,* I; E. G. Bourne, *Spain in America;* J. H. Von Campe, *Cortez; or the Conquest of Mexico;* E. Channing, "The Companions of Columbus" (Winsor, *Narrative and Critical History,* I, Chap. III).

C. E. Chapman, *A History of California; the Spanish Period*, Chaps. V and VI; R. Fernández Guardia, *History of the Discovery and Conquest of Costa Rica;* John Fiske, *The Discovery of America*, I; G. Folsom, ed., *The Dispatches of Hernando Cortés;* C. W. Hackett, "Delimination of Political Jurisdictions in Spanish North America" (*Hispanic American Historical Review*, I, 1); A. Helps, *The Life of Cortés;* ——, *The Spanish Conquest in America*, I; J. J. Lockhart, ed., *The Memoirs of . . . Bernal Díaz;* F. A. McNutt, *The Life of Hernán Cortés;* ——, tr., *The Letters of Hernán Cortés;* R. B. Merriman, *The Rise of the Spanish Empire*, II, Chap. XVII; E. J. Payne, *History of the New World called America*, I; W. Prescott, *The Conquest of Mexico;* ——, "The Lustre of Ancient Mexico" (*National Geographic Magazine*, XXX, 1); William Robertson, *The History of America*, I; W. S. Robertson, *History of the Latin American Nations*, Chaps. II, III; Kate Stephens, *The Mastering of Mexico;* J. Winsor, "Cortés and His Companions" (*Narrative and Critical History*, II, Chap. VI.) L. Alamán, *Disertaciones sobre la historia de la República Mexicana;* M. Cuevas, ed., *Cartas y otros documentos de Hernán Cortés;* B. Dorantes de Carranza, *Sumaria relación;* F. Fernández del Castillo, *Doña Catalina Xuárez Marcayda;* P. de Gayangos, ed., *Cartas y relaciones de Hernán Cortés;* F. L. de Gómara, *Historia de las conquistas de Hernando Cortés;* C. Polavieja, *Hernán-Cortés (estudios de un carácter)*; A. de Saavedra Guzmán, *El peregrino indiano;* J. Suárez de Peralta, *Noticias históricas de la Nueva España; Un crimen de Hernán Cortés.*

Chapter IV. Establishment of the Viceroyalty.—E. Armstrong, *The Emperor Charles V;* Bancroft, *Mexico*, II, Chaps. I-XXVI; ——, *History of the North Mexican States and Texas*, I; F. Bandelier, *The Journey of Álvar Núñez Cabeza de Vaca;* H. E. Bolton, *Spanish Explorations in the Southwest, 1542-1706;* F. W. Hodge and T. H. Lewis, *Spanish Explorers in the Southern United States, 1528-1543;* W. Lowery, *Spanish Settlements within the present Boundaries of the United States, 1513-1561.* H. Stevens, and F. W. Lucas, *The New Laws of the Indies for the good Treatment and Preservation of the Indians;* B. Moses, *The Establishment of Spanish Rule in America;* ——, "The Early Political Organization of Mexico" (*Yale Review*, November, 1895, and February 1896); H. I. Priestley, "Spanish Colonial Municipalities" (*California Law Review*, September, 1919; reprinted in Spanish, Genaro Estrada, ed., Mexico, 1921, and in English, Louisiana Historical Society, *Quarterly*, April 1922 [1923]); G. P. Winship, *The Coronado Expedition 1540-1542;* I. Wright, *The Early History of Cuba.*

El Liceo Mexicano, "Galeria de los vireyes de Mexico," contains biographies of Mendoza, Luis de Velasco, Montesclaros, and numerous later viceroys; *Cartas de Indias;* Castañeda de Nájera, *Relation du voyage de Cibola*, in Ternaux-Compans, *Voyages . . .* serie I, Tom. IX; Cervantes de Salazar, *Crónica de la Nueva España;* A. Herrera. *Historia general*, Decadas IV-VII; B. de Las Casas, *Historia de las Indias;* Mota Padilla, *Historia de la conquista de la . . . Nueva Galicia;* Motolinía, *Historia de los indios de Nueva España;* Oviedo y Valdés, *Historia general;* V. Riva Palacio, ed., *México á través de los siglos*, Tom. II; A. Rivera, *Principios críticos sobre el vireinato de la Nueva España;* B. Smith, ed., *Colección de varios documentos para la historia de la Florida;* J. A. Tello, *Libro segundo de la crónica miscelanea . . . de Xalisco;* Torquemada, *Primera [segunda, tercera] parte de los veintiún libros rituales.*

Chapter V. The Age of Philip II in New Spain.—H. H. Bancroft, *History of Mexico*, II, Chaps. XXVII-XXXIV; E. G. Bourne, *Spain in*

America, Chap. XV; C. E. Chapman, *A History of Spain*, Chap. XXIII; J. S. Corbett, *Drake and the Tudor Navy;* ——, *Sir Francis Drake;* W. Lowery, *Spanish Settlements*, II; E. J. Payne, *Elizabethan Seamen;* W. H. Prescott, *History of the Reign of Philip II;* I. B. Richman, *California under Spain and Mexico;* ——, *The Spanish Conquerors;* J. A. Robertson, "Legaspi and Philippine Island Colonization" (American Historical Association *Report*, 1907); J. G. Shea, "Ancient Florida" (Winsor, *Narrative and Critical History*, II); J. Sparks, *Life of Ribault*.

Alsedo y Herrera, *Piraterías y agresiones de los ingleses;* Barcia, *Ensayo cronológico para la historia general de la Florida;* A. Cavo, *Los tres siglos de México;* L. González Obregón, *Los precursores de la independencia;* Herrera, *Decada* VIII, *lib.* VII, *cap.* XIV *et seq;* C. Navarro y Lamarca, *Compendio de la historia general de América*, II, 245-285 (Bib.); M. Orozco y Berra, *Noticia histórica de la conjuración del marqués del Valle;* E. Ruidíaz y Caravia, *La Florida; Pedro Menéndez de Avilés;* J. Suárez de Peralta, *Noticias históricas de la Nueva España;* N. de Zamacois, *Historia de Méjico.*

CHAPTER VI. SIXTEENTH CENTURY RELIGION.—H. H. Bancroft, *History of Mexico*, II, Chaps. XV, XIX, XXVI, XXXI, XXXII; H. E. Bolton, "The Mission as a Frontier Institution in the Spanish American Colonies" (*American Historical Review*, Vol. XXIII, No. 2); E. G. Bourne, *Spain in America*, Chap. XX; Mrs. J. W. Butler, *Historic Churches in Mexico, with some of their Legends;* J. Klein, "The Church in Spanish American History" (*Catholic Historical Review*, III, No. 3, October, 1917); H. C. Lea, *The Inquisition in the Spanish Dependencies*, Chap. VI; J. G. Shea, *History of the Catholic Missions among the Indian Tribes of the United States*, Chaps. I–IV; J. Sierra, ed., *Mexico, its Social Evolution*, Vol. I, Book II, Part II; E. Vacandard, *The Inquisition.*

F. J. Alegre, *Historia de la Compañía de Jesús en Nueva-España;* J. Arlegui, *Chronica de la provincia de . . . Zacatecas,* J. D. Arricivita, *Crónica seráfica . . . del colegio . . . de la Santa Cruz de Querétaro;* P. Beaumont, *Crónica de la provincia de . . . Michoacán;* A. Dávila Padilla, *Historia de la . . . provincia de Santiago de México;* J. Díez de la Calle, *Memorial y noticias sacras;* J. D. Espinosa, *Crónica apostólica . . . de todos los colegios de Propaganda Fide;* A. Fernández, *Historia eclesiástica de nuestros tiempos;* F. Frejes, *Historia breve de la conquista de los estados independientes del Imperio Mexicano;* G. García, ed., *La Inquisición de México;* ——, *El clero de México;* González Dávila, *Teatro eclesiástico;* G. Mendieta, *Historia eclesiástica indiana;* Moreno, *Fragmentos de la vida . . . de Quiroga;* J. de Ortega, *Historia del Nayarit (Apostólicos afanes de la Compañía de Jesús);* M. Ramírez Aparicio, *Los conventos suprimidos en México;* Remesal, *Historia de . . . Chiapas; A.* de Vetancurt, *Crónica de la provincia del Santo Evangelio;* ——, *Menología franciscano.*

CHAPTER VII. SOCIAL AND POLITICAL ORGANIZATION.—Bancroft, *History of Mexico*, III, Chap. XXXIV; ——, *History of Mexico* (1914), Chap. XXVIII; E. G. Bourne, *Spain in America*, Chaps. XV–XX; S. Hale, *The Story of Mexico*, Chap. XXII; W. Lowery, *The Spanish Settlements*, I, Chaps. II–III, II, Chap. I; B. Moses, *The Establishment of Spanish Rule in America*, Chaps. II–IV; H. I. Priestley, *José de Gálvez*, Chap. II; W. S. Robertson, *History of the Latin American Nations*, Chap. IV; Wm. Robertson, *History of America*, III, Book VIII; Wm. Russel, *History of America*, I, Book II, Chaps. I–II; D. E. Smith, *The Viceroy of New Spain.*

M. Chevalier, *Le Mexique ancien et modern*, Partie troisième; A. Cravioto *El alma nueva de las cosas viejas;* G. Estrada, *Visionario de la Nueva España,*

L. González Obregón, *México viejo;* ——, *Las calles de México; Instrucciones que los virreyes de la Nueva España dejaron;* J. M. Marroqui, *La ciudad de México.*

CHAPTER VIII. NEW SPAIN IN THE SEVENTEENTH CENTURY.—Bancroft, *History of Arizona and New Mexico,* Chaps. VI–X; ——, *History of the North Mexican States,* I, Chaps. I–XIV; H. E. Bolton, *Kino's Historical Memoir of Pimería Alta;* ——, *The Spanish Borderlands;* R. C. Clark, *The Beginnings of Texas, 1684–1718;* W. W. H. Davis, *The Spanish Conquest of New Mexico;* J. C. Dunlop, *Memoirs of Spain during the Reigns of Philip IV and Charles II, from 1621 to 1700;* W. E. Dunn, *Spanish and French Rivalry in the Gulf Region of the United States, 1678–1702;* G. P. Garrison, *Texas, a Contest of Civilizations,* Chaps. I–VI; C. W. Hackett, "The Revolt of the Pueblo Indians of New Mexico in 1680" (Texas State Historical Association *Quarterly,* XV); ——, "The Retreat of the Spaniards from New Mexico in 1680" (*Idem;* XVI); C. H. Haring, *The Buccaneers in the West Indies in the XVII Century;* ——, *Trade and Navigation between Spain and the Indies in the Time of the Hapsburgs;* M. A. S. Hume, *The Court of Philip IV; Spain in Decadence;* A. P. Newton, *The Colonizing Activities of the English Puritans, the last Phase of the Elizabethan Struggle with Spain.* M. Venegas, *A Natural and Civil History of California,* I.

F. J. Alegre, *Historia de la Compañía de Jesús;* Antúnez y Acevedo, *Memorias históricas sobre la legislación y gobierno del comercio de los españoles;* G. Artíñano y Galdácano, *Historia del comercio con las Indias durante el dominio de los Austrias;* A. Cavo, *Los tres siglos de México;* F. X. Clavigero, *Historia de la antigua ó baja California; Diccionario mexicano de geografía y estadística;* Fonseca and Urrutia, *Historia general de Real Hacienda;* G. García, *Juan de Palafox y Mendoza;* J. Gutiérrez de Rubalcava, *Tratado histórico político y legal del comercio de las Indias Occidentales;* A. de León, *Títulos y confirmaciones de tierras; El Liceo Mexicano,* "Galeria de los virreyes," I, II; M. A. de la Mota Padilla, *Historia de la conquista de la Provincia de ia Nueva Galicia;* M. de Navarrete, "Introducción" to *Relación del viage hecho por las goletas Sútil y Mexicana . . .* (H. I. Priestley, tr., MS); M. Orozco y Berra, *Apuntes para la historia de la geografía en México;* A. Pérez de Ribas, *Historia de los triumphos de nuestra santa fee;* V. Riva Palacio, ed., *México á través de los siglos,* Tom. II, 549–750; M. Rivera Cambas, *Los gobernantes de México,* I; J. de Solórzano Pereira, *Política indiana;* F. Sosa, *El episcopado mexicano.*

CHAPTER IX. THE REFINEMENTS OF COLONIAL LIFE.—Bancroft, *Essays and Miscellany,* Chap. XVI; ——, *History of Mexico,* II, Chap. XXIV; ——, *Native Races,* II, Chaps. VIII, XVII, XVIII; S. Baxter, *Spanish Colonial Architecture in Mexico;* R. Campbell, *Campbell's new revised Complete Guide;* A. Coester, *The Literary History of Spanish America;* Goldberg, *Studies in Spanish American Literature;* Mary G. Holway, *Art of the Old World in New Spain and the Mission Days of Alta California;* T. A. Janvier, *The Mexican Guide;* H. I. Priestley, "The Old University of Mexico" (*University of California Chronicle,* XXI, No. 4); J. Sierra, ed., *Mexico, its Social Evolution,* Vol. I, Book II, Viceregal Period, Vol. II, Pts. V, VI, VII.

Bernardo Couto, *Diálogo sobre la historia de la pintura en México;* A. García Cubas, *The Republic of Mexico* [*songs and dances*]; A. Herrera y Ogazón, *El arte musical en México;* F. E. Mariscal, *La patria y la arquitectura nacional;* N. Mariscal, *El arte en México; Monografías mexicanas de arte* (Jorge Enciso, ed.): 1. *Catedral y Sagrario,* 2. *Residencias coloniales de México,* 3. *Iglesias y con-*

ventos de la ciudad de México; F. Pimentel, *Historia crítica de la literatura . . . en México;* V. G. Quesada, *La vida intelectual en la América española durante los siglos XVI, XVII, y XVIII;* M. G. Revilla, *El arte en México en la época antigua y durante el gobierno virreinal;* M. Romero de Terreros, *Arte colonial;* F. Sosa, *Las estatuas de la Reforma, Noticias biográficas;* —— L. G. Urbina, *La vida literaria de México;* A. F. Villa, *Breves apuntes sobre la antigua escuela de pintura en México.*

CHAPTER X. THE EIGHTEENTH CENTURY.—J. Addison, *Charles III of Spain;* F. W. Blackmar, *Spanish Institutions of the Southwest;* H. E. Bolton, *Texas in the Middle Eighteenth Century;* E. Burke, *An Account of the European Settlements in America;* C. E. Chapman, *The Founding of Spanish California,* Chaps. IV, IX, X; Wm. Coxe, *Memoirs of the Kings of Spain of the House of Bourbon;* A. Humboldt, *Political Essay on the Kingdom of New Spain;* W. R. Manning, *The Nootka Sound Controversy* (American Historical Association Annual *Report* (1904); J. Pinkerton, *Modern Geography;* H. I. Priestley, *José de Gálvez,* Chaps. VII–X; W. R. Shepherd, *Latin America;* D. E. Smith, *The Viceroy of New Spain.*

J. Álvarez, *Estudios sobre la historia general de México,* III; Marqués de Croix, *Corréspondance;* José de Gálvez, *Informe general;* J. V. Revillagigedo, *Instrucción reservada que dió a su sucesor;* V. Riva Palacio, *México á través de los siglos,* II, Libro III; A. Rivera, *Principios críticos;* G. Torres Quintero, *México hacia el fin del virreinato español;* H. Villarroel, *México por dentro y fuera.*

CHAPTER XI. PRECURSORS OF REVOLUTION.—Bancroft, *History of Mexico,* IV, Chaps. I, II; ——, *History of Mexico* (1914), Chaps. XXIX, XXX; Challice, *The Secret History of the Court of Spain during the last Century;* Fortier and Ficklen, *Central America and Mexico,* Chap. VII; A. Humboldt, *Political Essay on the Kingdom of New Spain;* A. H. Noll, *From Empire to Republic,* Chap. I; C. Oman, *A History of the Peninsular War,* Vol. I, Sec. I; W. S. Robertson, *Francisco de Miranda and the Revolutionizing of Spanish America;* W. R. Shepherd, *The Hispanic Nations of the New World* (Chronicles of America, Vol. L, Chap. II); Wm. Walton, *Present State of the Spanish Colonies;* G. F. White, *A Century of Spain and Portugal (1788–1898).*

L. Alamán, *Historia de Méjico,* I; J. L. Cancelada, *Conducta del . . . virrey Iturrigaray;* G. García, *El plan de independencia de la Nueva España en 1808;* J. Servando Teresa de Mier, *Historia de la revolución de Nueva España,* I; J. M. L. Mora, *Méjico y sus revoluciones,* III; Castillo Negrete, *México en el siglo XIX,* I; N. de Zamacois, *Historia de Méjico,* VI; L. de Zavala, *Ensayo histórico de las revoluciones de Méjico,* I.

CHAPTER XII. "EL GRITO DE DOLORES."—G. Abbott, *Mexico and the United States,* Part II; Bancroft, *History of Mexico,* IV, Chaps. V–XI; ——, *History of Mexico* (1914), Chaps XXXI–XXXV; F. C. Baylor, "Hidalgo, the Washington of Mexico" (*New Princeton Magazine,* V.); B. Mayer, *Mexico, Aztec, Spanish, and Republican,* I, Book III, Chap. I; A. H. Noll and McMahon, *The Life and Times of Miguel Hidalgo y Costilla;* Noll, *From Empire to Republic,* Chap. II; J. Poinsett, *Notes on Mexico;* W. S. Robertson, *Rise of the Spanish-American Republics,* Chap. III; F. Robinson, *Mexico and her Military Chieftains;* H. G. Ward, *Mexico in 1827,* I, Bk. II; P. Young, *History of Mexico,* Book II.

C. M. Bustamante, *Cuadro histórico de la revolución mexicana;* J. M. Fuentes, *Apuntes y documentos sobre las familias Hidalgo y Costilla;* C. Hernández, *Mujeres célebres de México;* Hernández y Dávalos, *Colección de documentos;*

J. M. de Licéaga, *Adiciones y rectificaciones á la historia de México;* J. M. L. Mora, *Méjico y sus revoluciones,* III; Castillo Negrete, *México en el siglo XIX,* II; M. Rivera, *Historia antigua y moderna de Jalapa,* I; N. de Zamacois, *Historia de Méjico,* Tomo VI; L. de Zavala, *Ensayo histórico de las revoluciones de Méjico* . . . I; A. Zerecero, *Memoria para la historia de las revoluciones en México.*

CHAPTER XIII. THE EPOCH OF MORELOS.—Bancroft, *History of Mexico,* IV, Chaps. XII–XXIX; ——, *North Mexican States and Texas,* I; —— *History of Mexico* (1914), Chaps. XXXVI–XXXVIII; I. J. Cox, "Monroe and the Early Mexican Revolutionary Agents" (American Historical Association *Report,* 1911, Vol. I); H. C. Lea, "Hidalgo y Costilla and Morelos" (*American Historical Review,* IV); A. H. Noll, *From Empire to Republic,* Chap. III; G. L. Rives, *The United States and Mexico 1821–1848,* I; W. D. Robinson, *Memoirs of the Mexican Revolution;* W. S. Robertson, *Rise of the Spanish American Republics,* Chap. III; H. G. Ward, *Mexico in 1827,* I.

F. de P. Arrangoiz, *Méjico desde 1808 hasta 1867;* M. Arroniz, *Biografía del . . . iniciador de la independencia;* F. Bulnes, *La guerra de independencia, Hidalgo-Iturbide;* C. M. Bustamante, *Campañas del General D. Félix María Calleja;* P. del Mendíbil, *Resumen histórico de la revolución de los Estados Unidos Mejicanos;* A. Teja Zabre, *Vida de Morelos;* M. Torrente, *Historia de la revolución hispano-americana.*

CHAPTER XIV. ITURBIDE AND THE FIRST EMPIRE.—Bancroft, *History of Mexico* (1914), Chaps. XXXIX–XLI; ——, *History of Mexico,* IV, Chaps. XXVI–XXXIII; C. De Beneski, *A Narrative of the Last Moments of the Life of Iturbide;* J. B. Henderson, *American Diplomatic Questions,* Chap. IV; A. H. Noll, *From Empire to Republic,* Chaps. IV, V; Noll and McMahon, *Life and Times of Hidalgo;* W. S. Robertson, *Rise of the Spanish American Republics,* Chap. IV; P. Young, *History of Mexico.*

F. Bulnes, *La guerra de independencia, Hidalgo-Iturbide;* A. Iturbide, *Breve diseño crítico de la emancipación y libertad de la nación mexicana;* C. Navarro y Rodrigo, *Iturbide;* J. T. Parisot, tr., *Mémoires autographes de . . . Iturbide;* J. J. Pesado, *El libertador de México;* R. H. Valle, *Como era Iturbide.*

CHAPTER XV. MILITARY ANARCHY.—Bancroft, *History of Mexico,* V. Chaps. I–VI; ——, *History of Mexico* (1914), XLII–XLIV; M. Beaufoy, *Mexican Illustrations, Founded upon Facts;* F. E. Calderón de la Barca, *Life in Mexico;* W. R. Manning, "British Influence in Mexico, 1822–1826" (*The Pacific Ocean in History,* 1917); ——, *Early Diplomatic Relations Between the United States and Mexico;* A. H. Noll, *From Empire to Republic,* Chap. VI; J. Poinsett, *Notes on Mexico;* G. L. Rives, *Mexico and the United States,* I; F. Robinson, *Mexico and her Military Chieftains;* J. H. Smith, *The War with Mexico,* Chaps. I–II; H. G. Ward, *Mexico in 1827;* P. Young, *History of Mexico.*

J. M. Bocanegra, *Memorias para la historia de México independiente,* I; F. Bulnes, *Las grandes mentiras de nuestra historia;* F. Iglesias Calderón, *Tres campañas nacionales; Muerte política de la República Mexicana;* G. Prieto, *Memorias de mis tiempos, 1828–1840* (Tomo I; tomo II includes 1840–1853).

CHAPTER XVI. THE SECESSION OF TEXAS.—E. D. Adams, "English Interests in the Annexation of California" (*American Historical Review,* XIV); ——, *British Interests and Activities in Texas, 1838–1846;* E. C. Barker, "The Annexation of Texas" (*American Historical Review,* XVII); ——, "California as a Cause of the Mexican War" (*Texas Historical Review,* II);

BIBLIOGRAPHY 471

——, "President Jackson and the Texas Revolution" (*American Historical Review*, XII); ——, "The United States and Mexico" (*Mississippi Valley Historical Review*, I, 3); ——, "The San Jacinto Campaign" (Texas State Historical Association *Quarterly*, IV); C. R. Fish, *American Diplomacy;* G. P. Garrison, "The First Stage in the Movement for the Annexation of Texas" (*American Historical Review*, X); ——, *Texas, a Contest of Civilizations;* ——, *Westward Extension, 1841-1850;* W. F. Johnson, *America's Foreign Relations;* J. H. Latané, *The Diplomatic Relations of the United States and Spanish America;* G. L. Rives, *The United States and Mexico, 1821-1848*, I; J. H. Smith, *The Annexation of Texas.*

V. Filísola, *Memorias para la historia de la guerra de Tejas;* R. Martínez Caro, *Verdadera idea de la primera campaña de Tejas;* C. Pereyra, *Tejas, la primera desmembración de la República Mexicana;* A. de L. Santa Anna, *Manifiesto de sus operaciones en la campaña de Tejas;* J. M. Tornel, *Tejas y los Estados Unidos.*

CHAPTER XVII. THE APOGEE OF CENTRALISM.—Bancroft, *History of Mexico*, V, Chaps. XI, XII, XIII; Calderón de la Barca, *Life in Mexico;* C. J. Folsom, *Mexico in 1842;* G. P. Garrison, *Westward Extension, 1841-1850,* Chaps. XIII-XV; L. S. Hasbrouck, *Mexico from Cortés to Carranza,* Chaps. XVI, XVII; B. Mayer, *Mexico as it was and as it is;* ——, *Mexico, Aztec, Spanish, and Republican;* A. H. Noll, *From Empire to Republic,* Chap. VII; F. Robinson, *Mexico and her Military Chieftains;* J. H. Smith, *The War with Mexico*, I, Chaps. II-VI; W. Thompson, *Recollections of Mexico;* E. B. Tylor, *Anahuac; or Mexico and the Mexicans;* P. Young, *History of Mexico.*

C. L. de Bazancourt, *Le Mexique contemporain;* C. M. Bustamante, *Apuntes para la historia del gobierno del General Santa Anna;* E. Domenech, *Histoire du Mexique*, II; M. Rivera, *Historia . . . de Jalapa,* III; M. Rivera Cambas, *Los gobernantes de México*, II; V. Salado Álvarez, *De Santa Anna a la Reforma.*

CHAPTER XVIII. WAR WITH THE UNITED STATES.—Bancroft, *History of California*, IV; F. Bishop, *Our First War with Mexico;* W. E. Conelley, ed., *Doniphan's Expedition;* P. S. G. Cooke, *The Conquest of New Mexico and California;* J. E. Cowan, *Condensed History of the Mexican War;* J. Klein, "The Treaty of Guadalupe" (University of California *Chronicle*, VII); C. C. Kohl, "Claims as a Cause of the Mexican War" (New York University *Series of Graduate School Studies*); C. H. Owen, *The Justice of the Mexican War;* G. L. Rives, "Mexican Diplomacy on the Eve of the War with the United States" (*American Historical Review*, XVIII, 275); ——, *The United States and Mexico, 1821-1848;* J. S. Reeves, "The Treaty of Guadalupe Hidalgo" (*American Historical Review*, X);——, *American Diplomacy under Tyler and Polk;* R. S. Semmes, *Service Afloat and Ashore;* E. K. Smith, *To Mexico with Scott;* J. H. Smith, *The War with Mexico.*

R. Alcáraz, *Apuntes para la historia de la guerra entre México y los Estados Unidos;* C. M. Bustamante, *El nuevo Bernal Díaz del Castillo;* G. García, ed., *Las guerras de México con Tejas y los Estados Unidos;* E. Castillo Negrete, *Invasión de los Norte-Americanos en México;* I. M. Mota, *Reflecciones sobre la guerra;* J. F. Ramírez, *México durante su guerra con los Estados Unidos;* J. M. Roa Bárcena, *Recuerdo de la invasión Norte-Americana;* J. Suárez y Navarro, *Historia de México y del General . . . Santa Anna.*

CHAPTER XIX. THE REVOLUTION OF AYUTLA.—G. D. Abbott, *Mexico and the United States* (contains biography of Juárez); Bancroft, *History of Mexico,*

I, (1914) Chap. XLVII; U. R. Burk, *Life of Juárez;* S. Hale, *The Story of Mexico;* A. H. Noll, *From Empire to Republic;* Fortier and Ficklen, *Central America and Mexico.*

Arrangoiz, *Historia de Méjico,* II; M. Aznar, *Observaciones histórico-políticas sobre Juárez y su época;* F. Bulnes, *Juárez y las revoluciones de Ayutla;* I. Comonfort, *Política del General Comonfort;* M. de Fossey, *Le Mexique;* G. García, *Los gobiernos de Álvarez y Comonfort;* ——, *La revolución de ayutla según el archivo del General Doblado;* L. Gonzaga Cuevas, *El porvenir de México;* J. M. Lafragua, *Historia de la revolución de México contra la dictadura del General Santa Anna;* Rivera, *Historia . . . de Jalapa,* IV; M. Villa-Amor, *Biografía del General Santa Anna;* N. Zamacois, *Historia de Méjico,* XIV.

CHAPTER XX. THE WAR OF THE REFORM.—Bancroft, *History of Mexico,* V; U. R. Burke, *A Life of Juárez;* W. Butler, *Mexico in Transition;* J. W. Foster, "The Contest for the Laws of Reform in Mexico" (*American Historical Review,* XVI); T. B. Gregory, *Our Mexican Conflicts;* A. H. Noll, *From Empire to Republic;* A. Raganel, *What the Catholic Church has done to Mexico, . . . with a Reply by Cardinal Farley;*

J. J. Álvarez, *Parte general . . . sobre la campaña de Puebla;* G. Baz, *Vida de Benito Juárez;* F. Bulnes, *El Verdadero Juárez;* M. Galindo y Galindo, *La gran decada nacional;* G. García, *Juárez; refutación . . . a Bulnes;* F. Iglesias Calderón, *Las supuestas traiciones de Juárez;* A. Molina Enríquez, *La reforma y Juárez;* A. de la Portilla, *Méjico en 1856 y 1857;* M. Ocampo, *Obras completas;* E. Rabasa, *La organización política de México;* V. Riva Palacio, ed., *México á través de los siglos,* V; J. Sierra, *Benito Juárez, su obra y su tiempo;* M. Valdés, *Memorias de la Guerra de Reforma;* F. Zarco, *Historia del Congreso Constituyente;* R. Zayas Enríquez, *Benito Juárez, su vida, su obra;* A. Zerecero, "Biografía de Benito Juárez" (In *Memorias para la historia de las revoluciones en México*).

CHAPTER XXI. FOREIGN INTERVENTION; THE SECOND EMPIRE.—M. Alvensleben, *With Maximilian in Mexico;* A. W. Barber, *The Benevolent Raid of General Lew Wallace;* J. M. Callahan, *The Evolution of Seward's Mexican Policy;* W. H. Chynoweth, *The Fall of Maximilian;* G. Cluseret, *Mexico and the Solidarity of Nations;* J. F. Elton, *With the French in Mexico;* J. W. Foster, "Maximilian and his Mexican Empire" (Columbia Historical Society *Records,* XIV); F. Hall, *The Invasion of Mexico by the French;* P. Kollonitz, *The Court of Mexico;* P. F. Martin, *Maximilian in Mexico;* G. P. Messervy, *The Quickstep of an Emperor;* J. Musser, *The Establishment of Maximilian's Empire in Mexico;* J. M. Taylor, *Maximilian and Carlota.*

S. Basch, *Recuerdos de México;* Ch. Bauzet, *La intervención francesa en México;* Ch. Blanchot, *Mémoires;* J. R. Castro, *La cuestión mexicana;* P. L. Détroyat, *L'intervention française au Mexique;* F. Iglesias Calderón, *El egoismo norte-americano durante la intervención francesa;* E. Kératry, *La créance Jecker;* E. Lefévre, *Le Mexique et l'intervention Européenne;* C. Pereyra, *Juárez discutido como dictador y estadista;* V. Salado Álvarez, *La intervención y el imperio;* E. Schmit von Tavera, *Geschichte der Regierung des Kaisers Maximilien I.*

CHAPTER XXII.—THE RECONSTRUCTION PERIOD.—Bancroft, *Biography of Porfirio Díaz;* Burke, *A Life of Juárez;* A. Lee, *The Reformation in Mexico;* Salm-Salm, *Diary.*

R. García Granados, *Historia de México desde la restauración de la República en 1867 hasta la caída de Porfirio Díaz;* Riva Palacio, *Historia de la adminis-*

tración de Lerdo de Tejada; P. Tovar, *Historia parlamentaria;* E. Velasco, *Planes de Tuxtépec y Palo Blanco.*
CHAPTER XXIII. THE RISE OF PORFIRIO DÍAZ.—H. Baerlein, *Mexico, the Land of Unrest;* E. I. Bell, *The Political Shame of Mexico;* F. Bulnes, *The Whole Truth about Mexico;* J. Creelman, *Díaz, Master of Mexico;* C. M. Flandrau, *Viva México;* C. de Fornaro, *Díaz, Czar of Mexico . . .;* D. Hannay, *Díaz;* C. Lummis, *The Awakening of a Nation;* W. Thompson, *The People of Mexico;* R. W. Smith, *Benighted Mexico;* J. K. Turner, *Barbarous Mexico;* E. B. Tweedie, *Porfirio Díaz;* C. Whitney, *What's the Matter with Mexico?* F. Bulnes, *El verdadero Díaz y la revolución;* C. B. Ceballos, *Aurora y ocaso;* F. Colina, *Madero y el General Díaz;* J. H. Cornyn, *Díaz y México;* C. Díaz Dufoo, *Limantour;* F. Hernández, *Un pueblo, un siglo y un hombre;* J. López-Portillo, *Elevación y caída de Porfirio Díaz;* R. Rodríguez, *Historia auténtica de la administración del Sr. Gral. Porfirio Díaz;* J. Rodríguez Castillo, *Historia de la revolución social de México;* R. Zayas Enríquez, *Porfirio Díaz.*
CHAPTER XXIV. FRANCISCO I. MADERO.—Bancroft, *History of Mexico* (1914), Chap. LXII; Bell, *The Political Shame of Mexico;* A. B. Case, *Thirty Years with the Mexicans;* T. H. Russell, *Mexico in Peace and War,* Chaps. I-IV; Smith, *Benighted Mexico,* Chaps. X, XI, XII; E. D. Trowbridge, *Mexico Today and Tomorrow;* E. B. Tweedie, *Mexico from Díaz to the Kaiser;* G. B. Winton, *Mexico Today;* Zayas Enríquez, *The Case of Mexico.*
J. Fernández Rojas, *De Porfirio Díaz á Victoriano Huerta;* F. Hernández, *Más allá del desastre;* F. I. Madero, *La sucesión presidencial en 1910;* A. Manero, *El antiguo régimen y la revolución;* A. Molina Enríquez, *Los grandes problemas nacionales;* G. Ponce de León, *El interinato presidencial de 1911* (de la Barra); R. Prida, *De la dictadura á la anarquía;* C. Trejo Lerdo de Tejada, *La revolución y el nacionalismo.*
CHAPTER XXV. VICTORIANO HUERTA.—F. Bulnes, *The Whole Truth about Mexico;* M. Calero, *The Mexican Policy of President Woodrow Wilson;* E. L. O'Shaughnessy, *A Diplomat's Wife in Mexico;* ——, *Intimate Pages of Mexican History;* ——, *Diplomatic Days;* R. Zayas Enríquez, *The Case of Mexico.*
De cómo vino Huerta y cómo se fué; M. Doblado, *El Presidente Huerta;* G. N. Espinosa, *La decena roja . . .;* M. L. Guzmán, *A orillas del Hudson;* R. Guzmán, *El intervencionismo de Mr. Wilson en México;* L. Lara Pardo, *De Porfirio Díaz a Francisco Madero.*
CHAPTERS XXVI and XXVII. CARRANZA'S PROGRAM OF REFORM.—C. W. Ackerman, *Mexico's Dilemma;* G. H. Blakeslee, ed., *Mexico and the Caribbean* (Clarke University Addresses); V. Blasco Ibañez, *Mexico in Revolution;* W. H. Burges, *A Hot-house Constitution;* G. A. Chamberlain, *Is Mexico Worth Saving?;* L. J. De Bekker, *The Plot against Mexico;* E. J. Dillon, *Mexico on the Verge;* C. Fornaro, *Carranza and Mexico;* T. E. Gibbon, *Mexico under Carranza;* C. L. Jones, *Mexico and its Reconstruction;* D. Lawrence, *The Truth about Mexico;* Mexican Bureau of Information, *"Red Papers" of Mexico; an Exposé of the great Científico Conspiracy to eliminate . . . Carranza; The Mexican Oil Controversy as told in Diplomatic Correspondence between the United States and Mexico;* J. Vera Estañol, *Carranza and his Bolshevik Régime.*
M. Aguirre Berlanga, *Génesis legal de la revolución constitucionalista;* R. Alducín, *La revolución constitucionalista;* S. Alvarado, *La Reconstrucción de México;* V. Blasco Ibañez, *El militarismo mejicano;* A. Breceda, *México re-*

volucionario; L. Cabrera, *La herencia de Carranza;* M. Calero, *Un decenio de política mexicana;* M. Gamio, *Forjando patria;* E. González-Blanco, *Carranza y la revolución de México;* F. González Roa, *El aspecto agrario de la revolución mexicana;* F. F. Palavicini, ed., *El primer jefe; Tres intelectuales hablan sobre México; El movimiento educativo en Mexico;* L. Vasconcelos, ed., *La caída de Carranza.*

INDEX

INDEX

Oropesa, Conde de, 54
Orozco, Pascual, 398, 399, 401, 405, 406, 413, 420, 421
Orozco, Pascual, Jr., 407
Ortega, General, see González Ortega, Jesús
Ortiz, Fray Tomás, 100
Ortiz, Josefa María, 208, 209
Ortiz de Letona, Pascasio, 215
Ortiz Rubio, General Pascual, 452
Osorio, Diego, archbishop; 24th viceroy, 1664, 148
Osorno, José Francisco, 240
Otero, Mariano, 298
Otomis, 17, 68, 91
Otumba Valley, 42
Oviedo, Manuel, 414

Pacheco, Alonzo, 79
Pacheco, General Carlos, 380, 381
Pacheco Osorio, Rodrigo, marquis of Cerralvo, 15th viceroy, 1624–1635, 147
Pachuca, 142
Pacific Coast, 3, 7, 87, 92, 93, 137, 214, 332; Ocean, 2, 3, 4, 5, 22, 35, 45, 93, 127, 143, 179, 181, 185, 299, 310, 335
"Pact of the Ciudadela", 415
Paesiello, Giovanni, 161
Painting in Mexico, 156–8
Palafox, Juan de, bishop of Puebla, 18th viceroy, 1642; visitor-general, inquisitor-general, 147
Palavicini, Félix F., 452
Palenque (Chiapas), 29
Palmas, Río de las, 36
Palo Alto, battle, 306
Palo Blanco, Plan de, 372, 373
Panamá, 1, 35, 36, 46, 332
Pani, Alberto, 451
Pánuco, province, 44, 87, 94, 101, 127; River, 17, 37, 61, 78
Pápagos, 17
Papantzin, Princess, 33
Parada, Alonzo de, 51

Paraguay, Jesuit Republic, 138
Paredes y Arrillaga, General Mariano, president, 1846, 293, 294, 296, 297, 305–6, 318, 376
Paris (France), 346, 355, 402, 403
Parma, Duchy of, 196
Parra, Licientiate, 208
Parral (Chihuahua), 399
Parras (Coahuila), 308
Paso del Norte [Ciudad Juárez], 309, 357, 358
"Pastry War", 292–3
Pattie, James O., 277
Pátzcuaro, 153, 206
Paul IV (Pope), 77
Paz, Fray Hernando de la, 104
Peage, defined, 132, 135
Pearl Coast, 35
Pearls, 92, 138
Pearson's Magazine, March, 1908, cited, 396
Pedrarias de Ávila, 35, 36
Peláez, General Manuel, 431
Peña y Peña, Manuel de la, President, 1847, 313, 318
Pensacola (Florida), 80, 137, 149
Peralta, Gastón de, viceroy, 1566, 85
Pereyra, Carlos, cited, 255
Pérez, Juan, 180
Pérez Alegre, Antonio, 407
Perry, Colonel, 244, 278
Pershing, General John, 432–3
"Personal service", 74, 75, 82, 131
Peru, 47, 71, 77, 87, 143, 146, 181
Petroleum, 12, 13–4, 392, 437–9, 443, 453–4
Philip II, of Spain, 72, 74, 82, 85, 89, 90, 95, 111, 142, 149, 171
Philip IV, of Spain, 147
Philip V, of Spain, 149, 173–4, 183
Philippines, 60, 81–2, 103, 148, 185
Pico, Andrés, 310, 311
Piedmont (Italy), 353
Piedras, Colonel José de las, 283
Piedras Negras, 29

GOLFO DE MEXICO

SKETCH MAP OF